My Double Life

SUNY series, Women Writers in Translation
Marilyn Gaddis Rose, Editor

My Double Life

The Memoirs of Sarah Bernhardt

SARAH BERNHARDT

Translated by
VICTORIA TIETZE LARSON

State University of New York Press

Cover photo: Paul Nadar/©Arch.Phot./CNMHS, Paris
Sarah Bernhardt, photographed by Nadar ca. 1864. Photo courtesy of the
Caisse Nationale des Monuments Historiques et des Sites, Paris.

Published by
State University of New York Press, Albany

For information, address State University of New York Press,
State University Plaza, Albany, N.Y. 12246

Production by Marilyn P. Semerad
Marketing by Dana E. Yanulavich

Library of Congress Cataloging-in-Publication Data

Bernhardt, Sarah, 1844–1923.
    [Ma double vie. English]
    My double life : the memoirs of Sarah Bernhardt /
Sarah Bernhardt ; translated by Victoria Tietze
Larson.
        p.   cm. — (SUNY series, women writers in
translation)
    Includes bibliographical references and index.
    ISBN 0-7914-4053-2 (hc. : alk. paper). — ISBN
0-7914-4054-0 (pbk. : alk. paper)
    1. Bernhardt, Sarah, 1844–1923. 2. Actors—France-
-Biography. I. Larson, Victoria Tietze, 1954–   .
II. Title. III. Series.
PN2638.B5A3   1999
792'.028'092—dc21
    [B]   98-30036

10 9 8 7 6 5 4 3 2

Contents

Preface

Sarah Bernhardt, French actress of German Jewish descent and illegitimate birth, was born in Paris probably in 1844[1] and died there in 1923. At her death she was in the process of making a film, apt symbol of the fact that her career—which was her life—finished at the point when popular entertainment was about to shift focus from the theater to the celluloid screen, and when the kind of international star status that she had enjoyed in the theater would pass henceforth to movie stars. Always attuned instinctively to significant people, moods, and moments, Sarah was ready to adapt her theatrical acting skills to a new medium whose potential she sensed—just as, during the first of her many visits to America, she had sought out Thomas Edison who was instrumental in developing so many of the technologies, including film, that were to usher in the modern era and bring to an end the world to which Sarah belonged.

In fact Sarah's art belonged to the nineteenth century not only in the technological sense but also, in some ways, aesthetically. Her style of acting—a blend of romantic passion combined with academic technique, dedicated often to the presentation of dying heroines in plays by conventional dramatists—had much more in common with the theater of the past than it had with contemporary experimental theatre, and for that reason it bordered at its worst, in the opinion of her vocal critics such as Chekhov[2] and George Bernard Shaw, on the side of the "flagrantly vulgar and commercial . . . hackneyed and old-fashioned."[3] At her best, however, Sarah was seen as the heir of the great *tragédienne* Rachel (1820–1858), especially in her performance of Racine's Phèdre.[4] Moreover, as with Rachel, so with Sarah, audiences and critics characterized the erotic undertones of their acting as "serpentine," and insisted with revulsion on their emaciated physiques (which, by present-day standards, were not exceptionally thin). Both were marginalized in bourgeois French society by their "foreign" connections (Rachel was born near Basel to itinerant peddlars), Jewish heritage, independent life styles, many lovers, and illegitimate children. Both were internationally celebrated stars who toured the world and made enormous fortunes. Both were immortalized by great novelists: Rachel as Vashti in Charlotte Bronte's *Villette*, Bernhardt as Berma in Proust's *A la recherche du temps perdu*. Most importantly, however, like Rachel Sarah had a powerfully charismatic stage presence that overrode the boundaries of time and makes her memory live: in Sarah's case it seems to have been a compound of her remarkable and beautiful voice and crystalline intonation,[5] her ability to represent and induce intense emotion, and her physical grace.

Sarah's autobiography, *Ma double vie*, describing the years 1844 to 1880, was published in 1907 (although it may have been composed many years before),[6] when Sarah was sixty-three and still had sixteen action-packed years to live—for she was possessed of formidable energy and continued a hectic performance schedule even after the amputation of her leg in 1915 and until not long before her death. The title of her memoirs, *Ma double vie* ("My Double Life"), entices the reader with its suggested promise of revealed secrets, yet no such revelations are forthcoming. In fact the autobiography is remarkable for what it leaves out. Sarah makes no mention, for example, of the circumstances surrounding, or the effect on her life of, the birth of her illegitimate son Maurice in 1864 (a catastrophic event if judged by prevailing standards of bourgeois morality) or of her many liaisons with actors and, if rumor is to be believed, with statesmen, men of letters, and royalty. As she herself candidly remarks in chapter XXXI, "I wish to set aside in these memoirs everything that directly touches intimacy in my life. There is a family 'I' that lives another life and whose sensations, joys, and sorrows are aroused and extinguished for a very small group of hearts."

It is not surprising that a woman who manipulated her relationship with the public through publicity in a thoroughly modern way—and in whose eccentric private life the public took great interest—should publish her autobiography. What *is* surprising is that it is written so well, with a novelist's sense of composition and moments of powerfully visual prose—so well, in fact, that some wondered when it was published whether Sarah had actually written it. But as Max Beerbohm said, "there is no use in pretending that she did not write this book herself. Paris contains, of course, many accomplished hacks who would gladly have done the job for her and would have done it quite nicely. But none of them could have imparted to the book the peculiar fire and salt that it has—the rushing spontaneity that stamps it, for every discriminating reader, as Sarah's own."[7] As Beerbohm points out, Bernhardt was surprisingly accomplished too in painting and sculpture, talents equally outside her profession.

In a way, however, each of these artist-roles (writer, painter, sculptor) formed an extension of Sarah's acting career, since she was highly self-conscious of herself as an artist, having herself photographed in a Worth-designed white silk "artist's" outfit with the accoutrements of the artist around her. Both her enemies and friends concurred in the view that she did not separate her life from her art. She acted in both of them. Thus *Ma double vie* does not so much tell us the "facts" of Sarah's life, but rather fashions a persona for her, transforming her life into drama and her self into a character. It is striking, for example, how often in the memoirs she refers to her physical appearance, indicating a self-conscious tendency to see herself, as though by an audience on a stage. For example she repeatedly emphasizes her slim and fragile physique and delicate health. While it is true that by contemporary standards she was considered excessively thin (and thus, like Rachel, was caricatured as a skeleton by cartoonists), her repeated emphasis on these physical traits, along with her insistence on her early religious mysticism, creates a stereotypical Jeanne d'Arc-like image (a role she acted on the stage) of fragile, innocent vulnerability. This image ill accords with that presented by some of her biographers of a woman who, like her mother and sisters, led the life of a courtesan from an early age. Probably both images are equally incomplete and two-dimensional.

A telling example of Sarah's tendency to romanticize and dramatize her life emerges from a comparison of her account of a visit in 1880 to Thomas Edison with an account of the same visit by Marie Colombier, one of the actresses who accompanied her on this American tour and wrote an account of it in *Le Voyage de Sarah Bernhardt en Amérique*. Colombier says that the train left New York at 6 P.M. for an hour's journey to Menlo Park in New Jersey (then a tiny rural hamlet about twenty-five miles from New York, now swallowed up by dismal suburban malls and strip development), while Bernhardt says the train left New York at 10 P.M. and arrived at Menlo Park at 2 A.M.! Colombier's account emphasizes the prosaic and banal—"We are in the middle of the countryside. Not a house anywhere. There is snow as far as the eye can see, horrible melting snow. We can't walk—we paddle. It's not very nice in satin slippers"[8]—whereas Sarah's account is pure melodrama:

> The night was a deep black. Snow was falling silently and heavily. . . . We looked like conspirators. The dark night, the two mysterious carriages, the silence imposed by the freezing cold, us, all muffled up in furs and throwing worried looks here and there—all of this gave our visit to the great Edison the atmosphere of a scene from an operetta.

The present new annotated translation of selections from *Ma double vie* replaces a 1907 translation by an anonymous translator rendered in dated English with many inaccuracies and unacknowledged omissions.[9] Owing to the current economic realities of academic publishing, I have had to abridge the original two-volume text (summarizing the omitted portions) to reduce its length. Deciding what to leave out was an unhappy and necessarily unsatisfying task: I tried to omit nothing of importance pertaining to Sarah's evolution as an actress or to the political and social background of the memoirs, but abridgment must inevitably impair somewhat the dramatic or "novelistic" coherence of the original work. Extensive notes have been provided especially on the actors and actresses and plays and playwrights mentioned by Bernhardt, material that is collected here in English for the first time.

From the notes a fascinating picture may be glimpsed of the theater in nineteenth-century France: of the kinds of people who acted in it and the lives they led, of the kinds of plays that were performed, and of the dramatists who wrote them (many of them now forgotten although they were then household names). Notes are also provided on the statesmen and historical events Sarah discusses, as well as on now unfamiliar aspects of nineteenth-century life, such as styles of clothing, types of fabric, and carriages. As far as these three latter items are concerned, I have preserved the French term if it was used in nineteenth-century English and have explained its meaning in a note. Particularly helpful for visualizing the appearance of the many different items of dress described by Sarah is the exhaustively illustrated C. Willett Cunnington's *English Women's Clothing in the Nineteenth Century* (New York, 1990)—English women's clothing at the time in its terminology and style being largely borrowed from France. Information on the types of carriages described may be obtained from D. J. M. Smith, *A Dictionary of Horse-Drawn Vehicles* (London, 1988). Photographs and portraits of the actors and actresses mentioned by Bernhardt can be found in *La Comédie-Française: 1680–1980*, eds. Sylvie Chevalley et al. (Paris, 1980), Frédéric Lolliée, *La Comédie-Française: 1658–1907* (Paris, 1907), and Henry Lyonnet, *Dictionnaire des comédiens français (ceux d'hier)* (Geneva, n.d.) 2 vols. Those who wish to obtain further information in English on the plays and dramatists mentioned may consult Anthony Levi, *Guide to French Literature 1789 to the Present* (Chicago and London, 1992) or *The Oxford Companion to French Literature*, ed. Paul Harvey (Oxford, 1959). I have found particularly helpful for its information about the more minor dramatists who are not listed in these two works Ernest Pronier's *Sarah Bernhardt: une vie au théâtre* (Geneva, n.d.), which also contains the most complete list available of the plays in which Sarah performed.

I would like to thank Dr. Carol Bové of the Department of Foreign Languages, Westminster College, Pennsylvania, for first interesting me in this project. I would also like to thank my "readers," Dr. Anna St. Léger Lucas of the Department of French, McMaster University, Canada, and Professor Susan Bassnett of the University of Warwick, UK, for many useful suggestions. For helpful information on the question of "overscoured silk" I would like to thank Dr. Owen Morgan of the Department of French, McMaster University, and for her kind response to my queries, Ruth Brandon, author of *Being Divine*. For generous advice on certain difficult points of translation my thanks go to Dr. Daniel Mengara of the Department of French, Montclair State University, New Jersey.

VICTORIA TIETZE LARSON

My Double Life

Chapter I

$\mathcal{M}$y mother loved to travel. She would go from Spain to England, from London to Paris, from Paris to Berlin—from there to Christiania;[1] then she would come home to kiss me and set off again for Holland, the country in which she was born. She would send my nurse clothes for her and cakes for me. She would write to one of my aunts, "Look after little Sarah, I'll be back in a month." A month later she would write to another sister, "Go and see the child at her nurse's, I'll be back in two weeks."

My mother was nineteen, I was three. One of my aunts was seventeen, the other twenty. Another was fifteen and the eldest was twenty-eight. But she lived in Martinique and already had six children. My grandmother was blind. My grandfather was dead. My father had been in China for two years—why, I have no idea. My young aunts would promise to come and see me, but rarely kept their word.

My nurse was a native of Brittany and lived near Quimperlé in a little white house with a low thatched roof, on which grew wild stocks. This was the first flower to delight my childish eyes, and I have loved ever since this flower petalled with the setting sun, its leaves thickset and gloomy. Britanny is far away, even in our era of high-speed travel, but at that time it was at the end of the world. Happily my nurse was, it seems, a good woman, and since her child was dead, I was all she had left to love. But she loved in the way that poor people love—when she had the time.

One day, when the hired hand was sick, she had gone to the fields to help with the potato harvest. The sodden soil was rotting the potatoes so the work was urgent. She entrusted me to the care of her husband, who was stretched out on his Breton bed, riven by lumbago. The good woman had set me in my high chair. She had made sure to peg in place the narrow tray that held me in, and on this she had put some little things for me to play with. As she was leaving she threw a faggot on the fire and said to me in Breton (until the age of four I understood only Breton), "You'll be good Milkblossom?" (This was the only name I answered to at that time.) As soon as she was gone, I

3

strained to pull out the wooden peg so carefully put in place by my poor nurse. When I eventually succeeded, I pushed away the little rampart, thinking, foolishly, to spring onto the floor. Instead I fell into the gaily crackling fire. The cries of Nurse's husband, who was unable to move, brought the neighbors. I was thrown, smoking all over, into a pail of fresh milk.

My aunts were notified and they alerted my mother. For four days this peaceful spot was plowed up by a succession of carriages. My aunts arrived from everywhere. My panic-stricken mother rushed from Brussels with Baron Larrey[2] and one of his friends, a young up-and-coming doctor and an intern. I was told afterward that my mother's despair could not have been more painful or charming. Dear Baron Larrey! I often saw him after this and I was destined to meet him again later in life. He delighted me with his story of the love of these good people for "Milkblossom," and he couldn't help laughing at so much butter. There was butter everywhere he said—on couches, on sideboards, on tables, and hanging in skins from hooks. All the neighbors had brought butter to make poultices for "Milkblossom." Mama, ravishingly beautiful— Madonna-like with her golden hair and eyes fringed with lashes long enough to cast shadows on her cheeks when she lowered her eyelids— gave money to everybody. She would have given her golden hair, her childlike feet, her very life, to save this child about whom she had been so little concerned only a week before. Yet she was just as sincere in her despair and her love as she had been in her unconscious forgetfulness.

Baron Larrey went back to Paris, leaving my mother, my aunt Rosine, and the intern with me. Six weeks later, Mama triumphantly took my nurse, her husband, and me back to the good city of Paris, where she installed us at Neuilly on the banks of the Seine. Apparently I hadn't a single scar—nothing except an excessively rosy complexion. My mother, happy and confident, set off on her travels again, once more leaving me to the care of my aunts. Two years passed by in this little garden at Neuilly, which was full of horrible crowded dahlias, colored like balls of yarn. My aunts never came. Mama sent money, candy, and toys.

Nurse's husband died, and she married the concierge at 65 rue de Provence. Not knowing where to find Mama, and not knowing how to write, my nurse took me to her new location without notifying anybody. I was delighted by the move. I was five years old, and I remember that day as though it were yesterday. Nurse's lodgings were located just above the carriage entrance-way and the bull's-eye window was framed by the heavy monumental gateway. From the outside I found this great gateway handsome, and I clapped my hands when I saw it. It was dusk, around five o'clock on a November day. I was put in my little bed and must have gone to sleep, for my memories of the day stop there.

The next day, however, I was overwhelmed by tremendous sorrow: the little room in which I slept was windowless. I began to cry. I escaped from my nurse's grasp as she dressed me and ran into the adjoining room to the round window. I pressed my obstinate little forehead against the glass and began to howl with rage because I could see no more trees, boxwood border, or falling leaves. Nothing except stone . . . cold, grey, ugly stone and windowpanes opposite. "I want to go away! I don't want to stay here! It's dark! It's nasty! I want to see the ceiling of the street!" I sobbed. My poor nurse took me in her arms, wrapped me in a blanket, and took me down into the courtyard: "Lift your head, Milkblossom, and look! There it is! The ceiling of the street!" It consoled me a little to see that there was sky in this ugly place, but sadness had taken hold of my whole soul. I no longer ate, I grew pale and anemic, and I would certainly have died of consumption if it had not been for a real *coup de théâtre*.

One day, while I was playing in the courtyard with Titine, a little girl who lived on the second floor—I cannot recall either her face or her real name—I saw Nurse's husband crossing the courtyard with two ladies, one of whom was very elegant. I only saw them from behind, but my heart missed a beat when I heard the voice of the elegant woman. My poor little body started to shake convulsively.

"There are windows that look out onto the courtyard?" she asked.

"Yes, Madame, those four there." And he pointed out four open windows on the first floor. The lady turned round to look.

I cried out in joy as one who had been delivered, "Aunt Rosine! Aunt Rosine!" I threw myself at the skirt of the pretty visitor. I buried my face in her furs, stamped, sobbed, laughed, and ripped her long lace sleeves.

She took me in her arms and tried to calm me. As she questioned the concierge she stammered to her friend, "I don't understand it at all! It's little Sarah, my sister Youle's daughter."

My cries had attracted attention. Windows opened. My aunt decided to take refuge in the lodge while she heard the explanation. My poor nurse told her all that had happened—the death of her husband, her second marriage. What she said to excuse herself I don't remember.

I clung to my aunt who smelled so good . . . so good, and I didn't want her to leave ever again. She promised to come for me the next day, but I didn't want to stay in the dark any longer. I wanted to leave at once, at once, with my nurse. My aunt gently stroked my hair and spoke to her friend in a language that I did not understand. She tried in vain to make me understand something or other . . . but I wanted to leave with her at once. Gentle, tender, cajoling, but without true affection, she said sweet things to me, stroked me with her gloved hand, smoothed down my ruffled dress, and made a thousand other playful, charming, cold gestures. She left, taken off by her friend, after emptying the contents of her little purse into Nurse's palm.

My poor nurse was in tears, and taking me in her arms, she opened the window saying, "Don't cry any more Milkblossom. Look at your pretty aunt. She'll come back. You'll be able to go with her." And big tears rolled down her beautiful round calm face. But all I could see was the unalterable black hole behind me. In a fit of despair I hurled myself toward my aunt who was about to climb into the carriage—and then nothing . . . darkness . . . darkness . . . a distant roar of distant voices, all very distant.

I had escaped from poor Nana. I had smashed onto the pavement at my aunt's feet. I had broken my arm in two places and my left kneecap. I did not wake up until some hours later in a large sweetly scented bed in the center of a large bedroom with two beautiful windows—a delight for me for one could see "the ceiling of the street." My mother, hastily summoned, came to look after me.

I came to know my family, my aunts, my cousins. My little head could not understand why so many people now loved me at once, when I had spent so many days and nights loved by one person alone. I stayed here two years recovering from this terrible fall, poor in health, my bones weak and brittle. I was carried almost everywhere I went.

I pass over these two years of my life which have left only a confused memory of cuddling and drowsiness.

Chapter II

One morning my mother took me on her knee and said, "How big you are now! You must learn to read and write." Indeed, at seven I didn't know how to read, write, or count, as I had lived with my nurse until I was five and had been ill for the last two years. Playing with my curls, my mother said, "It's time to be a big girl now. You are going to go to boarding school."

That meant nothing to me. "What's boarding school?"

"It's a place where there are lots of little girls."

"Are they sick?"

"Oh no," replied Mama, "they are very healthy, as you are now, and they play and are jolly." I jumped up and down, bursting with joy. But Mama pulled me close to her, her eyes brimming with tears.

"And you? And you, Mama? Will you be all alone? You won't have your little girl any more?"

Mama bent over my small form. "Our good Lord has told me He's going to send me a bunch of flowers and a little baby to console me."

With an even noisier outburst of joy I cried out, "So I'll have a little brother—or a little sister—Oh, I don't want one of those! I don't like girls!"

Mama kissed me tenderly and made me dress right there. I remember a blue dress of velours épinglé,[1] in which I gloried.

Thus arrayed, I waited anxiously for my aunt Rosine's carriage, which was to take us to Auteil. She arrived around three o'clock. Our maid had left with my things an hour before, and it had given me great pleasure to see my little trunk and toys piled up in the carriage. Slowly and calmly Mama climbed first into my aunt's magnificent vehicle. I climbed up in turn, making a bit of a to-do of it, because the concierge and some shopkeepers were watching. My aunt jumped up lightly, her skirts swirling, and gave the order in English to the coachman, sitting stiff and ridiculous, to go to the address written on the paper she handed him. Another carriage followed ours in which three men had taken their places: Régis,[2] my godfather, who was my father's friend, General de Polhes, and a painter of equestrian and hunting scenes

7

which were the fashion at the time, who was called Fleury I believe. I
found out on the way that these gentlemen were going to order dinner
at a fashionable nightclub on the outskirts of Auteuil, and the whole
party was to meet up there later with some other friends.

I paid little attention to what my mother and aunt were saying.
From time to time, when they were talking about me, they spoke in
English or German, throwing me as they did so tender smiling glances.
The long drive filled me with delight. With my face pressed to the glass
I gazed fixedly at the road as it rolled by, grey, muddy, and studded with
ugly houses and scrawny trees. I found it beautiful because it constantly
changed. Eventually the carriage stopped at 18 rue Boileau, Auteuil.
Fastened to the railings was a long blackened metal sign with gold
lettering. I looked up at it. Mama said to me, "You'll soon know how
to read what it says there, I hope." My aunt whispered in my ear, "Boarding school of Mme. Fressard" and I replied confidently to Mama, "It
says 'Boarding school of Mme. Fressard.' " Mama, my aunt, and the
three gentlemen roared with laughter at my ladylike self-possession.

Mme. Fressard came to meet us. She impressed me. She was of
average height, a little heavy, with greying hair in the style of Mme. de
Sévigné,[3] beautiful big eyes like George Sand's,[4] very white teeth gleaming in a slightly swarthy face, dimpled hands, and long fingers. She
looked and spoke well. She took me gently by the hand, and dropping
down on one knee to put her face on a level with mine, said to me in
her musical voice, "You're not afraid, my little girl?" I blushed and did
not reply. She addressed several questions to me. I refused to reply. The
adults encircled me: "Go on, you baby, answer!" "Come on, Sarah, be
nice!" "Oh, what a horrible little girl!" To no avail. My lips were sealed.

After the usual tour around the dormitories, refectory, and sewing
room, after a thousand exaggerated compliments—"How well kept it
is!" "How clean!"—and a thousand similar stupid remarks on the comfort of this juvenile jail, my mother drew Mme. Fressard aside. I clung
to my mother's knees and prevented her from walking.

"Here are the doctor's orders," she said as she handed over a long
list of things that had to be done.

Mme. Fressard smiled slightly sarcastically. "You know, Madame,"
she said, "that we can't curl her hair like this?"

"Much less uncurl it," said my mother, passing her gloved fingers
through my hair. "This isn't hair, it's a mop! Please don't ever try to
untangle it without brushing it first—you'll never get to the end of it
and you'll hurt her. What do the children have at four o' clock?" she
continued.

"A piece of bread, of course, and whatever their parents give them
in addition."

"Here are twelve jars of different preserves, because she's fussy. Give her preserve one day and chocolate the next. Here are six pounds of it."

Mme. Fressard smiled, still ironic but kindly. She picked up a pound of chocolate and said aloud, "From Marquis's! So, little one, you're spoiled!" and she tapped me on the cheek with her white fingers. Then her eyes fixed in some surprise on a big pot.

"This," said my mother, "is some cold cream that I made myself. I want my daughter's face, neck, and hands rubbed with it every evening at bedtime."

"But . . . " Mme. Fressard began.

Mama cut in impatiently. "I'll pay double for laundering the sheets." My poor darling mother! I remember quite clearly that my sheets were changed once a month, at the same time as everybody else's.

Finally, the moment of parting came and Mama was carried off by a sympathetic group amidst an outpouring of consolatory words and phrases: "It'll do her good!" "She needs this!" "You're going to find her changed next time you see her!" etc. General Polhes, who was very fond of me, took me in his arms and, lifting me up high, said, "You're in the army now, little nipper! You're going to have to march in time!" As I pulled his long moustache he said, "Better not do that to the lady!" winking in the direction of Mme. Fressard who had a slight moustache. My aunt shrieked with laughter. My mother's lips tightened as she suppressed a smile. The troop departed in a whirl of skirts and conversation, while I was dragged off to the cage in which I was to be emprisoned.

I spent two years at this boarding school. I learned to read, write, and do arithmetic. I learned many games I didn't know. I learned how to sing rondos and how to embroider handkerchiefs for Mama. I was relatively happy because we went out on Thursdays and Sundays and these walks gave me a feeling of freedom. The dust in the street seemed to me to be of other stuff than the soil of the big garden at the school.

Then there were little rituals at Mme. Fressard's, which always threw me into a state of mad excitement. Occasionally, on Thursdays, Mlle. Stella Colas, who had just made her début at the Théâtre-Français,[5] would come and recite verse. The night before I wouldn't sleep a wink. In the morning I combed my hair carefully and got myself ready with beating heart to hear things I did not understand at all, but which cast a spell on me. Plus there was a legend attached to this pretty personage: she had thrown herself almost under the horses of the Emperor's carriage to attract the sovereign's attention and obtain his pardon for her brother, who had conspired against the Emperor's life. The sister of Mlle. Stella Colas, Clotilde, was a boarder at Mme. Fressard's. She is now the wife of M. Pierre Merlou, the Minister of Finance.

Stella Colas was short and blonde, with blue eyes that had a slight hardness to them, but which were nevertheless full of depth. She had a deep voice and I would thrill in every fiber when this frail, blonde, pale girl tackled the dream of Athalie.[6] How many times, seated on my child's bed, did I try to say in a deep voice, "*Tremble! fille digne de moi . . .* " I would lower my chin, blow out my cheeks, and begin "*Tremble . . . trem . . . ble . . . trem-em-em-eble . . .* "[7] But it would always finish badly because I would start off in a very low muffled voice and then unconsciously raise it. Then the other girls would wake up and burst out laughing. I would jump up and furiously lash out right and left with kicks and slaps, which were returned a hundred fold.

Mlle. Caroline, the adopted daughter of Mme. Fressard, whom I met again a long time afteward as the wife of the famous painter Yvon, would appear, furious and implacable, and would hand out punishments to all of us for the day after. As for me, I would be gated and given five strokes of the ruler on the knuckles. Oh! Mlle. Caroline and that ruler! I reproached her for it when I saw her again thirty-five years later. She would make us wrap our fingers round the thumb and then hold out our hands very straight in front of her. Smack! Smack! With her wide ebony ruler she would deal out a nasty hard dry blow that made tears spring.

I took a dislike to Mlle. Caroline. She was beautiful, but it was a beauty that bored me: her skin was very white and her hair, which she wore with a central parting in waved bandeaux on either side of her head, was very black. When I saw her a long time afterward, she was brought to my house by a relative of mine who said, "I bet you don't recognize this lady? And yet you know her very well." I was leaning against the large mantelpiece in my hall and I saw approaching from the far end of the main drawing room a tall person with a slightly provincial air, who was still quite beautiful. When she had descended the stairs into the hall the daylight revealed her arched forehead framed by the tightly parted hair. "Mlle. Caroline!" I exclaimed, and with a furtive movement I hid my hands behind my back. I never saw Mlle. Caroline again. The rancor that I had harbored toward her since childhood must have penetrated my politeness as a hostess.

I was not too unhappy at Mme. Fressard's and it seemed natural to me that I should stay there until I was quite big. My uncle Faure, who is now a member of the Carthusian order, had stipulated that his wife, my mother's sister, should take me out often. He owned a magnificent estate at Neuilly, through which a stream flowed, and I used to fish there for hours with my two cousins, a girl and a boy. In short, these two years passed by peacefully and uneventfully, disturbed only by my terrible tantrums, which would throw the boarding school into disarray and leave me two or three days at a time in the infirmary.

One day my aunt Rosine suddenly appeared to withdraw me from the school. An order from my father stated the place to which I was to be transferred. The order was categoric. My mother who was travelling had notified my aunt, who had hurried off—between two waltzes, as it were—to carry this out.

The idea that my wishes and mode of life were once again being violated without my consent threw me into an unspeakable rage. I rolled on the floor, shrieked, and hurled reproaches against Mama, my aunts, and Mme. Fressard for not finding a way to keep me. After two hours of struggling, during which I escaped twice from the hands that tried to dress me, and ran into the garden to climb up trees and throw myself into the little pool in which there was more slime than water, I was eventually carried off in my aunt's carriage, exhausted, tamed, and sobbing.

I stayed with her for three days with such a fever that they feared for my life. My father came to my aunt's. At that time she lived at 6 rue de la chaussée d'Antin, and my father was friendly with Rossini[8] who lived at no. 4 in the same street. He often brought him round and Rossini made me laugh with his hundreds of clever stories and his comical faces. My father was as handsome as a god and I regarded him with pride. I knew him very little as I rarely saw him, but I loved him for his enchanting voice and his slow gentle gestures. He was quite imposing and I noticed that my excitable aunt calmed down in his presence.

I had regained my equilibrium, and Dr. Monod, who was seeing me at the time, said that I could be moved without risk. We had waited for Mama, but she was ill in Haarlem. My father refused my aunt's offer to take me to the convent. I can still hear my father's gentle voice saying, "No, her mother will take her to the convent. I've written to the Faures. They're going to look after the little one for two weeks." And as my aunt was about to protest he said, "It's calmer than here, my dear Rosine, and the child needs calm more than anything."

I arrived that evening at my aunt Faure's. I did not like her very much as she was cold and affected. But I adored my uncle. He was so gentle and calm and his smile was charming. His son was a devil like me—adventurous and a bit crazy. We liked to be together. My other cousin, adorable Greuze, was reserved and always afraid of dirtying her dress and even her apron. The poor darling married Baron Cerise and died in childbirth at the height of her beauty and her youth, because her timidity, reserve, and narrow upbringing made her recoil from accepting medical attention when this was absolutely necessary. I loved her very much and wept many tears over her, and still a mere moonbeam will evoke in my imagination her blonde apparition.

I stayed three weeks at my uncle's, wandering with my cousin, spending hours on my stomach, fishing for shrimps in the little brook that crossed my relatives' estate. This estate was enormous and encircled by a wide ditch. How many times I laid a bet with my cousin and his pretty sister that I would jump across the ditch: "I bet you five pins!" "I bet you three sheets of paper!" "I bet you my two pancakes!"—we ate pancakes every Tuesday—and I would jump. Most of the time I fell in the ditch, floundering in the green water, shrieking because I was afraid of frogs, howling with terror because my two cousins pretended to be leaving.

When I went in and my worried aunt caught sight of me from the step where she was watching for our return—what a reprimand! What a cold look! "Go and change, Mademoiselle, and stay in your bedroom! Your supper will be brought up to you without dessert!" Passing the big mirror in the hall, I would catch a glimpse of myself looking like a worm-eaten log, and I would see my cousin signaling, with his hand to his mouth, that he would bring me dessert. Greuze would let her mother cuddle her as she seemed to say, "Thank God *you* are not like this little gypsy!" This was the name my aunt reproached me with when she was angry. I would go up to my bedroom heavy-hearted, ashamed, remorseful, swearing never to jump over the ditch again. But once I got to my room the gardener's daughter—a big peasant girl who had been appointed to wait on little me—would be there laughing at me: "Oh, how ridiculous Mademoiselle looks like that!" And she would laugh so much that she would make me proud of being so ridiculous, and I would already be thinking, "The next time that I jump over the ditch I'm going to *cover* myself in grass and mud."

Once undressed and washed I would put on my little flannel nightdress and wait in my room for supper. They would bring me soup, meat, bread, and water. I hated and still hate meat. I would throw it out of the window, taking care to cut off the fat and leave it on the side of my plate, for my aunt would come up to check on me.

"You have eaten, Mademoiselle?"

"Yes, Aunt."

"Are you still hungry?"

"No, Aunt."

"Write out the Lord's Prayer and the Creed three times, little pagan" (I had not yet been baptized).

A quarter of an hour later, my uncle would come up. "Did you eat well?"

"Yes, Uncle."

"Did you eat your meat?"

"No, I threw it out of the window. I don't like it."

"You lied to your aunt?!"

"No! She asked me if I had eaten. I said yes, but I didn't say that I had eaten my meat."

"What punishment do you have?"

"I have to write out three Lord's Prayers and three Creeds."

"Do you know them off by heart?"

"No, Uncle, not very well. I keep making mistakes."

And this adorable man would dictate the Lord's Prayer and the Creed, which I copied down devotedly, because he dictated them with love.

He was devout, very devout, my uncle Faure. After the death of my aunt he joined the Carthusian order. At this very moment I know that he is digging his own grave, old and sick and bent with pain, giving way under the weight of the spade, imploring God to take him, and thinking often of me, his "dear little gypsy." The dear sweet man! I owe him what is best in me and I love him with respect and devotion. How many times, at difficult periods in my life, have I remembered him and mentally asked for his advice! For after my aunt decided to break off relations with Mama and me I no longer saw him. But he has always loved me and has occasionally conveyed advice to me—advice full of generosity, honesty, and good sense. Not long ago I went to the rural spot where the Carthusians have their refuge. I sent in a male friend to see the saintly man and I cried when I heard the words that my uncle had dictated to him to be repeated to me.

But to return to my story. . . Once my uncle had left, Marie, the gardener's daughter, would come in nonchalantly with her pockets bulging with apples, biscuits, nuts, and raisins. Greuze's brother would send me dessert; but Marie, grand girl, would clear out the contents of all the appetizer dishes! So I would say to her, "Sit down, Marie, and shell the nuts, while I do my Creeds and Lord's Prayers. We'll eat them after I've finished." Then Marie would sit on the floor so as to be able to hide everything quickly under the table, should my aunt come back. But my aunt would not come back. She would be playing music with Greuze while my uncle taught mathematics to her brother.

Finally Mama let us know that she was coming. This caused an upheaval in my uncle's house. My little trunk was readied for me. The convent of Grand-Champs that I was about to enter had a uniform. My cousin, who loved sewing, furiously marked all my things with "SB" in red thread. My uncle gave me the silver place-setting and goblet. Everything was marked with "32," my identification number. Marie gave me a big muffler in shades of purple, which she had been knitting me in secret for days. My aunt put around my neck a little scapular which had been blessed, and when Mama arrived with my father everything was ready.

A big farewell dinner was given, to which were invited two gentlemen who were friends of my mother, as well as my aunt Rosine, and four other members of the family. I felt very important. I was neither happy nor sad. I felt important and that was enough. Everybody was talking about me. My uncle stroked my hair. Greuze blew me kisses from the end of the table.

Suddenly my father's voice made me turn to him. "Listen Sarah, if you are very well-behaved in the convent, I will fetch you in four years and take you with me far away on some fine trips."

"Oh, I'll be good! As good as Henriette!" She was my aunt Faure. Everybody smiled.

After dinner, as it was fine weather, we strolled in the park. My father took me aside and said some serious things to me, sad things that I had never heard before, but which I understood in spite of my youth, and which made me cry. He was sitting on an old bench and held me on his lap. Leaning against him, my head on his chest, I listened and cried, not speaking, disturbed. My poor Papa, I was never to see him again, ever, ever...

Chapter III

slept badly and at eight o'clock the next morning we left by post-chaise for Versailles. I can still see plump Marie, the gardener's daughter, in tears, the household gathered on the top step, my little trunk, the toy chest Mama had brought along, a kite my cousin had made himself, which he gave to me just as the carriage started to move. I can still see the great square house, which grew smaller and smaller as we drew further away. I stood up, steadied by my father, and waved the blue scarf that I had taken from around his neck. Then I fell asleep and did not wake up until we were in front of the heavy door of Grand-Champs convent.

I rubbed my eyes, trying to orient myself. I jumped out of the carriage and looked around curiously. The paving stones were small and round and grass grew between them. A wall, a big door with a crucifix above it, and then behind it nothing . . . one could see nothing. On the left there was a house. On the right the Satory barracks. There was not a sound, not a footfall, not even an echo.

"Oh, Mama, am I going in there? Oh no! I want to go back to Mme. Fressard's!"

Mama shrugged and pointed to my father, giving me to understand that she had nothing to do with it. I threw myself at him. He was already ringing the bell. He took my hand, and as the door opened led me in gently. Mama and Aunt Rosine followed. The courtyard was enormous and gloomy, but now there were buildings and windows to be seen and the curious faces of children. My father said something to the extern sister and we were shown into the parlor.

It was a huge room with a polished floor divided along its full length by a black grille. There were red-velvet upholstered benches along the walls and then some chairs and armchairs near the grille. There was a portrait of Pius IX, a full-length portrait of St. Augustine, and a portrait of Henri V. My teeth were chattering. I seemed to remember having read a description of a prison in some book and it was exactly like this. I looked at my father and mother, my suspicions aroused. People said so often that I was an uncontrollable child, that I needed an iron hand, that I was a real devil. My Aunt Faure said so often, "This child will turn out badly; she has some crazy ideas . . . " etc. etc. I was seized with fear.

"Papa! Papa! I don't want to go to jail! This is a jail, I'm sure of it! I'm scared, I'm scared!"

A door opened on the other side of the grille. I stopped and looked. A little short round woman had just come in. She came up to the grille. Her black veil was pulled down as far as her mouth. I could not see any of her face. She recognized my father. Doubtless they had already conferred when arrangements were being made for my admission. She opened a door in the grille and we went into the second room.

Seeing that I was pale and that my tearful eyes were full of terror, she gently took my hand, and turning her back to my father, lifted up her veil. I saw the most gentle and smiling face possible. Big blue childlike eyes, a turned-up nose, a full smiling mouth, fine strong white teeth. Her air of kindness, strength, and gaiety made me throw myself at once into the arms of Mother Sainte-Sophie, the Mother Superior at the convent of Grand-Champs.

"Ah! Here we are friends—already!" she said to my father as she lowered her veil.

And we went off; I held Papa and Mother Sainte-Sophie by the hand and two other nuns accompanied us—Mother Préfète, a tall cold woman with pursed lips, and Sister Séraphine, blanched and willowy like a sprig of lily of the valley.

We started by looking round the building, particularly at the big workroom where all the pupils gathered on Thursdays for the lecture, which was almost always given by Mother Sainte-Sophie. The pupils worked all day long at needlework, some working on tapestry, others embroidering, some working with transfers. The room was large. On St. Catherine's Day and certain other occasions there was dancing there. It was also in this room that once a year the Mother Superior gave each sister the penny that represented her year's wages. The walls were decorated with religious engravings and with some oil paintings done by pupils. But the place of honor belonged to St. Augustine: a magnificent large engraving depicted his conversion. Oh, how often I have looked at this engraving! St. Augustine certainly stirred great emotions in me and troubled my childish heart.

Then Mama admired the cleanliness of the refectory. But she wanted to know where my place would be, and when it was shown to her she vehemently objected to my being put there.

"No," she said. "The child has a very delicate chest and will be right in a draft there! I don't want her to be there."

My father backed up my mother. It was agreed that I would be put at the back of the refectory and the promise was kept.

When it was time to climb the wide staircase that led to the dormitories, Mama was alarmed for a moment: the staircase was wide, very wide . . . the steps were low and easy, but there were so many of them to climb to get to the first floor. For a moment, staring vacantly, her arms hanging limply, Mama hesitated, discouraged.

"Stay there, Youle," said my aunt. "I'll go up."

"No, no," said Mama sorrowfully. "I want to see where the child will sleep. She is so delicate."

My father half carried her up and we found ourselves in one of the immense dormitories. It was like a much larger version of the dormitory at Mme. Fressard's, except that it had a tiled floor without any carpet or anything.

"This is impossible!" exclaimed Mama. "The little one can't sleep here. It'll be the death of her. It's too cold."

Mother Sainte-Sophie, the Mother Superior, made my mother sit down and tried to calm her. She was very pale. She already had a weak heart. "Look here, Madame. We will put your little girl in this dormitory." She opened a door into a fine room containing eight beds. It had a parquet floor. It was the room adjoining the infirmary, where the delicate or convalescent children slept.

Mama was reassured and we went down to the gardens. There were the "little wood," the "middle wood," and the "big wood." Then there was an orchard that stretched as far as the eye could see. In it was the building for the pauper children, who received free schooling and helped with the big weekly wash. The sight of these immense woods in which were gymnastic equipment, swings, and hammocks, filled me with joy. I would be able to wander about amongst all of this. Mother Sainte-Sophie said the "little wood" was reserved for the eldest pupils and the "middle wood" for the little girls. As for the "big wood," all the classes gathered together there on holidays, as well as for collecting chestnuts and gathering acacias. Mother Sainte-Sophie noted that each child could have her own little garden, and that sometimes two or three girls would get together in order to have a pretty garden.

"Oh, I can have a garden of my very own?"

"Yes," said my mother, "of your very own."

The Mother Superior called the gardener, old Larcher, who, apart from the chaplain, was the only man on the convent's staff. "Larcher," said the dear lady, "here is a child who wants a beautiful garden. Pick one out for her in a nice spot."

"Very well, Reverend Mother," said the good fellow. I saw my father slip a coin into his hand and the gardener thanked him with some confusion.

It was getting late. It was time to say goodbye. I remember well that I felt no sadness. All I could think about was my garden. The convent no longer seemed like a prison to me, but a paradise. I kissed Mama and my aunt. Papa held me close to him for a moment. When I looked at him his eyes were full of tears. But I had no desire to cry. I gave him a big kiss and murmured, "I'm going to be good, good, and work hard so that I can leave with you in four years." Then I went over to Mama who was giving the same instructions to Mother Sainte-Sophie as she had to Mme. Fressard: cold cream, chocolate, preserves, etc. etc. Mother Sainte-Sophie wrote down all the instructions. She took care later to follow them scrupulously.

After my family had left I felt close to tears. But the Mother Superior took my hand and led me to the "middle wood" to show me where my garden would be. That was all that was needed to distract me.

∞∞

[In the remainder of the chapter: *Sarah's life at the convent where, although the life was rigorous and some of the nuns excessively strict, she greatly loved Mother Sainte-Sophie and was regarded as a "personality" by her peers. Overhearing Mother Sainte-Sophie praise her, following her rescue of a drowning four-year old girl, Sarah becomes devoutly religious.*]

Chapter IV

An event very simple in itself, but which was, however, to shatter the calm of our cloistered existence, had the effect of completing my attachment to the convent where I wanted to stay forever. The Archbishop of Paris, Monseigneur Sibour, was visiting chosen communities, and ours was among those selected.

The news was delivered to us by Mother Saint-Alexis, the dean, who was so tall, so thin, and so old, that I found it impossible to accept her as a human being, or even as a living creature. She seemed to me to be jointed and stuffed. She frightened me. I would not come near her until she was dead. We had been assembled in the big room we used on Thursdays. Standing on the little platform supported by two lay sisters, she announced to us in a voice coming from far, far away . . . Monseigneur was coming. He was to come on St. Catherine's day, fifteen days hence.

In our peaceful convent it was as though a hornet had entered a beehive. Our study hours were shortened so that we could devote ourselves to making garlands of roses and lilies. The massive carved wooden throne was uncovered so that it could be rubbed and polished. We hung the lights with crystal balls. The grass in the courtyard was pulled up. I don't know that anything was left undone in honor of this visit!

Two days after the announcement made by the dean, the Mother Superior read us the program of festivities. The youngest of nuns—delightful Sister Séraphine—was to read a speech honoring Monseigneur. Then Marie Buguet would play a piece on the piano by Henri Herz. Marie de Lacour would sing a song by Loïsa Puget. Then a little three-act play written by Mother Sainte-Thérèse would be performed called *Tobie recouvrant la vue.*[1] I have here in front of me the little manuscript, yellowed and torn, and I can just decipher the gist of it and one or two sentences.

Scene I: Young Tobias bids farewell to his blind father, Tobit. He vows to bring back to him the ten talents he had lent to Gabael, a relative.

19

Scene II: Tobias sleeping on the banks of the river Tiber. The angel Raphael watches over him. Struggle with a monstrous fish, which had attacked Tobias as he slept. The fish now killed, the angel advises Tobias to take its heart, liver, and gall and to treasure them religiously.

Scene III: Return of Tobias to his blind father. The angel advises him to rub his father's eyes with the innards of the fish. The old father regains his sight. The angel Raphael, pressed by Tobit to accept a reward, reveals who he is. With a hymn to the glory of God he vanishes toward heaven.

The little play was read by Mother Sainte-Thérèse in the room we used on Thursdays. We were all in tears after the reading, and Mother Saint-Thérèse had to make a great effort not to commit, even if only for a moment, the sin of pride. I was wondering anxiously to myself what part I would play in this pious comedy. I did not doubt that, with my little personality, I would be given some part in it. And I trembled with anticipation. I began to get quite nervous, my hands went cold, my heart thumped, my temples throbbed. So when Mother Sainte-Thérèse said in her calm voice, "Mesdemoiselles, listen, please. Here is the casting of the parts," I refused to approach her and stayed brooding on my stool. She called out:

Old Tobit: Eugénie Charmel.
Young Tobias: Amélia Pluche.
Gabael: Renée d'Arville.
The Angel Raphael: Louise Buguet.
Mother of Tobias: Eulalie Lacroix.
Sister of Tobias: Virginie Depaul.

I had been listening surreptitiously. I was struck by outraged and furious amazement when Mother Sainte-Thérèse added, "Here are your scripts, Mesdemoiselles," and gave each one a little text of the play.

Louise Buguet was my best friend. I went up to her and asked her for her script, which I reread feverishly.

"Will you let me say it to you when I've learned it off by heart?"

"Oh, of course," I replied.

"Oh, how scared I'm going to be!" my little friend kept saying.

She had been chosen as the angel, I think, because she was as pale and blonde as a ray of moonlight. She had a gentle timid voice; and sometimes we would make her cry just to see how pretty she looked. Limpid pearly tears would flow from her large grey questioning eyes.

She immediately set about learning her part, while I, like a shepherd dog, trailed on the heels of the Chosen. The play did not concern

me, but I wanted to be a part of it. Mother Superior went by and
stroked my cheek as we were curtseying.

"We certainly thought about you, dear, but you are always so timid
when you are asked anything."

"Oh, that's because it's history or arithmetic . . . It's not the same
thing. I wouldn't have been afraid."

She smiled doubtfully and went on.

We rehearsed for a week. I asked to be the big monster. I wanted
to be involved at any price. But it was César, the convent dog, who was
to be the monstrous fish. A competition was held for the fish costume.
I had gone to great trouble cutting out cardboard scales that I had
painted and then sewn together. I had made some enormous gills which
were to be put on a collar round César's neck. However, it was not my
project that was adopted, but that of a tall, stupid girl whose name
escapes me. She had made a big tail from a piece of leather and a mask
with big eyes and gills. But there were no scales. It was César's hairy
coat that one would see. In spite of this setback, I busied myself with
Louise Buguet's costume on which I worked with Sister Sainte-Cécile
and Sister Jeanne, who were in charge of the linen room.

At rehearsals nobody could get a word out of the Angel Raphael.
Louise, our angel, would stand openmouthed on the stage, her beautiful eyes pearling with tears. She would bring the play to a standstill, all the time throwing me looks of tearful appeal. I would whisper
the words to her. I would get up and run toward her and kiss her
and whisper in her ear the whole speech. I was starting to be part
of it all.

Finally, two days before the solemn event, the dress rehearsal was
held. As soon as the Angel Raphael appeared—oh, so pretty!—he collapsed on the bench, sobbing and imploring, "Oh, no! I'll never manage it!" "Indeed, she never will . . . " sighed Mother Sainte-Sophie.

Then, emboldened by pride and joy and full of self-assurance, and
forgetting my little friend's sorrow, I leaped onto the stage and standing on the bench on which wept the stricken Angel Raphael, I cried
out, "Mother, Mother, I know her part! Do you want me to say it?"

"Yes, yes!" cried out everyone from their seats.

"Yes, yes, you know it well," said Louise Buguet, and she tried to
put her headband on me.

"No, let me rehearse like this first."

We started the second scene again, and I made my entrance armed
with a long willow branch. I started, "Fear nothing, Tobias, I will be
your guide. I will clear you path of stones and thorns. Weariness over-
whelms you. Rest! I will watch over you." And Tobias, overcome, lay

down on the bank . . . of five yards of blue jaconet,[2] which snaked across the stage to represent the river Tigris. Then I continued with a prayer to God while Tobias slept.

Then César appeared as the monstrous fish and the little audience trembled with fear. César, who had been well trained by old Larcher, the gardener, came out slowly from under the blue jaconet, his fish mask on his head; two enormous whitened cockleshells, with a hole in the middle of each to allow César to see out, had been wired to his collar, which also held up two enormous gills like palm leaves. César, with his nose on the ground, growled, roared, and then threw himself wildly at Tobias who killed him with the first blow of his club. César fell on his back, his four paws in the air, and then collapsed onto his side, playing dead. The audience went wild with joy. They clapped their hands and stamped their feet. The smallest girls stood up on their stools and cried out, "Oh, good César! Clever César! What a good doggy he is!" The sisters shook their heads, touched by the goodwill of the guardian of the convent. As for me, I had forgotten that I was the Angel Raphael and was kneeling to stroke César—"Oh, how well he played at being dead, Madame!"—and I kept kissing his paws, lifting up one after the other. César, inert, continued to play dead.

The little bell recalled us to order. I got up and, to the accompaniment of the piano, we entoned a Hosannah to the glory of God who had just saved Tobias from the frightful monster. Then the little green serge curtain fell, and I was surrounded by girls praising and petting me. Mother Sainte-Sophie came up to us on the little stage. She gave me an affectionate kiss. As for Louise Buguet, she was cheerful again now and her pretty angelic face shone: "Oh, how well you knew the part! Besides, we can hear *you*. Thank you!" She kissed me and I hugged her with all my strength. Finally! I was in it!

The third scene started. It took place in the house of the old father. The angel, Gabael, and young Tobias were handling the innards of the fish and looking at them. The angel was explaining how they should be used to rub the eyes of the blind father. I felt a bit nauseous because I was holding the liver of a skate and the heart and gizzard of a chicken. I had never touched such things before. At moments I felt myself retching and my eyes watered. Finally, the blind father came in, guided by Tobias's sisters. Gabael, kneeling on one knee in front of the old man, gave him the ten silver talents and recounted at length the exploits of Tobias in Media. Finally, Tobias went up to his father and after holding him in a long embrace rubbed his eyes with the liver of the skate. Eugénie Charmel grimaced, but, after having her eyes rubbed, cried out, "I can see! I can see! Kind God! Clement God! I can see! I can see!" In an ecstatic posture with her arms outstretched and her eyes open she advanced, and the whole little innocent and loving audience wept.

Everyone was kneeling on stage, giving thanks to God, except for old Tobit and the angel. After this prayer of thanks for blessings received, the audience, moved by inbred piety, repeated "Amen." Then Tobias's mother came forward and spoke to the angel, saying, "Noble stranger, take a place at our hearth. Henceforth you shall be our guest, our son, our brother!" But I came forward and in a long speech of at least thirty lines made myself known as the envoy of God, the Angel Raphael. Quickly picking up the blue tarlatan,[3] which had been concealed for the final effect, I wrapped myself in this diaphanous fabric to simulate my ascension to Heaven. The little green serge curtain dropped on this apotheosis.

∞·∾

[In the remainder of the chapter: *Sarah is enraptured when Monseigneur Sibour promises to return for her baptism in the spring, but before this can happen news reaches the convent that he has been assassinated. Sarah has a premonition—which proves to be correct—that her father has died. Her mother and aunts Rosine Berendt and Henriette Faure (also her godmother), her uncle Faure, her godfather Régis, M. Meydieu (her sister Jeanne's godfather), General Polhes (her sister Régina's godfather), and her sisters' godmothers, along with various cousins, all descend on the convent for the joint baptism of Sarah, Jeanne (six years old), and Régina (not yet three). After her first communion, a few days after her baptism, which she embraces in a spirit of overwrought mysticism, Sarah is taken on a vacation by her mother to Cauterets in the Pyrenees. They are accompanied by Jeanne, Mme. Guérard and her son, and Marguerite, an old family servant.*]

Chapter V

[*Sarah returns to the convent for ten more months, and, although she is nearly fourteen, remains very much a child. She learns "nothing," but continues to cherish a dream of becoming a nun. During a vacation she spends much time with Sophie Croizette,[1] whose mother, a former ballet dancer, and Sarah's mother, had struck up an acquaintance. One day, back at the convent after this vacation, a soldier's cap comes flying over the wall into the grounds, tossed there by the soldier's friend as a prank. Sarah seizes it and, egged on by the other girls' laughter, retreats to the top of a climbing frame and refuses to give it back. The other girls are sent inside and Sarah is left outside until night falls when, frightened, cold, and tired, she finally consents to come down. As a result of her chill she contracts pleurisy and is taken away from the convent to convalesce. In fact, however, she never returns to Grand-Champs, much to her sorrow. Instead her education is entrusted to a governess, Mlle. de Brabender, an old spinster, who lives in a convent and had served as a governess in an aristocratic household in Russia. Mlle. de Brabender is very ugly but is liked and respected by Sarah.*]

Chapter VI

I got up one September morning, gaiety welling up inside me. It was eight o'clock. I pressed my forehead to the window pane and looked. At what? I don't know! I had woken up with a start in the middle of some dream and had leaped toward the light, hoping to find in the infinite grey sky something to illuminate my anxious but joyous sense of expectation. Expectation of what? Could I have said what at the time? Can I say now, today, after long reflection? No.

I was nearly fifteen. I was waiting for life to start, and this morning seemed to me to herald a new era. I was not mistaken, for this September day decided my future.

I remained at the window in a trance, my forehead on the glass, seeing in the mist formed by my breath houses, palaces, carriages, jewels, pearls. Oh, how many pearls there were! Princes . . . kings . . . yes, I went as far as kings! The imagination moves fast, and reason, its enemy, always leaves it to wander on its own. In my pride and enthusiasm I rejected princes, kings, pearls, and palaces and retorted, "I want to be a nun!" For in the infinity of grey sky I caught a glimpse of the convent of Grand-Champs, my white dormitory, and the little lamp swaying above the little Virgin, Whom we had decorated with our own hands. I preferred the throne of the Mother Superior (which it was my vague ambition to have at some distant point in the future) to the throne that the king offered me. And the king would die of despair! Oh my God yes! I preferred the rosary beads that I could feel slipping through my fingers to the pearls offered me by princes! And no outfit could compete with the veil of black barège[1] falling like a soft shadow on the snowy white batiste[2] that framed the beloved faces of the nuns of Grand-Champs.

I don't know how long I had been dreaming in this way when I heard Mama's voice asking Marguerite, our old maidservant, whether I was awake. I leaped into bed and buried my nose under the sheet. Mama opened the door a crack and I pretended to wake up.

"How lazy you are today!"

I kissed my mother and said cajolingly, "It's Thursday today and I have no piano lesson."

"And you are glad?"

"Oh yes!"

My mother frowned.

I hated the piano and Mama adored music. She adored it so much that in order to force me to learn it, and although she was nearly thirty, she took lessons to arouse my spirit of emulation. What a torture for me! Spitefully I set about putting my mother and the piano teacher at odds, and it came to pass over the question of which of the two was the more nearsighted. When my mother had studied a piece of music for three or four days she knew it by heart and could play it quite well without music, much to the astonishment of Mlle. Clarisse, the old and unbearable teacher, who followed the music with her nose to the paper. So it was with great delight one day that I heard a quarrel arise between Mama and the nasty Mlle. Clarisse:

"There's a quaver there!"

"No there isn't!"

"That's a flat!"

"No, you're forgetting the sharp! But you are crazy, Mademoiselle," added my mother and a few moments later she went into her room.

Mlle. Clarisse left, grumbling. As for me, I was suffocating with laughter in my room. With the help of one of my cousins who was a very good musician, I had added some sharps, flats, and quavers, and had done it so well that even a practiced eye would have had difficulty noticing them at first. Mlle. Clarisse was dismissed and I had no more lessons from that day onward.

Mama stared at me for a long time with her mysterious eyes, the most beautiful eyes I have ever seen. "After dinner there is going to be a family council," she said to me slowly.

"Alright. What dress shall I put on, Mama?" I spoke for the sake of speaking, to keep myself from crying.

"Put on your blue silk dress. You will look more serious."

At this moment Jeanne threw open the door with a burst of laughter, jumped on my bed and quickly slipped under the sheets, crying, "I touched goal!" Marguerite came in after her, all out of breath and scolding. The child had slipped away from her just as she was about to give her her bath, saying, "The goal is my sister's bed!" My sister's gaiety at a time that seemed of such gravity for me made me burst into tears. My mother, unable to understand why I was so sorrowful, shrugged her shoulders and ordered Marguerite to fetch the little one's slippers. When she took her two little feet in her hands and kissed them tenderly my sobbing doubled in intensity. Mama had an obvious preference for my sister, and this preference, which normally did not bother me, wounded me cruelly today. Mama went out impatiently.

I tried to forget everything by going to sleep and was woken by Marguerite who helped me dress, as I would otherwise have been late for dinner.

As guests that day there were my aunt Rosine, Mlle. de Brabender, my godfather, and the Duc de Morny,[3] a great friend of my father and mother. The dinner was a gloomy occasion for me. I was waiting for the family council. Mlle. de Brabender kept trying to make me eat with gentle words and tender gestures. My sister burst into laughter when she saw me. "You have eyes like that," she said, putting her little thumb over the end of her index finger, "and that serves you right because you've been crying, and Mama doesn't like crying . . . do you, Mama?"

"Why have you been crying?" the Duc de Morny asked. I did not reply, despite Mlle. Brabender's kind but pointed elbow gently nudging me. The Duc de Morny intimidated me a little. He was mildly mocking. I knew that he held a high position at Court and that my family regarded his friendship as an honor.

"It's because I told her there's going to be a family council after dinner," my mother said slowly. "There are times when she disappoints me."

"Oh come now!" exclaimed my godfather. My aunt Rosine said something in English to the Duc de Morny who smiled subtly into his fine moustache. Mlle. de Brabender scolded me under her breath. *Her* reproaches were heavenly to me. Finally, when the meal was finished, Mama told me to serve the coffee. With Marguerite's help I set out the cups and went into the drawing room.

The lawyer from Le Havre, Maître C***, whom I hated, was already there. He represented my father's family after my father died at Pisa in circumstances that were never explained, and are still a mystery. My childish hate was not misplaced. I learned later that this man had been my father's mortal enemy. He was so very ugly! His whole face seemed to rise toward his scalp. It was as though he had been hung for a long time by the hair and that his eyes, mouth, cheeks, and nose had been pulled up toward the crown of his head. He should have had a cheerful face with all these upward-turning features, but his clean-shaven face was sinister. He had red hair rooted like couch grass, and on his nose he wore a pair of gold-rimmed spectacles. What an ugly man! The memory of this man who had been my father's evil genius haunts me like a hateful nightmare. My poor grandmother, who had never gone out since my father's death and who wept for her beloved son so soon departed, had placed all her trust in this man. He was, furthermore, the executor of my father's will and it was he who controlled the small inheritance that my dear father had left me. I was not to enter into possession of this inheritance until my marriage and my mother drew on the interest for my education.

My uncle Félix Faure was there, sitting near the fireplace. Grumpily buried in his armchair, M. Meydieu took out his watch. He was an old friend of the family who always addressed me as "girl," which irritated me. He addressed me with the familiar "tu" form[4] and thought I was stupid. When I offered him coffee he eyed me scornfully, "So it's for you my girl that so many good people have to be troubled. They really have better things to do than bother themselves over a sniveling kid like you. Now if we were talking about your sister, we could take care of it quickly. There wouldn't be any problem . . . " and he stroked my sister's hair with his stiff fingers as she sat on the floor, plaiting the fringe of the armchair in which he sat.

The coffee had been drunk, the cups removed, my sister led away. There was a short silence. The Duc de Morny wanted to leave, but my mother held him back: "Stay! You can give us your opinion." The duke sat down near my aunt with whom he flirted a little. Mama had drawn close to the window with her embroidery in front of her. Her pretty profile was outlined against the window in its clear pure lines. She seemed a stranger to what was happening. The hideous lawyer had risen. My uncle had drawn me close to him. My godfather, Régis, seemed to merge with M. Meydieu. They both had the same stubborn bourgeois soul. They both loved whist and good wine. And both found me unpleasantly thin.

The door opened quietly to reveal a pale creature with brown hair, poetic and charming. It was Mme. Guérard, "the lady upstairs," as Marguerite used to call her. My mother had befriended her. Her friendship was a little patronizing, but Mme. Guérard tolerated the little slights she suffered occasionally out of adoration for me. She was tall, willowy slim, supple, serious. She lived above us and had therefore come down without a hat, wearing a peignoir[5] of printed calico patterned with little chestnut-colored sprays. M. Meydieu muttered something morosely. The abominable lawyer scarcely acknowledged her. The Duc de Morny greeted her graciously—she was so pretty! My godfather nodded—Mme. Guérard counted for nothing with him. My aunt Rosine gave her a casual glance up and down. Mlle. de Brabender shook her hand warmly—Mme. Guérard was so fond of me! My uncle Félix Faure gave her a chair and kindly made her sit down, enquiring after her husband, a scholar, with whom my uncle had worked from time to time during the course of writing his book, *La Vie de Saint Louis*.[6] Mama glanced from under her lashes, but did not raise her head—Mme. Guérard did not prefer my sister!

"Well, we're here for this little one, so let's talk about her," said my godfather. I began to tremble and pressed close between "my little lady" (this is what I had called Mme. Guérard since childhood), and Mlle. de Brabender. Each one took my hand to give me courage.

"Yes," continued M. Meydieu with a guffaw, "so you want to be a nun?" The Duc de Morny exclaimed sceptically to my aunt Rosine who laughingly hushed him. Mama sighed as she drew some threads up close to her eyes, looking for the ones she wanted.

"But you have to be rich to enter a convent and you don't have a penny," growled the lawyer from Le Havre.

I leaned over toward Mlle. de Brabender and whispered in her ear, "I have the money Papa left me."

The nasty man heard me. "Your father left you that money to get married with!"

"Alright. Then I will marry the good Lord!" This time my voice was resolute, and I blushed. For the second time in my life I felt the desire and the will to fight. I was no longer afraid. I was too annoyed. I let go of my two tender protectors and advanced toward the group. "I want to be a nun! I want to! I know father left me the money for me to marry, but I also know that nuns marry the Savior. Mama told me she didn't mind, so I'm not hurting Mama. I am more loved in the convent than here!"

My uncle drew me toward him. "My darling, your faith seems mainly to be a need to love . . . "

"And to *be* loved," Mme. Guérard murmured.

Everybody glanced toward Mama, who lightly shrugged her shoulders. Her look seemed heavy with reproach and I felt a stab of remorse. I went up to my mother and threw my arms around her neck. "Isn't it true that you are quite willing that I should be a nun and that it wouldn't trouble you?"

"On the contrary, it *would* trouble me! Because you know very well that after your sister you are my greatest love," she said in her sweet slow voice. The sound of a little waterfall which drops clear and babbling from the mountain, taking with it little pebbles, then gradually swelling with thawing snow—this was how the trailing voice of my mother seemed to me at that moment.

I bounded back into the group, which was so appalled by my innocent whim. I went from one to another looking for an ally, trying to explain my desire with whatever reason came to mind. Finally, the Duc de Morny who was growing bored, stood up. "You know what

should be done with this child? She should be put in the Conservatoire."[7]
He patted my cheek, kissed my aunt's hand, and bade the men farewell. I overheard him say to Mama, "You would have made a poor
diplomat. But follow my advice, put her in the Conservatoire." Then
he disappeared.

In anguish at the word "Conservatoire," I looked at everybody.
What was it? I leaned over toward my teacher, Mlle. de Brabender. She
pursed her lips and seemed shocked, the way she did when my godfather made an off-color joke at the table. My uncle Félix Faure looked
at the floor, absorbed. The lawyer had a rancorous look in his eye.
M. Meydieu nodded his head with some "Well, perhaps," "Who knows?"
and "Hm, Hm!'s" Mme. Guérard remained pale and sad and looked at
me tenderly. So what was the Conservatoire? This word, uttered so
casually, had knocked everybody over. Each seemed to react differently
to it, but nobody seemed happy about it.

Suddenly, in the middle of the general confusion, my godfather
exclaimed brutally, "She's too thin to make an actress!"

"I don't want to be an actress!" I cried.

"You don't know what that is!" my aunt said.

"Yes, I do! I know what Rachel is!"

"You know Rachel?" said Mama, standing up.

"Yes, yes, at the convent. She came one day to see little Adèle
Sarony. She looked round the convent and had to be sat down in the
garden because she couldn't breathe any more. Some medicine was
fetched to put her back on her feet. She was pale, so pale that she upset
me, and Sister Sainte-Appoline told me that she was in a profession that
was killing her, that she was an actress. So I don't want to be an actress!
I don't want to!" I had said all that in one breath, my cheeks burning,
my voice firm. I remembered what Sister Sainte-Appoline and Mother
Sainte-Sophie had said to me. And I remembered that when Rachel
had left the garden all pale and supported by a lady, a girl had stuck
her tongue out at her. I didn't want anyone to stick out her tongue at
me when I was a lady. I did not want many things that I did not completely understand, but which I remembered.

My godfather was doubled up with laughter, my uncle still serious,
the others were engaged in discussion. My aunt was talking excitedly
with Mama who appeared tired and bored. Mlle. de Brabender and
Mme. Guérard were arguing in low voices. I thought about the man
who had just left. I resented him, for it was he who had had this idea
of the Conservatoire and the word scared me. It was he who wanted me
to become an actress. But he had left and I could not argue with him.
He had left calmly smiling, giving me a casual affectionate pat, but not

giving a damn for this little skinny thing whose future was being discussed. "Put her in the Conservatoire!" This sentence tossed out so lightly had fallen like a bomb on my life.

I, the dreaming child who only this morning rejected princes and kings; I, whose trembling hands fingered this morning the rosaries of dream; I, who only a few hours ago had felt my heart beat with an unfamiliar emotion and had risen expecting some great event! Everything had crumbled under the leaden weight of this sentence as deadly as a cannon ball: "Put her in the Conservatoire!" I realized that this sentence was the signpost of my life. All these assembled people had stopped at this crossroads—"Put her in the Conservatoire!" I wanted to be a nun. Everyone thought that absurd and senseless. But "Put her in the Conservatoire!" had opened up the field of discussion and revealed to everyone the horizon of my future.

Only my uncle Félix Faure and Mlle. de Brabender were against the idea. They tried in vain to make my mother accept that with the hundred thousand francs that my father had left me I would find a husband. But Mama replied that I had told her that the idea of marriage horrified me, and that I would wait until I reached the age of majority and then go into a convent.

"In these circumstances," she kept saying, "Sarah will not have her father's money!"

"No, certainly not," agreed the lawyer.

"And," continued my mother, "she would go into the convent as a servant, and I don't want that! As for me, my wealth is all in the form of a life-annuity, so I will leave nothing to my children. I want to give them careers!" Exhausted by so much talk, my suffering Mama stretched out in an armchair.

I was becoming unbearably tense and my mother urged me to go to my room. Mlle. de Brabender tried to console me. Mme. Guérard thought this career had some points in its favor. Mlle. de Brabender thought the convent had a certain charm for an introspective nature. The latter was pious, a devout practicer, whereas "my little lady" was pagan in the purest sense of the word. Nevertheless, these two ladies understood one another because they both adored me. Mme. Guérard adored my proud rebellious nature, my prettiness, and my physical grace. Mlle. de Brabender felt tender toward me because of my fragile health; she consoled me in my grief at not being loved like my sister; but, above all, she loved my voice—she used to say that it had the accent of prayer, and my taste for the convent seemed quite natural to her. She loved me with a gentle religious tenderness. Mme. Guérard loved me with pagan love. These two women, the memory of whom I still cherish, had shared out my nature between them and adapted marvellously to my faults and my virtues. I certainly owe both of them my self-knowledge.

This day was to finish in the most incongruous way. I had stretched out in the little wicker armchair, which was the finest piece of furniture in my bedroom when I was a girl, and had dozed off, holding Mlle. de Brabender's hand. Mme. Guérard had gone back upstairs to her apartment. The door of my bedroom opened and my aunt entered, followed by Mama. I can still see my aunt in her dress of purple silk trimmed with fur, her chestnut-brown velvet hat tied under the chin with two long wide ties. Mama had taken off her dress and put on a white woollen peignoir. Mama hated staying in formal dress. Seeing her changed, I realized that everyone had gone and that my aunt was also preparing to leave. I got up, but Mama made me sit down.

"Rest a bit longer! This evening we are going to take you to the Théâtre-Français." I realized that they were trying to lure me, and therefore showed no pleasure, although deep down I was delighted at the thought of going to the Théâtre-Français. The only theater I knew, in fact, was the Robert-Houdin where I was sometimes taken with my sister, and I think it was chiefly for her sake, because I was a little too old to enjoy the shows. "Will you come with us?" Mama said to Mlle. Brabender.

"With pleasure, Madame," replied the dear lady. "Please allow me to get changed."

My aunt laughed at my sulkiness. "Ah! You little mask!" she said as she was leaving. "You are hiding your pleasure. Well, tonight you will see some actresses."

"Is Rachel performing?"

"Oh no, she is ill." She kissed me and left, saying, "See you to-night!"

My mother followed her. Mlle. de Brabender stood up all in a bustle. She had to leave immediately to dress and give notice that she would not be back until very late, as in the convent special permission had to be obtained to return after ten o'clock.

Now alone, I rocked in the wicker chair, although it was not a rocking-chair. I started to think: a critical faculty was beginning to germinate in me. So, all this disturbance of serious people—the lawyer summoned from Le Havre, my uncle torn away from work on his book, the old boy M. Meydieu disturbed in his routine, my godfather kept from the Stock Exchange, and the elegant and sceptical Duc de Morny grounded for two hours in this little bourgeois milieu—the upshot of all of this was the decision, "We are going to take her to the theater." I don't know what part my uncle had played in this farce, but I doubt it was to his taste. Nevertheless, I was happy to be going to the theater. I felt more important than usual. I had got up in the morning still a child, but in the space of a few hours events had made me into a young woman. I had been the subject of discussion. I had been able to express my wish. It was true that it had not been accepted, but I had nevertheless expressed it. Finally, it was now felt necessary to pamper and spoil me to get my consent. I could not be forced to do what others wanted. My consent had to be sought. I felt so joyful and proud of that, that I was mollified and almost inclined to give it. But, I said to myself, I would make them beg for it all the same.

After dinner we piled into a carriage—Mama, my godfather, Mlle. de Brabender, and I. My godfather had presented me with a gift of twelve pairs of white gloves. As I climbed the stairs at the Théâtre-Français I trod on the dress of the woman in front, who turned round and called me "little fool." I leaped backward into the enormous belly of an old gentleman, who pushed me away forcefully. Once we were all in the box—I in the first row with Mama, and Mlle. de Brabender behind me—I felt more at ease. I was pressed up against the front wall of the box and could feel Mlle. de Brabender's pointed knees in my velvet chair back, which gave me confidence. I leaned back in order to feel them even more.

When the curtain slowly rose I thought I was going to faint. It was, in fact, the curtain of my life which was rising. Those columns (it was a performance of *Britannicus*)[8] would be my palace. That backdrop would be my sky. That floor would give under my light weight. I heard nothing of *Britannicus*. I was far, far away, in my dormitory at Grand-Champs.

When the curtain dropped my godfather exclaimed, "Well, what do you say?" I did not reply. He turned my head around. I was crying big tears that slowly rolled down my cheeks—silent unending tears. My godfather shrugged and left the box, slamming the door. Mama turned impatiently to survey the crowd with her opera glasses. Mlle. de Brabender gave me her handkerchief. Mine had dropped and I did not dare to pick it up.

The curtain went up on the second play, *Amphitryon*.[9] I made an effort to listen to please my sweet amiable teacher. I remember only one thing: that I found Alcmène so unhappy that I burst into noisy sobs and the audience, much amused, stared at our box. My irritated mother led me away with Mlle. de Brabender, leaving behind my furious godfather who growled, "Stick her in a convent and let her stay there! Good God! What an idiot this child is!"

Such was the début of my artistic career.

Chapter VII

I was beginning to think, however, about my new career. Everybody sent me books: by Racine, Corneille, Molière, Casimir
Delavigne, etc. I opened them, but as I did not understand them I
quickly closed them, and reread La Fontaine,[1] whom I loved passionately. I knew all his fables. One of my joys was to make bets with my
godfather, or M. Meydieu, his learned and unbearable friend, that they
would not be able to recognize some of the fables if I started with the
last line and went backward toward the first, and often I won the bet.

One day a note arrived from my aunt, informing us that M. Auber,
then the director of the Conservatoire,[2] would be expecting us the
following morning at nine o'clock. I was going to put my foot in the
stirrup!

Mama sent me with Mme. Guérard. M. Auber, who had already
heard about me from the Duc de Morny, received us very kindly. His
was a fine head. His magnificent black eyes contrasted glowingly with
his white hair and ivory complexion. He was slim and distinguished.
His appearance and melodious voice, combined with my knowledge of
his fame, made a strong impression on me.

I hardly dared reply to his questions. Gently he made me sit down
close to him. "Do you like the theater very much?"

"Oh no, sir!"

This unexpected reply astounded him. He lifted his heavy-lidded
eyes to Mme. Guérard who said, "No, she doesn't like the theater, but
she doesn't want to get married and therefore will have no money,
since her father left her a hundred thousand francs, which she can only
have if she gets married. So her mother wants her to have a career
because Mme. Bernhardt has only a life-annuity which is quite good,
but which she cannot leave to her daughters. This being the case, she
wants Sarah to be independent. But Sarah would rather enter the
convent."

M. Auber said slowly, "That isn't an independent career, my child.
How old is she?"

"She's fourteen and a half," replied Mme. Guérard.

"No!" I cried out, "I'm nearly fifteen!"

The pleasant old man smiled. "In twenty years," he said, "you'll be less of a stickler for exact figures." Then, feeling that the interview had lasted long enough, he got up. "It seems," he said to "my little lady," "that the girl's mother is very beautiful?"

"Oh, very pretty!" she replied.

"Will you tell her that I was sorry not to have seen her, and give her my thanks for sending such a gallant substitute," and he kissed Mme. Guérard's hand, who blushed slightly.

I report this conversation word for word. Every movement and gesture of M. Auber's engraved itself on my mind, for this little man, full of charm and gentleness, all alone held my future in his delicate hand.

He opened the drawing-room door and said, as he touched me on the shoulder, "Never fear, my dear. Believe me, you will thank your Mama for having forced your hand. And don't look so sad! Life should be lived seriously but gaily." I stammered a few words of thanks. As I was getting ready to leave I was jostled by a beautiful woman with a rather heavy build and an excessively ebullient manner. "And especially," murmured M. Auber bending down to me, "don't let yourself put on weight like this great singer. Fat is the enemy of women and artists."

Then, while the servant was holding the door open to let us out, I heard M. Auber say as he went back into the drawing room, "Well, that's the most ideal woman . . . etc." I went downstairs a little bewildered and did not say a word in the carriage. Mme. Guérard recounted the story of our interview to Mama, but she interrupted her with "Good, good, thank you," and did not let her finish.

As the examination was to take place a month after this visit I had to start preparing for it. Mama did not know anyone in the theater. My godfather advised me to learn the part of Phèdre but Mlle. de Brabender was against that, as she found it rather shocking, and refused to help me if I chose it. M. Meydieu, our old friend, wanted me to work on Chimène in *Le Cid*,[4] but first he said that I didn't round the "o's" or roll the "r's" enough, and then he gave me a little exercise book. I reproduce the contents of this exactly, as my poor dear Guérard treasured everything that related to me, and it is she who gave me a large quantity of documents that are very useful as I write. Here are the instructions of my odious friend:

> Every morning practise *"te, de, de"* to the scales to improve your vibration. Before breakfast say forty times *"Un très gros rat*

dans un très gros trou" to open your "r's." Before dinner say forty times *"Combien ces six saucisses-ci?—C'est six sous ces six saucisses-ci!—Six sous ces six saucissons-ci?—Six sous ceux-ci! Six sous ceux-là! Six sous ces six saucissons-ci!"* to learn not to whistle your "s's." At night before going to bed, say twenty times *"Didon dîna, dit-on, du dos d'un dodu dindon"* and twenty times *"Le plus petit papa, petit pipi, petit popo, petit pupu."*[5] Open your mouth wide for the "d's" and purse it for the "p's."

He handed over this work to Mlle. de Brabender with great seriousness. She, with equal seriousness, wanted me to follow his instructions. Mlle. de Brabender was charming and I loved her, but I could not help bursting into lunatic laughter when, after having made me do the *"te, de, de,"* which I could manage, and *"le très gros rat,"* she started on the *"saucissons."* In her toothless mouth they made a cacophony of whistles likely to make all the dogs in Paris howl. And when the *"Didon dîna"* was thrown in, into the bargain, together with some *"plus petit papa,"* I thought that my dear teacher had lost her senses altogether: her eyes half-closed, her face red, her moustache bristling, her demeanour pompous and bustling, her mouth taking on now the form of a piggy-bank slot, now creasing up into a little round, she rumbled, whistled, dingdonged, and putt-putted without stopping. I collapsed into my wicker chair. Laughter strangled me. Big tears spurted through my lashes. My feet beat the floor. My arms thrown out to right and left groped and twisted with spasms of laughter. I bent over now forward now backward. My mother, drawn by the uproar, opened the door a crack. Mlle. de Brabender explained very seriously that she was demonstrating M. Meydieu's "Method." Mama remonstrated with me, but I could not listen, I was delirious with laughter. She took away the teacher and left me alone, fearing that I would have a fit of hysterics otherwise. Left alone, I gradually calmed down. I closed my eyes and pictured the convent. The *"te, de, de"* mingled for a moment in my confused state of mind with the Lord's Prayer that I used to have to repeat fifteen or twenty times as a penance. Finally I regained my senses, got up, washed my face in cold water, and then went to join my mother whom I found playing whist with my teacher and godfather. I gave an affectionate kiss to Mlle. de Brabender, who kissed me in return so kindly that I was taken aback.

The days passed. The only exercises of Meydieu I did were the *"te, de, de"* accompanied by the piano. My mother woke me every morning to do this exercise, which I hated. My godfather had made me learn Aricie,[6] but I understood nothing that he said to me about the poetry.

It was his opinion, as he explained to me, that the verse itself should be pronounced without any particular stress except on the rhyme. It was deadly boring to listen to and impossible to put into practice. In addition, I did not really understand the character of Aricie, who seemed to me not to love Hippolyte at all, and to be a wily coquette. My godfather explained to me that this was the way people loved in antiquity. And when I said to him that Phèdre seemed to love him more, he took my chin and said, "Look at this little mask! She pretends not to understand and would like someone to explain it all to her."

It was all too stupid. I understood nothing and asked no questions. But how bourgeois, sneaky, and lewd this man was in spirit. He did not like me because I was thin; but I interested him because I was going to be an actress. For him this word meant all the most superficial aspects of the art. He was incapable of seeing its beauty, nobility, and benevolent power. At the time it was difficult for me to sort out all of this, but I felt ill at ease in the presence of this man whom I had known since childhood and who was almost a father to me.

I did not want to continue learning Aricie. Most importantly, I could not discuss it with my teacher who did not want to hear about this play. So I learned *L'Ecole des femmes* and Agnès[7] was explained to me by Mlle. de Brabender. The dear lady did not see very much in it. The whole story seemed childishly simple to her. And when I rehearsed *"Il m'a pris . . . il m'a pris le ruban que vous m'aviez donné "*[8] she would smile unsuspectingly as Meydieu and my godfather roared with laughter.

Chapter VIII

$\mathcal{F}$inally the day of the examination arrived. Everybody had given me words of advice, but no one had given me any solid advice. No one had thought of hiring a professional to prepare me for the exam.

I got up early in the morning feeling heavy-hearted and uneasy. Mama had had made for me a black silk dress with a slightly décolleté neckline edged with a gathered bertha.[1] The dress was rather short and showed my broderie anglaise[2] pantaloons, their embroidered hems resting on my ankle-boots of bronze kid. From my black bodice there emerged a white chemisette,[3] which encircled my excessively slender neck; my hair was parted on my forehead and framed my head however it liked; no pin or ribbon could restrain it. I also wore a big straw hat although it was late in the year. Everybody came to inspect my attire. I was turned around and back twenty times. I had to curtsey . . . just to see how I would look.

Finally everybody seemed content. "My little lady" came down with her serious husband and kissed me, very moved. Old Marguerite made me sit down and put in front of me a cup of cold broth, which she had simmered long and tenderly to a delicious jelly that I could swallow in a second. I was in a hurry to leave.

As I rose from my chair I got up so quickly that my dress tore on some tiny splinter. Mama turned around in annoyance to a visitor who had come in five minutes before and was standing in admiring contemplation. "See! Here is the proof of what I kept telling you; all these silks tear with the slightest movement."

"But," this person shot back, "I told you that that silk was overscoured,[4] and I gave it to you at a good price for that reason." He was a young Jew, quite good-looking, shy, a Dutchman. He was gentle but tenacious. I had known him all my life. His father, a friend of my maternal grandfather, was a rich businessman and father of a large tribe. He sent his sons, endowed with a small allowance, to seek their fortune wherever their fancy took them. Jacques, the one I am describing, had come to Paris. He had at first sold matzos and as a young boy

41

he had often come to the convent to bring me some along with the treats that Mama used to send. Then what a surprise, one day that I was home from school, to see him offering Mama rolls of the kind of oilcloth that is used for tablecloths for the breakfast table. I remember that one of these fabrics had a border of medallions representing all the kings of France. It was on this cloth that I was best able to learn my history. Anyway for a whole month he had been the owner of quite an elegant little fabric store and he sold overscoured silks. He is now one of the most important jewellers in Paris.

The tear in my dress was quickly mended and, knowing now that it was made of overscoured silk, I treated it with care. Finally we parted, Mlle. de Brabender, Mme. Guérard, and I in a little carriage for two. I was happy that the carriage was so small because I was squeezed between these two kind ladies, my dress of overscoured silk delicately spread out on their knees.

When I entered the room in which one waited before entering the audition room, there were already fifteen or so boys there and about twenty girls. All of the latter were accompanied by their mother, father, aunt, brother, or sister, etc. A smell of beef marrow mixed with vanilla hit me and made me retch. As the door opened for me I felt every eye on me and blushed to the roots of my hair. Mme. Guérard led me in gently and I turned back to find Mlle. de Brabender's hand. She came in timidly, redder than I and even more embarrassed. Everybody was looking at her and I could see the girls nudge each other and nod toward her. One girl jumped up and ran to her mother, "Look at that sight!" My poor teacher felt awkward, while I was getting angry. I thought she looked a thousand times better than all these fat and vulgar mothers with their plumage. Of course, Mlle. de Brabender *did* look different with her salmon-colored dress, her Indian shawl tightly wrapped round her shoulders and pinned at the front by a very large cameo, and her hat framing her face with such tight ruching that it made one think of a nun's wimple. She very certainly did not look like this ugly crowd with the exception of about ten people among them. The boys were clustered in a tight squad near the windows, laughing and making comments in dubious taste, I think. The door opened. A girl who was very flushed and a boy who was positively scarlet had just recited their scene. Each of them went back to their families, chattering away and complaining each about the other. A name was called: "Mlle. Dica-Petit." I saw a tall girl, blonde and distinguished, go forward confidently.[5] She stopped to kiss a pretty woman, fat, pink and white, and all dolled up. "Don't worry, Mama darling . . . " then she said something in Dutch and disappeared, followed by a boy and a skinny little girl who was to make responses for him. This detail was explained to me by

Léautaud, who was calling out the names of the students and taking the names of the reciters and responders. I had not known about that. Who would make responses for me in my role as Agnès? He suggested several young people, but I stopped him.

"No, no, Monsieur, I don't want to ask anyone to do that. I don't know anybody. I don't want to do that!"

"Well what will you recite then, Mademoiselle?" asked Léautaud in the most blasé tones.

"I'll recite a fable."

He sniggered as he wrote down my name and the title, *Les Deux Pigeons*,[6] that I gave him. I heard him still chuckling into his big moustache as he continued to make his rounds. Then I saw him go into the audition room of the Conservatoire. I began to feel feverish, which worried Guérard for unfortunately my health was very delicate. She made me sit down and put some drops of eau de cologne behind my ears.

Smack! "That will teach you to wink like that!" A tremendous slap across the prettiest face possible. The mother of Nathalie Manvoy had just hit her daughter. I stood up, trembling with fear, hopping with anger. I wanted the ugly woman to be slapped in return. I wanted to kiss the pretty head that had received the insult. But I felt myself forcefully held back by my two guardians. Dica-Petit coming out of the audition room set everybody's thoughts in a new direction. She was radiant and pleased with herself. Oh, very pleased! Her brother handed her a little flask in which there was some kind of cordial (and I would have been happy to have some, for my throat was dry and burning). Her mother folded a little woollen scarf over her chest before fastening her coat and all three disappeared. Other girls and boys were called before it was my turn. Finally, my name was called, which made me jump like a sardine pursued by a big fish. I shook my hair back. "My little lady" stroked my second-quality silk. Mlle. de Brabender told me to remember my "o's," "a's," "r's," "p's," and "t's", and I went into the room all on my own.

I had never been alone for a single hour in all my life. As a little child I was always clinging to my nurse's skirts; at the convent always hanging on to a friend or one of the sisters; at home always between Mlle. de Brabender and Mme. Guérard, or, if they were not there, in the kitchen with Marguerite. And here I was all alone in this strange room with a platform at one end, a big table in the middle, and all round the table growling men, either grousers or jeerers. There was a single woman with a high and mighty manner, holding pince-nez, which she only put down to pick up her lorgnette. I felt their eyes behind me as I climbed the few stairs. Once I was on the platform Léautaud leaned over and whispered, "Curtsey, then start, and stop when the chairman rings." I looked at the chairman. It was M. Auber. Indeed, I had forgotten that he was the director of the Conservatoire. I had forgotten everything. So I curtseyed and started:

> Deux pigeons s'aimaient d'amour tendre.
> L'un d'eux s'ennuyant au . . . [7]

I heard a deep growl and a ventriloquist droned, "We're not in class here. What an idea to recite fables!" It was Beauvallet,[8] the tragedian with the booming voice from the Comédie-Française. I stopped, my heart beating.

"Continue, my child," said a man with silver hair: it was Provost.[9]

"Yes, it will be shorter than a scene," exclaimed Augustine Brohan,[10] the only woman present. I started again:

> Deux pigeons s'aimaient d'amour tendre.
> L'un d'eux s'ennuyant au logis
> Fut assez . . . [11]

"Louder, my child, louder," a little man with frizzy white hair said kindly. It was Samson.[12] I stopped terror-struck, overcome with nerves, ready to cry, to scream. Seeing this, M. Samson said to me, "See, we are not ogres." He had just spoken in a low voice to Auber. "Come along, start again, and louder this time."

"Oh no!" exclaimed Augustine Brohan. "If she starts again, it's going to be longer than a scene!" This outburst made everyone at the table laugh. During this time I took hold of myself. I thought these people malicious to laugh at this poor little trembling thing who had been handed over to them with her hands bound. I felt a slight, although indefinable, contempt for this merciless jury. I have often since thought about this ordeal, and I have come to the realization that good, intelligent, compassionate people turn into inferior beings when they are part of a crowd. The absence of personal responsibility awakens evil instincts. Fear of ridicule chases away the good ones.

Having regained my self-possession, I started the fable again, unconcerned about what might happen. My voice had become more liquid with the effect of my emotions, the desire to make myself heard made the timbre of my voice sing. Silence fell. Before the end of the fable the bell rang. I made a sign, and descended a few steps, exhausted.

M. Auber stopped me as I went past. "Well, little one, that was very good. Here are M. Provost and M. Beauvallet who want to have you in their class." I recoiled a bit when he pointed out M. Beauvallet. It was the ventriloquist who had frightened me so much. "Well, which of these gentlemen do you prefer?" I did not reply, but pointed to Provost. "There you are! Perfect! Take out your handkerchief, my poor Beauvallet. I entrust this child to you, my dear Provost."

I understood, and cried out mad with joy, "So I am accepted!"

"Yes, you're accepted. And I have only one regret, and that is that your pretty voice is not destined for music."

But I was no longer listening. I was crazy with joy. I did not thank anybody. I ran to the door. " 'My little lady,' Mademoiselle, . . . I'm accepted!" As they pressed my hand and asked questions I said nothing except, "Yes, yes, I've been accepted!" I was surrounded and questioned: "How do you know you've been accepted?" "One never knows in advance." "Yes, yes, I know! M. Auber told me. I am going into the class of M. Provost! M. Beauvallet wanted me but I didn't want his class. His voice is too loud!"

A spiteful girl exclaimed, "Have you quite finished?! . . . Alright, so they're fighting all over you!"

A girl who was pretty, but too swarthy for my taste, came up to me quietly, "What did you recite, Mademoiselle?"

"I recited the fable of *Les Deux Pigeons.*" She was astonished. Everybody was astonished. And I was overjoyed because I was causing astonishment.

I clapped my hat on my head, swept up my skirts, and carried off my two friends as I danced out. They wanted me to eat something in the cake shop, but I refused. We got into the carriage. Oh! How I would like to have pushed it along! On all the shop fronts, I read "I've been accepted!" When the carriage stopped in some traffic jam, it seemed to me that people were looking at me in astonishment, and I was surprised to find myself nodding my head as though to say, "Yes, yes, it's true, I've been accepted!" I gave no further thought to the convent. I felt only pride that I had succeeded in the first endeavor I had undertaken. An endeavor whose success depended on me alone. It seemed to me that the coachman would never get to 265 rue Saint-Honoré. I kept putting my head out of the window and saying, "Quicker, please, quicker, coachman!"

Finally, we arrived at the house. I jumped out of the carriage to get to the house quickly and shout the good news to my mother. I was stopped by the daughter of the concierge. She was a corset maker and worked in a little attic opposite the window of the dining room where I worked when I was having lessons with my teacher, so that I could not help staring at her ruddy, lively little face. I had never spoken to her but I knew who she was. "Well, Mlle. Sarah, are you happy?" "Yes, yes,

I have been accepted!" And I lingered a second, unable to resist the joyful surprise of the concierge's whole family. I slipped away however to run to Mama, but as I entered the courtyard I found myself rooted to the spot. Anger and sorrow possessed me as I saw "my little lady" standing there, her hands cupped to her mouth, her head thrown back, shouting to Mama who was leaning out of the window, "Yes, yes, she's been accepted!" I hit her in the back with my fist and started to cry with rage, for I had prepared for Mama a complete little story, which was to finish with a wonderful surprise. I was to enter the room with a sad air, regretful and confused, so as to make myself a target for her usual comment: "It doesn't surprise me, you are so silly, my poor little thing." Then I would throw my arms round her neck and say, "It's not true, it's not true, I've been accepted!" And in my imagination I could see their faces light up: old Marguerite, my godfather guffawing, my sisters dancing . . . And here was Mme. Guérard trumpeting the news aloud and preempting the effect I had so well prepared.

I must say that the lovely lady continued to do this until her death, which is to say for most of my life. It was in vain that I made violent scenes; when I was recounting an adventure that I wanted to make an impression, she could not help bursting into laughter before the end. And if I was sketching out a story with a sad ending, she would sigh and roll her eyes and keep murmuring "Alas!" which would ruin the whole effect that I intended. This drove me crazy, so that finally I would say, "Guérard, go out, my darling," before I started a story, and she would go out, laughing at the thought of the blunders she could have made.

Still cursing Guérard, I went upstairs to Mama whom I found standing at the wide open door. She kissed me tenderly and seeing my sulky face said, "So you're not happy?"

"Yes, but it's Guérard. I'm furious with her. Be a sport, Mama. Act as though you knew nothing. Close the door. I'm going to ring. And I rang. Marguerite opened it. Mama arrived. She acted surprised. And my sisters, and my godfather, and my aunt . . . And when I embraced Mama and yelled, "I've been accepted!" everybody exclaimed in joy. I was happy once again. I had made an impression after all. My career was already taking possession of me without my realizing it.

My sister Régina, whom the sisters did not want to keep at the convent and had sent home to Mama, started to dance a folk dance called the *bourrée*. She had learned this dance from her nurse and danced it on every occasion, always finishing with this little couplet:

> Mon p'tit ventr' 'éjouis toi,
> Tout ce ze gagn' est pou' toi . . . [13]

Nothing was more comic than this chubby little girl with her serious manner. Régina never laughed. Hardly a smile would part her thin lips or relax her very small mouth. Yes, nothing could be funnier than watching her so seriously and brutally dancing the *bourrée*, and on this day she was funnier than ever because she was excited by everyone's joy. She was four years old and nothing bothered her. She was wild and insolent. She hated society and people in general. When she was forced to appear in the drawing room, she would embarrass everyone with her strange and wild remarks, her aggressive replies, her kicking and punching. This *enfant terrible* had platinum hair, a pearly complexion, blue eyes too large for her face, and lush eyelashes which shadowed her cheek when she lowered her eyes and touched her eyebrows when her eyes were open. She was obstinate and melancholy. Sometimes four or five hours would go by without her opening her mouth, refusing to answer any question put to her. Then she would jump up from her little chair and start singing her head off as she danced the *bourrée*.

Today she was in a very good mood. She stroked me tenderly and relaxed her clenched lips to smile at me. My sister Jeanne kissed me and made me tell the story of my audition. My godfather gave me a hundred francs. M. Meydieu, who had just arrived to find out the result of my audition, promised to take me next day to Barbedienne's so that I could choose a clock for my room: it was a dream of mine.

Chapter IX

rom this day a change began to take place in me. My childish soul persisted with me for quite some time longer, but intellectually I had a much clearer perception of life. I began to feel the need to create a personality for myself. It was the first awakening of my will. I wanted to be someone. At first Mlle. de Brabender told me that this was pride. It seemed to me that it was not that at all. But I found it difficult at the time to define what motivated this desire. I did not understand till several months afterward why I wanted to be someone.

A friend of my godfather's proposed to me. This man was a rich tanner. A nice man, but so brown, so black, so hairy, so bearded, that he disgusted me. I refused. So my godfather asked my mother's permission to talk to me in private. He made me sit down in my mother's room and said, "My poor child, you are stupid to refuse M. Bed***. He has an income of sixty thousand francs. He has prospects." It was the first time I had heard this word, and when he explained what it meant to me, I wondered what "prospects" had to do with it all. "Of course they're important," said my godfather, "your romantic ideas are idiotic. Marriage is a business arrangement and must be regarded as such. Your future father-in-law and mother-in-law are bound to die just like you and I, and it's not unpleasant to think that they will leave two million to their son and thereby also to you if you marry him!"

"I don't want to marry him."

"Why?"

"Because I don't love him."

"But one doesn't always love before marriage," replied my pragmatic counsellor. "You will love him afterward."

"After what?"

"Ask your mother. But listen to me. That's not important just now. You have to get married. Your mother has a life-annuity left by your father. But this annuity comes out of the income from the factory that your grandmother owns, and she cannot stand your mother. Your mother's going to be dispossessed of her income and will be left with

49

nothing, with three children on her hands. It's that cursed lawyer from Le Havre who has arranged all this. The whys and the wherefores would take too long to explain. Your father handled his affairs badly. So you have to marry, if not for yourself, at least for the sake of your mother and sisters. You'll give your mother the hundred thousand francs that your father left you which can't be touched. M. Bed*** will put three hundred thousand francs in your name. I've arranged everything. If you want you can give that to your mother and with four hundred thousand francs she will live very well."

I burst into tears and asked for time to think it over. I found Mama in the dining room. She asked me gently, almost timidly, "Your godfather has spoken to you?"

"Yes, mother, yes. Will you let me think about it?" I threw my arms about her and sobbed on her shoulder. Then I shut myself up in my room, and, for the first time in a long time I longed for the convent. My whole childhood rose up before me and I cried even more. I felt so unhappy that I wanted to die. Little by little, however, I calmed down and went carefully over the facts and over what had been said. I definitely did not want to marry this man. Since I had been at the Conservatoire I had learned certain things. Vaguely, oh, very vaguely, for I was never alone! But, in any case, I understood enough not to want to marry without love.

However, I had to endure an unexpected attack. Mme. Guérard asked me to go up to see the embroidery she was doing on a frame for Mama's birthday. Imagine my surprise to find there M. Bed***. He begged me to change my mind. It gave me a lot of pain to see this dark man crying. "Do you want a more impressive dowry?" he asked me. "I will assign you five hundred thousand francs."

But that wasn't it, and under my breath I said, "But, Monsieur, I don't love you!"

"But, Mademoiselle, *I* will die of sorrow if you won't marry me." I looked at this man ... die of sorrow ... I felt confused, sorry, and enchanted ... for he loved me the way people love in plays. I vaguely recalled phrases I had read and heard. I repeated them to him without conviction and I left him without coquetterie.

M. Bed*** did not die. He is still living and is very wealthy. He is much better than he was when he was all black, for now he is all white.

Apart from this, I had just passed my first examination with flying colors, especially in tragedy. M. Provost, my teacher, had not wanted me to use a scene from *Zaïre*,[1] but I had insisted. I found the charming scene between Zaïre and her brother Nérestan very much to my taste. But at the moment when Zaïre, overcome by her brother's reproach, falls at his feet, and says, "*Frappe! dis-je, je l'aime ... !*"[2] Provost wished me to say these words with violence, whereas I wanted to say them gently and with the resignation that comes from almost certain death. I argued for a long time with my teacher, and eventually I pretended to give in to him during the classes. But on the day of the examination I fell on my knees in front of Nérestan with outspread arms. With a sob I offered my heart full of love to the mortal blow that I expected as I murmured, *"Frappe! dis-je, je l'aime!"* So convincing and tender was the effect that the whole theater erupted into cheers and two rounds of applause. I was awarded the second tragedy prize, to the great displeasure of the audience who would like to have seen me win the first prize.[3] And yet it was just. My youth and inexperience justified this second place. I won an honorable mention for comedy in the role of false Agnès.

So I felt that I had the right to refuse the marriage proposal. My future was revealing itself. Consequently my mother would not lack for anything should she should lose her income. In fact, a few days after the examination, M. Régnier,[4] a professor at the Conservatoire and *societaire*[5] of the Comédie-Française, came to ask my mother if she would allow me to act at the Vaudeville[6] in a play of his (*Germaine*). The directors would give me twenty-five francs per performance. I was amazed, seven hundred and fifty francs a month for my début! I was over the moon. I begged my mother to accept the terms offered by the Vaudeville. She told me to do as I pleased. I asked for an interview with M. Camille Doucet, Director of Fine Arts. As Mama refused as usual to accompany me, Mme. Guérard came with me. My little sister Régina begged me to take her and I agreed. It was the wrong decision, for we had only been in the director's office five minutes when my sister, who was five years old at the time, started climbing on the furniture, jumping over a stool, and finally sitting on the floor where she pulled the waste-paper basket placed under the desk toward her and spilled out all the shreds of paper it contained. Seeing this, Camille Doucet remarked gently to her that she was not a very well-behaved little girl.

My sister, with her head in the waste-paper basket replied in her hoarse voice, "Mister, if you annoy me I shall tell everybody that you could poison even holy water. My aunt says so!"

I blushed with shame and stammered, "Don't believe that, M. Camille Doucet, my little sister is lying."

But Régina had leaped up and clenching her fists she hurled herself at me like a little animal. "Aunt Rosine didn't say that? It's you who are the liar... the proof is she said that to M. de Morny who replied that..." I no longer remembered and still do not remember what the Duc de Morny had replied, but, horrified, I put my hand over my sister's mouth and rushed out dragging her with me. As she screamed her head off, we stormed through the crowded waiting room that adjoined the director's office. I exploded into one of those violent fits of anger that had made my childhood so turbulent, and threw myself into the first hackney carriage that passed. Once in the carriage I struck my little sister with such anger that Mme. Guérard was horrified and covered her with her own body, so that it was she who received my kicks, my punches, and all the other blows, for I threw myself right and left, beside myself with anger, sorrow, and shame. And this shame was all the greater for the fact that I liked Camille Doucet very much. He was gentle and charming, genial and sensitive. He had refused my aunt something or other and she, little used to refusals, had taken offense. But I was innocent of all of that. What was Camille Doucet going to think? And I had not even asked him about the Vaudeville. All my plans were ruined, and it was this little monster, as pale and blonde as an angel, who had shattered my greatest dream. Huddled in the carriage, her obstinate forehead creased with fear, her lips thin and tight, she watched me with half-closed eyes through her long lashes. Once I was back home I told my mother the whole story and she told my little sister that she would have no dessert for two days. Régina was fond of food, but her pride was stronger than her appetite. She twirled around on her little heels and began to dance the *bourrée* and sing, *"Mon p'tit ventr' se réjouit pas."*[7] I felt a great urge to smack the nasty little girl.

A few days later I found out in class that the Ministry had refused me permission to play at the Vaudeville. M. Régnier expressed his sympathy but added kindly, "Oh dear, the Conservatoire is holding on to you, dear child, and it is quite right to. So don't be too upset." When I replied, "I'm sure that Camille Doucet is the reason for this," he exclaimed, "Certainly not! Camille Doucet was your warmest advocate, but the Ministry doesn't want to spoil you for your début next year." From then on I nursed a feeling of strong and tender appreciation for this nice man, Camille Doucet, who had held no grudge against me for my little sister's stupid outburst.

I set to work again with real fervor. I never missed a class. Every morning I went to the Conservatoire with my teacher. We left early because I preferred walking to taking the bus; and I kept the twenty *sous*[8] that my mother gave me every morning for both our bus rides and the eight *sous* for cakes. We were meant to come back on foot, but every other day we took a cab with the forty *sous* saved in this way. Mama never suspected this little deceit in which my dear Brabender took part, not without remorse.

I never missed a class.[9] I even went to the classes on deportment where poor M. Elie, an old fop with his curled hair, makeup, and lace frills, gave us the most comical lessons imaginable. There were very few of us at these classes so old Elie took revenge on us for the absence of the others. We all came in for it at every class. Old Elie used to address us as *"tu."* We were his objects. And all five or six of us had to get up on the stage. Standing with his black baton in his hand (why this baton?) he would shout, "Come on ladies, body back, head high, toes down . . . there . . . perfect . . . One, two, three, march!" And we would march, toes down, head high, casting downward glances to see where our feet were going. We walked with all the nobility and solemnity of camels. Then he would teach us how to leave with nonchalance, dignity, or fury. It was a sight to see these girls heading toward the doors, with a dragging step or a sprightly one or a heavy one, depending on the sentiment that was supposed to be expressed. Then there was the miming of "That's enough sir! Please leave!" for old Elie did not want a single word to be uttered. "Everything," he used to say, "is in the look, gesture, and posture." There was also what he called an *"assiette,"* that is sitting down with dignity or collapsing with fatigue. There was also the *assiette* that said, "I'm listening—speak, sir!" That *assiette* was incredibly difficult. One had to put everything into it: the desire to know, the fear of hearing, resignation to the possibility of sending away the interlocutor combined with the wish to retain him . . . What tears this *assiette* cost me! Poor old Elie! I bear him no ill will, but I have done my best to forget what he taught me, for nothing is more useless than instruction in deportment. Every being moves according to its own proportions. Very tall women take strides, those with hunched shoulders walk like orientals, women who are too fat waddle like ducks, those with short legs stump along, very short women skip, and cranes walk like cranes. Nothing can be done about it. Deportment classes are no longer held and that is the way it should be. It is the gesture that should express thought. It is either harmonious or silly depending on whether the actor is intelligent or not. In the theater it is better to have long arms, long rather than short: an actor with short arms can never make a fine gesture! It was vain for Elie to tell us this or that—we were stupid and clumsy—and he was comical, the poor man, oh, so comical!

I also took fencing lessons. My aunt Rosine had put this idea in Mama's head. It was the famous Pons who taught the lessons once a week. What a horrible man he was . . . brutal, vulgar, cocky! An outstanding fencing master, he rebelled against the idea of giving lessons to "little brats," as he called us. But he was not rich and this class— I believe, although I can't confirm it—had been created for him by a patron of high position. He always had his hat on his head—which shocked Mlle. de Brabender—and a cigar in his mouth, which made his students, who were already winded from repeated sallies, cough. What a torture these classes were! From time to time he would bring along friends who very much enjoyed the spectacle of our clumsiness. This caused a scandal one day, for when one of these happy spectators made an excessively insolent remark to a student named Châtelain, the latter wheeled around and slapped him. A brawl followed in which Pons tried to intervene and himself received a couple of blows. All of this caused a great brouhaha, and from that day onward the class was closed to visitors. It was a great relief when I obtained my mother's permission not to go to these classes anymore.

Of all my classes, the one I liked by far the best was Régnier's. He was gentle, well bred, and taught us to speak "true." However, I owe what I know to the variety of classes that I took and seriously pursued. Provost taught us to act in the grand manner, with diction that was rather pompous but elevated. He especially preached amplitude of gesture and inflection. Beauvallet, in my opinion, taught nothing of value. He had a deep and prepossessing voice, but that belonged to him alone. He could not give it to anybody else and, while it was an admirable instrument, it did not in itself invest him with talent. He was clumsy in his gestures, his arms were too short, and his head was without distinction. I detested this teacher. Samson was quite the opposite. His voice was frail and piercing, his dignity was acquired but flawless. His method was to aim for simplicity. Provost sought grandeur, Samson exactitude, and he was especially concerned about final cadences. He would not allow us to let our intonation drop at the end of a sentence. Coquelin,[10] who had been a student of Régnier's I think, had much of Samson's speaking style, retaining at the same time the concern for verisimilitude that he had learned from his first teacher. I remember these three teachers, Régnier, Provost, and Samson as though it were only yesterday.

The academic year slipped by uneventfully for me. However, two months before my second examination, I had the misfortune to change teachers. Provost fell very ill and Samson took me into his class. He had high hopes for me, but he was authoritarian and stubborn. He forced on me two very bad scenes in two very bad plays: Hortense in *L'Ecole des vieillards* by Casimir Delavigne,[11] for comedy, and *La Fille du Cid*, again by Delavigne, for tragedy. I did not feel at ease in these two roles, which were written in harsh and bombastic language.

The day of the examination arrived. I was ugly. Mama had demanded that I have my hair done by her hairdresser. I had cried and sobbed when I saw this barber making rows in my hair in all directions in order to try and make a parting in my rebellious mop. It was this idiot's idea to do this and it was he who had suggested it to Mama. My head was in his stupid hands for an hour and a half, for he had never dealt with hair like this before. He kept mopping his brow every five minutes and saying, "What hair! My God! It's horrible! It's like rope! This is the hair of a blonde negress!" Then, turning to my mother, he said, "Mademoiselle's hair should be shaved and her hair regimented while it grows back." "I'll think about it," said Mama distractedly. I turned around so quickly that I was burned on the forehead by the curling iron this man was holding. But this curling iron was being used to uncurl my hair. Yes, he felt that my hair curled in an unruly way, that it was necessary to uncurl it so that it would wave and give a more dignified look to my face. "Mademoiselle's hair is being arrested in its growth by this crazy frizziness! All the girls in Tangiers and negresses have hair like this! Mademoiselle, who is destined for the stage, would be much more beautiful if she had hair like Madame . . . " he said, bowing with respectful admiration toward my mother, who did indeed have the most beautiful hair in the world—blonde, and so long that she could stand up with the ends of her hair under her heels and still be able to bend her head (although it is true that Mama was very short!)

Finally I escaped from the hands of this wretch, dead with fatigue after an hour and a half of blows with the comb, the brush, the curling iron, pins, and fingers turning my head from left to right, then from right to left, etc., etc. . . . I was disfigured, I no longer recognized myself. My hair was drawn back from the temples, my ears visible and detached, unseemly in their nudity. Above my head was a packet of little sausages arranged side by side in imitation of the Roman diadem style. I was hideous! My forehead, which I always saw under the golden fluff of my hair, looked immense and implacable. I did not recognize my eyes, used as I was to see them veiled by the shadow of my hair. My head weighed a ton. I used to fix my hair with two pins and I still do. This man had put in five or six packets. It was all so heavy on my poor head!

It was already late. I had to get dressed quickly. I was crying with rage. My eyes were getting smaller, my nose was growing larger, my veins were swelling. But it was the last straw when it came to putting on my hat. It would not stay on top of the packet of sausages. My mother quickly wrapped my head in a piece of lace and pushed me toward the door. As soon as I reached the Conservatoire I dashed with "my little lady" toward the waiting room. Mama had made her way to the auditorium. I snatched off the poor lace that covered my head and, cowering on a bench, I gave up my head to my friends after telling them in a few words the saga of my hair. All of them loved and envied my hair that was so supple, light, and golden. They all took pity on my distress.

All of them were upset to see my ugliness, except for the mothers who were reveling in spiteful joy. All these young hands took out the pins and Marie Lloyd,[12] a delightful creature and a closer friend of mine than the others, took my head and kissed it tenderly, saying "Oh, your beautiful hair! What have they done to it?" as she took out the last pins. This tenderness made me burst into tears again. Finally I stood up triumphant without pins and sausages! But my poor hair, weighed down by the lard with which that miserable hairdresser had coated it, and separated by the furrows he had made to create these sausages, fell in greasy weeping locks about my face. I shook my hair for five minutes in a mad rage and managed to separate it a little, then I pinned it up as best I could with two pins.

But the examination had started. I was to perform in tenth place. I no longer knew what I had to say. Mme. Guérard wiped my temples with some cool toilet water. Mlle. de Brabender, who had just arrived, looked at me without recognizing me and was looking for me everywhere. The poor woman had broken her leg three months before. She was using crutches, but she had wanted to come. Mme. Guérard was just beginning to tell her the dramatic story of my hair when my name rang out in the hall, "Mlle. Chara Bernhardt!" It was Léautaud who later became prompter at the Comédie-Française and who had a strong *auvergnat* accent.[13] "Mlle. Chara Bernhardt!" I jumped up without a word, my mind a blank, scanning the room for the student who was supposed to make responses for me. I went on stage with him.

I was surprised by the sound of my voice, which I did not recognize. I had cried so much that my head was thick and my voice nasal. I heard a woman's voice say, "Poor little thing, they shouldn't have allowed her to compete. She has a frightful cold, her nose is running and her face is swollen." I finished my scene. I curtseyed and went off to meager and plaintive applause. I walked like a sleepwalker and fainted in the arms of Mme. Guérard and Mlle. de Brabender. A request for a doctor was made in the theater and the rumor, "The little Bernhardt girl has fainted! The little Bernhardt girl is unconscious!" reached my mother who, huddled at the back of a box, was growing extremely bored. When I came round my eyes opened on the beautiful face of Mama. A teardrop hung on her long lashes. I put my head against hers and cried silently, but this time they were sweet tears, without salt, and did not burn my eyelids. I stood up, smoothed myself out, and looked at myself in the greenish mirror. I was less ugly. My face was calmer, my hair had regained its suppleness; I certainly looked better than I had just previously.

The tragedy competition was over. The prizes were announced. I had not won one. I had received nothing in the way of an award. My second prize from the previous year had been mentioned, but I was empty-handed. Oh, it gave me no pain, it was what I had expected! A few people protested on my behalf. Camille Doucet, a member of the jury, had argued for a long time, apparently, that I should be given the first prize, in spite of my bad performance during the competition, saying that most weight should be given to my excellent examination grades, and to my class grades, which were the best. But nothing could overcome the bad effect produced that day by my nasal voice, swollen face, and heavy locks of hair.

After a half-hour interval during which I was made to drink some port and eat a *brioche*[14] the signal was given for the beginning of the comedy competition. I was fourteenth on the list so I had the time to make a complete recovery. And now I began to feel my instinct for battle take over. A sense of injustice roused the rebel in me. I had not deserved the tragedy prize on that day, but I felt I should have been given it anyway. I resolved to have the first prize for comedy. And, with the exaggeration that I have always brought to everything, I lifted my head and declared to myself that if I did not get the first prize I would have to give up acting. My tender and mystical love for the convent took hold of me more strongly than ever. Yes, I would go to the convent! But only if I did not win the first prize. There began in my silly young girl's head the most crazy battle one could possibly imagine. I felt all my yearnings for the convent in my distress at having failed to win a prize, and all my vocation for the theater in my hope of winning one. I recognized in myself, with natural partiality, a gift for all the denial, sacrifice, and devotion which ought to seat me gently on the throne of the Mother Superior at the convent of Grand-Champs. On the other hand, I bestowed on myself with liberal indulgence all the gifts necessary for the realization of my other dream: to become the best, most famous, and most envied of actresses, and I counted off on my fingers all my qualities—grace, charm, distinction, beauty, mystery, piquancy. Oh, everything! I believed I had them all. And when logic and good faith raised a doubt or a "but" as I concocted this fairy-tale list of qualities, my combative and paradoxical ego found a cutting and incontrovertible response.

It was in these special circumstances and in this state of mind that I presented myself on stage when my turn came. The role of a reasonable and reasoning married woman for my comedy act was a stupid choice. I was a child who appeared much younger than I was. I acted nevertheless a very radiant, very reasonable, and very gay part and was warmly applauded. I was transfigured. I was delighted, I had my first prize! I had no doubt that it would be awarded to me unanimously. The competition finished. During the delay necessary for the committee to debate the awards I asked for something to eat. A chop was brought from the Conservatoire's baker, and I devoured it, to the great joy of Mme. Guérard and Mlle. de Brabender, for I hated meat and always refused to eat it.

Finally, the members of the committee took their places in their box. The audience fell silent. The young men were called on stage first. No first prize. Then Parfouru was called to receive the second prize for comedy. Parfouru is today M. Paul Porel, the director of the Vaudeville and the husband of Réjane.[15]

Then it was the girls' turn. I stood in the doorway, ready to throw myself on stage. "The first prize for comedy. . . " I took a step forward, pushing past a girl who was head and shoulders taller than I. "First prize by unanimous decision: Mlle. Marie Lloyd!" And the tall girl that I had pushed aside leaped, elegant and radiant, onto the stage. There were a few protests. But her beauty, her distinction, and her timorous charm got the better of everyone and everything. Marie Lloyd was applauded. She came up to me and kissed me tenderly. We were very close and I loved her very much, but as a student I had always rated her as nothing. I do not remember whether she had received a prize the year before, but no one had expected her to receive this prize. I was terror-stricken.

"Second prize for comedy: Mlle. Bernhardt!" I had not heard it. They pushed me on stage, and as I curtseyed, I saw hundreds of Marie Lloyds dancing in front of me, some grimacing at me, others blowing kisses; some were fanning themselves, others waving . . . They were tall, tall, all these Marie Lloyds . . . they were taller than the ceiling, they were walking on people's heads, and they were coming toward me, squashing and suffocating me, crushing my heart. Apparently my face was as white as my dress.

Back in the wings, I sat down on a bench without saying a word and watched Marie Lloyd, surrounded by an admiring crowd. She was wearing a dress of pale blue tarlatan, a bunch of forget-me-nots pinned to her bodice, and a sprig of forget-me-not in her black hair. She was tall, very tall, with delicate white shoulders emerging modestly from her low-necked dress—very low-necked . . . but there was no risk in that. Her fine head, a little haughty, was very graceful and beautiful. Although she was very young she had more of a woman's charm than any of us others. Eyeing me sidelong with her large bronze-colored eyes, her little round mouth smiled maliciously, and her wonderfully sculpted nose flared at the nostrils. Where the hairline bordered the oval of her beautiful face were two little perfect ears, pearly and transparent. A long flexible white neck supported this charming head. It was a prize for beauty that Marie Lloyd had won! And the jury had awarded it in good faith. She had gone on stage laughing and radiant as Célimène,[16] her competition piece, and in spite of her monotonous delivery, her sloppy diction, and her impersonal performance, she had brought in the votes because she was the personification of Célimène, the twenty-year-old coquette who was so unconsciously cruel. She had realized for everybody Molière's ideal. All these thoughts came together later in my mind. This first painful lesson served me well in my career and I have never forgotten Marie Lloyd's prize.

Every time that I start to work on a role I see the character in my imagination in costume, with hair styled, walking, greeting, sitting down, standing up. But that is only the materialized vision from which there suddenly emerges the soul, which must dominate the character. Listening to the author read his work, I try to define his will in the hope of identifying myself with it. On occasion I have tried, along with the dramatist, to force the audience to return to the truth and to destroy the legendary aspect of certain characters whose true nature modern historians have revealed; but the audience has not followed me. I soon came to the realization that legend always triumphs over historical fact, and maybe that is a blessing for those who think with the crowd . . . Jesus, Joan of Arc, Shakespeare, the Virgin Mary, Mohammed, and Napoléon I have all entered into legend. It is thus impossible for us to imagine Jesus or the Virgin Mary carrying out humbling human functions. They led the life we live and death has chilled their sacred limbs, but only rebelliously and sorrowfully will we accept this. We throw ourselves into pursuit of them in the ethereal heavens or in the infinity of dream. We discard their humanity as dross, in order to leave them clothed in idealism and seated on a throne of love. We do not want Joan of Arc to be a crude strapping peasant woman violently pushing away the rough soldier who wants to joke, mounting like a man the broad-backed draft horse, laughing freely at the soldiers' crude jests, and, subject as she was to the shameless lack of privacy typical of this still barbarous era, deserving all the more credit for remaining a heroic virgin. We want none of these useless truths. In legend she remains a frail being, led by a divine spirit. Her girl's arm, holding up the heavy standard, is supported by an invisible angel. The beyond is reflected in her child's eyes from which the warriors draw their strength and courage. It is thus that we wish her to be. And the legend remains triumphant.

Chapter X

But let us return to the Conservatoire.

Almost all the students had left. I remained silent and confused on my bench.

Marie Lloyd came to sit next to me. "You're upset?"

"Yes, I wanted to have the first prize, and you have it. It's not fair!"

"I don't know whether it's fair or not," replied Marie Lloyd, "but I swear I didn't do it on purpose!" I couldn't help laughing. "Shall I come and have supper with you?" she asked, her beautiful eyes moist and pleading. She was an orphan and not happy. On this day of triumph she deserved a little family. I felt my heart melt with infinite tender pity. I threw my arms round her neck and all four of us left: Marie Lloyd, Mme. Guérard, Mlle. de Brabender, and I. Mama had sent a message to say she would wait for me at home.

In the carriage my "couldn't care less" character asserted itself. We chatted about this boy and that girl: "Oh, my dear, how ridiculous she was!" "Oh, her mother... did you see her hat?" "And Estebenet's father... did you see his white gloves? He must have stolen them from a policeman!" And we laughed like maniacs.

"And poor old Châtelain with his hair curled!" added Marie Lloyd. "Did you see it?"

But I was no longer laughing. I remembered that I had had *my* hair straightened, and that, thanks to that, I had lost my first prize for tragedy.

Once we got back home to Mama's we found already there my aunt, my godfather, our old friend Meydieu, Mme. Guérard's husband, and my sister, Jeanne, with her hair all curled. Seeing this gave me a stab in the heart. She had straight hair, which they had curled to beautify her, although she was gorgeous anyway, but they had straightened *my* hair and made me ugly.

Marie Lloyd was welcomed by Mama with that charming and distinguished indifference that was peculiar to her. My godfather hurried to her side. For this middle-class girl her success was complete. My godfather had seen my young friend a hundred times before without being struck by her beauty or touched by her poverty, but today he claimed to have foreseen a long time ago the triumph of Marie Lloyd. Then he came up to me and putting his two hands on my shoulders forced me to face him, "Well, you have completely failed! But why are you so set on acting? . . . You are thin, short . . . and your face which is nice enough close up is ugly from a distance, and your voice doesn't carry!"

"Yes my girl . . . your godfather is right," said M. Meydieu, "so why don't you marry the miller who has proposed, or this stupid Spanish tanner who is losing his brainless head over your beautiful eyes? You will never do anything with the theater! Get married!"

M. Guérard came over to shake my hand. He was close to sixty years old, whereas Mme. Guérard was not even thirty. He was sad, gentle, and timid. He had received the Legion of Honor, wore a long and worn frock-coat, had aristocratic gestures, and was private secretary to M. de la Tour Desmoulins, a deputy who was much in favor. M. Guérard was a mine of knowledge.

My sister Jeanne muttered to me, "My sister's godfather" (that was how she referred to my godfather), "said when he came back that you were as ugly as can be." I gave her a little push.

We sat down to eat. Throughout the meal I longed again for the convent. I hardly ate anything and was overcome by such tiredness after lunch that I had to go to bed. Once I was alone in my bedroom, stretched out between the sheets, my limbs racked, my head heavy, my heart swollen with repressed sighs, I tried to ponder on my sad situation. But sleep conspired with my youthfulness to restore me, and I slept deeply.

When I woke up I could make no order out of my thoughts. What time was it? I looked at my watch. Ten o'clock! I had been sleeping since three o'clock in the afternoon. I listened for a moment. All was quiet in the house. On the table next to my bed on a little plate were a cup of chocolate and a brioche. There was also a sheet of writing paper, propped up so that it could not be missed, against the cup. I took the paper with a trembling hand. I never received letters and I wanted to make out what it said by the weak light of my night-light. I managed to do this with difficulty and was able to read these lines written by "my little lady" (Mme. Guérard):

> While you were sleeping, the Duc de Morny sent a note to your mother telling her that Camille Doucet had just assured him of your engagement with the Comédie-Française. So don't be unhappy, my dear child, and have confidence in the future.

> "Your little lady"

I pinched myself to make sure I was awake. I dashed to the window. I looked outside. The sky was dark. Yes, dark for everybody but starlit for me. Yes, the stars shone. I looked for mine, and chose the biggest and the most brilliant. I went back to my bed and amused myself jumping up and down on it, and when I stumbled I laughed like crazy. I swallowed all my chocolate and almost choked myself on the *brioche*. Standing on my bolster I made a long speech to the figure of the Virgin Mary placed at the head of my bed. I adored the Virgin Mary. I explained to her the reasons why I could not take the veil in spite of my vocation. I laid on the charm. I tried to persuade her and kissed her gently on the foot that crushed the serpent. Then I searched for the portrait of Mama, which I could only just make out in the shadows. I blew it kisses. I clutched the letter from "my little lady" in my hand and went back to sleep. What must have been my dreams that night?

The next day everybody was nice to me. My godfather arrived early. Nodding his head in a satisfied way he said to my mother, "She ought to take some air. I'll hire a landau." The outing was a delight as I could dream, since my mother hated to talk in a carriage.

Two days later, our old maid Marguerite breathlessly handed me a letter. In one corner of the envelope there was a large crest around which were emblazoned the words "Comédie-Française." I looked questioningly at my mother. She reprimanded Marguerite for giving me a letter without first asking her permission, but signaled to me that I could open it. "It's for tomorrow, Mama! . . . It's for tomorrow!" My younger sister was eight years old, but I, on that day, was only six.

I climbed the stairs to the floor above to tell Mme. Guérard, whom I found laundering children's white dresses and aprons. She took my head and kissed me tenderly, and her two hands which were full of lather left me with a snowy slab on either side. I went back downstairs like this taking the stairs four at a time and made a noisy entry into the drawing room. My godfather and M. Meydieu, my aunt, and Mama were starting a game of whist. I kissed them all in turn, laughing as I left each one with a bit of foam on their face. But today everything was permitted. I was somebody.

The next day, Tuesday, I was to go at one o'clock to the Théâtre-Français to be interviewed by M. Thierry, at that time the director of the Comédie.[1] What was I to wear? That was the big question . . . Mama sent for the milliner. She came over right away with the hats and I chose one of white ribbed cotton with a sky-blue crown, blue ties, and a white bavolet.[2] My aunt Rosine had sent one of her dresses, for all mine were too . . . little girl, my mother thought. Oh, this dress! I will never forget it. It was hideous—cabbage-green trimmed with a black-velvet Greek key pattern. I looked like a monkey in it, but I had to wear it. Luckily it was covered by a mantle, a gift from my godfather—a pretty mantle of black grosgrain[3] with white top-stitching. They thought that I ought to be dressed like a lady, but my wardrobe was full of little girl's clothes. Mlle. de Brabender gave me a handkerchief she had embroidered and Mme. Guérard a parasol. Mama gave me a pretty turquoise ring.

The next day, dressed in this fashion, pretty under my white bonnet, ill at ease in my green dress, but consoled by my grown-up mantle, I went with Mme. Guérard to see M. Thierry in my aunt's carriage. She had insisted on lending it to me, thinking that it would be more appropriate. I later found out that arriving like this in a carriage with footmen created a very bad impression. I have never wanted to find out exactly what the theater people thought about it, but it seems to me that my youthfulness ought to have protected me from all suspicion.

M. Thierry received me kindly and delivered me a pompous and incomprehensible little speech. Then he unfolded a piece of paper which he gave to Mme. Guérard, asking her to take note of it and sign it. It was my contract. "My little lady" replied that she was not my mother.

"Ah!" said M. Thierry as he stood up. "Take this paper away with you then and have Mademoiselle's mother sign it." He took my hand. His hand horrified me. It was soft, limp, and somehow lacking in sincerity. I disengaged mine quickly and scrutinized him. He was ugly, with a red face and a shifty look.

As I went out I met Coquelin who had waited for me, knowing that I was there. He had made his successful début a year ago. "Well that's it then!" he said gaily. I showed him the contract and shook hands with him. I went down the stairs four at a time, and just as I was going out found myself thrown into a group of people who were barring the door.

"Are you happy?" asked a gentle voice that came from the group.

"Oh yes, M. Doucet, thank you."

"But I had no part in it, my dear child. Your performance in the competition was very bad . . . but . . . "

"But that doesn't prevent us from putting our faith in you," M. Régnier said. Then turning to Camille Doucet he said, "What do you think your Excellency?"

"I think this child will be a very great artist."

There was a silence. "Well you have some carriage there!" Beauvallet crudely remarked, breaking the silence. He was the foremost tragedian of the Comédie and the most ill-mannered man in France . . . or anywhere else besides!

"This carriage belongs to Mademoiselle's aunt," said Camille Doucet as he shook my hand in a kindly manner.

"Ah! That makes it better then!" said the tragic actor.

I got into the carriage which had created such a to-do. Once I got home Mama signed the contract that I gave her without reading it, and I made the ardent resolution to be someone "no matter what."

A few days after I was contracted with the Comédie-Française, my aunt held a big dinner party. The Duc de Morny was there, Camille Doucet, M. de Walewski, the Minister of the Fine Arts, Rossini, my mother, Mlle. de Brabender, and myself. In the evening a great many people came. My mother had dressed me very elegantly. For the first time I wore a dress with a very low neckline. My God, how embarrassed I was! However, everybody paid me great attention.

Rossini asked me to recite some verse. I did so with good grace, happy and proud to be a little someone. I recited *L'Ame du purgatoire* by Casimir Delavigne. "You must recite that to music!" exclaimed Rossini when I had finished. Everybody applauded this idea and Walewski said to Rossini, "Mademoiselle will start again and you will improvise, my dear Master." I was delirious. I began again and Rossini improvised a delicious harmony that filled me with emotion. My tears flowed without my realizing it and my mother said as she kissed me, "This is the first time that you have really moved me." Mama adored music, and what had moved her was Rossini's improvisation.

The Comte de Kératry was there, a young and elegant hussar who paid me some big compliments and invited me to go and recite some verse at his mother's house. My aunt sang a fashionable romantic song and was much applauded. She was charming, flirtatious, and a little jealous of this nothing-at-all niece who detracted even an instant of attention from her worshipers.

I went back home a different person. I remained for a long time, all dressed, seated on my young girl's bed. So far I had known life only through my work and my family, but now I had had a glimpse of society. I was struck by the hypocrisy of some people and the fatuousness of others. I asked myself anxiously how I would manage, since I was so shy and so frank. I thought about what Mama did. But she did not do anything. Everything was all the same to her. I thought about my aunt Rosine. She, quite the opposite, involved herself in everything. I remained staring at the floor, my mind in a muddle, my heart disquieted. Only when I was thoroughly chilled did I get into bed.

The days following passed without incident. I worked away furiously at Iphigénie as M. Thierry had informed me that this was the role in which I would make my début. Indeed I was summoned to rehearsal of *Iphigénie*[4] at the end of August. Ah, this first notice of rehearsal! How it made my heart beat! I did not sleep all night. Daylight could not come soon enough. I kept on getting up to look at the time. It seemed to me that the clock had stopped. I had dozed, and I woke up amazed to see that it was still night when I had thought it was dawn. Finally, a streak of light through the panes seemed to me like a triumphant sun lighting up my bedroom. I sprang up, drew the curtains, and murmured my part to myself as I got dressed.

I thought about the fact that I was going to rehearse with Mme. Devoyod, the principal tragic actress at the Comédie-Française, with Maubant, with . . . and I trembled, for Mme. Devoyod had the reputation of having little indulgence to spare.[5] I arrived for the rehearsal an hour early. The stage manager, good old Davenne, smiled when he saw me and asked if I knew my part.

"Oh yes!" I exclaimed with total certainty.

"Come and say it for me then will you?" and he led me to the stage. I followed him along the long corridor of busts that leads from the green room to the stage. He told me the famous names that all these busts evoked. I stopped for a minute in front of that of Adrienne Lecouvreur.[6]

"I like this actress!" I told him.

"You know her story?"

"Yes, I've read everything written about her."

"That's very good, my dear child," said the nice man. "You must, indeed, read everything concerning your art. I will lend you some interesting books." And he drew me toward the stage.

The mysterious shadows, the stage sets rising like ramparts, the bare floor, the innumerable quantity of cords, weights, beams, backdrops, and battens suspended above my head, the abyss of the completely black auditorium, the silence broken only by the creaking of the floorboards, the cellar-like cold that took hold of you . . . all of this frightened me. I did not feel I was entering into the shining realm of living artists who every evening raised applause in the theater by their laughter or their tears. No. I had found myself in a cavern of dead glories, and the stage seemed to be filled with the illustrious ghosts of those just named by the stage manager. My highly strung and always vivid imagination saw them come toward me and stretch out their hands. These ghosts wanted to drag me away. I put my hands over my eyes and stood motionless.

"Are you ill?"

"No, no thank you . . . Just a dizzy spell, Monsieur. No, thank you."

M. Davenne's voice had chased away the ghosts. I opened my eyes and attended willingly to the advice of the good man who, with the script in his hand, explained to me the positions that I should take up, the moves that I should make etc. etc. He was quite happy with my way of reciting. He told me about certain traditions. One thing of note that he told me was, "At this point Mlle. Favart[7] would create a great sensation." The line in question was, *"Eurybate, à l'autel conduisez la victime."*[8]

The artists arrived gradually, grumbling, throwing me a glance and then rehearsing their scene without concerning themselves with me. I wanted to cry, but more than anything I was angry. I heard obscenities hurled by now one and now another. I was still unused to this rather brutal kind of language. At my mother's house we were careful with our language, at my aunt's we were affected, and it goes without saying that I had never heard an improper word at the convent. It is true that I had come from the Conservatoire, but I mixed with nobody there except for Marie Lloyd and Rose Baretta, the elder sister of Blanche Baretta, today a member of the Comédie-Française.

When the rehearsal was over it was agreed that we would rehearse the next day at the same time in the public foyer. The wardrobe mistress came to ask me to try on my costume. Mlle. de Brabender, who had arrived during the rehearsal, came up with me to the costume room. She wanted my arms to be covered, but the wardrobe mistress gently explained to her that that was impossible in a tragedy. So she tried on me a very ugly white woollen dress with such a stiff veil that I refused it. She tried on my head a wreath of roses that was so ugly that I refused that too.

"Well," the wardrobe mistress said to me rather dryly, "you will have to pay for the costume yourself then, Mademoiselle, for this is the Comédie's costume."

"Fine, I will pay for it," I said, reddening.

Back at home I told the sad tale of my costume to my mother, and Mama, who was very generous, immediately bought me a veil of silky white barège, which fell in beautiful large supple pleats, and a wreath of wild roses, which gleamed white and discrete in the dark. She ordered me some buskins from the Comédie's shoemaker.

We also had to think about getting a makeup case. Mama entrusted this task to Mme. Dica-Petit, the mother of my friend at the Conservatoire. So I went with Mme. Dica-Petit to the father of Léontine Massin (a student at the Conservatoire) who was a manufacturer of cosmetics cases. We climbed the six floors of the house located in Réaumur Street. As we stopped at a humble door we read MASSIN, MAKER OF MAKEUP CASES.

I knocked at the door and a little hunch-backed girl opened it. I immediately recognized Léontine's sister; she sometimes came to the Conservatoire. "Ah!" she exclaimed, "what a surprise! I say, Titine, it's Mlle. Sarah!"

Léontine Massin ran in from the next room. Gentle, calm, and pretty, she embraced me. "How happy I am to see you! You are going to start at the Comédie! I saw that in the papers." I blushed up to the roots of my hair. I was in the papers! "*I'm* going to start at the Variétés!"[9] she said, and she talked and talked so long and so fast that I was dazed.

Mme. Petit remained cool and tried unsuccessfully to separate us. She had replied with a nod and a "Not bad thank you" to the questions that Léontine had addressed to her about the health of her daughter. Finally, when the pretty girl's outburst was over, she was able to say to me, "You must order your case, that's what we are here for."

"Ah yes, you'll find Papa in the back at his workbench, and if you're not going to be long I will wait for you. I have a rehearsal at the Variétés."

Mme. Petit choked out, "No! It's impossible!" She did not like Léontine Massin. The latter, annoyed, turned her back on her and shrugged her shoulders. Then when she had put on her hat she kissed me and gravely shaking hands with Mme. Petit said, "I hope, Mme. Fatty, that I will never see you again!" and she disappeared with a peal of ringing young laughter. I heard my companion murmur some nasty remark in Dutch, the meaning of which I did not understand until later.

We ventured into the room at the back of the house and found old Massin there at his workbench, planing some little planks of white wood. The hunchback bustled around singing joyfully, while the father remained gloomy, surly and worried. After we had ordered the case we were going out, Mme. Petit leading the way, when Léontine's sister held me back by the hand. "Father was not polite because he's jealous, as my sister Léontine is not going to the Théâtre-Français." I felt slightly troubled by this confidence, as I vaguely glimpsed the close-knit and painful drama that moved the inhabitants of this poor dwelling in such different ways.

Chapter XI

*O*n September 1, 1862, the day of my début, I found myself planted in front of the theatre posters on the rue Duphot. At that time they occupied a large billboard on the corner of the rue Duphot and the rue Saint-Honoré. It said on the poster for the Comédie: "The début of Mademoiselle Sarah Bernhardt." I do not know how long I stayed there drawn by the letters of my name, but I remember that each person who stopped seemed to look at me after reading the notice, and I could feel myself blushing up to the roots of my hair. Finally, I made my way to the Théâtre-Français at five o'clock.

I had a dressing room up high that I shared with Mlle. Coblentz.[1] This room was on the other side of the rue Richelieu, in a house rented by the Comédie-Française. A little enclosed walkway bridged the street and it was by means of this that we reached the Comédie.

I took an infinitely long time getting dressed. I couldn't decide whether I looked good or bad. "My little lady" thought I was too pale. Mlle. de Brabender thought I was too red. My mother was to make her way directly to the auditorium. My aunt Rosine was on vacation. When the beginning of the performance was announced I was seized by a cold sweat from head to toe. I nearly fainted. I went down trembling, staggering, my teeth chattering. By the time I reached the wings the curtain was going up. A gentle and serious voice made me turn round. It was Provost, my first teacher, who had come to comfort me. I threw my arms round him, glad to see him again. Samson was there too; I think in fact that he was performing that night in a Molière comedy.

There were these two so different men. Provost, tall, his silver hair all windblown, a droll expression on his face; Samson, on the other hand, short, stiff, neat, his white shiny hair in tight curls. These two men had been moved by the same protective instinct for this poor fragile being, nervous and so full of faith—both of them knew how passionately I worked at my art, and how my tenacious will constantly struggled with my physical weakness. They knew that my motto "No matter what" had not come about accidentally, but had been chosen purposely. Mama had told them how, at the age of nine, I had chosen

69

this motto after a bad fall into a ditch. No one could jump across it and my young cousin had challenged me to try it. I had disfigured my face, broken a wrist, and bruised my whole body. While I was being carried away I kept crying out in rage, "Yes, yes, I will try again no matter what, if I am challenged again! And I'll do what I want all my life!" In the evening, when my aunt, feeling sorry for me, asked me what I would like, my whole little bandaged body jumped for joy and wheedling, but consoled, I whispered, "I would like some of my very own writing paper with my motto on it." When my mother mockingly insisted on knowing what this motto was, I remained silent for a moment and then I hurled into the attentive silence such a furious "No matter what!" that my aunt Faure recoiled, murmuring, "What a terrible child!" So Samson and Provost reminded me of this story, and tried to give me courage by reminding me of it. But my pulse was thumping in my ears and I heard nothing. It was with a push from Provost, who had heard my cue, that I went on stage.

I dashed toward Agamemnon, my father. I did not want to leave him, I needed someone to hold onto. I threw myself at my mother Clytemnestre. I stammered out my lines. And when I left the stage I rushed back up to my dressing room. I was undressing feverishly when Mme. Guérard asked me in alarm if I was crazy. I had only done the first act and there were still four others. Then I realized that I would really be in danger if I let my nerves take hold of me in this way. I made an appeal to my self-imposed motto and, looking at myself in the eye in the mirror, I ordered myself to gain control and calm down! My jangled nerves submitted to my reason. I finished the play. I was insignificant.

When Mama saw Sarcey's column in L'Opinion nationale early next day she sent for me and read these lines to me herself:

> Mlle. Bernhardt who made her début yesterday in Iphigénie is a tall and pretty young person with a very slim figure and a very agreeable face; the top portion of her face is especially beautiful. She holds herself well and enunciates with perfect clarity. This is all one can say at the moment.

Drawing me toward her she said, "This man is stupid. You were charming." And she herself prepared me a little cup of coffee with cream. I was happy, but not completely.

When my godfather arrived in the afternoon he exclaimed, "My God, my poor little one, what thin arms you have!" It was true, there had been some laughter. I had heard it clearly when I stretched out my arm to Eurybate and said to him the well-known verse from which

Favart drew the effect that had become legendary... *I* had drawn no effect from it, except some smiles at my long thin arms.

My second début was in *Valérie*[2] in which I had some success, and my third début provoked this outburst from Sarcey against the whole Comédie:

> *L'Opinion nationale*, September 12. On the same evening *Les Femmes savantes*[3] provided the occasion for the third début of Mlle. Bernhardt who played the role of Henriette. She was just as pretty and just as insignificant as in her roles in *Junie* (this was an error, he meant *Iphigénie*) and in *Valérie* with which she was entrusted earlier. This performance was really poor, and raises some thoughts that are less than sanguine. That Mlle. Bernhardt is inadequate is her own business. She is a beginner, and it is only natural that among the beginners with whom we are presented, there are some who are not at all successful. It takes several tries to find a good one. But what is sad is that the actors who surrounded her were not much better than she, and yet these are *sociétaires*! The only advantage they had over their young colleague was a greater familiarity with the stage. They are today what Mlle. Bernhardt could be in twenty years if she stays at the Comédie-Française.

I did not stay there. In fact, one of those small things that determine the course of one's life certainly determined mine. I had entered the Comédie with the intention of staying there forever. I had heard my godfather explain to my mother the different stages of my career: the little one will earn so much for the first five years... so much afterward, and finally, after thirty years, she will have the pension of a *sociétaire* if she becomes one, about which he seemed to have some doubts.

My sister Régina was again the cause, although unwittingly this time, of the little drama which made me leave the Comédie. It was the anniversary of Molière's birthday. Tradition required that all the artists of the great house come and salute the bust of the great writer. It was the first time that I had taken part in the ceremony and my young sister, who had heard me talking about it at home, had begged me to take her along. I obtained permission from Mama, who sent with us our maid Marguerite.

The whole Comédie was assembled in the foyer, men and women in different costumes, but all dressed in the famous Doctor's robe. The announcer came to warn us that the ceremony was about to start and everybody pressed into the corridor where the busts were. I held my little sister by the hand. In front of us walked the very fat and very solemn Mme. Nathalie, a member of the Comédie, old, nasty, and fierce. As Régina tried to avoid standing on the trailing robe of Marie Royer,[4] she found herself stepping instead on Nathalie's.[5] The latter turned around and swiftly pushed the child, so violently that she fell against a column supporting a bust. Régina cried out and turned to me, her pretty face all bloody. "Nasty bitch!" I shouted, throwing myself at the fat lady, and just as she was about to reply I gave her a couple of slaps. There followed fainting of the old *sociétaire*, tumult, brouhaha, indignation, approbation, suppressed laughter, a sense of satisfied vengeance, sympathy for the poor little girl from those actresses who were mothers, etc. etc.

Two groups formed. One around the nasty Nathalie who was still in a swoon, the other around little Régina. It was quite strange to see the composition and different aspect of the two groups. Around Nathalie there were men and women who were solemn, cold, and upright, some fanning the big slumped heap with handkerchiefs, the others with fans. One *sociétaire*, young but severe, sprinkled some water on her. But Nathalie, feeling this, suddenly woke up, and putting her hands to her face murmured in a voice that was still faint, "That's stupid! You are going to spoil my makeup!" Around Régina young women were crouching down to wash her pretty face and the little girl kept saying in her hoarse voice, "I didn't do it on purpose big sister, I swear! She's a big cow who let rip for nothing!" For Régina—this blonde seraph who could have made the very angels envious of her ideal and poetic beauty— had a mouth on her like a coachman's, and nothing at all had worked to change it. Her gross outburst made the little friendly circle burst into laughter while it raised the hackles of the enemy circle.

Bressant,[6] the most charming and popular of the actors, came to me and said, "We must try to fix things, dear Mademoiselle, for Nathalie's short arms are very long. Between you and me, you were a little lively, but I like that, and then the kid is so funny and so pretty," he said pointing to my little sister. The audience was growing impatient in the theater as this scene had caused a delay of twenty minutes. We had to go on stage.

Marie Royer kissed me, "You're a case little chum!"

And Rose Baretta[7] drawing close to me said, "How did you dare? A *sociétaire* . . . "

As for myself, I was not really clear as to what I had done but my instinct told me that I was going to pay dearly for it.

The next day I received a letter from the director asking me to go to the Comédie for a matter that concerned me personally. I had cried the whole night, more out of irritation than remorse, and I was especially irritated by the thought of the attack that I was going to have to endure from my whole family. I hid the letter from my mother as she had conferred adult independence[8] on me from the day I had joined the theater. So I received my letters directly without her checking them first and I came and went without a chaperone.

At one o'clock precisely I presented myself at the director's office. M. Thierry, very cold, his nose even more congested than ever, his eye more shifty, gave me a deadly sermon, faulted my indiscipline, my lack of respect, and my scandalous conduct, and finished his pitiable harangue by advising me to seek the pardon of Mme. Nathalie. "I have brought her here," he added. "You will make your apologies in front of three members of the Committee.[9] If she consents to pardon you the Committee will decide whether it is appropriate to impose a fine on you or terminate your contract."

I remained a few moments without replying. I saw in my mind my mother sad, my godfather guffawing with bourgeois laughter, my aunt Faure triumphant with her "This child is terrible!" I saw my dear Brabender, wringing her hands, her moustache drooping, her little eyes welling with tears, so touching in her silent prayer. I could hear my gentle and shy Guérard arguing with everybody, emboldened by her faith in my future.

"Well, Mademoiselle?" said Thierry dryly. I looked at him without speaking. He grew impatient. "I'm going to ask Mme. Nathalie to come in and I ask you to act as quickly as possible, as I have other things to do than make amends for your foolishness."

"Oh no, sir, don't call Mme. Nathalie, I won't ask her pardon. I am going to resign immediately."

He was thrown into confusion, and his arrogance melted in great pity for this indomitable and wilful child, who was going to wreck her future for the sake of her pride. He became gentler and more polite. He asked me to sit down, which he had not yet done. Sitting facing me, he spoke gently to me about the advantages of the Comédie, of the risk involved in leaving this illustrious house to which I had been honored with admittance, and a hundred other very good sensible reasons, which softened me. But when he saw I was moved and he wanted to have Mme. Nathalie come in, the little beast in me revived.

"Oh don't let her come! I'll slap her again!"

"Then," he said "I must ask your mother to come."

"Oh sir, my mother never inconveniences herself!"

"Well, I will go and see her then."

"There's no point, sir. My mother has given me my independence. I am free to direct my own life. I alone am responsible for my acts."

"Well, Mademoiselle, I will let you know," and he stood up to signal that the interview was over.

I went back home having resolved that I would say nothing to my mother, but my little sister, who had been questioned about her wound, had told the whole story in her own way, exaggerating yet further, if possible, the brutality of the *sociétaire* and the audacity of my action. Rose Baretta came to see me and wept, saying that my contract would surely be terminated. The whole family was excited, argumentative, sorry; *I* was tense. I reacted badly to the reproaches I received and worse still to the advice. I shut myself up in my room and double-locked the door. The next day the whole house avoided me, so I went up to see Guérard, for it was in her that I found comfort and consolation.

A few days passed without my services being required at the theater. Finally one morning, I received a summons to a reading: *Dolorès* by M. Bouilhet.[10] It was the first time I had been summoned for the reading of a new play. I was going to be given a "creation." All my sorrows flew away like a cloud of black butterflies. I shared my joy with Mama who concluded logically that, since I had been called for a reading, the idea of terminating my contract and of making me ask Nathalie's forgiveness had been abandoned.

I went to the theater. How surprised I was to receive from M. Davenne himself the role of Dolorès, the lead role in the play by Bouilhet. I knew that Favart, to whom this part by rights belonged, was ill. But there were other actresses . . . and I could not get over my joy and surprise. And yet I felt worried . . . From early on I had an anguished premonition of events that were about to devolve on me.

I had been rehearsing for five days when, as I was climbing up the stairs one day, I found myself face to face with Nathalie who was sitting under the great portrait of Rachel, a portrait by Gérôme nicknamed "the chili pepper." I did not know whether I should go back down or carry on regardless. But my hesitation was noticed by this nasty woman who said, "Pass, pass, Mademoiselle, I forgive you, as I have got my revenge: you're not going to keep this role that you like so much." I passed without saying a word, crushed by what she had said as I sensed that it was true.

I said nothing to anyone. I rehearsed. This scene took place on a Tuesday. The following Friday when I arrived for the rehearsal I was sorry to learn that Davenne had not come in, the rehearsal was canceled. Just as I was getting into my carriage the doorkeeper came running after me with a letter from M. Davenne. The poor man had not dared to deliver the blow that he foresaw would be so painful to me. He explained to me in his letter that in view of my extreme youth, the difficulty of the role . . . such responsibility weighing on such frail shoulders . . . that finally since Mme. Favart had recovered from her illness, it was wiser that . . . I continued the letter through my tears, but anger quickly took the place of sorrow.

I dashed up the stairs and presented myself at the director's office. He could not see me at the moment. "That's alright, I'll wait." Tired of waiting after an hour, I brushed away the boy, and the secretary who tried to hold me back, and went into M. Thierry's office. In a flood of words punctuated by sobs I poured out all that despair, anger at injustice, and rage at hypocrisy can inspire. The director looked at me stunned. He could not conceive of such audacity or such violence in a girl so young. When I finally fell exhausted into an armchair he tried to calm me but it was vain.

"I want to leave immediately, sir! Give me my contract. I will return mine to you."

Finally, tired of begging, he called his secretary, gave her some orders, and she came back with my contract. "Here is the contract signed by your mother, Mademoiselle. You are free to return it to me within forty-eight hours. After that I will consider you as no longer a part of the house. But, believe me, you are wrong. Think it over for forty-eight hours."

I left without replying. The same evening I returned to M. Thierry the copy of the contract that he had signed and tore up my mother's.

I had broken with the House of Molière and would not return there until twelve years later.

Chapter XII

*T*his act, so violently decisive, turned my life at home upside
down. I was no longer as happy in the company of my family.
They constantly reproached me for my violence. Both my aunt and my
young sister dropped annoying innuendoes. My godfather, whom I had
quite bluntly sent packing, no longer dared to attack me openly, but he
put Mama up to it. The only place I was happy was with Mme. Guérard.
Consequently I went up to see her all the time. I amused myself helping
her with her domestic chores. She taught me how to make scrambled
eggs, *galettes*,[1] and chocolate. It took my mind off my problems and my
gaiety quickly returned.

One morning I found Mama looking mysterious. She kept looking
at the clock and was worried that my godfather, who always had lunch
and dinner with us, had not yet come. "It's strange," Mama kept saying,
"yesterday after our game of whist he said, 'I'll be there tomorrow
before lunch.' It's strange . . . " Normally so calm, she paced up and
down and told Marguerite, who put her head in to ask if lunch should
be served, to wait a while.

Finally, the doorbell made my mother and sister Jeanne (who was,
no doubt, in the secret) jump up. "Well, it's settled," said my godfather
as he gently shook the snow from his hat. "Here, read this, hot-head!"
and he gave me a letter with the letter-heading of the Gymnase theater.[2]

It was a letter from Montigny, the director of this theater, to M. de
Gerbois, a friend of my godfather's whom I knew well. The letter, which
was very friendly in its tone toward M. de Gerbois, finished with the
words "And, just to please you, I will hire your protégée, who seems to
have a lousy temper." I blushed when I read these lines and thought
that my godfather was very tactless. He could have made me really
happy without dealing me this little wound. But his was the most insen-
sitive soul that ever existed. Mama seemed so happy that I thanked my
godfather and kissed Mama's pretty face.

Oh, how I loved to kiss this pearly face, always fresh and softly
flushed with pink! When I was little I used to ask her to make a "butterfly"
on my cheek with her long eyelashes. She would put her face up close

to mine and flutter her eyelids doing "tickles" on my cheek, and I would lean back swooning with pleasure. On this day I suddenly took her by the head and said, "Do 'butterfly' on your big daughter's cheek."

She pulled me toward her saying, "What a big baby you are! You're shameless!" and she did a "butterfly" on my cheek. The whole of the rest of the day was bathed in sunshine by the kiss of those long lashes.

The next day I went to the Gymnase. I had to wait for some time in the company of five other girls. Then M. Monval, an old cynic who was stage manager and almost general manager, inspected us. At first sight I had liked him because he looked like M. Guérard, but I quickly went off him. His way of looking at me, speaking to me, in fact of sizing me up, put me on my mettle at once. I replied dryly to his questions, and our conversation, which seemed to have taken on a hostile tone, was interrupted by the arrival of M. Montigny, the director of the theater.

"Which of you is Mlle. Sarah Bernhardt?" I got up. "Would you come into my office, Mademoiselle?" Montigny was an old actor, round and good natured.[3] He seemed rather infatuated with his own personality, with his own ego, but that did not matter to me. After a little friendly chat, during which he preached to me a little about my flight from the Comédie, and made me many promises about the roles that he was going to have me play, he drew up my contract and asked me to bring it back to him signed by my mother and other guardians.

"I'm legally independent and my signature is valid," I said.

"Ah, it's ridiculous to have given independence to someone as headstrong as you. Your family really didn't do you a service by doing that!"

I was going to reply that what my family did was no business of his, but I restrained myself, and went back home happy.

At the beginning, Montigny kept his word. He made me an understudy for Victoria Lafontaine,[4] a young actress who was charmingly gifted and very popular at the time. I played in *La Maison sans enfants* and I replaced her at a moment's notice in *Le Démon du jeu*, a play that was very successful. I was not bad in these two plays. But Montigny, in spite of my pleas, did not come to see me in them, and the malicious stage manager played a thousand nasty tricks on me. Anger began to well up inside me and I struggled with all my might to calm my nerves.

One evening, as I was leaving the theater, I was given an audition notice for the next day. Montigny had promised me a good role and I went to sleep cradled by the fairies as they transported me into a land of success and glory.

When I arrived at the theater I found already there Blanche Pierson[5] and Céline Montaland[6]—the two prettiest creatures that it has ever pleased God to create. One of them was as fair as the rising sun, the other was as dark as a starry sky, for she was luminous in spite of her black hair. There were also some other women, also very pretty. The play that we were going to read was entitled *Un Mari qui lance sa femme.* It was by Raymond Deslandes.[7] I did not like the play from our reading of it. It seemed stupid to me. I waited anxiously to find out what role I was going to be given. I was to know only too soon. It was the character of Princesse Dunchinka: air-headed, silly and giggling, eating and dancing all the time. This role did not suit me at all. I was very inexperienced on the stage and had a certain awkward shyness. Plus I had not worked so persistently and faithfully for three years only to play the part of a tart in an idiotic play.

I felt desperate. The craziest ideas came into my head. I wanted to give up the theater and start a business. I spoke about it to that old friend of the family, unbearable Meydieu, who encouraged me in this idea and wanted me to take a store on the boulevard des Italiens, a confectioner's! Yes, that was the good man's obsession. He loved candy, and he knew piles of recipes for unusual ones that he wanted to market. I remember one called a "bonbon nègre" as he wanted to call it. It was a mixture of chocolate and coffee essence rolled in toasted licorice. It was like black praline and it was very good. Persisting in my idea I went with Meydieu to visit a shop. But when he showed me the tiny mezzanine that was to be my apartment I felt so discomforted that I abandoned forever the idea of going into business.

However, every day I rehearsed this insipid play. It put me in a bad mood. Finally the first performance took place. I was neither successful nor unsuccessful. I was just unnoticed. In the evening Mama said, "My poor child, you were ridiculous in your role as the Russian princess! You made me very sorry." I did not say a word, but I had a very real desire to kill myself.

I slept badly and went up to see Mme. Guérard at about six o'clock in the morning. I asked her for some laudanum which she refused to give me. When she saw how insistent I was the poor dear lady realized what I intended to do. "Well," I said to her suddenly, "swear on the heads of your children that you won't tell anyone what I am going to do, and I won't kill myself." An idea had suddenly started to germinate in my head and I wanted to put it into action without further ado. She swore, and I told her that I was going to leave immediately for Spain, a country that I had wanted to see for a long time. She started.

"What? Go to Spain? With whom? When?"

"With my savings! This very morning! Everyone is sleeping at home. I'm going to pack my trunk and leave immediately—with you!"

"No, no . . . I can't leave!" cried Mme. Guérard. "What about my husband? What about my children?" Her daughter was only just two years old.

"Well, 'my little lady,' give me someone to accompany me."

"I have nobody. My God! My God!" she said in tears, "Give up this idea, my little Sarah, I beg you!"

But my mind was made up and I was determined to do it. I went down to pack my trunk and then came back up to the Guérards' apartment. Then I opened a window and threw a pewter fork wrapped up in paper against one of the panes of a dormer window opposite. The window was thrust open and the sleepy and furious face of a young woman appeared at the window. Cupping my hands round my mouth I shouted, "Caroline, do you want to leave right away for Spain?" Her stupefied expression suggested that she had not fully understood what I had said, but she said, "I'm coming, Mademoiselle!" and quickly closed the window.

Ten minutes later Caroline was tapping on Mme. Guérard's door. Mme. Guérard had collapsed in an armchair. M. Guérard had already asked twice from behind the closed bedroom door what was going on. "It's little Sarah. I'll tell you everything in a little while." Caroline occasionally worked at Mme. Guérard's as a dressmaker. She had offered her services to me as a chambermaid. She was good-natured and rather daring. She accepted my proposal immediately.

⚬⚬⚬

[*Sarah sets off with Caroline that morning leaving letters for her mother and Montigny, director of the Gymnase. From Marseille they take a six-day voyage on a dirty merchant ship to Alicante, where they spend the first night in a disreputable hotel. Sarah awakes to see a man entering their room. Their screams bring the police and a French-speaking Hungarian vice-consul to the hotel. He offers Sarah hospitality in his own home and it turns out that his wife's father had been a friend of Sarah's father. The next day Sarah leaves for Madrid where, introduced into society by letters of introduction, she is welcomed with open arms. She attends bull fights and enjoys herself tremendously, forgetting all about her worries back home. She toys with the idea of staying in Spain permanently but a telegram from Mme. Guérard telling her that her mother is seriously ill takes her back to Paris, where her mother is (by now) convalescent. Sarah finds that in her absence her grandmother has agreed to allow her access to half the money her father had left her in the event of her marriage. On the basis of this income Sarah decides to move out into an apartment of her own, since the constant visits of her detested godfather, who adores her mother, make her mother's house odious to her. Sarah's mother does not wish to marry him and impose on herself*] *a new master because, like Sarah, she is strong willed and, though usually placid, prone to violent rages.*]

∽⌒∾

I said nothing about my plans to the dear invalid; but I asked our old friend Meydieu to find me an apartment. This old man who had so tormented me as a child had softened toward me since my début at the Théâtre-Français. In spite of the slap I had given Nathalie, and in spite of my abscondment from the Gymnase, he was prepared to take me as I was. When he came to see us the day after my return I stayed to talk to him for a while in the drawing room and shared my idea with him. He approved of it, and said that the relationship between my mother and myself could only gain from the separation.

I took an apartment on the rue Duphot, very close to our house. Guérard took it upon herself to furnish it. When my mother had completely recovered I got her to agree, after several days, that it was better that I should live on my own in my own way. The idea was accepted. Everything seemed to be turning out for the best. My sisters were present during the conversation. My sister Jeanne stole close to Mama. Suddenly my sister Régina, who had refused to speak to me or look at me during the three weeks that I had been back, leaped onto my knee and said, "Take me with you this time! I'll kiss you if you do." I looked at my mother in some confusion.

"Oh take her! She is so unbearable," she said.

Régina jumped down and started to dance the *bourrée* and murmur vulgar and crazy things. Then she kissed me as though to suffocate me, leaped onto Mama's chair and said as she kissed her here, there, and everywhere, on her hair, on her eyes, "So are you happy that I'm going away? You'll be able to give everything to your Jeannot!"

Mama blushed slightly, but her expression melted into one of ineffable love as it fell on Jeanne. She gently pushed Régina away, who then took up her *bourrée* again, and leaned her head back on Jeanne's shoulder, "It'll just be the two of us," she said. There was so much unconscious emotion in these words and in the way she looked at Jeanne that I was astounded. I closed my eyes as though to shut it out. All I could hear was the distant jigging of my sister as she chanted in time to each step, "Us two, just the two of us, just the two of us!"

It was a painful drama played out by these four hearts in their little bourgeois setting.

Chapter XIII

settled permanently into the rue Duphot with my young sister.
I kept Caroline to wait on me and hired a cook. "My little lady"
spent nearly every day with me and every evening I dined with my
mother.

I had kept in touch with an actor from the Porte-Saint-Martin[1]
who had become stage manager of this theater, then directed by Marc
Fournier. At this time they were putting on a *féerie*[2] that was all the rage,
called *La Biche au bois.*[3] For the principal role they had engaged a
wonderful artist from the Odéon called Mlle. Debay,[4] who played tragic
princesses very charmingly. I often had seats at the Porte-Saint-Martin
and I enjoyed *La Biche au bois* very much. Mme. Ugalde,[5] who sang the
role of the young prince very well, totally astonished me. And Mariquita,
who danced, charmed me. Oh, how charming gorgeous Mariquita was!
Her dancing was always so full of spirit, character, and distinction.

Thanks to old Josse, I was somewhat acquainted with everybody.
But imagine my surprise and terror when, as I came to the theater at
five o'clock one day to take my seat, Josse cried out as he saw me, "Here
she is, our princess, our little Doe in the woods, here she is! It's the god
of the Theater who sends her to us!"

I struggled like an eel in a net, but it was no use. M. Marc Fournier,
a great charmer, gave me to understand that I was really doing him a
favor, and saving the day. Josse, who divined my hesitation, said, "But
my dear little one, you will not be abandoning your great art, for Mlle.
Debay from the Odéon theater plays the princess' role, and Mlle. Debay
is the foremost artist in the Odéon, and the Odéon is an imperial
theatre, so the role would not be a disgrace to your training."

Mariquita, who had just arrived, also pressed me. They sent for
Mme. Ugalde to rehearse the duets with me, for I would have to sing.
Yes, I was going to sing with a real singer, the foremost artist of the
Opéra-Comique![6] Time was passing. Josse made me rehearse my role,
which I knew almost in its entirety as I had often seen the play and had
an extraordinary memory. Minutes passed, leading to quarters of an
hour, which made up half hours, which became full hours. My eyes did

not leave the clock, the big clock in the director's office where we were. Mme. Ugalde made me rehearse. She thought I had a pretty voice, but I kept on singing out of tune. She supported and encouraged me.

They dressed me in the costume of Mlle. Debay and the curtain went up. Poor me! I was more dead than alive! But I regained my courage after a triple round of applause for my waking couplet that I began as though I were murmuring Racinian verse. Once the performance was over Marc Fournier offered me through Josse a three-year contract, but I asked for time to think it over.

Josse had introduced me to a playwright, a charming man with real talent: Lambert Thiboust. The latter thought I would be ideal for his heroine, the Bergère d'Ivry, but M. Faille, a former actor and the new director of the Ambigu,[7] was as good as owned by a certain de Chilly, who had made his reputation in the role of Rodin in *Le Juif-errant*[8] and had then married a wealthy woman and retired from acting to take up the directorship. He had, I think, just handed over the Ambigu to Faille. De Chilly had taken under his wing a charming girl named Laurence Gérard.[9] She was sweet and bourgeois, quite pretty but without real beauty or grace. Faille told Lambert Thiboust that he was negotiating with Laurence Gérard, but that he would nevertheless bow to the wishes of the author. "However," he said, "I must ask that your protégée come for an audition."

I submitted to the desire of the poor devil who must, I thought, be just as much of a nonentity as a director as he had been as an actor. So I went through a rehearsal on the stage of the Ambigu, illuminated by the gloomy "servante" (a little transportable lamp), while right under my nose one yard away was M. Faille, swaying on his chair, one hand on his belly, plunging the fingers of the other into his enormous nostrils. It was horribly disgusting. Lambert Thiboust was sitting close to him; I could see his smiling face looking at me encouragingly. For my audition I used *On ne badine pas avec l'amour*.[10] I didn't want to recite verse, as the play I was supposed to perform in was in prose. I think I was totally charming and this was Lambert Thiboust's opinion too. But when I had finished, poor Faille stood up in a slow and pretentious manner, spoke in a low voice to the author, and dragged me into his office.

"My child," said the good but stupid director, "my child, you have no talent for the theater!" I was about to demur. "None at all!" he continued. The door opened. "And look," he said, pointing to a person who had just entered, "M. de Chilly, who was in the theater listening to you, will tell you the same as I."

M. de Chilly nodded, and shrugged his shoulders. "Lambert Thiboust is crazy, no one has ever seen a shepherdess so thin!" he murmured. He rang for the boy and said, "Bring in Mlle. Laurence Gérard."

I understood. Without saying goodbye to these two peasants I left the office, but I had a heavy heart. I made my way to the foyer to get my hat that I had taken off for the audition. I found there Laurence Gérard who was called in a few seconds later. Seeing myself close to her in the mirror, I was struck by our dissimilarity. She was plumpish, with a wide face, magnificent black eyes, a rather coarse nose, thick lips, and an overall patina of the ordinary. I was blonde, thin, and frail like a reed. I had a long pale face, blue eyes, a rather sad mouth, and my whole being was imprinted with distinction. This slight glimpse of our two persons consoled me for my failure. Besides, I realized how much of a nonentity this Faille was, and how common de Chilly!

I was destined to see them both again in my life—Chilly shortly afterward as director of the Odéon; Faille twenty years later in a situation so sad that tears came to my eyes when he came to me and begged that I would perform at his benefit. "Oh, I beg you," said the poor man, "please come! You are the whole attraction at this performance. I count on you alone for my revenue." I shook hands with him. I do not know whether he remembered our first interview and my audition. As for me, I had only one desire—that he would not remember it.

Five days later Mlle. Debay had recovered and resumed her role. Before definitively contracting myself to the Porte-Saint-Martin, I wrote to Camille Doucet. The next day I received a note inviting me to a meeting with the minister. I felt some emotion at seeing this nice man again.

He was standing waiting for me as I was ushered in. He put out both hands and pulled me gently toward him. "Oh, what a terrible child!" he said, making me sit down. "Look here, you must calm down. You must not waste all your wonderful talents in travel, abscondment, and slaps." I was touched by his kindness. I looked at him with eyes full of regret. "Don't cry, my dear child, don't cry. Let's see now, how are we going to set right all this folly?" He remained silent for a moment, then he opened a drawer and took out a letter. "Here is something that perhaps will save us," he said. It was a letter from Duquesnel who had just been named director of the Odéon in association with Chilly.[11] "I have been asked for some young actors to revive the troupe at the Odéon. Well, we'll take care of that," he said, "and," as he stood up and led me to the door, "we will succeed."

Once I was back home I went over all my Racine roles. I waited anxiously for several days, calmed by Mme. Guérard who reassured me.

Finally I received word and went at once to the minister. A radiant Camille Doucet awaited me.

"It's done," he said, "but not without some difficulty. You are very young but you are already famous for your wilfulness. I had to give my word that you would be as meek as a little lamb."

"Yes, I will be, I promise," I told him, "even if it's only out of gratitude to you. But what must I do?"

"Here is a letter from Félix Duquesnel. He's expecting you." I thanked Camille Doucet a thousand times. He said, "I'll see you in a less formal capacity at your aunt's on Thursday. I received an invitation to dinner this morning. You can tell me then what Duquesnel says."

It was ten-thirty in the morning. I went home to make myself beautiful. I put on a dress of canary yellow covered by an overskirt of black silk lace and a conical-shaped straw hat covered with ears of wheat, tied under the chin with black velvet. I must have looked delightfully dashing.

Dressed like this, joyful and full of confidence, I went to see Félix Duquesnel. I waited for a few moments in a little sitting room which was furnished very artistically. A young man appeared—elegant, smiling, charming. I could not get used to the idea that this blonde and smiling young man would be my director. After a short conversation we found ourselves in agreement on all points. "Come to the Odéon at two o'clock," Duquesnel said by way of farewell. "I will introduce you to my associate. According to etiquette I should put it the opposite way," he added laughing, "but we are talking theater." He came down a few steps with me and stopped, leaning on the railing as he said goodbye.

At two o'clock exactly I was at the Odéon. I waited more than an hour. I began to grind my teeth and only the promise that I had made to Camille Doucet prevented me from leaving. Finally Duquesnel appeared. "You are going to see the other ogre," and he led me toward the director's office. On the way I pictured to myself an ogre as charming as his associate. So I was very disappointed to see the very ugly man that I recognized as Chilly. He rudely eyed me up and down, pretended not to recognize me, and signaling me to sit down, he passed me a pen without saying a word, pointing to the place where I had to sign.

Mme. Guérard stopped my hand. "Don't sign without reading it!"

Chilly raised his head. "You are Mademoiselle's mother?"

"No," she replied, "but I'm almost as good as."

"Well, you are right. Read it quickly and sign it or not; but be quick!" I felt a blush rising up my cheeks. This man was odious. But Duquesnel said to me in a low voice, "He has no grace, but he's a good man, don't take offense." I signed the contract and handed it back to the ugly associate.

"You know," he said, "he's responsible for you, for I personally would not have hired you for anything in the world."

"Believe me, sir," I replied, "if only you were involved in this I would not have signed it. So we are quits," and I took my leave immediately.

I went right away to let Mama know, for I knew it would give her great joy. Then, on the very same day, I set out with "my little lady" to buy everything that was necessary to furnish my apartment.

In the evening I went to the convent in the rue Notre-Dame-des-Champs to visit my dear teacher, Mlle. de Brabender. She had been sick for thirteen months, racked by severe rheumatism in all her joints. Stretched out straight in her little white bed, pain had rendered her unrecognizable. A turban concealed her hair, her big nose had collapsed in her sickness, her pale eyes seemed to have no irises. Only her formidable moustache bristled under the repeated pangs of pain. However, I found her changed in such a strange way that I searched for the cause. When I approached to kiss her gently I examined her so curiously that she sensed it. She signed to me with her eyes to look at a table close to her; in a glass I saw all my dear old friend's teeth. I put in the glass the three roses that I had brought for her and kissed her, apologizing for my impertinent curiosity.

I left the convent with a very heavy heart, for the Superior, who had led me into the garden, informed me that my dear Mlle. de Brabender could not live long. So I went back every day to see my gentle teacher.

But rehearsals began at the Odéon and I had to space out my visits. One morning around seven o'clock they came from the convent to fetch me in haste, and I was present at the sad death throes of the gentle creature. At the last moment her face lit up with such great joy that I suddenly wished to die. I kissed her hands, already cold, which held the crucifix. I was given permission to come back at the time when her body was to be put in the casket.

When I arrived at the appointed time next day I found the sisters in a state of such consternation that I was afraid. "My God, what's happened?" They pointed to the door of the cell without saying a word. Ten nuns surrounded the bed on which rested the strangest sight possible. My poor teacher lying stiff on her death bed had the face of a man. Her moustache had lengthened and a beard half an inch long surrounded her chin. This moustache and beard were red, while her long white hair framed her face. Her mouth which had caved in without the support of her teeth had allowed her nose to fall onto this red moustache. This terrible and ridiculous mask had replaced the sweet face of my friend. It was the mask of a man while her small fine hands were those of a woman. The young nuns had eyes big with fear. In spite of the reassurance of the sister nurse who had dressed the poor dead body, in spite of her assurance that the body was that of a woman, the little nuns trembled and crossed themselves over and over.

The day after the doleful ceremony I made my début at the Odéon in *Le Jeu de l'amour et du hasard*.[12] I was not made for Marivaux, who demands qualities of coquetterie and preciosity which I did not have then, and which I do not have now. In addition, I was a little too thin. I was not a success.

Chilly passed in the hallway as I was chatting with Duquesnel, who was encouraging me, and said to him as he pointed at me, "Grain for the birds, but there's no kernel there!"[13] I was outraged by the insolence of this man. Blood turned my face crimson, but in the haloes I saw with my half-closed eyes there was the face of Camille Doucet, this face always clean-shaven and youthful under its crown of white hair. This was, I thought, a mental vision that appeared to me, constantly on the alert as I was to the promise that I had made. But no, it was the real Doucet.

He came up to me. "What a pretty voice you have! How much we will enjoy your second début!" This man was always courteous but truthful. In fact, this début had given him no pleasure at all, but he had promised himself that the second would be great. And he had spoken truly. I had a pretty voice. That was all one could ascertain from this first test.

So I stayed at the Odéon, working hard, always ready to replace someone as I knew all the parts. I obtained some success, and the students had already made a favorite out of me. My arrival on stage was always greeted with bravos from the young people. A few old grousers looked down at the pit to impose silence, but the young people couldn't care less.

Finally, my day of success dawned. Duquesnel had had the idea of staging a revival of *Athalie* with the Mendelssohn choruses. Beauvallet, the odious professor, was a charming colleague. It was he who, by special permission of the minister, was to play Joad. For my part, I was to play Zacharie. Some students from the Conservatoire were to recite the spoken choruses, while the music students performed the musical part. But it was going so badly that Duquesnel and Chilly were in despair. Beauvallet, more friendly than formerly, but still foul mouthed, kept uttering terrible oaths. We started again, and yet again. Nothing worked. The wretched speaking choruses were abominable. Suddenly Chilly cried out, "Well, let the little one say the choral parts; she can do it all on her own with her pretty voice!"

Duquesnel did not say a word. But he pulled on his moustache to hide his smile. His colleague was coming around . . . he was coming around to his little protégée! He nodded his head indifferently to the questioning glance of Chilly, and we started again with myself reading the spoken choruses. Everybody applauded and the conductor especially exulted. The poor man had suffered so!

The day of the first performance was a real little triumph for me. Oh, very small, but so full of promise for my future! The audience was taken by the sweetness of my voice and its pure crystal tone and made me repeat the spoken choruses. I was rewarded by three rounds of applause. After the act, Chilly came up to me and said, "You are adorable!"

His use of the familiar "tu" offended me a little, but I retorted mischievously addressing him in kind, "You must think I've put on weight!" He left roaring with laughter. From this day on we always addressed each other with the familiar "tu," and we became the best friends in the world.

The Odéon! It is the theatre that I most liked and that I left only with regret. We were all friends there and everybody was jolly. This theater was almost a continuation of school. All the young people went there. Duquesnel was a director full of wit, gallantry, and youthfulness. Often during the rehearsals several of us would go to the Luxembourg for a ball game during the acts that we were not in. I would remember the months I had spent previously at the Comédie-Française—such a starchy, gossipy, jealous little group. I recalled my several months at the Gymnase. There we had talked of nothing except dresses and hats. We chattered about a thousand things that had nothing to do with art.

At the Odéon I was happy. We only thought about putting on plays. We rehearsed in the morning, the afternoon, all the time. I loved that. In the summer I lived in a lodge attached to the villa Montmorency at Auteil. I arrived in a *"petit-duc"*[14] that I drove myself. I had two marvellous ponies that my aunt Rosine had given me because they had almost killed her when they had bolted at Saint-Cloud at the sight of a merry-go-round. I rode along the river at full tilt. But despite the sparkling light of July, despite the gaiety of the sounds outside, it was with real joy that I climbed the cold cracked steps and headed quickly for my dressing room, distributing greetings as I ran. Then, once I had taken off my coat, hat, and gloves, I would bound onto the stage, happy to be at last in this infinite shadow. The meager light of the *"servante"*

struck here or there a tree, a turret against the wall, or a bench, while
the faces of the actors were only fitfully illuminated. I found nothing
more vivifying than this air full of microbes, nothing gayer than this
shadow, nothing brighter than this darkness! One day my mother was
curious to come and see the wings. I thought that she was going to die
of disgust. "You unlucky child! How can you survive in there?" she
murmured, and once she was outside she breathed in great breathfuls
of air.

Yes, I could survive in there. In fact I was only really alive when I
was there. Since then I have changed a little. But I still have a great
liking for this dark factory in which, as joyous jewellers of our art, we
cut the precious stones furnished us by the poets.

The days slipped by bringing occasional little disappointments,
but a new day brought a new dream, and life seemed to be composed
of eternal happiness. I played in turn in *Le Marquis de Villemer*[15] (the
part of the crazy baroness, an experienced woman of thirty-five—I was
only just twenty-one and looked seventeen), and in *François le Champi*[16]
in the role of Mariette in which I was very successful. I treasure the
memory of the rehearsals of *Le Marquis de Villemer* and of *François le
Champi*.

Mme. George Sand, a sweet and charming creature, was extremely
shy. She spoke very little and smoked all the time. Her large eyes were
always dreamy. Her mouth was a bit heavy and vulgar, but her face had
a very kind look to it. She had been perhaps of medium build, but she
gave an impression of heaviness. I would watch this woman with a
romantic tenderness. Had she not been the heroine of a beautiful love
story? I would sit very close to her. I would take her hand and hold it
as long as possible in mine. Her voice was gentle and charming.

Prince Napoléon,[17] nicknamed Plon-Plon by the public, often came
to rehearsals of George Sand. He liked her tremendously. The first time
that I saw this man I became pale and felt my heart stop. He looked so
much like Napoléon I that I immediately bore him a grudge—for by
resembling him he diminished him, by robbing him of his distance and
bringing him close to us. Mme. Sand introduced me to him, in spite of
my protests. He looked at me in an impertinent fashion. I did not like
him. I hardly replied to the compliments that he offered me and huddled
up close to George Sand. He began to laugh and cried out, "This little
girl's in love with you!" George Sand gently stroked my cheek. "She's
my little Madonna, don't torment her." I stayed close to her, throwing
furtive and unhappy glances at the prince.

However I gradually came to like listening to him. For this man's
conversation was brilliant, serious, and witty. He studded all his conver-

sation with words that were a little crude, but everything that he said was interesting and instructive. He was spiteful, and I heard him say things about little Thiers[18] that were treacherous and horrible, but which contained a grain of truth. One day he painted such an amusing portrait of nice Louis Bouilhet that George Sand, who liked him, could not help laughing, at the same time that she reproached him for his nastiness.

The prince did not stand on ceremony, and yet he did not like to be treated without respect. One day an actor called Paul Deshayes, who was performing in *François le Champi*, went into the green room where there were Prince Napoléon, Mme. George Sand, the curator of the library—whose name I have forgotten—and myself. This actor was common and somewhat of an anarchist. He greeted Mme. Sand and to the prince he said, "You are sitting on my gloves, sir." The prince raised himself only slightly and sent the pair of gloves to the floor saying, "I say, I had thought the seat was clean." The actor blushed, picked up his gloves, and went out murmuring some vulgar threat.

I played in *Le Testament de César Girodot* in the role of Hortense. In *Kean*, by Alexandre Dumas,[19] I played the role of Anna Damby. At its première (February 18, 1868) the audience was very nasty and very hostile toward Alexandre Dumas *père*, on account of a personal affair that had nothing to do with his art. The political situation had been arousing strong emotions for some months, and there was a popular movement in favor of bringing Victor Hugo back from exile.[20] When Dumas entered his box he was greeted by booing. Then the many students who were there began to call in unison for *Ruy Blas*. Dumas got up and asked to speak. Silence fell. Dumas began, "My young friends . . . " but a voice shouted out, "We will be happy to listen to you, but only if you are alone in your box!" Dumas protested vehemently. Several members of the orchestra took his side, for he had invited a woman into his box, and no matter who this woman might be, it was not right to insult her in such an outrageous fashion. I had never witnessed such a scene before. I was watching through the crack in the curtains, feeling very interested and very nervous. I saw the great Dumas, pale with anger, shaking his fist, shouting, swearing, storming. Then suddenly there was a burst of applause. The woman had slipped out of the box, taking advantage of the moment when Dumas leaned out of the box to reply, "No! No! This woman will not leave!" At this very moment she disappeared. The delighted audience cried out, "Bravo!" and allowed Dumas to speak. But he was only heard for a few moments and then the cries of "*Ruy Blas!* Victor Hugo! Victor Hugo!" were heard again amidst the infernal din.

We had been waiting for an hour to begin the performance. Finally Chilly and Duquesnel came on stage. "Have courage, folks! The audience is out of control. Let's start anyway, and whatever happens, happens!"

I said to Dusquesnel, "I'm afraid I'm going to faint!" My hands were icy and my heart was thumping. "Tell me, what should I do if I'm too afraid?"

"Be afraid! Perform! And don't faint, no matter what you do!"

The curtain lifted in the midst of the storm: the bird calls, cat meows, and the dull rhythmic chorus of "Ruy Blas! Ruy Blas! Victor Hugo! Victor Hugo!"

My turn came. Berton senior,[21] who played Kean, had been badly received. I entered wearing an eccentric costume of "an Englishwoman in 1820." I heard a burst of laughter, which riveted me to the threshold on which I had just appeared. At the same moment the applause of my dear little student friends could be heard over the spiteful laughter. I took my courage in my hands and even felt an urge to fight. But I did not need to, for after the second interminable speech in which I betray my love for Kean, the delighted audience gave me a great ovation. Here is what "Ignotus" said in *Le Figaro*:

> Mlle. Sarah Bernhardt appeared in an eccentric costume which increased the uproar yet further. But her warm voice—that astonishing voice of hers—moved the audience. She tamed it like a little Orpheus.

After *Kean* I played in *La Loterie du mariage*.[22] While I was rehearsing this play Agar[23] came to find me in my usual corner, where I would sit on a little stool that I kept in my dressing room with my feet on a straw-bottomed chair. This was my favorite place because there was a gaslight there which allowed me to work while I was waiting for my turn to go on stage. I loved doing embroidery, lacework, or needlepoint. I had a pile of little projects started and I would take up this one or that as the fancy took me.

Mme. Agar was a wonderful creature who had been created for the pleasure of the eye. She was tall, pale, brown-haired, with large soft dark eyes. Her mouth was tiny with small rounded lips which lifted at the corners in an imperceptible smile and she had beautiful teeth. Her head was crowned with a marvellous abundance of glossy hair. She was the living incarnation of the ancient Greek ideal. Her hands were beautiful, long and rather soft. Her slow and slightly heavy walk completed the evocation. She was the great star of tragic roles at the Odéon theater. She came toward me with her measured step. Behind her was a young man between twenty-four and twenty-six years old. "Here my darling," she said kissing me, "you can make a poet happy." She introduced me to François Coppée.[24] I gestured to the young man to sit down and took a better look at him. His handsome face, emaciated and pale, was that of the immortal Bonaparte. My whole being surged with emotion for I love Napoléon I. Bonaparte above all.

"You are a poet, Monsieur?"

"Yes, Mademoiselle." (His voice also trembled, for he was even more timid than I.) "I have written a little play and Mlle. Agar is sure that you would be willing to perform in it with her."

"Yes, my darling," said Agar. "You will play in it for him. It's a little masterpiece and I'm sure that you will be tremendously successful in it."

"Oh, and you too! You will be so beautiful!" said the poet gazing at her rapturously.

I was called on stage. I came back a few moments later. The young poet was talking in a low voice to the beautiful tragic actress. I was coughing a little. Agar had taken possession of my armchair. She wanted to give it back to me and when I refused she pulled me onto her knee. The young man pulled up his chair and we chatted like that, our three heads touching. It was agreed that after I had read it I would take the play to Duquesnel, as he was the only one, out of the two directors, who was capable of appreciating poetry. After that we would obtain permission from the two directors to perform the play at a benefit performance which was due to take place after our première. The young man was delighted and gave me a pale grateful smile as he shook my hand nervously.

Agar escorted him as far as the little landing that projected over the stage. I looked at this magnificent statue next to the slim figure of the young writer. Agar might have been about thirty-five. She was really beautiful but, in my opinion, lacking in charm. I could not understand why this poetic Bonaparte was in love with this young matron—for it was as clear as day, and she seemed to be smitten too. I found it extremely interesting. I saw them shake hands lingeringly. Then with an abrupt and almost awkward gesture he bent over her beautiful hand and kissed it slowly. Agar came back over to me, her cheeks a bit flushed, which was unusual for her, as her complexion was usually a marble white. "Here, here's the manuscript!" she said giving me a little scroll.

The rehearsal had just finished. I took leave of Agar and read the play in the carriage. I was so enchanted by it that I turned around and went back so that I could have Duquesnel read it immediately. I met him on the stairs.

"Please, come back up!"

"Oh my God," he said. "What's the matter? Have you won the lottery?"

"Well, almost. Come!"

Once we were in his office I said, "Read this, please!"

"Give it to me. I'll take it away with me."

"No, read it, here, right now! Do you want me to read it to you?"

"No, no! Your voice is a sorceress that makes the worst verse sound like ravishing poetry. Give it to me!"

And the young director sat himself in his armchair and started to read while I leafed through newspapers.

"It's delicious!" he exclaimed. "In fact it's a real masterpiece!"

Jumping for joy I said, "So you'll make Chilly adopt it?"

"Yes, yes, don't worry. But when do you want to put it on?"

"Well, let's see. The author seems to be in a hurry and Agar too."

"And you too," he said laughing, "as this is the role of your dreams!"

"Yes, little Duq, me too! If you want to be really nice, let me do it at the benefit performance for Mme.*** in two weeks' time. That way it won't interfere with any other performance and our poet will be so happy!"

"Alright," said Duquesnel, "I can arrange that . . . but what are we going to do about scenery?" he murmured, biting his nails (his favorite meal when he was preoccupied).

I had already thought about that and I offered to walk back home with him where his wife was waiting so that I could explain my plan to him on the way. The scenery would be borrowed from *Jeanne de Ligneris*, a play that had just recently been staged but had died as a result of the derisive response it had received. It had a superb Italian park setting with statues, flowers, and even the staircase. As for the costumes I knew that if we mentioned it to Chilly, no matter how inexpensive they might be, he would scream like Rodin! Agar and I would supply the costumes.

We had reached Duquesnel's house. "Come up and say hello to my wife and while you're at it talk to her about the costumes," he said.

So I went up, and after I had kissed the prettiest face that one could imagine I shared our plot with the fair mistress of the household. She fully approved of our plan and promised immediately to set about looking for pretty designs for our costumes. While she was talking I compared her in my mind with Agar. How much I preferred this ravishing blonde head with its enormous limpid eyes and its two little rosy dimples, and the soft hair that formed a halo around the forehead and the fine wrists attached to which were the prettiest pair of hands that one could ever hope to see—hands that are, in fact, still famous.

I left the nice couple and went to see Agar to tell her everything that had happened. The poor thing kissed me over and over. There was a priest there who was her cousin, who seemed very pleased by my story: he must have been aware of the whole situation. There was a timid ring on the doorbell and François Coppée was announced. "I'm off," I said to him on the doorstep as I shook his hand. "Agar will tell you everything."

Chapter XIV

[*Coppée's play* Le Passant *is tremendously successful, making Coppée famous overnight, and after the benefit performance there follow more than one hundred more performances. Sarah and Agar are invited to give a performance of it at the Tuileries palace for the Emperor and Empress. Sarah is embarassed when she is caught unawares by the amused Emperor practising her curtsey in an ante-room as she waits with Mme. Guérard to be presented to him. Sarah finds both the Emperor and the Empress more attractive than in their portraits, but the Empress' charm is ruined by an unattractive voice.*

After the success of Le Passant *Chilly softens in his attitude toward Sarah. Meanwhile she has become the star attraction of his theater, especially with the students in the audience.*

Sarah now lives at 16 rue Auber, which she has furnished with antique Dutch furniture given to her by her blind, Jewish, grandmother—a tall and beautiful but cold woman who has come to live with Sarah. Sarah plans to obtain fire insurance for her apartment but sends the agent away without sign-ing the policy since she feels depressed and uneasy. The unease grows into a premonition of disaster which occurs the next evening in the form of a fire, while Sarah is giving a dinner party for Rose Baretta, Charles Haas[1] (tall, charming, witty, and elegant), and Arthur Meyer, a young journalist. After rescuing her grandmother (whose only concern is to save her trunk), her baby son,[2] and the servants, Sarah finds out the next day that all her possessions have been de-stroyed, and realizes that her financial situation is now precarious, although a benefit performance at which Adelina Patti sings helps her to recover.

She takes an apartment on the rue de Rome and installs her grandmother in a retirement home. She performs in the plays Le Bâtard[3] *and* L'Affranchi,[4] *in* l'Autre *by George Sand and* Jean-Marie *by André Theuriet.*][5]

Chapter XV

War had been declared! And I hate war! It exasperates me, it makes me shudder all over. And from time to time I would start in terror, overwhelmed with grief at voices crying in the distance. War! Infamy! Shame! Pain! Theft and crime sponsored, pardoned, and glorified!

Recently I visited a large steelworks. (I won't say in what country, because everyone there was very hospitable to me—I am not a spy or an informer, but a storyteller!) So I was visiting one of these frightful factories in which engines of death are made. The owner, a millionaire, was introduced to me. He was a pleasant man, devoid of conversation but with a preoccupied and dissatisfied air to him. I learned from my guide that this man had just lost a large sum of money, more than sixty million he said.

"My God! How did he lose it?"

"Oh!" exclaimed my interlocutor, "He didn't lose it, but he failed to make it, which is the same thing." And as I looked at him in bewilderment he said, "Yes, this is how it happened—you know that there was talk of war between France and Germany over Morocco?"

"Yes."

"Well, this prince of steel hoped to sell cannon, and activated for that purpose one of his factories which is working overtime at the moment, day and night. He gave huge bribes to influential members of the government, and bought newspapers in France and Germany in order to stir up the two nations. But all has failed, thanks to the intervention of wise and humanitarian men. And the millionaire is in despair. He has lost sixty, maybe even a hundred million."

I looked contemptuously at this wretched man and ardently wished that I could see him suffocated by his millions, since remorse was doubtless an unknown emotion to him. And how many others are just as contemptible as this man! Almost all those who call themselves munition suppliers, in all the countries of the world, are frenzied propagators of war.

Let every one be a soldier in the moment of danger, yes, a thousand times yes! That everyone should arm himself for the defense of his country, and that one should kill to defend oneself and one's own, makes sense. But that there are still, in these modern times, young men whose only dream is to kill other people in order to make themselves a career—that passes the bounds of comprehension! Without a doubt it is necessary to guard our borders and our colonies; but since everybody is a soldier, why not derive this defense from this "everybody"? There would be schools only for officers and no more of these horrible barracks that are so offensive to the eye. And when sovereigns visit us and are shown a parade of the troops, wouldn't they be more impressed by the strength of a people that was embodied in one millionth of its potential power picked randomly by lottery from the mass of its soldiery, than by the elegant evolution of an army trained specifically for parade? I have seen so many of these magnificent parades in all the countries that I have visited! And yet I know from history that the army that prances so gracefully on parade, may be the selfsame one that flees irrationally before the enemy.

Thus on July 19 war[1] was seriously declared. Paris became the theater of both touching and comic scenes. Being highly strung and of delicate health I could not bear the sight of all these young people gone mad, shouting *La Marseillaise* and running around the streets in serried ranks, yelling repeatedly, "To Berlin! To Berlin!" My heart beat, for I also believed that we were heading for Berlin. But I felt that they were preparing themselves for this great act in a disrespectful and ignoble manner. Yet, I understood their rage, as those people had provoked us without good reason. My helplessness disgusted me. And when I saw all those pale mothers, their eyes swollen with tears, holding their boys in their arms and kissing them desperately, my throat tightened in anguish. I wore myself out with constant crying. And yet nothing could have made one foresee the final horrible catastrophe.

The doctors decided that I should leave immediately for Eaux-Bonnes. I did not want to leave as the general fever was gaining a hold on me. But I grew steadily weaker each day and on July 27 I was carried onto a train almost by force. Mme. Guérard, my manservant, and my chambermaid accompanied me and I had brought my child along. At the stations there were notices everywhere announcing that Emperor Napoléon had gone to Metz to assume command of the army.

When I got to Eaux-Bonnes I had to go to bed. My condition seemed very grave to Dr. Leudet, who told me later that he had been sure I was going to die. I was vomiting blood and had a piece of ice between my teeth the whole time. However after twelve days I was able to leave my bed. I quickly regained my strength and peace of mind and went for long rides on horseback. Plus the news of the war suggested that victory was imminent. It was thrilling and moving to hear that the young Prince Imperial had been baptized by fire at Saarbrück in the battle commanded by General Frossard. Life seemed beautiful again. I had confidence in the outcome of the war and I pitied the Germans for embarking on it.

Alas! The fine cavalcades of glory that galloped in my imagination were thrust aside by the terrible news of the battle of Saint-Privat. The news was posted each day in the little garden of the casino at Eaux-Bonnes. That was where people found out what was happening. As I hated the crush, however, I would send my manservant to copy out the dispatches. How painful the dispatch from Saint-Privat informing us in its laconic style of the frightful butchery, of the heroic defense put up by Maréchal Canrobert,[2] and of Bazaine's first act of treachery in not going to the aid of his comrade![3] I knew Canrobert and liked him very much. Later on he became one of my devotees and I treasure the memory of exquisite hours spent listening to him tell stories of the heroism of others (never his own). What a wealth of anecdotes he had! What wit! What charm!

The news of the battle of Saint-Privat brought back my fever. My nights were full of nightmares. Again I was ill. Each day the news was worse. Gravelotte with its thirty-six thousand men, both French and German, mown down in a few hours, followed Saint-Privat. Then there was MacMahon's sublime but impotent struggle as he was pushed back to Sedan. And then there was Sedan! Sedan . . . [4]

Ah! The horrible moment of awakening!

The month of August had died the night before amidst the din of weapons and death rattles, but in the moaning of the dying there was still a suggestion of hope. The month of September, as yet hardly born, was already cursed. Its first war cry was stifled by the brutal and cowardly hand of Destiny. A hundred thousand men—a hundred thousand Frenchmen—had to concede defeat. The Emperor of France had to give his sword to the Emperor of Prussia. Nothing can wipe out the memory of that cry of pain and rage uttered by the whole nation!

On September 1, about ten o'clock, Claude, my manservant, knocked on my door. I was awake. He gave me a copy of the first dispatches: "Battle of Sedan. Mac-Mahon[5] wounded, etc. . . . " "I beg you," I said, "go back down there and as soon as a new dispatch comes in bring it to me. I sense something big, something incredible! Something else is going to happen, and we have suffered so much for the last month that it can only be something good and beautiful. For in His scales God balances joy and suffering. Go back there Claude dear, go back." I went to sleep full of trust. I was so tired that I slept till one o'clock. When I woke up my chambermaid, Félicie, the most delightful girl that one could ever imagine, was sitting next to my bed. Her pretty face and big dark eyes looked so sad that my heart stopped beating. I looked at her anxiously. She handed me the copy of a dispatch that had arrived: "Emperor Napoléon III has just surrendered his sword." Blood rushed to my face and my lungs were too weak to hold back the surge. I dropped my head on the pillow and blood flowed from my lips along with the plaint of my whole being.

For three days I hovered between life and death. Dr. Leudet sent for a friend of my father's, a shipowner named M. Maunoir. He hurried to my bedside with his young wife who was also ill, more so than I in fact, despite her healthy appearance, for she died six months later. Thanks to their solicitude and to the energetic care of Dr. Leudet, I emerged from this crisis alive. But I resolved to return to Paris at once. A state of siege was going to be proclaimed. I did not want my mother, my sisters, and my niece to remain in the capital. In fact everybody at Eaux-Bonnes, invalid and tourist alike, was suddenly seized with a desire to leave. I found a stagecoach that took me for an exorbitant price to the first train that came along.

In that train we managed to find more or less satisfactory seats for ourselves, but once we got to Bordeaux it was impossible to find five places on the express train. My manservant was allowed to go up next to the driver. Mme. Guérard and my chambermaid stowed themselves somewhere or other, and I got into a compartment where nine people were piled one on top of another.

An ugly old man tried to push out my little boy as I steered him into the compartment ahead of me, but I pushed him back forcefully saying, "No human force will make us get out of this compartment, ugly old man! We are here and here we'll stay!"

A fat lady who took up more space to herself than three ordinary people cried out, "This is wonderful! We're already suffocating. It's shameful to have eleven people in a compartment when there is only space for eight."

"Well, get out then," I flashed back, "and with you gone there will be only seven!" The stifled laughter of the other passengers told me I had won over my audience. Three young men offered me their seats. I refused them and declared my intention to stand. The young men got up and declared *their* intention to stand.

So the fat lady hailed a conductor. "Conductor! Listen . . . " The conductor stopped in mid track, his foot poised to continue walking.

"It's shameful! There are eleven of us in this wagon! It's impossible to move."

"Don't believe a word of it," cried one of the young men. "Look, there are still three empty places, we are all standing, send us some more people!"

The conductor went away, laughing and muttering against the complaining woman, who violently accosted the young man. He bowed respectfully to her and said, "Madame, if you will calm down you'll find that you are going to be very happy. We seven, including the child, will sit on this side and you four will stay on that side."

The ugly old man, who was thin and short, glanced sidelong at the fat lady, "Four . . . " he murmured, "four . . . " indicating with his look and tone of voice that the fat lady took up far more than one place.

This tone and look were not lost on the young man, and before the ugly old man knew what was happening he said, "Here sir, you put yourself over on this side in this nice little corner, then all the slim ones will be together." In the old man's place he installed a placid, sweet Englishman who was between eighteen and twenty. He had a wrestler's torso and a fair baby face. A very young woman sitting opposite the fat lady was crying with laughter. All six of us on the slim side managed to find a space, a bit squashed together, but cheered by this little argy-bargy. And we were in need of cheering.

The young man who had so wittily arranged everything was a tall handsome boy, with a fair complexion, blue eyes, and hair that was almost white, which gave his face an attractive freshness and youthfulness. During the night he took the child on his lap. As for the others, apart from the child, the fat lady, and the young Englishman, nobody else slept. The heat was overwhelming. We talked about the war. One of the young men said to me after some hesitation that I looked like Sarah Bernhardt and I replied that it was with good reason. The young men then introduced themselves to me: Albert Dépit, the one who had recognized me, Baron van Zelern or van Zerlen, I don't remember which, a Dutchman, and Félix Faure, the young man with the blonde hair, who told me that he was from Le Havre and knew my grandmother very well.

I remained in friendly contact with these three men, except for Albert Dépit, who later became my enemy. All three of them are now dead. Albert Dépit died a desperate man, having tried everything and succeeded at nothing. The Dutch baron died in a train crash, and Félix Faure died as President of France.[6]

When the young woman heard my name she also introduced herself. "I think we are distantly related," she said. "I am Mme. Laroque."

"From Bordeaux?" I asked.

"Yes."

So we could talk about our family, for the wife of my mother's brother was a Laroque from Bordeaux.

The journey passed quite quickly in spite of the heat and our thirst, and the fact that there was so little space. However, our arrival at Paris was more depressing. We shook each other's hand warmly. The fat lady's husband was waiting for her at the station. Without saying a word to her he handed her a telegram. When she had absorbed what it said the poor thing shrieked and fell sobbing in his arms. What misfortune had just struck her? I looked at her. She was certainly no longer ridiculous, the poor woman. I felt a pang at the thought that we had laughed at her so much, when she was already touched by such misfortune.

Back at home I sent word to my mother that I would go and see her that day. She, however, came round immediately wanting to know what kind of state of health I was in. It was then that we arranged all the details of my family's departure, except for mine, since I wanted to stay in Paris during the siege. My mother, my little boy and his nanny, my sisters, my aunt Annette who ran my household, and my mother's chambermaid, were all ready to leave the next day. I had booked rooms at Le Havre at Frascati's for the whole shabang.

But wanting to leave was one thing, being able to leave another. I had sent my manservant to book a compartment. He came back three hours later with his clothes torn and suffering from numerous kicks and punches. "Madame cannot mingle with this crowd," he said to me, "it's impossible. I would not be able to protect her alone. If Madame were travelling alone, it would be one thing . . . but with Madame's mother, the young ladies, and the children . . . it's impossible, impossible." I hastily fetched three of my male friends, explained the situation to them and begged them to accompany me. I stationed alongside my manservant my butler and a servant of my mother's who brought along with him his young brother, a priest, who was quite willing to join us. We left all together in a railway bus. There were seventeen of us altogether, although only nine were really travelling. I can tell you that eight defenders was not an excessive number, since those who were trying to buy tickets were not human beings, but hunted wild beasts spurred on by the desire to flee. These animals saw nothing except for the little ticket office, the gate that led to the train, and the train that would ensure flight. The presence of the young priest was very helpful to us, as his religious mien protected us from some of the jostling.

All of my loved ones were settled in a compartment and blew me kisses as the train started. All at once I felt a shiver of terror, as I realized that I was suddenly alone. It was the first time that I had been parted from the little being who was the dearest of all to me in the world. Just then two arms tenderly encircled me and a voice murmured, "My little Sarah, why didn't you leave? Your health is so delicate. Will you be able to bear being without your little one?" It was Mme. Guérard who arrived too late to kiss the child, but remained to console the mother.

I gave myself up to my despair. Now I regretted that I had sent my son away. And yet what if the fighting should reach Paris? Not for one moment did the idea occur to me that I might have left with him. I felt I could be useful in Paris. Useful for what? Stupid to believe this no doubt, but I was convinced of it. I felt that all who were in good health should remain in Paris—and in spite of my delicacy I felt that I was healthy (not without reason, as I have proved since). I remained there without knowing what I would do there.

I passed several days dazed by the absence of life and love which normally surrounded me.

Chapter XVI

$\mathcal{M}$eanwhile the defense was getting organized. I resolved to use my strength and intelligence to take care of the wounded. But where could I set up a military hospital? The Odéon had closed its doors. I moved heaven and earth to get permission to set up a military hospital at the Odéon.[1] Thanks to Emile de Girardin[2] and Duquesnel my wish was granted. I went to the Ministry of War and made my statement and request. My application to set up a military hospital was granted, but I needed provisions. I wrote a note to the Préfet de police.[3] A courier arrived shortly after I had sent my message and gave me this note from the Préfet:

> Madame, if it is possible for you to come right away I will wait for you until 6:00 P.M. If not, I will see you tomorrow morning at 8:00 A.M. Forgive the early hour, but I am busy in court from 9:00 A.M., and as I understand that you wish to discuss a matter of great urgency I am anxious to serve you if it is in my power.
>
> Comte de Kératry

I remembered a Comte de Kératry who had been introduced to me at my aunt's, the evening when I had recited some verse accompanied by Rossini. But he was a young lieutenant, a handsome lad, witty and dashing. He had introduced me to his mother. I had sometimes recited poetry at the countess' soirées. The young lieutenant had left for Mexico. We had corresponded for some time and then had lost touch with one another. I asked Guérard if she thought that the Préfet was a close relative of my young friend and she said she thought so. We talked about it in the carriage in which we were travelling, for I left immediately for the Tuileries in which the prefecture was located.

My heart thumped as I arrived at the front door. I had come there a few months previously one morning in April with Mme. Guérard. As today an officer had opened the door of my carriage, but then a mild April sun had lit up the steps and glanced off the shining lamps of the carriages which criss-crossed the court in all directions. Then there had

107

been an exhilarating bustle of young and elegant officers exchanging greetings. But today the November sun sneaking through mist turned to lead everything it touched. The black and soiled cabs succeeded one another, catching on the grating, chipping at the steps, moving forward or backward to the vulgar banter of the coachmen. Greetings were exchanged to the tune of "How are you old man?" "Oh, what a hangover!" "So, have you any news?" "Yes, we are f————"! etc. The prefecture was a different place. The atmosphere had changed. The light fragrance left in the air by the passage of elegant women had disappeared. A vague odor of tobacco, greasy clothing, and dirty hair weighed on the air. Ah, the pretty French empress! I could see her in her blue dress embroidered with silver, calling to her aid Cinderella's fairy[4] to help put back on her little slipper.[5] I could see the delightful Prince Imperial helping me to arrange some pots of verbena and michaelmas daisies, and holding in arms too weak an enormous pot of rhododendrons hiding his handsome face. Finally I saw in my mind's eye also Emperor Napoléon III, applauding with his half-closed eyes the rehearsal of the curtsey destined for him.

The blonde empress had fled in her American dentist's carriage, for it was not even a Frenchman who had the courage to protect this unfortunate woman, but a foreigner. The gentle and idealistic emperor had vainly tried to kill himself on the battlefield. Two horses were killed beneath him, but he received not a scratch. He had given up his sword and we had all wept of rage, shame, and pain on learning of its surrender. What courage this brave man must have had to accomplish this act! He had wanted to save a hundred thousand men, spare a hundred thousand lives, reassure a hundred thousand mothers. Poor dear emperor! History will one day do him justice, for he was good and humane and trusting—alas!

I stopped a moment before going in to the Préfet's living quarters. I wiped my eyes and to alter my train of thought I said to "my little lady," "Would you find me pretty if you were to see me for the first time?"

"Oh, yes!" she replied emphatically.

"So much the better! I need this old Préfet to think me pretty because I have so many things to ask of him."

What a surprise it was to recognize the lieutenant who had become captain and then Préfet de police! My name, called out by the officer who ushered me in, made him bound from his chair and he advanced toward me with his hands outstretched and a smile on his face. "Well? Had you forgotten me?" he asked, as he offered a friendly greeting to Mme. Guérard.

"But I didn't think that it was you, and I am very glad to see that it is—you will grant all my wishes."

"There you are!" he said bursting into laughter. "Well, Madame, give me your orders!"

"Here they are then. I want some bread, milk, meat, vegetables, sugar, wine, brandy, potatoes, eggs, coffee," I said all in one breath.

"Ah, let me breathe!" cried out the préfet and count. "You talk so fast that you're suffocating me."

I stopped and began again a moment later. "I have set up a military hospital at the Odéon, but as it is a military one the municipality will not give me any provisions. I already have five wounded, I am managing; but I have been informed that others are coming and they have to be fed."

"Your wishes will be more than granted. There are in the prefecture several months' worth of provisions prepared by the unfortunate empress. I will send you all that except for the meat, bread, and milk. As far as that is concerned I am going to have orders issued that your hospital should be made part of the municipal service, even though it is a military hospital. Also, here is a chit for salt and some other commodities that you will fetch from the new Opéra."

I looked at him incredulously. "At the new Opéra? . . . but it is under construction, there is nothing but scaffolding."

"Yes, that's right. You take the little door under the scaffolding which opens onto the rue Scribe. You go up by the spiral staircase, which leads to the provisions office, and someone will help you there."

"I have one more request."

"Let me hear it! I am at your service."

"I'm very worried. A gunpowder store has been set up in the cellars of the Odéon. If Paris were bombarded and if a shell fell on this site we would all be blown up and that's not my goal."

"You're absolutely right," said the nice man, "and nothing could be more stupid than to have stored gunpowder in this place. But as far as this matter is concerned I am going to have more difficulty, because I am dealing with a bunch of obstinate burghers who want to organize the defense in their own way. Try to get me a petition signed by the most influential landowners and businessmen in the district. Are you happy?"

"Yes," I said, giving him a warm handshake, "yes, you are good and charming, thank you."

I moved toward the door and then stopped, hypnotized by an overcoat lying on an armchair. Mme. Guérard, who had followed my gaze, pulled me gently by the sleeve. "Oh, my little Sarah, don't do that!" But I slipped a begging glance toward the young Préfet.

He did not understand and said to me, "What else can I do for you, pretty Madame?" I pointed to the overcoat and tried to look as charming as possible.

"I beg your pardon," he said dumbfounded, "I don't understand at all." I continued to point at the designated object. "Give it to me?" I said to him.

"My overcoat?"

"Yes."

"What for?"

"For my wounded convalescents."

He burst into laughter and fell into a seat. A little annoyed by his inextinguishable laughter I said, "What I said is not so funny. Listen to me. I have a poor boy whose only injury is two fingers blown away. He doesn't want to stay in bed, which is understandable. His military greatcoat is not warm enough and I find it very difficult to heat the big foyer of the Odéon where the stronger men are. At the moment this man is warm because I took the overcoat of Henri Fould who came to see me the other day, and as my wounded patient is a colossus and Henri Fould is a giant I would never have found such an opportunity again. But I am going to need a lot of overcoats and this one seems to me to be very warm." I was stroking the fur lining of the coveted garment.

The young Préfet was snorting with laughter. He emptied the pockets of his overcoat, and showing me a magnificent white silk scarf that he took from the deepest one, he said, "You permit me to keep my scarf?" I nodded with an air of resignation. He rang the bell and assuming a solemn expression, in spite of the laughter in his eyes, he said to the officer as he gave him the overcoat, "Carry that to these ladies' carriage." I thanked him and left very happy.

I came back twelve days later with a list filled with signatures of the most influential landowners and businessmen of the district around the Odéon. But I stood petrified on the doorstep of the Préfet's office, for the latter, instead of coming toward me, dashed toward a cabinet, opened it violently, threw something in it, then slammed it shut. Then he leaned on it as though to forbid me access to it, saying to me in his witty and teasing voice, "Pardon me, but I caught a bad cold after your first visit. I have put my overcoat . . . Oh, an ugly old overcoat, not a warm one," he added vehemently, "but anyway an overcoat . . . I have put it in there— and look, I have the key!" Putting this key in his pocket he approached and sat me down.

But the conversation lost its playful tone, the news was sad. The wounded had been piling up in the hospitals for twelve days. Everything was going badly. Foreign policy, domestic policy. The Germans were advancing on Paris. The Army of the Loire was being assembled. Gambetta,[6] Chanzy,[7] Bourbaki,[8] Trochu[9] were organizing a desperate defense. We talked for a long time about these sad facts. I shared with him the painful impression I had received the last time that I had come here to the Tuileries; I recalled the splendid, refined, happy people who had once been there and who were today so terribly much to be pitied. We sat in silence. Then I shook his hand, saying that I had received everything he had sent, and I went back to the hospital.

Indeed, the Préfet had sent me ten barrels of red wine, two of brandy, thirty thousand eggs arranged in cases full of bran and lime, a hundred sacks of coffee, twenty canisters of tea, forty cases of Albert biscuits, a thousand canisters of preserves and a quantity of other things. M. Menier, the famous chocolate manufacturer, had sent me five hundred pounds of chocolate. One of my friends, a miller, had made me a gift of twenty sacks of flour, six of them maize flour. This miller was the one that had proposed to me when I was at the Conservatoire. Félix Potin, my former neighbor when I lived at 11 boulevard Malesherbes, had responded to my appeal and had sent me two barrels of raisins, a hundred cans of sardines, three sacks of rice, two sacks of lentils and twenty loaves of sugar. I had received from M. de Rothschild two barrels of brandy and a hundred bottles of his wine for the convalescents.

I received in addition a very unexpected present. Léonie Dubourg, a friend from Grand-Champs, sent me fifty tins containing four pounds of salted butter each. This girl had married a rich country gentleman who owned, it seems, numerous farms. I was very touched by the fact that she had remembered me, for I had not seen her since the convent.

I had in addition recquisitioned all my friends' overcoats and slippers. I had bought a consignment of two hundred flannel vests and my aunt Betzy who lived, and still lives, in Holland—she was the sister of my blind grandmother and she is ninety-three years old today—my aunt Betzy found a way to send me through the delightful ambassador of Holland three hundred nightshirts made in a wonderful Dutch fabric and one hundred pairs of sheets. I received linen and bandages from all corners of Paris. But it was especially to the Palace of Industry that I would go to stock up on linen and bandages. An adorable woman named Mlle. Hocquigny worked there as "bossess" of all the hospitals. Everything she did was done with smiling grace. Everything that she refused to do was refused with gracious sorrow. Mlle. Hocquigny was over thirty. She was an old maid who gave the impression of being a young woman. She had big, blue, dream-filled eyes, a smiling mouth, a delightful oval face, little dimples, and above this grace, this dream, this mouth (flirtatious and full of promise), a large forehead like those of the virgins of the Primitives, a large forehead which was a little curved, bordered by two wide bandeaux of very flat, very smooth hair, separated by a straight, fine, impeccable parting. This forehead was like a protective rampart to the delightful face. Mlle. Hocquigny who was

very much courted and adored remained unmoved by all the homage
she received. She was glad to be loved, but she did not permit anyone
to talk to her about it. The Palace of Industry had an extraordinary
staff of doctors and famous surgeons. All of them were in love with
Mlle. Hocquigny, even the patients. As she had conceived a great friendship for me she would share with me her comments and observations
and her sad disdain. Thanks to her I was never lacking for linen and
bandages.

I had organized my hospital using very few people. My cook was
installed in the public foyer. I had bought her an enormous stove and
she could make soups and broths for fifty men. Her husband was chief
male nurse. I had appointed two assistants to him. Mme. Guérard,
Mme. Lambquin, and myself were the female nurses. We had to do the
night shift two at a time, with the result that we were on two nights out
of three. But I preferred that to taking on a woman that I did not know.
Mme. Lambquin played duenna roles at the Odéon.[10] She had an ugly
face and a common bearing, but she was full of talent. She had an
arrogant and Gallic way of expressing herself. For her a spade was a
spade and she had no time for double-talk and innuendo. Sometimes
she was embarrassing with the crudity of her words and her thoughts,
but she was good, active, alert, and dedicated.

My male friends who were serving on the ramparts, would come
to serve me as secretaries during their leisure hours, for I had a book
which I presented every day to a sergeant from Le Val-de-Grâce[11]
who would come to find out if there were any admissions, deaths, or
discharges.

Paris was under siege. One could no longer go out very far. We
received no news. But the German circle had not reached the gates of
the city. Baron Larrey would come from time to time and I had as chief
surgeon Dr. Duchesne, who sacrificed all his days, nights, and talent
exclusively to the care of these unfortunate men during the five months
that this frightful and real nightmare lasted.

I cannot evoke these terrible hours without profound emotion. It
was no longer the thought of the fatherland in danger which kept my
nerves on edge but the suffering of all its children: those who were
fighting over there; those who were brought to us smashed or dying;
those noble housewives who lined up for hours and hours to receive a
piece of bread, of meat, the pitcher of milk needed to nourish the poor
kids. Ah, the poor women! . . . I could see them from the windows of
the theater. I could see them huddling against one another, blue with
cold, stamping their feet to stop them from freezing, for this winter was
the worst that we had had to endure in twenty years. Often one of these
silent heroines would be brought to me faint with fatigue, or taken with

a sudden congestion brought on by the cold. Three unfortunate women were carried to the hospital. One of them had frost-bitten feet—she lost a toe on her right foot. Another, a large woman who was nursing, had poor breasts harder than wood, she was screaming with pain. The youngest, a child of sixteen to eighteen years old, died of cold on the stretcher where I had put her to take her back home. On this day, 24 December, 1870, the temperature was fifteen degrees below freezing.

Quite often I would send Guillaume, our nurse, to comfort them with a bit of brandy. What suffering these desolate mothers, these frightened sisters, these worried fiancées endured! How excusable were their revolts in the Commune, even their murderous folly!

My hospital was full. I had sixty beds and had to improvise ten others. The soldiers were in the public foyer and the artists' foyer.[12] The officers were in a room formerly used as a theater buffet.

One day a young Breton was brought to me called Marie Le Gallee. He had received a bullet in the chest and another bullet had broken his wrist. After having bandaged his chest tightly and splinted his poor wrist with some little pieces of wood Dr. Duchesne said to me simply, "Give this man whatever he wants, he's dying."

I approached him. "Tell me, what you would like, Marie Le Gallee?"

"Soup!" he replied brusquely and laconically. Guérard hurried off toward the kitchen and came back shortly afterward with a large bowl of thick stock with some toast dunked in it. I put the bowl on the little portable plank with four legs that served as a table for the meals of my wounded men, and which, thanks to these four little legs, was extremely convenient.

The dying man stared at me. "Barra!" he said to me, "barra!" I gave him the spoon. He shook his head. I gave him the salt and the pepper. "Barra, barra!" he continued, and his poor punctured chest whistled with the repeated efforts of his energetic demand. I immediately sent word to the Ministry of the Marine where there were surely some Breton sailors. I explained my sad quandary and my ignorance of the Breton dialect. I received the reply, "*Barra* means 'bread.'" Happy, I ran to Le Gallee with a big piece of bread. His face lit up. He took the bread with his good hand, broke it with his teeth, and let the pieces fall into the bowl. Then he put the spoon in the middle of this strange soup and, as long as the spoon would not stand upright in the middle of the bowl, he piled up the bread. Finally the spoon stood upright without wavering and the young soldier smiled. He was getting ready to eat this horrible mixture when the young priest of Saint-Sulpice attached to my hospital, whom I had summoned after the sad words of the doctor, gently put a hand on his arm, arresting him just as he was about to satisfy his appetite. The poor man looked at the priest who showed him the sacred ciborium. "Oh! . . . " he said. Putting his big handkerchief over the steaming soup, he crossed his hands. We had placed around his bed the two screens which served to isolate the dying or the dead. He remained alone with the priest while I made my rounds of the sick to calm down the cocky ones or help the believers to rise for prayer. The young priest opened the light screen a crack. Marie Le Gallee, his face lit up, was eating his abominable bread soup. He fell asleep afterward, woke up to ask for something to drink, and died immediately afterwards with a slight suffocating spasm.

Happily I did not lose many of the men out of the three hundred who passed through my hospital, for the death of these unfortunates shattered me. But although I was very young—I was twenty-four at the time—I could distinguish between the cowardice of some and the heroism of many others. A young Savoyard of eighteen had had his index finger removed. According to Baron Larrey this lad had surely blown off the finger with his own gun. But I did not want to believe it. I observed, however, that in spite of the care given to this finger it did not heal. One day I wrapped his bandage in a different way without his noticing it and I had proof, the next day, that the bandage had been changed. I recounted the story to Mme. Lambquin who was on duty that night with Mme. Guérard. "Well, well," she said, "I'll watch out. Sleep my child and count on me." The next day when I arrived she told me that she had surprised the lad scratching the scar of his finger with his knife. I called the young Savoyard and told him that I was going to report it to Le Val-de-Grâce. He began to cry and swore to me that he would not do it again. Five days later he was cured. I signed his discharge papers and he was sent to active service. What became of him?

Another invalid surprised us just as much. Every evening that his scar was on the point of healing he would be seized by a frightful dysentery which retarded his recovery. This appeared suspicious to Dr. Duchesne who asked me to watch this man. After quite a long period of time, we were able to ascertain that he had conjured up the most comical invention. He slept near the wall and thus had no neighbor on one side. At night he worked at filing off the brass from his bed. He dropped the filings into a little pharmacist's pot, which had contained some ointment at one time. A few drops of water and some cooking salt mixed with the brass filings composed a poison which nearly cost the life of its inventor one day. I was disgusted by this trickery. I wrote to Le Val-de-Grâce and an ambulance came to pick up the unpatriotic Frenchman.

But, alongside these pathetic beings, what heroism! One day a young captain was brought to me, a big devil of herculean stature with a superb head and a frank gaze. He was registered in my book as Captain Menesson. He had received a bullet in the top of his arm near the shoulder. When I tried with the help of the male nurse to gently remove his greatcoat three bullets fell out of the hood that he had lifted over his head, and I counted sixteen bullet holes in his greatcoat. This young officer had remained standing for three hours serving as a target and covering the retreat of his men who fired unceasingly on the enemy. This happened in the vineyards of Champigny. He had been brought to me unconscious in an ambulance. He had lost a lot of blood, and was half dead with fatigue and weakness. He was gentle and charming and considered himself two days later to be sufficiently cured to return to battle; but the doctors opposed it and his sister, who was a nun, begged him to wait until he was almost well. "Oh, not completely well," she said gently, "but just enough to have the strength to fight." Shortly after his arrival they came to give him the cross of the Legion of Honor. This was a second very emotional experience. The unfortunate wounded who could not move turned their hurting heads toward him and their eyes shone through a veil of tears as they sent him a brotherly look. The stronger ones stretched their hands out to the hands of the young colossus.

That same evening, for it was Christmas, I had decorated the hospital with great garlands of greenery. I had made some pretty little shrines in front of my statues of the Virgin Mary and the young priest of Saint-Sulpice came to take part in our poor but poetic Christmas. He recited some sweet prayers and the wounded, among whom there were many Bretons, sang some sad and serious songs which were full of charm.

Porel, today the director of the Vaudeville theater, had been been wounded on the plain of Avron. He was convalescing. He was my guest, along with two officers who were ready to leave the hospital. The Christmas dinner remains in my memory as one of the most charming and yet most melancholy of times. We dined in the very small room that served us as a bedroom. Our three beds, covered by fabrics and furs that I had brought from my place, served as seats. Mlle. Hocquigny had sent me five yards of white sausage and the stronger of my poor soldiers enjoyed this delicate dish. One of my friends had made twenty big *brioches* and I had ordered some big bowls of punch whose iridescent flames greatly amused the big sick children. The young priest of Saint-Sulpice accepted a little piece of *brioche* and a drop of wine before leaving.

Oh, how charming and good this young priest was! And he was very adept at shutting up Fortin, an intolerable wounded soldier who gradually became more and more familiar and finished by declaring him "a good devil." Poor little priest of Saint-Sulpice! He was shot by the communards.[13] I cried for days and days about the assassination of the little priest of Saint-Sulpice.

Chapter XVII

January arrived. The enemy army held Paris strangled in an embrace that tightened every day. Rations became scarce. A deathly cold enveloped the city. The poor soldiers who fell, sometimes only slightly wounded, gently slipped into an eternal sleep, the head numbed, the body half-frozen.

We received no more news. However, thanks to the ambassador for the United States, who had wished to remain in Paris, I received a letter from time to time. In this way I received a little piece of paper, as thin and supple as a primrose petal, telling me, "We are all leaving for The Hague. Everyone well. Have courage. Much love.—Your mother." This impalpable missive had been sent seventeen days previously.

Thus Mama, my sisters, my little boy, everybody had been at The Hague since this time while my mind, which was constantly on their trail, had been lost on the road to Le Havre, where I thought they were settled and happy with a cousin of my paternal grandmother's. Where where they? With whom were they staying? I had two aunts at The Hague, but were they there? I could no longer orient my thoughts and starting from this moment I continued to be tortured by worry.

I did the impossible in order to obtain some wood. Before his departure by balloon on October 9 the Comte de Kératry had sent me a large supply of it, but I was on the point of running out. Thus I forbade anyone to touch what remained in the cellars in order not to be caught out in a crisis. I burned all the little seats in the theater of the Odéon, all the wooden cases which were used to hold props, quite a lot of old Roman benches, armchairs, and curule seats stuffed in the basement, in fact anything that came to hand. Finally, taking pity on my despair, pretty Mlle. Hocquigny had twenty-two thousand pounds of wood sent to me. I took courage once again.

There was much talk about a new system of conserving meat by which the meat lost neither its blood nor its nutritional value. I sent Mme. Guérard to the town hall that served the district where the Odéon was located, as the rations were being issued there, but a brute told her that I could have the provisions when I removed the religious bric-à-

brac from my hospital. In fact, the mayor, M. Hérisson, had come with
a highly placed official to visit my hospital. This important person asked
me to remove all the pretty white Virgins placed on the mantelpieces
and consoles and to take down the crucifix in each room where the
wounded were. When I refused in a rather insolent and decided way to
comply with the whim of my visitors, the famous republican turned his
back on me and gave the order that I should be given nothing at the
town hall. But I was obstinate. I moved heaven and earth and I succeeded, in spite of the order of the boss, in being included in the
distribution of rations. It is true to say, however, that the mayor was a
charming man.

So Guérard came back after the third visit to the town hall with a
child pushing a wheelbarrow containing ten enormous bottles of this
miraculous meat. I received the precious cargo with great joy, for my
men had been almost totally deprived of meat for three days and the
much loved stew pot was a necessary resource for the poor wounded
men. On the bottles a label gave instructions for the opening of the
bottle: "Soak the meat so many hours etc. . . . " Mme. Lambquin, Mme.
Guérard, all the hospital staff and myself gathered anxiously and curiously around the glass receptacles. I asked the chief male nurse to open
the biggest, in which one could glimpse, through the thickness of the
glass, the sight of an enormous piece of beef which was plunged in
thick muddy water. The string which held the paper cover on the cork
was cut, and just as the nurse was about to put in the corkscrew a
thunderous explosion was heard and a fetid odor filled the room.
Everybody fled in horror.

I called back the frightened and the sickened and showed them
the label on which they could read "Do not worry at all about the bad
odor when the bottle is opened." Courageous and resigned we took up
our task again, although constantly sickened by the abominable stench.
I took out the beef and put it in a big dish brought for the purpose.
Five minutes later the meat became blue then black and stank so unbearably that I decided to throw it away. But Mme. Lambquin, more
considered and reasonable than I, said, "No! Oh, no! My dear little
one, this is not a time when we can throw away meat, even rotten meat.
Let us put it back in the bottle and send it back to the town hall."

I followed her very wise counsel and was fortunate to have done
so, for a private hospital that had been set up on the Boulevard Médicis,
having felt the same disgust as we had on opening the bottles, threw
the contents into the street. A few moments later an excited crowd
unwilling to listen to reason hurled abuse at the "aristocrats," "church
bigots," and "spies" who would throw into the street good meat intended for the sick, which the dogs were eating when the people were

starving . . . etc. etc. It was very difficult to prevent the crazy wretches from invading the hospital and an unfortunate nurse who had come out was struck, harassed, and finally left half dead. She did not want to be taken into her hospital and the pharmacist asked me to take her. I kept her for a few days in an apartment on the second floor and when she had recovered she asked if she could stay as nurse at my hospital. I complied with her request and later kept her on as a second maid. This girl who was gentle, blonde, and shy was predestined for unhappiness. She was found dead in the Père-Lachaise cemetery after the brawl between the communards and the Versaillais. A stray bullet had hit her in the neck while she was praying at the grave of her little sister who had died two days earlier from smallpox. I had brought her to Saint-Germain where I had settled during the horrors of the Commune. I tried hard to dissuade her from going to Paris. Poor little girl!

As I could not count on this preserved meat I made a contract with a butcher who provided me with horse meat at quite a high price, and this was the only meat that we ate until the end. If it was well prepared and well seasoned it was very good.

Everyone had begun to despair. We lived in a state of suspense, although we did not know exactly what we were waiting for. An atmosphere of melancholy turned the sky to lead, and it was almost a relief when the bombardment started on December 27. Finally something new was happening! At least it was a new kind of suffering and there was noise. For the previous two weeks, not knowing what was going on had been killing us.

On January 1, 1871, we drank a toast to the health of the absent and to the peace of the dead, and the toast was strangled by our tight throats. Every night we heard under the windows of the Odéon a lugubrious cry of "Ambulance! Ambulance!" and we would go down to meet the head of the sad procession. One, two, sometimes three, carriages followed one another, full of poor wounded soldiers. They were there, ten or twelve of them, arranged on the straw, lying down or seated. I would say that I had one or two spaces and I would lift up the lantern and look in the carriage. Heads would turn slowly toward the lantern. Some would close their eyes, too weak to bear even this fleeting glow. Helped by the sergeant who accompanied the carriage and by our male nurse, I would carefully take down one of these unfortunate men onto the narrow stretcher that was to take him to the hospital. Oh, what painful anguish! When, as I lifted the head of a patient, I noticed that it was growing heavy, so heavy! . . . when I bent over the inert head and could no longer hear any breath . . . then the sergeant would give orders to back up, and the poor corpse was put back in its place in the carriage while we got out another wounded man. The other dying men would move back a little in order not to profane the dead. Imagine my sorrow when the sergeant said to me, "Try, please, to house one or two more. It's a pity to drive these poor devils around from hospital to hospital. Le Val-de-Grâce is full." "Alright, I'll take two more." And I would ask myself desperately how I would manage to find beds for them . . . So we would give them our beds and the poor men would be saved.

I should mention that since January 1 all three of us had slept every night at the hospital. We had long bathrobes of grey flannel, a little like the soldiers' greatcoats. The first one who was woken by a cry or a moan would jump out of bed, and, if it was necessary, would wake up the other two. One night, January 10, Guérard and I were sitting on benches in the artists' foyer waiting for the painful cry of "Ambulance!" There had been a fierce battle at Clamart and we knew that there would be many wounded. I was sharing with Guérard my fear that the bombs, which had already reached the Museum, the Sorbonne, Salpetrière, Le Val-de-Grâce, etc. etc., would also reach the Odéon eventually.

"Oh, my little Sarah," said the tender woman, "the hospital flag flies so high that they could not mistake it. They would have to do it on purpose, and that would be abominable."

"But my dear Guérard, why do you want to make our execrable enemy better than ourselves? Didn't we also act like savages in Berlin in 1806?"

"But in Paris there are some wonderful buildings . . . "

"But what about Moscow? Wasn't it full of masterpieces? And the Kremlin is one of the most beautiful buildings in the world! That didn't stop us from pillaging this wonderful city . . . No, my poor 'little lady,' don't be deceived! Whether the armies are Russian, German, French, or Spanish, they are armies, that is to say beings who form an impersonal 'everyone,' a ferocious and unconscious 'everyone'! The Germans would bombard the whole of Paris if they had the opportunity. My poor Guérard, you just have to accept it."

I had hardly finished my sentence when a terrible explosion woke up the sleeping neighborhood. Guérard and I, who were sitting facing each other, found ourselves in the middle of the room, huddled together and terrified. My poor cook, her face all white, came to me to get help.

The explosions followed one another at frequent intervals. The bombardment had begun in our direction that night. I went to the wounded. They were not disturbed. Only one, a child of fifteen whom we had nicknamed "Baby Rose," was sitting on his bed. As I went up to him to calm him he showed me a little medallion of the Virgin Mary. "It's thanks to her that I wasn't killed. If they were to put the Virgin Mary on the ramparts of Paris the bombs wouldn't come." And he lay down again, holding the little medallion in his hand.

The bombardment continued until six in the morning. "Ambulance! Ambulance!" Guérard and I went down. "Here," said the sergeant, "take this man, he is losing all his blood, he will never make it if I continue with him." The stretcher took the wounded man, but as he was a German I asked the noncommissioned offficer to take his papers to the Ministry. The man took the place of a convalescent that I installed elsewhere. I asked him his name and he told me in German that he was Franz Mayer, a private of the Silesian *Landwehr*. Then he fainted, weakened by the loss of blood. After he had been resuscitated I asked him if he wanted anything, but he did not reply. I thought then that this man did not speak French, and, as no one at the hospital spoke German, I postponed till the next day the task of fetching someone who knew this language.

I must say that the poor man was made most unwelcome by his companions in the dormitory. A soldier called Fortin who was twenty-three, a true Parisian, jocose, boisterous, funny, and good-natured, never stopped hurling insults at the young German, but the latter never said a word. I went several times to Fortin to ask him to keep quiet but it was useless. Put into a joyful mood by the uproarious laughter that he aroused at each sally, he continued with renewed vigor, preventing the others from sleeping and moving around violently in his bed, cursing out loud when too abrupt a movement revived his pain, for this unlucky man had had his sciatic nerve torn out by a bullet and he suffered atrociously. After my third fruitless appeal for silence I gave orders to the two male nurses to carry him into a room alone. He asked for me and promised that he would behave well all night. I lifted the order and he kept his word. The next day I had Franz Mayer carried into a room where there was a young Breton who had had his skull fractured by a shell and needed the utmost quiet. One of my friends who spoke German very well came to ask the Silesian if there was something he wanted.

The wounded man's face lit up on hearing his language spoken and then turning to me he said, "I understand French very well, Madame, and if I listened calmly to the horrors spewed out by your French soldier it's because I know that you can't hold out more than two more days, and I understand his exasperation."

"And why do you think we can't hold out?"

"Because I know that you have been reduced to eating rats."

Dr. Duchesne had just come and was bandaging the wounded man who had a horrible scar at the top of his thigh. "Well, my friend," he said to him, "when your fever has fallen you will eat a nice piece of chicken." The German shrugged his shoulders. "While you're waiting drink this, and you will tell me what you think of it." And he gave him a glass of water cut with an excellent cognac that the priest had sent to me. Besides, it was the only kind of tea that was ever taken by my soldiers. The Silesian said no more, but he took on the closed and circumspect air of people who know and do not want to say.

However, they continued to bombard us. The hospital flag surely served as a target for the enemy, for they fired with surprising accuracy and corrected their sights as soon as a bomb fell outside the area of the Luxembourg. Thus we received more than twelve bombs in one night. These lugubrious shells looked like fireworks when they exploded in the sky. Then the bright flashes fell, black and murderous.

Georges Boyer, who was at that time a young journalist, came to visit me at the hospital and I told him about the terrifying beauty of the night.

"Oh, I would very much like to see that!" he said.

"Come this evening, around nine or ten o'clock, and you will see."

We spent several hours at the little round window of my apartment which faced toward Châtillon. It was from there that the Germans fired the most. We listened in the silence of the night to the dull sounds coming from there; then, a light, a formidable distant thud, and the bomb reached us, dropping in front or behind, striking its target or exploding in the sky. One time we only just had the time to quickly draw back and, again, the blast of air struck us so violently that for a second we were under the impression that we had been struck. The shell had fallen beneath my apartment, touching the cornice which it dragged with it in its fall to the ground where it exploded feebly. But what astonishment to see a horde of children fall onto the burning fragments, like a flock of sparrows on fresh dung when a carriage has passed! The little vagabonds were arguing with one another over the debris left by the war engine. I wondered what they could do with that. "Oh, don't wonder," said Boyer, "these little famished children want to sell it!" And it was true. The male nurse who was sent to get information brought back a child of ten years old.

"What are you going to do with that, my little friend?" I said to him, taking the piece of shell which was still hot and dangerous by its jagged edges.

"I am going to sell it."

"What for?"

"To buy a place in the queue for meat rations!"

"But you risk your life, my little one. Sometimes the shells come one after another very fast. Where were you when the shell fell?"

"Stretched out there on the edge of the wall under the railings," and he pointed to the Luxembourg garden which was opposite the Odéon near the actors' entrance.

We bought all the little pieces from this child without daring to offer him seemingly sensible advice. For why command wisdom to this little creature, who had never heard talk of anything but massacres, fires, vengeance, reprisals, and all that in the name of honor, faith, and right? And then was it even possible to find shelter? All those who lived in the Saint-Germain district were exposed to the danger of bombardment, for very fortunately the enemy could only shell Paris in this direction and still not everywhere. No, it was our neighborhood which was by far the most dangerous.

One day when Baron Larrey had come to see Franz Mayer, who was very ill, he wrote a prescription, which a little helper was ordered to bring very quickly. As the child liked to dawdle I stationed myself at the window. "Toto!" I shouted. His name was Victor. The pharmacy was on the corner of the place Médicis. It was six o'clock in the evening. Toto looked up and, seeing me, began to laugh and skip as he ran along to the pharmacy. He had only four or five yards to go when I clapped my hands, as he looked back at the window, and shouted, "Good! Come back just as fast!" Alas! The poor child! Before he could open his mouth to respond he was split open by a shell, which had just fallen and rebounded a yard off the ground without exploding and struck the child full in the chest.

I gave such a shriek that everybody came running. But I could not reply. I brushed everyone aside and ran down the stairs gesturing to them to follow me, stuttering the words, "stretcher . . . the little one . . . the pharmacist . . . " Ah, the horror, the horror! When we reached the child his poor entrails were spilled on the ground, all his chest, his poor little rosy doll face were stripped of skin, no more eyes, no more nose, no more mouth, nothing, nothing except some hair at the end of a bloody rag a yard away from his head. It was as though two tiger's paws had opened the belly and skinned the poor little skeleton with refined rage. Baron Larrey, the best of men, went pale at this sight. He had certainly seen plenty of others, but this poor little one was an unredeemable holocaust.

Ah, the injustice of war! The infamy of war! Will the time we dream of when there will be no more war ever come? When a monarch who wants war will be deposed and imprisoned like a criminal? When there will be a cosmopolitan body where the wise of each country will represent their nation and where the rights of humanity will be discussed and represented? So many men think the same as I! So many women say the same as I! And then there are people who are so learned, such as chemists, who spend their time dreaming about, looking for, and finding, explosives which will destroy everything, bombs that are capable of wounding twenty or thirty men, guns that will repeat their murderous task until the bullet itself drops dead, after having blown apart the breasts of ten or twelve men.

I knew someone who carried out research into balloons whom I liked very much, for studying the direction of balloons was for me the realization of a dream: to fly in the breezes, to get close to heaven, to travel without any road either before one or behind one, without any ceiling other than the ether of the sky, under the feet the damp cotton wool of the clouds ... How interested I was in my friend's research!

But one day, all aglow with a new discovery he came to me saying, "I have discovered something that overjoys me!" He began to explain to me that his balloon could without danger contain inflammable substances, because of this, because of that, owing to this, owing to that ... "

"But what for?" I asked, bewildered by so many words and appalled by so many technicalities.

"What do you mean 'what for?' For war of course! One could shoot and drop terrible bombs from between three thousand and thirty-six hundred feet ... even from forty-five hundred feet up and it would be impossible to be touched in return at such a distance. My balloon, thanks to the coating (my invention) with which the canvas will be covered, will have nothing to fear from fire or gas!"

Interrupting him brusquely I said, "I don't want to know anything more either about you or your invention. I thought you were a humane scientist and instead you are a wild beast! You were studying the most beautiful manifestation of human genius, these celebrations in the sky that I already loved so much, and now you want to transform them into cowardly attacks against the earth—you horrify me! Go away!" and I left my friend with his little shame and his cruel invention. His efforts did not materialize as he had dreamed they would.

The remains of the poor kid were put in a very small casket, and Mme. Guérard and I followed the pauper's hearse on a morning so cold that the driver had to stop for a glass of hot wine, without which the unfortunate man would have been struck with congestion. We were alone in the carriage. The child had been brought up by his grandmother who knitted vests and wool stockings for a living because she was paralyzed in both legs. It was during a visit to order some vests and stockings for my men that I had met old Tricottin, as she was called, and her grandson Victor Durieux. At her request I had taken the child on as a little gofer, and the poor old woman was so grateful to me for that that I did not dare to go and see her to tell her of the death of the little boy.

It was Mme. Guérard who went to the rue de Vaugirard where the old woman lived. As soon as she saw her enter she realized from her sad face that something bad had happened. "Good God, my poor lady, is the skinny lady (that was me) dead?" Mme. Guérard told her then as gently as possible the painful news. But the old woman took off her glasses, looked at the visitor, wiped her glasses, put them back on her nose, and began to rail violently against her son, the father of the little dead boy, who had had this child with a whore, saying that she had known all along that unhappiness would befall them . . . and she continued, not to regret the death of the poor little one, but to insult her son, a soldier in the Army of the Loire.

In spite of the grandmother's lack of sorrow, I went to see her after the burial. "It's all finished Mme. Durieux. I rented a plot for five years for the poor little thing."

She turned round, comically furious: "That's crazy! Now that he is with the good Lord he no longer needs anything! Would have been better to buy me a patch of earth that would put something on the table! The dead don't grow vegetables!"

This outburst was so terribly logical that, in spite of her odious brutality, I acceded to the wishes of old Tricottin and gave her the same present as the child. Each one would have their patch of land: the little one, who had the right to life, in order to sleep there his eternal sleep; the old one to wrestle there with haunting Death over what remained to her of life.

I came back to the hospital sad and tense. Joy was waiting for me there however: a friend holding a tiny little piece of tissue paper on which were written two lines in my mother's hand—"We are very well and in Hamburg." Then I was seized with anger. In Hamburg! All my family was in Hamburg settled tranquilly on enemy soil! I racked my brains to divine by what strange concatenation of events my mother had gone to Hamburg. I knew that my pretty aunt Rosine had a lady friend on whom she descended every year, for she went to Hamburg every year for two months, two months at Baden-Baden, and one month at Spa, my aunt being the most playful creature that the good Lord had ever created. Those who were so dear to me were well! That was the most important thing. I *was* annoyed with my mother for going to Hamburg however.

I thanked a thousand times the friendly bearer of the little piece of paper sent by the American embassy, which did its utmost to give aid and consolation to Parisians. Then I gave him a note for my mother in case it should be possible to deliver it.

The bombardment of Paris continued. One night the Christian brothers came seeking hands and carriages to pick up the dead on the plateau of Châtillon. I gave my two carriages and wanted to go with them to the battlefield.

Ah, a horrible Dantesque memory! It was a freezing night. We advanced with difficulty. Finally some torches and lamps indicated that we were there. I got out with the male nurse and his aide. I was carrying a lantern. We had to advance slowly for at each step one stumbled against the dying and the dead. We passed murmuring, "Ambulance! Ambulance!" Then a groan would direct our steps. The first man that I found in this way was half-lying, his body leaning against a pile of dead. I lifted the lantern to his face. He had an ear and half his jaw blown away. Great clots of blood coagulated by the cold hung along his lower jaw. He had a crazed look. I picked up a straw and dipping it in the flask I drew up a few drops of brandy which I blew between the teeth of the poor child. I repeated this process three or four times. He revived a little and we carried him into one of the carriages. The same thing was done for the others. Some of them drank from the flask itself which shortened the task.

One of these unfortunate men was frightful to see. A shell had completely undressed him from head to foot. Only his two arms had kept some tattered sleeves at the shoulder. No trace of a wound. His poor naked torso was marbled with big black marks and blood flowed slowly from the corners of his mouth. I approached him for he seemed to me to be breathing. I made him take some drops of the reviving liquid. He half opened his eyes and said, "Thank you." We carried him into the carriage and the poor man died of a hemorrhage which covered the other wounded with an abundant flood of black blood. Daylight was coming gradually, a misty and sullen day. The lamps were being extinguished and we could make one another out. About a hundred people were there: little nuns, military and civilian nurses, Christian Brothers, other priests, and some ladies who, like myself, were putting all their strength and will into the service of the wounded. The spectacle was even more lugubrious in the light of day, for everything that night had concealed in its shadows was made visible in the pallid and tardy light of this January morning. There were so many wounded that we could not carry them all and I sobbed at my powerlessness. However, other carriages were arriving . . . but there were so many of them, so many! Many of them who were only slightly wounded had died from cold.

When I arrived back at the hospital I found at the door one of my friends, an officer in the marines, who had brought me a marine wounded at the Fort d'Ivry. He had received a bullet under the right eye. He was registered under the name of Désiré Bloas, first mate, twenty-seven years old. He was a magnificent lad of few words with a frank expression.

When he was settled in his bed Dr. Duchesne had a barber fetched to shave him as the bullet had plowed through his long thick whiskers and lodged into the saliva gland, dragging into the wound with it hairs and skin. The surgeon put tweezers into the wound to extract from it the pieces of skin which were blocking the opening; then extremely fine tweezers were needed to extract all the hairs which were mingled with this inextricable hash. When the barber gently shaved around the wound the poor man became deathly pale and an oath escaped him, but he turned toward me, "Pardon, Mademoiselle." I was very young but I looked still younger than my age, I looked like a very young girl.

I held in my hand the hand of the poor sailor and I comforted him with a thousand sweet words which come from the heart when women console mental or physical pain. "Ah! Mademoiselle!" poor Bloas said to me when his bandaging was finished, "you gave me courage." When he began to feel calmer I asked him if he wanted to eat something. "Yes," he said. "Well, my lad," cried Mme. Lambquin, "do you want some soup, some cheese, or some preserves?" And the strong solid fellow said smiling, "Yes, some preserves."

Désiré Bloas talked to me often about his mother who lived close to Brest. He seemed to adore his mother, but to feel real rancor against his father, for, one day, I asked him if his father were still living. He looked up with his bold eyes and fixed them with a challenging look of painful contempt on a being that only he could see. Alas! The good child was destined to meet a cruel end, I will describe how later.

The suffering of the siege was beginning to erode the morale of the Parisians. Bread had just been rationed: ten ounces for adults, five ounces for children. A subdued fury took hold of the people at this news. The women remained the most courageous, the men were getting irritated. Quarrels were becoming venomous. Some wanted all-out war, others wanted peace.

One day when I went into the room of Franz Mayer to take him his meal he flew into a comic fury, throwing his chicken on the floor and saying that he did not want to eat anything, anything at all, because they had lied to him when they had said that the Parisians only had enough for two days before they would have to surrender. He had been at the hospital for seventeen days and he was being given chicken. What the poor man did not know was that at the beginning of the siege I had bought forty chickens and six geese and I was raising them in my bathroom at the rue de Rome. Oh, my bathroom was very pretty! . . . But I let Franz believe that Paris was full of chickens, ducks, geese, and other domestic bipeds.

However, the bombardment continued. One night I had to carry all the sick into the cellars of the Odéon, for just as Mme. Guérard was helping a wounded man to get back into bed a shell fell on the bed itself, between her and the officer. I shudder still to think that three minutes later the unfortunate man, lying in his bed, would have been killed, although the shell did not explode.

We could not stay for long in the cellars. Water was rising and the rats tormented us. So I decided to move the hospital and I had the most sick patients moved to Le Val-de-Grâce. I kept about twenty men who were on the way to recovery. I rented an immense empty apartment to put them in at 58 rue Taitbout. There I waited for the armistice. I was nearly dead with worry. No news from my family for such a long time. I could no longer sleep. I had become a shadow of my former self.

Jules Favre[1] was in charge of negotiations with Bismarck. These two days of preliminaries were the most tense for the besieged. False news was brought: insane and exorbitant demands on the part of the Germans who were not merciful toward the conquered. There was a moment of stupefaction when it was learned that we would have to pay two hundred million then and there, and our finances were in such a sad state that we shuddered at the thought of not being able to find this two hundred million.

Baron Alphonse de Rothschild, imprisoned in Paris with his wife and two brothers, guaranteed the two hundred million. This fine gesture was quickly forgotten. There are even some who deny it. The ingratitude of the crowd is humiliating for civilized humanity, for ingratitude is the disease of white people, as the Red Indians used to say, and it is very true.

When we learned in Paris that the armistice had been signed for twenty days, a frightful sadness took hold of everyone, even those who most fervently desired peace. Each Parisian felt on his cheek the hand of the conqueror. It was the stigma, the slap given by the abominable peace treaty. I clearly remember this January 31, 1871! Anemic with deprivation, worn down by sorrow, tortured by anxiety for my family, I was going with Mme. Guérard and two friends toward the Parc Monceau.

Suddenly one of my friends, M. de Plancy, went as pale as death. I followed his gaze. A soldier was passing. He was unarmed. Then two others. They were unarmed. And they were so pale, these poor unarmed soldiers, these humble heroes. There was so much pain in the discouraged way in which they walked. In the expression with which they looked at women there was a look of "It's not our fault" so pitiful, so moving, that I burst into tears and wanted to go back home immediately. I did not want to meet any more disarmed French soldiers. I decided to leave as soon as possible to find my family.

Through Paul de Rémusat I got an interview with M. Thiers from whom I asked for a document to guarantee safe passage. But I could not leave alone. I was fully aware that the journey that I was about to undertake was very dangerous. M. Thiers and Paul de Rémusat had warned me; and I foresaw that I would need to be in the constant company of a travelling companion. Therefore I gave up the idea of taking my servant and decided to take a friend with me. I ran naturally to Guérard; but her mild-mannered husband formally forbade her to leave. He thought this was a crazy and dangerous journey. Crazy it was, in fact. Dangerous it was also.

I did not insist. I asked my son's young governess, Mlle. Soubise, to come and see me. I asked her if she wanted to come with me. I did not conceal from her any of the dangers of the journey. She jumped for joy and promised to be ready to leave in twelve hours. This girl is today the wife of Commander Monfils-Chesneau. And—how life is full of the unexpected!—she now teaches the two daughters of my son, her old pupil.

Mlle. Soubise was then a very young girl who looked like a Creole with her very beautiful black eyes, soft and timid, and her child's voice. To see the both of us one would have taken us for two kids, for, although I was the older of the two, my slimness and my face gave me the appearance of being younger. It would have been crazy to carry a trunk with us. I took a bag for both of us. There was nothing in it except a change of underwear and some stockings. I had taken my revolver and I offered one to Mlle. Soubise, but she refused it with horror and showed me an enormous pair of scissors in an enormous case.

"But what do you intend to do with those?"

"I will kill myself," she replied sweetly. "I will kill myself if we are attacked."

I was surprised by the difference in our characters. *I* took a revolver, determined to kill to defend myself; *she* was determined to kill herself to defend herself.

Chapter XVIII

$\mathcal{O}$n February 4 we finally set off on this journey which was meant to take three days and in fact took eleven. At the gate where I first tried to leave Paris I was rudely sent back. Exit permits were subject to the authorization of the German outposts. I went to another gate, but it was only at the postern of Poissonniers that I could get my guarantee of safe passage authorized. We were led into a little shed transformed into an office. A Prussian general was sitting there.

He eyed me disdainfully. "You are Sarah Bernhardt?"

"Yes."

"This girl is accompanying you?"

"Yes."

"You think you will get through easily?"

"I hope so."

"Well, you are mistaken. You would be better off returning to Paris."

"No. I want to leave. I am fully prepared for what might happen to me but I want to leave."

He shrugged his shoulders, called an officer, said something or other to him in German and went out, leaving us alone without our passports. We had been there perhaps a quarter of an hour when I heard a familiar voice. It was one of my friends, René Griffon, who had found out about my departure and had wanted to catch up with me to dissuade me from my plans. But his efforts were in vain. I wanted to go. The general returned some time later. Griffon was worried about what could happen to us. "Everything!" the officer told him, "And worse than everything!" Griffon spoke German and had a conversation with this officer about us which annoyed me a little for, as I did not understand, I imagined that he was encouraging the general to prevent us from leaving. But I resisted prayers, supplication, and even threats. A few moments later a very smartly equipped carriage stopped at the door of the shed. "There you are!" the German officer said to me brutally. "I am going to have you taken to Gonesse where you will find the supply train which leaves in an hour. I am sending a recommendation on your behalf

131

to the station master, General X . . . after that . . . may God preserve you!"

I got into the general's carriage and said goodbye to my poor desperate friend. We arrived at Gonesse and got down at the station where there was a small group of people speaking in low voices. The coachman gave me a military salute and, refusing what I wanted to give him, departed at high speed.

I approached the group, wondering whom I would address, when a friendly voice accosted me: "What's this? You are here? Where are you going?" It was Villaret, the fashionable tenor at the Opéra who, I think, was going to join his young wife of whom he had received no news in the last five months. He introduced me to one of his friends travelling with him whose name I cannot remember, and also to the son of General Pélissier and an old man so pale, sad, and haggard that I pitied him. He was called M. Gerson and was going to Belgium to take his grandson to his godmother. His two sons had been killed during this painful war. One of them was married and his wife had died of despair. He was taking the orphan to his godmother and hoped to die as soon as possible afterward. Ah, the poor man! He was only fifty-nine and yet despair had so cruelly ravaged him that I would have thought him seventy.

In addition to these five people there was also an unbearable blabbermouth called Théodore Joussian, a wine dealer. Without waiting for an introduction he burst out with, "Hello, Madame! How lucky we are—you are going to travel with us! Ah, this is going to be a hard journey! Where are you going? Two women travelling alone, that's risky, all the more as the roads are full of German and French irregulars, marauders, and robbers. I've demolished my share of these German irregulars! But shh . . . let's talk quietly . . . crafty people have a sharp ear." Then pointing to the German officers as they walked up and down he said, "Cunning devils! If I had my uniform and my gun they would not be walking quite so gallantly in front of Théodore Joussian. I've got six helmets at home . . . "

This man irritated me. I turned my back on him and looked about for the stationmaster. A tall young German with his arm in a sling and painfully dragging his leg came up to me. He handed an open note to me. It was the letter of recommendation that the general's coachman had given him. He offered me his good arm. I refused to take it. He bowed and I followed him in silence accompanied by Mlle. Soubise. Once we got into his office he made us sit down at a little table laid for two. It was three o'clock in the afternoon. We had eaten nothing. Not a drop of water since the night before. I was touched by his consideration and we did honor to this very simple but restoring meal given to us by the young officer. While we were eating I looked at him secretly. He was very young and his face bore the traces of recent suffering. I was overwhelmed by tender pity for this unfortunate person, lame in his leg for the rest of his life. My hatred for war intensified yet further.

Suddenly he said to me in rather bad French, "I think that I can give you news about one of your friends."

"His name?"

"Emmanuel Boucher."

"Ah! yes, certainly he is a good friend . . . How is he?"

"He is still a prisoner but he is very well."

"But I thought that he had been released?"

"Some of those taken with him have been, because they gave their word that they would not carry arms any longer against us, but he refused to give his word."

"Ah! Brave soldier!" I cried out in spite of myself.

The young German looked at me with his clear sad eyes, "Yes," he said simply, "a brave soldier."

Once our meal was finished I got up to join the other travellers, but he told me that the wagon which was to take us would not be there for two hours. "Please rest, Mesdames, I will come back to escort you at the appointed time." He went out and I was soon deeply asleep. I was dead with fatigue. Mlle. Soubise touched my shoulder to wake me up and we prepared to leave. The young officer walked next to me. I stood a little dumbfounded in front of the wagon into which I was asked to climb. This wagon was open to the sky and full of coal. The officer had several empty sacks piled one on top of the other to make my seat more comfortable. He sent for his officer's greatcoat and asked me to send it back to him, but I refused this odious disguise. It was deadly cold, but I preferred to die of cold than to deck myself out in this enemy greatcoat.

A whistle. A salute from the wounded stationmaster and the freight train moved off. There were Prussian soldiers in the wagons. As much as the German officers were polite and courteous, so the subordinates, the employees and the soldiers, were coarse and crude. The train kept stopping for no obvious reason, would restart again to stop again and halted for an hour in the freezing night.

Once we arrived at Creil, the stoker, the mechanic, the soldiers—everybody got out. I looked at all these people whistling, bawling, spitting, and guffawing as they pointed at us. Weren't they the conquerors, and we the conquered?

At Creil we were at a standstill for two hours. We could hear distant strains of carnival music and hurrahs from reveling Germans. All this uproar was coming from a white house five hundred yards away. We could make out the silhouettes of interlocked beings waltzing and twisting in a dizzy bacchanalia. I felt unbearably irritated, for chances were that this would continue until dawn. I got out with Villaret so that we could at least stretch our legs. I dragged him toward the white house. Then, not wanting to share with him my plan, I asked him to wait. But, very luckily for me, before I had time to cross the threshold of this ignoble dive an officer came out from a little door smoking a cigarette. He spoke to me in German. "French," I replied. So he came up to me and asked in French (they all spoke French) what I was come to do there. I was extremely tense and I told him feverishly about our lamentable odyssey since leaving Gonesse, and finally about our two-hour wait in a freezing wagon while stokers, mechanics, and drivers were dancing there in the house.

"But I didn't know that there were passengers in one of these wagons and it is I who gave permission to these men to drink and dance. The driver told me that he was carrying livestock and freight and did not need to arrive until eight o'clock in the morning and I believed him."

"Well, sir, the only livestock in this train is eight French people and I would be very obliged to you if you could give orders that we continue our journey."

"Don't worry, Madame. Do you want to come to my place to rest? I am conducting an inspection here and I'm staying for a few days at this inn. Do you want to have a cup of tea to warm you up? I told him that I had a companion who was waiting on the road and a friend who was waiting for me in the wagon.

"That's no problem, let's go and fetch them!" he said.

A few moments later we came upon poor Villaret sitting on a milestone. He had his head on his knees and was sleeping. I asked him to go and fetch Mlle. Soubise. "And," added the officer, "if your other companions want to come and have a cup of tea they will be welcome."

I went back with him and went in by the same little door that I had seen him come out of into quite a large room at ground level. There was matting on the floor, a very low bed, an enormous table on which there were two large maps of France (one of them was riddled with pins and little flags!), a portrait of Emperor Wilhelm stuck on board and held up by four pin tacks: all of this belonged to the officer. On the mantelpiece under an enormous glass dome there was a bridal wreath, a military medal, and a lock of white hair. On each side of the dome there was a porcelain oriental vase with a twig of boxwood in it. All of this, along with the table and the bed, belonged to the innkeeper, who had given up her room to the officer. Five straw-bottomed chairs around a table, a velvet-covered armchair, and against the wall a wooden bench covered with books. A saber and belt were on the table and two horse-pistols.

I was musing to myself over all these sundry objects when Mlle. Soubise, Villaret, young Gerson, and the unbearable Théodore Joussian arrived. (May he forgive me if he is still living, the poor man, but the mere memory of him still irritates me.) The officer served us with steaming tea and it was a real feast for us, for we were exhausted with hunger and cold. When the door was opened for a moment for the tea to be brought in Théodore Joussian had glimpsed through it the crowd of girls, soldiers, and others. "Folks!" he cried out bursting into laughter, "We are at His Majesty Wilhelm's, there is a reception and it's really smart, that's all I can tell you!" and he smacked his lips appreciatively. Villaret remarked to him that we were the guests of a German and that he had better keep quiet. "Enough, enough," he replied as he lit a cigarette.

A frightful uproar of curses and cries replaced the deafening sound of the orchestra and the incorrigible Southerner opened the door a crack. I could see the officer who was giving orders to two subordinates. The latter separated the groups and manhandled the stoker, mechanic, and others from the train in such a rough manner that I felt sorry for them. A kick in the back, a blow with the flat of the saber on the shoulders, a thump which knocked over the driver of the train (the ugliest brute that I had ever seen). All these people found themselves sobered up in a few moments and took the road back to our wagon, with a hangdog but glowering expression.

We followed them but I was not too happy about what might happen to us on the way with these rascals. The officer had no doubt had the same thought for he ordered a subordinate to accompany us as far as Amiens. This subordinate got into our wagon and we set off once again.

We arrived at Amiens at six o'clock in the morning. Daylight had not yet penetrated the clouds of night. A fine drizzle fell, hardened by the cold. No carriage. No porter. I wanted to go to the Hôtel du Cheval-Blanc, but a man who was there told me, "It's useless, my little demoiselle, there isn't a corner to put even a little stick like you. Go over there to the house with the balcony, they put up people there," and he turned his back on me.

Villaret had disappeared without saying a word. Old M. Gerson and his grandson had tucked themselves silently into a country wagon which was hermetically closed. A large matron, red-faced and stocky, was waiting for them. The coachman who was driving, however, had an air of class.

The son of General Pelissier, who had not said a word since Gonesse, had disappeared like magic. Théodore Joussian gallantly offered to accompany us, and I was so tired that I accepted. He picked up our suitcase and began to walk at top speed. We could hardly keep up with him. He puffed so much as he walked that he could not talk, which gave me a big rest.

Finally there we were. We went in. Imagine my horror on seeing that the hotel lobby had been transformed into a dormitory. We could hardly walk between the mattresses spread out on the floor and the snoring of the sleepers was not particularly charming. Once we got to the registration desk a young girl in mourning told us that there were no free rooms. I fell into a chair and Mlle. Soubise leaned against the wall, her arms hanging in despair. Then the odious Joussian screamed that two young women could not be left out on the sidewalk like that at night. He went up to the woman who owned the hotel and murmured to her something that I could not hear, although I distinctly heard my name.

Then the woman in mourning looked up at me with her moist eyes, "My brother was a poet. He wrote a very pretty sonnet about you for he saw you play in *Le Passant* more than ten times and he also took me to see you and I really enjoyed that evening. But it's all over," and with her two arms lifted above her head she sobbed as she tried to stifle her cries, "It's all over! He's dead! They killed him! It's all over! It's all over!" I got up, stirred to the depths of my being by this dreadful grief. I took the girl in my arms and kissed her as I wept. I murmured to her quietly words that calm and console.

Soothed by my words and touched by my fellowship she wiped her eyes, took my hand, and gently led me off. Mlle. Soubise followed us. I signed to Joussian that he was to stay where he was and we silently climbed the stairs to the third floor. At the end of a narrow hallway the girl opened a door. She took us into a large bedroom filled with the fumes of pipe smoke. A little night-lamp on a night table was the only light in this large room. Wheezy breathing was the only sound to disturb the silence. I looked at the bed and in the weak light of the night-lamp I could see a man almost sitting up and supported by a pile of pillows. It was an aged man rather than an old man, his beard and hair were white, his face bore the marks of pain: two big crevices were hollowed out from the corners of his eyes to the corners of his lips. How many tears must have flowed down this emaciated face!

The girl quietly approached the bed, beckoning to us to come right into the room and then closing the door. We tiptoed with our arms out for balance to the back of the room. I sat down carefully on a large empire-style sofa. Mlle. Soubise sat down next to me.

The man half opened his eyes. "What's the matter, my girl?"

"Nothing father, nothing serious. I just wanted to warn you so that you wouldn't be surprised when you woke up. I have just put up two ladies in your room. They are over there." He turned his head peevishly and tried to make us out throught the gloom. "The blonde one," continued the girl, "is Sarah Bernhardt, you know, the one that Lucien liked so much?"

The man got up and putting his hand over his eyes plunged into the room. I approached him. He looked at me in silence then he made a gesture. The girl brought him an envelope that she took out of a little desk. The hands of the wretched father trembled. He drew out of the envelope very slowly three sheets of paper then a photograph. He looked fixedly at me and then at the portrait. "Yes, it's certainly you, it's certainly you . . . " he murmured. I recognized a photograph of myself in *Le Passant* smelling a rose. "You see," said the poor man, his eyes misted with tears, "you were the idol of this child." He read me in a softened voice with a slight Picardy accent a very pretty sonnet which he refused to give me. Then he unfolded a second piece of paper on which were scribbled some words to Sarah Bernhardt. The third was a kind of triumphal song which celebrated all our victories over the enemy. "The poor boy still had hope when he died," said the father. "He died only five weeks ago. He got three bullets in the head. The first fractured his jaw bone but he did not fall and he continued to fire on the devils like one possessed. The second bullet took off his ear. The third struck him in the right eye. He fell never to rise again. His comrade told us all of this. He was twenty-two years old. And there it is. Everything is over." The wretched man's head fell back on the pile of pillows. His two lifeless hands had let go the papers. Big tears flowed down his pale cheeks in the furrows hollowed out by grief. A strangled sob came from his lips. The girl had fallen on her knees, her head in the covers to deaden the sound of her sobs.

Mlle. Soubise and I were overwhelmed. These stifled sobs and deadened cries throbbed in my ears. I felt everything collapse. My hands stretched out into emptiness. I closed my eyes. Soon there was a distant rumbling which grew and advanced, then shrieks of pain, bones clashing together, horse hooves bursting human brains with a dull thud, then armed men passing like a tornado crying, "Long live war!" And all the women on their knees with their arms outstretched cried, "War is an infamy! In the name of the wombs that have borne you, the breasts that have nursed you, the pains of childbirth and the anxieties of rearing you, stop!" But the tornado passed, crushing the

women. I stretched out my arms in a supreme effort which suddenly
woke me. I was lying in the girl's bed. Mlle. Soubise was standing near
me and holding my hand. A stranger, whom I subsequently heard addressed as doctor, laid me back gently on the bed. I found it difficult
to collect myself. How long had I been there?

"Since this evening," replied the gentle voice of Mlle. Soubise.
"You fainted and the doctor told us that you had a fever. I was really
afraid."

I turned to the doctor. "Yes, dear Madame, you must be sensible
for another forty-eight hours, then you can set off again. You have
experienced a lot of shocks for one with such delicate health. You must
be careful, you must be careful!" I took the medicine that he gave me,
apologized to the hotel proprietor who had just come in, and turned
my face to the wall. I had such a longing for rest.

Two days later I left my sad but kindly hosts. My travelling companions had all disappeared. I went downstairs, meeting at every turn
of the staircase a Prussian, for the wretched man had been invaded
physically and by decree by the German army. He scanned the face of
every soldier and every officer trying to find out whether this one or
that one had killed his poor little boy. At least this was what I thought,
although he did not say this to me. I had a feeling that this was what
he was thinking and that this was the meaning of the expression in his
eyes.

In the carriage in which I was installed to go to the station the nice
man had put a little basket of provisions and he gave me a copy of the
sonnet and a copy of the photograph of his son. I left the two mourners
with profound emotion. I kissed the girl. Mlle. Soubise and I did not
exchange a word during our journey to the station, both of us being
absorbed, by the same agonizing thoughts.

At the station we found that there also the Germans were in authority. I asked for a first-class compartment for us alone, or for a
subcompartment—whatever they liked, as long as we were alone. I could
not make myself understood. Then I noticed a man who was greasing
the wheels of the cars. He looked French to me. I was not mistaken. He
was an old man, kept on partly out of charity and partly because he
knew the ropes and because he spoke German as he was Alsatian. This
good man led me to the ticket office and explained my desire to have
a first-class compartment to myself. The man in charge of selling tickets
burst into laughter. There were no first- or second-class compartments.
It was a German train and I would travel like everybody else. The wheel-
greaser's face turned bright red but he had to suppress his fury. He had
to watch his step, his wife had tuberculosis and was caring for their son,
who had just been discharged from hospital with an amputated leg

which had not yet healed—but there were so many people at the hospital! He told me all this as he led me to the stationmaster.

The latter spoke French very well but was not at all like the other German officers that I had met. He hardly acknowledged me and when I explained to him what I wanted he replied dryly, "That's impossible. We will reserve you two places in the officers' car."

"But that's what I want to avoid," I exclaimed, "—traveling with German officers!"

"Well then, we will put you with German soldiers!" he barked furiously, and putting on his cap he went out slamming the door. I stood confused and wounded by the insolence of this ignoble brute.

I was so pale, apparently, and the blue of my eyes had become so pale that Mlle. Soubise, who knew my temper, was very afraid. "I beg you, Madame, calm down. We are two women alone amongst these nasty people who, if they wished to, could do us harm. We must attain the goal of our journey and see your little Maurice again." Charming Mlle. Soubise was very shrewd and her little speech had the desired effect. To see my son again was indeed my goal! I calmed down and swore to myself that I would not give in to my temper during this journey which promised to be rich in incidents. And I almost kept my word.

I left the office of the stationmaster and found the poor Alsatian at the door. He swiftly hid the two *louis*¹ that I gave him and shook my hand fit to break it. Then he pointed to the purse hanging round my neck. "You should not keep that in such a visible place, it's very dangerous, Madame." I thanked him but took no notice of his advice.

The train was about to depart. I climbed into the only first-class compartment. There were two German officers there. They greeted us. I regarded this as a good omen. The whistle blew. What good fortune! No one else was getting on. Ah! Yes! The train had not made ten turns of its wheels when the door was violently opened and five German officers poured into our compartment. Now we were nine. What torture! The stationmaster made a gesture of farewell to one of the officers and both of them burst into laughter as they gestured in our direction. I looked at the stationmaster's friend. He was a military doctor. He wore on his arm the military hospital armband. His wide face was puffy. A red and tufty beard encircled his face. Two little shining eyes which were constantly in movement gave a furtive light to this rubicond face. Broad-shouldered and stocky-legged he gave the appearance of nerveless strength. The ugly man was still laughing when the station and its master were already far behind us. But the latter had evidently said something very funny.

I was in a corner with Mlle. Soubise opposite me and, on either side of us, the two young German officers, both gentle and polite, and one of them quite charming in his youthful grace. The army surgeon took off his helmet. He was very bald with a little mulish forehead. He started to talk with the other officers. Our two young guards participated little in the conversation, but among the others there was a tall conceited boy whom they addressed as Baron. He was tall, slim, very well groomed, and very strong. Seeing that we did not understand German he spoke to us in English; but Mlle. Soubise was too shy to answer and I speak English very badly. So he resigned himself with regret to speaking to us in French. He was nice, too nice. He was certainly well-bred but he was also tactless. I made him understand this by turning away to look at the countryside outside.

Absorbed in our thoughts, we had been traveling for a long time already when I felt myself being suffocated by smoke which was filling the compartment. I looked and saw that the army surgeon had lit a pipe. With half-closed eyes he was puffing smoke up to the ceiling. With my throat tight with indignation and my eyes smarting with smoke I was overcome by an attack of coughing which I exaggerated to attract the attention of the army surgeon. But it was the baron who tapped him on the knee and tried to make him understand that he was bothering me. He replied with some kind of insult and a shrug of the shoulders and continued to smoke. So in exasperation I lowered the window on my side. The freezing cold quickly penetrated the compartment but I preferred that to this nauseating pipe smoke. Suddenly, the army surgeon got up putting his hand over his ear. I noticed then that his ear was full of cotton wool. He swore like a trooper and, knocking into everything and standing on my feet and Mlle. Soubise's, he swiftly shut the window again, still grumbling quite uselessly, as I did not understand him. He then took up the same pose with his pipe and insolently blew out some enormous puffs of smoke. The baron and the two young Germans who had got on the train first seemed to be pleading and remonstrating with him, but he sent them packing and even started to insult them. Feeling a calm satisfaction at the rising anger of the nasty man, and amused at his earache, I once again opened the window. Once again he leaped up furious, showed me his ear and his swollen cheek, and I understood the word "periostitis" in the explanation he gave me as he closed the window and threatened me. So I gave him to understand that I had a weak chest and that smoke made me cough, which the baron explained to him acting as my interpreter. But it was easy to see that the army-surgeon did not give a jot about that and he once again took up his pipe and his favorite posture.

For five minutes I let him think that he had won, then, with a sudden blow from my elbow I broke the window. The army-surgeon looked dumbfounded. His face went white. He stood up very straight but the two young men got up at the same time while the baron guffawed noisily. The army-surgeon took a step in our direction but he met a bulwark: another officer had joined the two young ones and this one was a rough solid lad with a herculean build. I do not know what he said to the surgeon-major but it was short and sharp. The latter, not knowing how to relieve his anger, turned toward the baron who was still laughing and insulted him so violently that the baron replied to him in a way which made me realize the two men were challenging one another. Little I cared, besides. They could kill one another, each of them being as ill-bred as the other.

The compartment fell silent and became freezing cold, for the wind blew in furiously through the broken window. The sun had set. The sky was becoming misty. It could have been five thirty. We were approaching Tergnier. The army-surgeon had changed corners with his companion in order to protect his ear as much as possible. He was moaning like a badly slaughtered beast.

Suddenly the repeated whistling of a distant locomotive made us prick up our ears. Then there were two, three, four explosions under our wheels. We clearly felt the mechanic's effort to slow down the train, but before he could succeed, we were thrown against one another by a terrible shock. Cracking, explosions, the locomotive jerking as it spat out steam in irregular bursts, desperate cries, pleas, oaths, a sudden collapse in a moment of calm, and then thick smoke torn by flames. Our car was upended like a horse thrown down on its hind legs. Impossible to regain our balance.

Who was hurt, who was not? There were nine of us in the compartment. As for myself, I felt as though all my bones were broken. I moved a leg. I tried the other one. Then, delighted to find they were not broken, I did the same with my arms. I had not broken anything. Mlle. Soubise neither, but she had bitten her tongue and was bleeding, which frightened me. She seemed not to understand anything. The great blow had stunned her and she was without memory for several days. I had a deep graze between the eyes. I had not had time to put out my arms and I had struck my forehead against the pommel of the saber held by the officer next to Mlle. Soubise. Help was being rushed to us on every side. It took quite a long time to open the door of our car. Night had drawn in. Finally the door gave way and a lantern feebly lit up our dislocated car. I tried to find our one suitcase but I let it go as soon as I picked it up. My hand was red with blood. Whose blood was it? Three men were not moving, among whom was the army-surgeon who seemed to be deathly pale. I closed my eyes in order not to know and allowed myself to be pulled out of the car by the men who had come to our aid. After me one of the young officers got out. He took Mlle. Soubise, almost unconscious, from the arms of his companion.

The imbecilic baron got out also. He had a dislocated shoulder. Among those who had run up to help there was a doctor. The baron held his arm out to him and bade him reset his arm, which the doctor set about doing immediately. The French doctor took off the officer's greatcoat and handed it to two of his team to hold. Leveraging his weight against the baron he pulled on his poor arm. The baron went very pale and whistled under his breath. Once his arm was reset the doctor shook his other hand and said, "By Gad, I must have really hurt you but you have certainly have some courage." The German saluted and they helped him put his greatcoat back on. People came looking for the doctor and I saw that he was being led to our car. I shivered in spite of myself.

We were finally able to learn the reasons for our accident. A locomotive carrying only two wagons of coal had been manoeuvering to move onto the siding and let us pass. But one of the wagons had derailed, and the locomotive had been sounding the alarm at the top of its lungs while men had run ahead of us throwing down detonators for warning. However, it was all in vain and we had collided with the derailed wagon.

What were we going to do? The waterlogged roads were plowed up by cannon. We were four miles from Tergnier. A fine penetrating rain glued our clothes to our bodies. There were four carriages there but there were the wounded to transport. Other carriages were to come but there were the dead to carry away. An improvised stretcher carried by two ambulance men passed by. The surgeon-major was stretched out, so covered in blood that I clenched my fists digging my nails into my skin. One of the officers wanted to question the doctor who was following but I cried out, "Oh, no! I beg you, I beg you! I don't want to know. The poor man!" and I covered my ears as though I were about to hear something horrible. I never knew.

We had to resign ourselves to walking. We did a mile as bravely as possible but then I stopped exhausted. The mud, which was sticking to my shoes, weighed them down. The effort that one had to make at every step to pull one's feet from the cesspool was exhausting. I sat down on a milestone and declared that I would go no further. My gentle companion was crying. So the two young German officers who were acting as our bodyguards made me a seat from their crossed hands and we did another half-mile in this way, but my companion could do no more. I offered her my place but she refused. "Well, let's wait here." Totally exhausted we leaned against a little broken tree. Night had come, a night so cold! . . . Huddled up against Mlle. Soubise as we tried to warm one another I started to fall asleep, seeing pass before my eyes the wounded of Châtillon who died of cold as they sat against little bushes. I wanted never to make another movement and this feeling of numbness seemed delicious to me.

However, a cart passed on its way back to Tergnier. One of the young men hailed it and once the price was set I felt myself being lifted off the ground, carried into the cart and carried away with the jolting roll of two wobbly wheels which scaled the hillocks, got stuck in the quagmire, and jumped over piles of pebbles while the carter whipped up his beasts and shouted them on. In his way of driving there was an air of "I don't give a damn! Come what may!" which was in tune with the times. I sensed all that as I dozed, for I was not actually sleeping, but I did not want to reply to any question. I stubbornly reveled in this annihilation of my being.

However, a brutal jolt indicated that we had arrived at Tergnier. The cart had stopped in front of the hotel. We had to get out. I feigned a slumped, sleeping body but all the same I had to wake up. The young men helped me to go up to my room. I had asked Mlle. Soubise to pay for the cart before our brave little companions left. They were very sorry to leave us. I gave each one of them my signature on a piece of hotel paper for a photograph of myself. Only one of them claimed it six years later and I sent it to him.

The hotel at Tergnier could only give us one room between the two of us. I invited Mlle. Soubise to sleep in the bed and I fell asleep completely dressed in an armchair. In the morning I sought information about the train to Le Cateau but I was told that there was no train. We had to work miracles to get a carriage. Finally Dr. Meunier (or Mesnier) consented to lend us a cabriolet. So that was something . . . but there was no horse. The poor doctor had had his horse requisitioned by the enemy.

I paid a small fortune to a cartwright to hire a colt which had never been harnessed and which panicked when the harness was put on it. The poor animal calmed down when it was soundly whipped, but its panic changed to stubbornness. Standing full square on its four legs which trembled with fury, the colt refused to advance. With its neck stretched toward the ground, its eye fixed and nostrils dilated it stood as stiff as a post. So two men began to hold the light carriage; the halter was lifted up behind; the colt snorted a moment, shook its head, and thinking that it was free and unhindered, began to walk. It kicked up his hind legs twice and began to trot a tiny little trot. Then a young lad stopped it and gave it some carrots and stroked its mane. The halter was put back on. It stopped suddenly. The kid jumped into the cabriolet and lightly holding the reins he urged him to move again with words of encouragement. The colt made a timid start and feeling no resistance began to trot for a quarter of an hour bringing us back to the door of the hotel. I had to leave four hundred francs' deposit with the local notary in case the colt should die.

Ah, what a journey! The young lad, Mlle. Soubise, and I were squeezed into this little cabriolet whose wheels cracked at every jolt. The wretched colt steamed like a saucepan with the lid off. We had left at eleven in the morning and when we stopped because the poor animal could not take any more it was five o'clock in the afternoon. We had not covered even five miles. Oh, the colt was pitiful! The three of us combined were not much weight but we were still too much for it.

We were a few yards from a squalid house. I knocked on the door. An old and obese woman opened it. "What d'you want?"

"An hour's hospitality and a stable for our horse."

She glanced into the road and noticed our vehicle. "Eh, father! Come and see this!" she screeched. An obese man, just as obese but older than her, came out limping heavily. She pointed out the strangely harnessed cabriolet.

He burst into laughter and said to me with an insolent manner, "What d'you want?"

I began my sentence again, "An hour's hospitality etc."

"Chances are we can help you, but it'll cost yer." I showed him twenty francs.

The old woman elbowed him. "Goddam it . . . times being what they are, it's worth at least forty."

"So be it! It's agreed, forty francs."

He let me enter with Mlle. Soubise and sent his boy to lead the lad, who led in the colt holding it by the mane. He had tenderly removed its halter and thrown my blanket over its steaming haunches. The poor animal was quickly unharnessed and led into a little enclosure at the back of which some disjointed rafters served as a stable for an old mule, which was kicked awake by the fat woman and chased into the enclosure. The colt took his place and when I asked for some hay for it I was told, "It might be possible to find some, but that's not included in the forty francs." "Alright!" I gave our lad a hundred *sous* to go and fetch some hay but the shrew took it from him and gave it to her lad saying, "Go along, you know where it is. Be quick." The kid stayed near the colt which he rubbed down as best he could.

I went into the house and found Mlle. Soubise with her sleeves rolled up, washing two glasses and plates for us with her very delicate hands. I asked if it was possible for us to have some eggs.

"Yes, but . . . "

I interrupted our monstrous hostess. "I beg you, Madame, don't tire yourself out; it is understood that the forty francs is for your tip and that I will pay for everything else."

She was stuck for words for a moment and shook her head, but I begged her to give me the eggs. She brought me five eggs and I prepared an omelette, for my culinary masterpiece is the omelette. The water was nauseating so we drank cider. I sent for the lad and had him eat before me because I feared that the ogress would give him too stingy a meal.

When I paid the fantastic price of seventy-five francs—including the forty francs of course—the matron put on her glasses and taking a gold piece examined it on both sides, made it sound on a plate, then on the ground, and she did the same thing with the three *louis*.[1] I couldn't help laughing.

"There's nothing to laugh at," she grumbled. "For six months we've had nothing but robbers coming by here."

"And you know something about those!" I said. She looked at me, trying to fathom my thought, but my joking manner allayed her suspicions. Fortunately so, for they were the kind of people who could give us difficulties, but I had taken the precaution, as I sat down at the table, of putting my revolver down next to me.

"You know how to shoot?" the lame one asked me.

"Yes, I shoot very well," I said, which was not true.

Our vehicle was quickly prepared for the road again and we set off on our way. The colt seemed joyful. He struck the ground, kicked a little, and began to walk with a fairly regular step. Our villainous hosts showed us the road that led to Saint-Quentin and we left after numerous attempts to stop from our poor colt. Dead tired I fell asleep.

After travelling for an hour the carriage stopped all of a sudden and the wretched animal began to snort and rear up on his four legs which were tense and trembling. The day had been overcast. A low sky, full of tears, seemed to be settling slowly on the earth. We had stopped in the middle of a field plowed in every direction by the heavy cannon wheels. The rest of the ground had been trampled by horse hooves. The cold had hardened the little crests of soil and deposited ice here and there which glinted lugubriously in the gloom. We got down out of the carriage to find out what was making our little animal tremble so. I screamed with horror. Five yards away some dogs were savaging a corpse which was still half buried. Fortunately it was an enemy soldier. I took the whip from our young driver and I whipped the foul beasts as best I could. They backed off for a moment baring their teeth and then came back again to continue their voracious and abominable work, growling at us as they did so. The child got down and led the snorting colt by the reins.

We advanced with painful slowness, trying to find the road amid this devastated plain. An icy-cold night descended. The moon feebly parted its veil and illuminated the landscape with a wan and sorrowful light. I began to feel a deadly fear. It seemed to me that the silence was peopled with calls from those below. Each little pile of earth looked like a head to me. Mlle. Soubise hid her face in her hands and wept. After half an hour we saw approaching from a distance a little group of people who were carrying lanterns. I went up to meet these people as I wanted to ask directions. But I was silenced as I approached—the sound of sobbing reached us.

I saw a poor fat woman being supported by a young priest. Her whole being shook with the spasms of grief. She was followed by two noncommissioned officers and three other people. I let the woman pass and questioned the people who were following her. I learned that she was looking for the bodies of her husband and son who had both been killed on the plain of Saint-Quentin² a few days previously. She came every day at nightfall in order to avoid attracting attention. Her search had been fruitless so far but she was hopeful this time, for one of the noncommissioned officers who had just come out of hospital was taking them to the place where he had seen the husband of this poor creature fall, mortally wounded, in the same place where he had himself fallen and had been picked up by ambulance.

I thanked these people who pointed out to me the sad road that I had to follow, the best one across this cemetery still warm under the ice. Now we could make out groups who were searching. It was unbelievably horrible. Suddenly the child who was driving the carriage pulled my coat sleeve. "Madame! Look at that rogue stealing over there!" I looked and saw a man stretched out on the ground with a bag next to him. He had a veiled lantern which he was directing toward the ground. Then he would get up, his silhouette etched against the horizon, and look all around him. He would then go on with his work. When he noticed us he extinguished his lantern and lay at full stretch hugging the ground. We walked silently toward him. I had taken the colt by the reins on the other side from the child who, doubtless understanding my intention, let himself be led. I walked toward the man, pretending not to notice him. The colt recoiled, but we pulled it and forced it to advance. We were so close that I shivered at the thought that this wretch might perhaps allow himself to be run over by the carriage rather than reveal his presence.

But fortunately I was mistaken. A stifled voice murmured, "Watch out! I'm wounded! You're going to crush me!" So I took the lantern from the cabriolet (we had veiled it with a jacket and the moon illuminated our way better than its light) and I directed it onto the face of the wretch. I was amazed. It was a man of sixty-five to seventy with furrowed face framed by long dirty white whiskers. He had a scarf around his neck and wore a dark-colored cloak. Around about him the moonlight glinted off belts, brass buttons, the hilts of sabers, and other objects that the vile old man was filching off the dead.

"You are not wounded, you are a thief! A grave robber! I am going to shout till they kill you too! Watch out you miserable rascal!" and I moved so close to him that I could smell his breath tarnishing mine. He kneeled down, and linking his criminal hands implored me with a quavering and tearful voice. "Leave your sack there and all these objects, empty your pockets, leave everything and go! Run! When you are out of sight I will call one of these soldiers who is conducting a search and I will give him your booty. But I feel that I am doing the wrong thing in not handing you over yourself." He emptied his pockets moaning.

He was getting ready to leave when the kid whispered to me, "He's hiding some boots under his cloak." I was overcome by rage at this ignoble thief. I snatched from him his wide cloak.

"Let everything go, miserable man, or I'll call someone!" Six pairs of boots taken from the corpses fell with a thud to the hardened ground. The man bent down to pick up his revolver which had fallen from his pocket at the same time as the stolen objects. "Leave that and be off quickly! My patience is at an end!"

"But if I'm captured I'll not be able to defend myself," he cried in a fit of desperate rage.

"Then that will be God's will! Leave or I'll call." The man fled as he hurled invective at me.

Our little driver went to look for a soldier to whom I recounted the adventure and showed him the objects. "Oh! I'm not anxious to chase after him, there are enough dead here."

We continued on our way as far as a little crossroads where it was possible to take a road which was almost navigable. After having crossed Busigny and a wood where there were quicksands in which we nearly got stuck, our painful journey came to an end, and we arrived at Le Cateau in the middle of the night, half dead with fatigue, fear and despair.

Here I had to take a day of rest for I was laid up with a fever. We had two pretty rooms, only whitewashed but all spick and span—red shining tiles on the floor, a bed of varnished wood, and curtains of white lasting.[3] I called a doctor for dear Mlle. Soubise, who seemed to be even more ill than I. But he thought that we were both in a bad state. A nervous fever racked my limbs and burned in my head. She could not stay still, constantly seeing ghosts, fire, hearing cries, turning around quickly thinking that someone was touching her on the shoulder. The good man dealt with our exhaustion by giving us a calming potion. The next day a hot bath eased the stiffness of our limbs.

It was six days since we had left Paris and it would take me another twenty hours to reach Hamburg, for in those days trains were slower than they are now. I took the train to Brussels where I counted on buying a trunk and a few necessities. From Le Cateau to Brussels the journey was uneventful. We were able to take the train that same evening. I had bought some new items for our wardrobe which desperately needed replenishment. The journey passed without too many hitches as far as Cologne. But once we got to this city we had a cruel disappointment. The train had just entered the station and a conductor passed quickly through the carriages, shouting something or other in German. Everyone seemed in a hurry, men and women jostling one another rudely. I addressed another conductor and showed him our tickets. He obligingly took our suitcase and dashed off into the crowd. We followed him. I did not understand the panic until the man threw my suitcase into a compartment and signaled to me to get in quickly, quickly. Mlle. Soubise had already climbed onto the running board when she was violently pushed aside by a conductor who closed the door, and before I could fully take this in the train had disappeared. My suitcase had gone and our trunk had been put in a car which had been detached from the arriving train and attached just as it was to the departing express train.

I began to cry with rage. An employee took pity on us and took us to the stationmaster. He was a very distinguished man who spoke French quite well. He looked kind and compassionate. I collapsed into a big leather armchair and told him the whole misadventure sobbing nervously all the while. He immediately telegraphed to have my suitcase returned to me by the stationmaster at the first station, along with my trunk.

"You will get it back tomorrow around midday," he told me.

"So I can't leave this evening?"

"No. It's impossible, there's no train. The express to Hamburg doesn't leave till tomorrow morning."

"Oh my God! My God!" I cried, overcome with real despair which also affected Mlle. Soubise.

The poor stationmaster was quite embarrassed. He tried to calm me. "Do you know anyone here?"

"No, nobody. I don't know anybody at Cologne."

"Well, I will take you to the Hôtel du Nord where my sister-in-law has been staying for two days. She will take care of you."

Half an hour later her carriage arrived and he took us to the Hôtel du Nord, making a big detour to show us the city. But I did not admire anything German at this time. When we arrived at the Hôtel du Nord he introduced us to his sister-in-law, a young blonde woman, pretty, but too tall and strong for my taste. I must say though that she was kind and affable. She took two rooms for me near to her suite. She was staying on the ground floor.

She invited us to dinner which was served in her sitting room. Her brother-in-law came to spend the evening with us. This charming woman was very musical; she played some Berlioz, Gounod, and even Auber... I was extremely appreciative of this woman's sensitivity, for she played nothing except French composers. I asked her to play some Mozart and Wagner.

When she heard me mention the latter she turned to me and said, "You like Wagner?"

"I like his music, but I detest the man."

Mlle. Soubise whispered to me, "Ask her to play some Liszt." She overheard and with infinite good grace played some. I must say that this was a wonderful evening.

At ten o'clock the stationmaster (it's stupid, I can no longer remember his name and I cannot find it in any of my notes) told me that he would come to pick us up at eight o'clock the following morning and took leave of us. I went to sleep lulled by Mozart, Gounod etc. ... At eight o'clock a servant came to tell me that the carriage was waiting for us. A gentle tap-tap on my door and our lovely hostess of the night before said gently, "Come along, let's be on our way!" I was really touched by the delicacy of this pretty German woman. It was so fine that I asked her if we had time to go on foot. She said that we did, and all three of us set off for the station which was, in any case, very close to the hotel. A private compartment was waiting for us on the train and we settled in. The brother- and sister-in-law shook hands with us and wished us a good journey. The train left. I noticed in a corner a bouquet of forget-me-nots with the young woman's card and a box of chocolates from the stationmaster.

Finally, I was going to arrive at my destination. I was wild with excitement. Fancy seeing all those loved ones again! I would have liked to sleep, but I could not. My eyes widened by anxiety devoured the distance yet to travel quicker than the train. I cursed every stop. I envied the birds that I saw flying by. I laughed with joy as I imagined the surprised faces of the people that I was going to see again, and then I trembled with anxiety—would they all be there? If... Ah! The if's, the because's, the but's ... bristling with illnesses and accidents raised themselves in my mind, and I cried, and my poor little companion cried too.

Finally, here we are within sight of Hamburg! Twenty minutes more of the wheels turning and we will be entering the station. But, as though all the goblins and infernal devils have united to torture my patience, we stop. Everyone sticks his head out of the window. What? What's the matter? Why aren't we moving? A train has broken down in front of us with a defective brake. The track must be cleared. I fall back into the carriage, my teeth and fists clenched, trying to make out in the air the evil spirits who are hounding me. Then I resolutely close my eyes. I murmur some nasty insult to the invisible goblins and declare that as I do not want to suffer any longer I am going to sleep.

And I slept deeply, for this is a gift that God has given me: to be able to sleep when I want. In the most frightful circumstances and at the cruelest moments, when I have felt my sanity threatened by a shock too violent or too painful, my will has taken grip on my mind, as one would take hold of a nasty little dog that wanted to bite, and it has controlled it saying, "That's enough! Tomorrow you can reassume your suffering, your plans, your worries, your grief, your anguish. That's enough for today. You are going to collapse under the weight of so many blows and you will drag me with you. I don't want that! We are going to forget everything for so many hours and sleep together!" And I slept, I swear!

Mlle. Soubise woke me up as soon as the train was in the station. I was revived and calm. A moment later we were in a carriage: "7, Ober Strasse."

There we were! All my loved ones were there, both big and small, all well! Ah! What happiness! I could feel my heart beating in all my veins. I had suffered so much that I burst into laughter and delicious tears. Who will ever describe the infinite pleasure of crying tears of joy?

I stayed in Hamburg for two days, two days during which yet more crazy things happened to me, which I will not describe for they seem so unbelievable—such as the fire which broke out in our house, our flight in our night-clothes, camping in five feet of snow for six hours etc. etc.

Chapter XIX

As everybody was safe and sound we set off for Paris. But when we got to Saint-Denis, there were no trains. It was four o'clock in the morning. The Germans were masters of all the suburbs of Paris and the trains ran only to serve them. After an hour of petitions, parleys, and rebuffs, I met an officer of higher rank who was better-bred and nicer than the rest, who had a locomotive started up to take us to the station of Le Havre (Saint-Lazare).

The journey was very amusing. My mother, my aunt, my sister Régina, Mlle. Soubise, the two maidservants, the children, and I all chatted in a tiny little compartment in which there was a tiny little narrow bench belonging to the signalman typical of those days. The train moved slowly as the track was obstructed in many places by trucks and wagons. Having left at five o'clock in the morning we arrived at seven. At a place that I could not pinpoint exactly, our German drivers had been changed for French ones.

Then I enquired and found out that Paris was troubled by revolutionary movements. The mechanic with whom I was chatting was a very intelligent person of great foresight. "You would do better," he told me, "to go somewhere other than Paris, for there will be violence here before long."

We were there. I got out of the train with my tribe to the great amazement of the station employees. I was no longer very rich, but I gave twenty francs to a man who consented to take our six suitcases. We would have to go and get my trunk and those of my family later. But at this hour when not a single train was expected it was impossible to find a carriage . . . The children were so tired . . . what were we to do? I lived at 4 rue de Rome which was not far away, but my mother almost never walked, as she had a weak heart, and the babies were so so tired with their puffy half-open eyes and their little limbs all stiff with the cold and with sitting for so long. I was beginning to despair but when I saw a milk-cart passing I asked the station employee to hail it.

"Twenty francs to take my mother and the two babies to 4 rue de Rome?"

"And you too, my little miss," the milkman said. "You're thinner than a sparrow and won't add much weight." I did not ask him to repeat it, although I was a little annoyed.

After I had installed my mother, rather hesitant, next to the milkman, and the babies and myself in the cart, next to the churns of milk, some empty and some full, I said to the driver, pointing to the group that remained, "You don't mind coming back for them? That'll be another twenty francs."

"Right you are!" said the good man. "Good day! Don't wear out your hooves you others! I'll be right back!" and whipping his skinny horse he carried us off at high speed. The children rolled around, I hung on, Mama clenched her teeth and did not say a word, but she slipped me a look of annoyance from under her long lashes. Once we got to the door the milkman stopped his horse so short that I thought that Mama was going to fall onto the horse's mane. Finally we got out and the milk-cart left again at top speed.

Mama sulked at me for an hour. Poor pretty Mama! It was not her fault.

I had left Paris eleven days previously. I had left a sad city, but from this painful sadness resulted great and unexpected misfortune. No one dared to lift their heads, fearing that they would be buffeted by the wind which blew the German flag, displayed over there near the Arc de Triomphe.

I found Paris simmering with discontent. The walls were plastered with multicolored posters. All these posters contained the craziest harangues imaginable. Fine and noble thoughts jostled absurd threats. The workmen going to work would stop there in front of the posters. One of them would read them out loud and as the crowd grew in size he would read them again. And these calls to vengeance struck a chord with these people who had just suffered so much in this abominable war. It was very excusable, alas! This war had dug out from beneath their feet an abyss of ruins and mourning. Misery had reduced the women to rags and tatters. The deprivation of the siege had discouraged the children. The shame of defeat had demoralized the men. Hence these appeals to revolt, these anarchic cries, this howling of the crowd: "Down with the throne! Down with the Republic! Down with the rich! Down with the Church! Down with the Jews! Down with the Army! Down with the bosses! Down with the workers! Down with everything!" These cries woke up those who were sleeping.

The Germans who fomented all these riots, unintentionally rendered us a real service. Those who were abandoning themselves to a state of resignation were shaken from their torpor. Others who were demanding "revenge" found nourishment in their dormant strength. Nobody was in agreement. There were ten or twenty different parties mutually devouring and threatening one another. It was terrible! But it was the awakening. It was life after death.

I had among my friends ten or so political leaders of different persuasions and they all interested me, both the most foolish and the most wise.

I often saw Gambetta at the home of Girardin, and it was a joy for me to listen to this wonderful man. What he said was so wise, considered, and persuasive. When this man spoke he took on an aura of beauty in spite of his pot belly, short arms, and big head. Besides, Gambetta was never common or ordinary. When he took snuff the gesture of his hand as he brushed away the scattered grains was always full of grace. He smoked big cigars and knew how to smoke without bothering anybody else. When he was tired of politics he would talk about literature and this was a unique pleasure. He knew everything and recited verse admirably. One evening after dinner at Girardin's we acted together the whole scene in the first act of *Hernani*[1] between Hernani and Doña Sol, and though he may not have been as fine as Mounet-Sully[2] he was also admirable in his way. Another time he recited the whole of *Ruth et Booz* starting with the last verse. But I preferred yet more than all of this his political discussions, especially when he leaped on an opinion contrary to his own. The pre-eminent qualities of this man's talent were logic and level-headedness, and his persuasive force was his patriotism. The paltry death of this great mind was a disconcerting challenge to human pride.

Occasionally I saw Rochefort[3] whose mind delighted me. But I felt uneasy in his presence for his was the cause of the fall of the Empire. And although I am very republican, I liked Emperor Napoléon III. He had been overly confident but he was also very unlucky, and it seemed to me that Rochefort insulted him too much after his misfortune.

I also saw very often Paul de Rémusat,[4] the cherished protégé of Thiers. His was a great mind, both sensitive and tolerant, and he had elegant manners. Some accused him of Orleanism.[5] He was a republican, and a much more progressive one than M. Thiers. Anyone who thought that he was anything other than what he said he was, knew him very little. He had a horror of falsehood. He was sensitive, upright, and firm in character. He took no active part in politics except in closed circles and his opinion always prevailed even in the House, even in the Senate. He would speak nowhere except in offices. A hundred times he was offered the portfolio of the Fine Arts and a hundred times he refused it. Finally, because I insisted, he once almost allowed himself to be named Minister of Fine Arts; but at the last moment he refused the position and wrote me a wonderful letter from which I give here several passages. As the letter was not written for publication I do not claim the right to reproduce it in full. But I can without fear make public these few lines:

> Permit me, my dear friend, to stay in the shadow. I can see more clearly there than in the blinding light of honors. You are occasionally grateful to me for being attentive to the miseries that you point out to me. Leave me in my independence. It is more agreeable to me to have the right to succour everybody than to be forced to have to succour no matter whom . . .
>
> In art I have created for myself an ideal of beauty which would rightly seem too perfect . . .

It's a great shame that the rectitude of this sensitive man did not permit him to accept this post. The reforms that he suggested were very necessary and are so still . . . Anyway . . .

I also knew and often saw a madman full of wild utopic fantasies: this man was called Flourens. He was a tall and handsome boy. He fired on the soldiers, without thinking about the fact that his means of procuring happiness and fortune for everyone involved the unhappiness of a few. Reasoning with him was impossible, but he was charming and brave. I saw him two days before his death. He came with a very young girl who wanted to dedicate herself to acting. I promised him that I would take care of it. The next day the unhappy child came to inform me of the heroic death of Flourens who, not wanting to surrender, had opened his arms wide and cried to the hesitant soldiers, "Fire then! I will not spare *you!*" and he fell under their bullets.

A less interesting man, whom I regarded as a dangerous madman, was a certain Raoul Rigault who was Préfet de police for a short time. He was very young, very audacious, and very ambitious, and determined to do anything to succeed. Evil deeds seemed to him easier to perform than good. This man was a real danger. He was part of the band of students who sent me poetry every day. They were wildly enthusiastic and were with me everywhere I went. In Paris they had been nicknamed the "Saradoteurs." One day he brought me a little one-act play. This play was so stupid and the verse was so flat that I sent it back to him with a note that he no doubt found offensive for he bore me a grudge over it.

And this is how he tried to take revenge. One day he visited me. Mme. Guérard was there when he was announced. "You know," he said, "that I am all-powerful today."

"Times being what they are, that does not surprise me," I replied.

"I have come to see you to make either peace or war."

This way of talking did not please me. I jumped up. "As I foresee that your conditions for peace will not suit me, dear sir, I will not give you the time to declare war. You are one of those whom one prefers, however spiteful they may be, to number among one's enemies rather than among one's friends." I asked my butler to take the Préfet de police to the door.

Mme. Guérard was in despair. "This man will do us harm, my little Sarah, I swear." Her presentiment was not mistaken. However, she was thinking of me and not of herself and it was against her that he carried out his first act of vengeance by demoting one of her relatives, a police commissioner, to a lower position and a dangerous one. Then he created a thousand miseries for me. One day I received the order to go immediately on urgent business to the Prefecture. I did not reply. The next day a courier on horseback delivered a note from his lordship Raoul Rigault, which threatened to have me picked up in a prison van. I paid no attention to the threats of this rascal who was shot shortly afterward and died without bravery.

However, life was no longer tenable in Paris. I decided to leave for Saint-Germain-en-Laye. I begged my mother to accompany me but she left for Switzerland with my younger sister.

Leaving Paris was not as easy as I had imagined. Communards with their rifles on their shoulders stopped the trains and searched them top to bottom: through bags, pockets, and even under the upholstery in the compartments. They were afraid that passengers might be taking newspapers to the supporters of Versailles. It was incredibly stupid.

Settling down in Saint-Germain-en-Laye was not an easy thing. Almost all of Paris had taken refuge in this little country place, which was as boring as it was pretty. From the height of the terrace where the crowd gathered morning and evening we could see the menacing progress of the Commune.[6] On all sides of Paris rose arrogant and destructive fires. Often the wind carried burned paper to us, which was immediately sent to the town hall. The Seine swept along quantities of it that boatmen picked up in sacks. On certain days, and these were the most agonizing, a thick veil of smoke enveloped Paris. No breeze permitted the flames to find a way out. The city burned stealthily and it was impossible for our anxious gaze to discern which homes were newly set on fire by these furious madmen.

I rode on horseback each day. I went across the forest. I would go as far as Versailles, but it was somewhat dangerous as one would often meet in the forest poor starving devils whom one would succour with joy; but also often prisoners escaped from Poissy, or communard irregulars who wanted to kill a soldier from Versailles at any price.

Captain O'Connor and I were coming back from Triel one day where we had been riding in the hills. Quite late in the evening we branched off into the forest to take the shortcut home, when, suddenly, a shot coming from a nearby copse made my horse jump to the left so abruptly that I was thrown off. Luckily I had a good horse. O'Connor hurried over to me, but when he saw that I was on my feet and ready to get back in the saddle he said, "Wait a minute, I want to investigate this copse," and quickly galloped over there. I heard a shot, then branches cracking under fleeing feet. There was another shot unlike the two previous ones, and my friend reappeared with his pistol in his hand.

"He didn't hit you?" I asked.

"Yes, the first time, lightly on the leg. He aimed too low. The second shot he fired at random. But I think he has one of my bullets in his body."

"But," I said, "I heard him running away."

"Oh!" sniggered the elegant captain, "He won't go far."

"Poor devil," I murmured.

"Oh no!" exclaimed the captain, "No, I beg you, don't pity them. Every day they kill quantities of our men; yesterday again five soldiers from my regiment were found on the main road to Versailles, not only killed but also mutilated," and grinding his teeth he finished his sentence with an oath.

I turned to him with a look of astonishment but he did not notice it. We continued on our way, going as quickly as possible given the obstacles of the forest. Suddenly our horses stopped, snorting and balking. O'Connor took his revolver and dismounted, leading his horse. A few yards from us a man was lying on the ground. "That must be my rascal from just now," and bending over the man he addressed him. A groan was the reply. O'Connor had not seen the man before and therefore did not recognize him. He struck a match. The man had no rifle. I dismounted and tried to lift the wretched man's head but brought my hand away full of blood. He had opened his eyes and fixed them on O'Connor, "Ah! It's you, the dog of Versailles! . . . It's you who fired on me! I missed you, but . . . " and his hand tried to retrieve the revolver in his belt, but the effort was too great and his hand fell lifelessly.

For his part, O'Connor had loaded his revolver. I placed myself before the man and begged him to leave him alone. But I hardly recognized my friend. This handsome blonde-haired man, very correct, a little snobbish, but charming, seemed to me to have turned into a brute. Leaning threateningly over the wretch with his lower jaw thrust forward, he ground under his teeth some inarticulate phrases. His hand clenched in anger with the same gesture as that with which one crumples up an anonymous letter to throw it away in disgust.

"O'Connor, will you leave this man, I beg you!"

He was as gallant a man as he was a good soldier. He calmed down and took stock of the situation. "Alright!" he said, helping me to get back on my horse. "When I have dropped you off at your hotel I will come back with the men to pick up this rascal."

We got back half an hour later without exchanging a single word during the journey.

I retained a feeling of great friendship for O'Connor, but I could never see him without thinking about this sad scene. And suddenly when he was talking to me this brute's mask in which he had appeared to me that time would adhere to his smiling face for a moment. Recently, in March 1905, General O'Connor, who was commanding in Algeria, came to see me in my box and told me about his disputes with the great Arab leaders. He exclaimed laughingly, "I think that we're going to have to go to battle over it!" and the captain's mask covered the face of the general. I did not see him again. He died six months later.

Finally, it was possible to return to Paris. With the abominable and shameful peace signed and the wretched Commune crushed, apparently everything was restored to order. But what a lot of blood! What a lot of ashes! What a lot of women in mourning! What a lot of ruined buildings! In Paris one breathed the acrid smell of smoke. Everything I touched at home left me with an almost imperceptible greasy discoloration on my fingers. A malaise infected the whole of France but especially Paris.

However, the theaters were opening their doors again and there was general relief at this. One morning I received notice of a rehearsal from the Odéon. I shook my hair, tapped my feet, and breathed in the air, like a young horse champing at the bit. My career was opening up again. Once more I could gallop through my dreams. The lists were open. The struggle was commencing. Life was starting again. It is really strange that the human spirit is such that it has oriented life toward perpetual struggle. When it is not war, it is still a battle, for a hundred thousand of us all have the same goal.

God has created the earth and man for each other. The earth is large. What a lot of uncultivated terrain! There are miles and miles and leagues and leagues of new world waiting for those who will find within them the treasures of inexhaustible nature; yet we remain crowded together—piles of people, famished, spying and spied upon.

The Odéon opened its doors to the public with offerings from its repertory, but we also began to study some new plays. One of them especially met with resounding success. This was *Jean-Marie* by André Theuriet in October, 1871.[7] This one-act play is a real little masterpiece and it took its author straight to the Academy. Porel,[8] who played Jean-Marie, was acclaimed. At that time he was slender and dashing and full of youthful enthusiasm. He was a little lacking in poetry, but the joyful laugh of his thirty-two teeth made up in sensual warmth for its absence and he was very good in spite of it. I played a young Breton woman tied to an old husband in an arranged marriage, who lived eternally with the memory of her lost fiancé who was possibly dead. It was a pretty and poetic part and was very moving when she made her sacrifice at the end. There was even a certain grandeur in the end of the play. It was, I repeat, tremendously successful, and enhanced my growing reputation.

But I was waiting for the event which would consecrate me as a star. I was not yet fully conscious of what I was waiting for, but I knew that the Messiah would come.

In fact, it was the greatest poet of the last century who would place on my forehead the crown of crowns.

Chapter XX

At the end of 1871 it was announced to us, in somewhat mysterious and solemn fashion, that we were going to stage a play by Victor Hugo.

At this period in my life, my mind was still closed to great ideas. I lived in a milieu that was rather bourgeois, as far as my family was concerned, but rather cosmopolitan as far as snobbish acquaintances and friends were concerned—both those of my family and those that I had made through my independent life as an artist. Since my childhood I had heard Victor Hugo spoken of as a rebel and renegade, and his works, which I had read with passion, did not prevent me from judging him with great severity. Today I blush with shame and rage at the thought of all the absurd prejudices that were held, either out of stupidity or bad faith, by the little court that flattered me.

I had, nonetheless, a great desire to perform in *Ruy Blas*.[1] The queen's role seemed to me to be so charming! I let Duquesnel know how I felt about it and he told me that the thought of giving this part to me had already occurred to him. However, Jane Essler,[2] an actress much in vogue at the time, although a little vulgar, had a greater chance of obtaining it than I. She was at that time very close to Paul Meurice, who was the close friend and adviser of Victor Hugo. A male friend of mine brought to my home Auguste Vacquerie, who was the Master's other close friend, and in fact a relative of his.[3] Auguste Vacquerie promised to speak to Victor Hugo. Two days later he came to see me and assured me that chances were I would get the part. Paul Meurice, a man of integrity and charm, had himself suggested me to the author. Then Geffroy,[4] a wonderful actor who had been plucked from the Comédie-Française to play Don Salluste, had said, it seems, that he knew of only one little queen of Spain worthy to wear her crown, and that was me. I did not know Paul Meurice, and I was a little astonished that these people knew me.

The reading rehearsal was announced for December 6, 1871, at two o'clock at Victor Hugo's house. I was spoiled by so much adulation and flattery that I felt a little wounded by the nonchalance of a man who did not deign to put himself out, but rather invited ladies to come to his house, when, in fact, the theater was there as a neutral territory where rehearsals could be held.

I announced this piece of unprecedented audacity at five o'clock to my little court, which was gathered at my house. Men and women alike exclaimed, "What? This nobody, an outlaw till yesterday and pardoned only today, dares to demand that our little idol, the queen of hearts, the fairy of fairies, should inconvenience herself?" Everyone in my little circle was up in arms and could not keep still. "She won't go!" "Write him this . . . " "Write him that . . . "

Impertinent and contemptuous letters were being drafted when Maréchal Canrobert was announced. At that time he belonged to my five o'clock circle. He was quickly apprised of the situation by my turbulent entourage. He flushed with anger at the imbecilities being uttered against the Great Poet. "You ought not," he said, "go to Victor Hugo's house, who has no good reason, as far as I can see, to excuse himself from following normal etiquette. Make the excuse that you are suddenly indisposed, and, if you trust my judgment, you will have for him the respect that genius deserves." I followed the advice of my great friend and this is the letter that I sent to the poet:

Monsieur, the Queen has caught a cold. Her Camerara Mayor forbids her to go out. You are acquainted better than anyone with the etiquette of the Court of Spain. Have pity on your Queen, Monsieur!

I had the letter delivered and this is the reply that the poet sent me:

I am your obedient servant, Madame.

—Victor Hugo

The next day the reading took place in the theater—I believe that the reading did not take place as originally planned at the Master's house, or at least only part of it.

It was thus that I became acquainted with the monster. For a long time I felt a grudge against those fools who had prejudiced me against him. The monster was charming. And so witty, refined, and gallant, with a gallantry that is complimentary rather than insulting. Kind toward the humble. Always gay. He was not, it is true, the ideal of elegance; but there was a moderation in his gestures and sweetness in his way of talking which had something of the old aristocracy about it. He engaged in lively repartee and expressed strong opinions, but did so with gentleness. He recited poetry badly, but loved to hear it recited well. He often made sketches during the rehearsals. To berate an actor he would often speak in verse. One day, while he tried to convince poor Talien during a rehearsal that his diction was bad, I grew bored with the long colloquy and sat down on the table swinging my legs. He sensed my impatience and stood up in the middle of the auditorium to cry out:

Une reine d'Espagne, honnête et respectable,
Ne devrait pas ainsi s'asseoir sur une table.[5]

I leaped off the table, a little embarrassed, trying to think of something biting or witty to say . . . but I could not think of anything and subsided into ill-humored confusion.

One day when the rehearsal had finished an hour earlier than usual, I was waiting with my face glued to the window for Mme. Guérard, who was coming to pick me up. I was looking at the sidewalk on the other side of the street, which ran alongside the railings of the Luxembourg Gardens. Victor Hugo had just crossed and was about to walk off, when an old woman attracted his attention. She had just put down on the ground a heavy load of laundry, and was wiping her forehead, which was beaded with sweat in spite of the cold. Her toothless mouth panted open and the expression in her eyes was one of overwhelming anxiety as she looked at the wide road she had to cross, which was full of carriages and omnibuses. Victor Hugo went up to her and after a short interchange drew from his pocket a small coin, which he gave to the poor old woman. Then he took off his hat and gave it to the woman to look after as, with a quick movement and a smile on his face, he lifted the bundle onto his shoulder and crossed the road, followed by the astounded woman. I dashed down the stairs to kiss him, but by the time I had reached the corridor, bumped into Chilly who wanted to retain me, and run down the steps, Victor Hugo had disappeared. I could see only the back of the old woman who, it seemed to me, was hobbling along with a lighter step than before.

The next day, I told the poet that I had witnessed his sensitive and charitable deed. "Ah!" said Paul Meurice to me, his eyes moist, "every day is a day of kindness for him." I kissed Victor Hugo and we went to our rehearsal.

I cannot forget the rehearsals for *Ruy Blas*. They were all replete with good grace and charm. When Victor Hugo arrived the whole place lit up, and when the Master was absent his two satellites, Auguste Vacquerie and Paul Meurice, who hardly ever left his side, tended the sacred fire.

Geffroy, severe, sad, and distinguished, often gave me advice. When we were not on stage I would sometimes pose for him, for he was a painter. There are two paintings of his in the foyer of the Comédie-Française which portray two generations of *sociétaires*, both male and female.[6] The paintings are not very inventive, nor very beautiful in terms of their coloring, but they are faithful portraits and quite felicitously composed.

Lafontaine,[7] who had the part of Ruy Blas, engaged from time to time in long disputes with the Master. Victor Hugo never yielded, and I have to say that he was always in the right. Lafontaine had conviction and style, but his elocution in reciting poetry was poor. He had had his teeth replaced by dentures, which slowed down his delivery and made a strange little sound as the false palate clicked against his own palate. One was often distracted by that sound if one tried to listen attentively to the beauty of the poetry.

As for poor Talien,[8] who played the part of Don Guritan, he copped it all the time. He had completely misunderstood his role, and Victor Hugo kept explaining it to him clearly and wittily. But although Talien was very good-natured, hard working, and conscientious, he was a stupid goose. What he did not grasp right at the beginning he never understood—that was it, for life. But as he was honest and loyal he put himself in the author's hands and completely suppressed his own ego. He would say, "That's not the way I understood it, but I will do what you say," and he would repeat word for word, gesture for gesture, what he had been told to do. It made me wince. In my empathy for him as an artist I felt it as a blow to my artistic self-respect. I would often take him aside and try, in vain, to make him rebel against this treatment.

He was tall. His arms were excessively long, his eyes were weary looking. His nose, tired of having grown so much, had collapsed, discouraged, on his upper lip. His forehead was framed by bushy hair and his chin seemed to flee hastily away from this badly constructed face. However, his whole being had an aura of great kindliness that was all his own. For this reason everybody loved him.

Chapter XXI

$\mathcal{J}$anuary 26, 1872, was a night of artistic celebration for the Odéon. The quintessence of Parisian society and the quintessence of vibrant youth found themselves united at this première in the large, solemn, dusty theater.

What a splendid and moving performance it was! What a triumph for Geffroy as Don Salluste, pale, sinister, and severe in his black costume. Mélingue as Don César de Bazan disappointed the audience a little, but they misjudged him.[1] The role of Don César de Bazan looks deceptively good and always attracts actors because of the first act. But the fourth act, which belongs entirely to this character, is overwhelmingly heavy and redundant. One could take it out of the play, like a winkle out of a shell, and the play would be none the worse for it.

This 26 January rent the veil which had, until then, obscured my future, and I realized that I was destined for celebrity. Until that night I had been the students' little fairy. But on that night I became the Chosen One. Breathless, dazed, delighted by my success, I did not know to whom to respond first amidst the unceasing flow of male and female admirers. Then, suddenly, I saw the crowd part and I caught sight of Victor Hugo and Girardin coming toward me. Instanteously all the stupid thoughts that I had had against this great genius flooded over me. I remembered my first stilted and barely polite words with this kind and indulgent man. I wished that at this moment, when my life was about to take flight, I could cry out to him my repentance and grateful devotion. But before I could speak he kneeled down and held my two hands to his lips, saying, "Thank you, thank you." Thus it was he who said thank you. He, the Great Victor Hugo of the beautiful soul, whose genius filled the world. He, whose generous hands threw pardons, like gems, to all who insulted him! How little and ashamed I felt! But how happy! He got up and shook hands with those who pressed around him, saying just the right thing to each person as he did so. He was so handsome that night with the light catching his broad forehead, his thatch of thick silvery hair like cut hay lying in the moonlight, and his laughing and luminous eyes.

163

As I did not dare to throw myself into the arms of Victo Hugo I fell into Girardin's arms, my staunch friend in the early days, and I wept.

He drew me into a corner of my dressing room and said, "Now, you must not allow yourself to get intoxicated with this great triumph. Now that you are crowned with laurels you must avoid taking any more risks. You will have to be more flexible, docile, and sociable."

I looked at him and said, "My sense is that I will never be flexible or docile. I will try to be sociable. That's all I can promise. As for my crown, I assure you that in spite of the risks that I will always take, it will not slip off."

Paul Meurice, who had joined us, reminded me of this conversation on the evening of the première of *Angelo*[2] at the Théâtre Sarah-Bernhardt, on February 7, 1905.

Once I got home I stayed up late, talking for a long time with Mme. Guérard, and when she tried to leave I begged her to stay a while. I had become so rich in hopes for the future that I was afraid of thieves. "My little lady" stayed with me and we talked on till daybreak. At seven o'clock we took a carriage. I took my dear friend back to her place and I took an hour-long walk.

I had already had quite a few successes—in *Le Passant, Le Drame de la rue de la Paix*,[3] as Anna Damby in *Kean*, and in *Jean-Marie*. But I sensed that the success of *Ruy Blas* eclipsed all of these and that, this time, my performance may have been subject to discussion, but it could not be dismissed. I often used to visit Victor Hugo in the morning. He was full of charm and kindness. When I had become quite at peace with him, I told him about my first impressions and all my stupid and irritated rebellion with respect to him, everything that I had been told, everything that I had believed in my naive ignorance of politics.

One morning the Master was enchanted by the conversation we were having together. He summoned Mme. Drouet,[4] a gentle spirit, the companion of his glorious and rebellious soul. He said to her with a melancholic smile, "The evil work of the wicked is to sow error in all earth, fertile or not." This morning engraved itself in my mind forever for the great man talked for a long time. Oh, not for me! But for what I represented to him. Wasn't I, in fact, the young generation whose spirit had been ruined by our middle-class and religious education, which had closed our minds to all generous ideas and toward any flight toward the New? When I left Victor Hugo I felt more worthy, on that morning, of his friendship.

I went to see Girardin. He had gone out. I wanted to talk with someone who loved the poet. I went to see Maréchal Canrobert. There

I had a great surprise for, just as I was getting out of my carriage, I nearly fell into the arms of the maréchal who was leaving his house. "What? What's the matter? Is is put off till another time?" he asked me laughing. I did not understand. I looked at him a little dumbfounded. "Well, have you forgotten that you invited me to lunch?" I was confused, I had completely forgotten.

"Well, so much the better!" I said. "I so much wanted to talk to you. Come, I'll take you there."

I told him about my visit to Victor Hugo. I repeated to him the fine things that he had said, forgetting that I had often spoken in opposition to his ideas. But this wonderful man knew how to admire and even if he could not, or would not, change his opinions, he approved of great ideas that might bring about great changes.

One day when he was at my house along with Busnach,[5] a violent political discussion arose. I was afraid for a moment that things might turn nasty, as Busnach was the wittiest and most vulgar man in France. It is true also that even if Maréchal Canrobert was a polite and well-bred man, he was just as sharp a wit as Busnach.

The latter, irritated by the cocky replies of the maréchal, cried out, "Maréchal, I challenge you to write about the odious utopias that you have just supported!"

"Oh, M. Busnach," replied Canrobert coldly, we do not use the same steel to write history. You use the pen, I the sword!"

The lunch that I had so completely forgotten turned out to be one that I had arranged several days previously. We found at the house Paul de Rémusat, charming Mlle. Hocquigny, and M. de Montbel, a young attaché at the embassy. I explained why I was late as well as I could and this morning finished with a most delightful harmony of thought. I never felt more than on this day the infinite joy of listening.

During a silence Mlle. Hocquigny leaned over toward the maréchal and said, "Don't you agree that our young friend ought to enter the Comédie-Française?"

"Oh no! No! I am happy at the Odéon! I made my début at the Comédie and I was unhappy for the little time that I stayed there."

"You will be forced, my dear friend, forced to go back there. Believe me, better sooner than later."

"Don't spoil my happiness today, I have never been happier!"

One morning a few days later my maid gave me a letter. There was a large round stamp on one corner of it around which it said "Comédie-Française." I remembered that ten years previously, almost to the day, Marguérite, our old servant, had given me with my mother's permission a letter in the same kind of envelope. At that time my face had flushed with joy. This time I felt the pale caress of fear on my face.

When events are about to disturb my life I always have a moment of recoil. I cling for a moment to what is. Then I hurl myself head first into what will be, just as a trapeze artist gets a firm grip on his trapeze in order to throw himself in full flight into the void. In a second, what is becomes for me what was, and I love it with a tender emotion as though it were something dead. But I adore what is to be. It is the unknown, the mysterious attraction. I always believe that it will be extraordinary and I shiver from head to foot with delicious unease.

I receive quantities of letters and I find that I never receive enough. I watch them pile up as I watch the waves of the sea. What are they going to bring me, these mysterious envelopes: little, big, pink, blue, yellow, white? What are they going to throw out on the rocks these great raging waves, darkened by seaweed? What corpse from the foam? What piece of wreckage? What are they going to throw up on the beach, these little waves, reflections of the blue sky, these little laughing waves? What pink starfish? What purple anemone? What pearly shell? And I never open my letters immediately. I look at the envelopes, try to recognize the handwriting and the seal, and it is only when I am quite certain who the letter is from that I open it. The others I have my secretary open or my kind friend Suzanne Seylor. My friends know this so well that they always put their name or initials in the corner of their letters. At this time I did not have a secretary, but "my little lady" acted as one.

I looked at the letter for a long time and finally I gave it to Guérard. "It's a letter from M. Perrin, director of the Comédie-Française," she said. "He asks if he could make an appointment with you, Tuesday or Wednesday afternoon, either at the Comédie or at your place?"

"Thank you. What day is it today?"

"Monday."

So I installed Guérard at my desk. "Will you tell him that I'll go tomorrow at three o'clock?"

I earned very little at the Odéon at this time. I lived on what father had left me, that is on the settlement made with the notary of Le Havre, and not much of it was left. So I went to see Duquesnel and I showed him the letter.

"Well," he said, "what are you going to do?"

"Nothing. I have come to ask your advice."

"Well, I advise you to stay at the Odéon. Besides, you have another year in your contract, I won't let you leave!"

"So will you give me a raise? They are offering me twelve thousand francs a year at the Comédie. Give me fifteen thousand francs here and I will stay, because I don't want to leave."

"Listen," replied the seductive director very amicably, "you know that I can't act alone. I will do what I can, I promise." Duquesnel always kept his word. "Come back tomorrow before you go to the Comédie, I will give you Chilly's response. But, listen, if he is determined not to give you a raise, don't leave! We will find a way. Plus . . . plus . . . I can't tell you any more!"

I came back next day as agreed. I found Duquesnel and Chilly in the director's office. Chilly addressed me quite brutally, "Duquesnel tells me that you want to leave? Where are you going? It's stupid! Your place is here! Think about it! At the Gymnase they only put on modern plays and mere fashion shows. That's not your kind of thing. At the Vaudeville the same thing. At the Gaîté you would ruin your voice. You are too distinguished for the Ambigu . . . " I looked at him without replying. I realized that his colleague had not spoken to him about the Théâtre-Français. He was embarrassed and muttered, "You agree with me?"

"No!" I said, "you have forgotten the Comédie!"

He collapsed in his large armchair. "No, my dear friend, don't give me that. They have already had a taste of your bad temper at the Comédie. I dined the other evening with Maubant.[6] When someone said that they ought to engage you at the Comédie-Française he almost choked with fury. And I assure you that the great tragic actor was not nice about you."

"Well, you should have defended me!" I exclaimed in irritation. "You know very well that I'm very serious about my acting."

"But I did defend you. I even added that the Comédie would be very lucky to have an actress with your spirit, that perhaps you would change the monotonous tone of the House, and I meant what I said. But this poor actor was beside himself. He doesn't think you have any talent. First of all, he claims that you don't know how to recite verse, that you open the a's too much . . . finally, out of arguments, he added that you would enter the Comédie-Française only over his dead body."

I remained silent for a moment weighing up the pros and the cons of the probable result of my initiative. Finally, making up my mind, I murmured, already upset, "So you don't want to give me a raise?"

"No! A thousand times no!" shouted Chilly. "You can blackmail me when your contract is finished, and then we will see. But until then I have your signature, you have mine, and I hold to the contract. The Théâtre-Français is the only theater besides this one that would suit you, and I am confident on that front."

"You are perhaps wrong."

He got up quickly and planting himself in front of me with his hands in his pockets he said in a familiar and odious tone, "So you take me for an idiot!"

I got up coldly and pushing him away gently with my hand I said, "Yes, I take you for a triple idiot!" and I dashed toward the stairs, Duquesnel calling me vainly. I flew down them two at a time.

Under the arcade of the Odéon I was stopped by Paul Meurice, who was coming on behalf of Victor Hugo to invite Duquesnel and Chilly to supper, to celebrate the hundredth performance of *Ruy Blas*. "I've just left your house," he said. "I left you a note from Victor Hugo."

"Good, good, it's alright." I jumped in my carriage and said, "I'll see you tomorrow, my dear."

"My God! You're in a hurry!"

"Yes, yes." I leaned forward and shouted to the coach driver, "To the Comédie-Française!" As I looked back to Paul Meurice to say goodbye, I saw him standing with his mouth open under the arcade.

When I arrived at the Comédie I had my visiting card sent into Perrin.[7] Five minutes later I was introduced to the glacial mannequin. There were two separate men in this man: the one that he really was, and the one that he had created to suit the demands of his career. Perrin was gallant, nice, witty, and slightly shy. The mannequin was cold, brusque, silent, and slightly affected.

I was received at first by the mannequin. He stood up and ostentatiously gave me his ladies' bow, his arm outstretched as he indicated the guest's chair. He affectedly waited until I was seated to sit down. Then picking up a paper knife to occupy his hands, he said to me in a rather blank voice—the mannequin's voice—"You have considered, Mademoiselle?"

"Yes, sir. Here I am to sign."

Before he had had time to ask me to use his desk, I drew up my chair, took a pen and prepared to sign. But I had not taken enough ink and I stretched out my arm across the width of the table again. I plunged the pen resolutely to the bottom of the inkwell. But this time I took too much and in the return journey a large drop of ink fell on the white paper placed in front of the mannequin. He bent his head with a rather grim eye, looking like a bird that spies a grain of hempseed in its millet. As he was about to remove the blotted paper I cried out, "Wait! Wait!" and took possession of it. "I'm going to see whether it's right or wrong to sign. If it's a butterfly, it's right. If it's anything else, it's wrong." I folded the paper in half down the middle of the enormous blot and pressed it firmly. Then Emile Perrin began to laugh, giving up his role as mannequin. He leaned over the paper close to me and we opened it very carefully, as one opens a hand in which one has imprisoned a fly. The paper opened up to reveal in the middle of its whiteness a magnificent black butterfly with wings outstretched. "Well?" said Perrin, having now completely abandoned his role as mannequin, "We did well to sign!" I said, and we talked like long lost friends.

This man was charming and very attractive in spite of his ugliness. When we left we were friends and delighted with one another.

I was performing in *Ruy Blas* at the Odéon in the evening. Around ten o'clock Duquesnel came to my dressing room. "You were a bit harsh on poor Chilly. And really, you were not nice. You should have come back when I called you. Is it true what Paul Meurice told us—that you went immediately to the Théâtre-Français?"

"Here, read it!" I said, giving him my contract with the Comédie.

Duquesnel took the contract and when he had taken it in he said, "Do you really want me to show it to Chilly?"

"Show it to him."

He came closer to me and said with a serious and sorrowful air, "You ought never to have done that without letting me know. It shows a lack of trust that I did not deserve." He was right, but the thing was done.

A moment later Chilly arrived, furious, gesticulating, crying, stammering with anger: "It's a disgrace! Treachery! You had no right! I will make you pay the penalty!" As I was in a bad mood I turned my back on him and excused myself with difficulty to Duquesnel. He was hurt, and I was a little ashamed, for this man had given me nothing except evidence of friendship; and it was he who, in spite of Chilly and so much other ill will, had held the door open for my future.

Chilly kept his word and sued me and the Comédie in a suit which I lost. I had to pay a penalty of six thousand francs to the directors of the Odéon.

A few weeks later Victor Hugo offered the actors in *Ruy Blas* a great supper in honor of the hundredth performance. It was wonderful for me. I had never been at a supper of this kind.

I had hardly spoken to Chilly since our scene. But that evening he was on my right and we had to make up. I was on the right of Victor Hugo. On his other side was Mme. Lambquin who played the part of the Camerera Mayor and Dusquesnel was next to her.

Facing the illustrious poet was another poet, Théophile Gautier.[8] He had a lion's head on an elephant's body. He had a delicious sense of humor, choice words, and a rich laugh. The bloated, soft, pallid flesh of his face was punctuated by two pupils veiled by heavy eyelids. His gaze was charming and distant. In this being there was an oriental nobility strangled by fashion and western ways. I knew almost all his poetry and I gazed tenderly at this tender person enamored of beauty. I amused myself dressing him in my mind's eye in superb oriental costumes. I saw him stretched out on great cushions, his beautiful hands rummaging through gems of every color. Some of his verse murmured on my lips and I was departing with him into the realm of infinite dream when a word from my neighbor Victor Hugo made me turn my head toward him.

What a difference! He, the great Poet, was the most ordinary being imaginable except for his luminous brow. His appearance was heavy although very active. His nose was common, the expression in his eye was coarse, his mouth was without beauty, only his voice had nobility and charm. I liked to listen to him while looking at Théophile Gautier.

And yet it was hard to look opposite me for next to the poet was an odious creature, Paul de Saint-Victor.[9] His cheeks looked like two vessels sweating oil, his hook-nose was acerbic, his eyes spiteful and hard, his arms too short, his belly too big. He looked jaundiced. He had a great deal of wit and talent, but he used both of them to say and write more evil than good. I knew that this man hated me and I returned his hatred.

In the toast made by Victor Hugo to thank everybody for their concerted effort in bringing back his play to the stage, everybody leaned toward the poet with their glass in the air. But the illustrious Master turned toward me, "As for you, Madame . . . " At this precise moment Paul de Saint-Victor put his glass down on the table so violently that it broke. There was a little moment of astonishment, but I leaned across the table toward him and handed my glass to Paul de Saint-Victor: "Take mine, sir. In drinking it you will know my thoughts, a response to yours, which you just expressed so clearly." The nasty man took my glass, but with what a look.

Victor Hugo finished his toast amidst applause and cheers. Then Duquesnel leaned backward and, calling me quietly, told me to warn Chilly that he had to respond to Victor Hugo. I did so, but he looked at me with a dull eye and a dead voice and said, "My legs won't move." I looked at him closely while Duquesnel asked for silence for M. de Chilly's speech. I saw his fingers grasping his fork desperately; the end of his fingers were white, the rest of his hand was purple. I took this hand. It was frozen. The other was hanging and lifeless under the table.

Silence fell. All eyes converged on Chilly. "Get up," I murmured, seized with fright. He made a movement and his head suddenly collapsed, crushing his face in his plate. There was a subdued uproar! The few women surrounded the poor man. Stupid, banal, and indifferent words were murmured like familiar prayers.

His son was sent for. Then two waiters came and lifted the body, alive but inert, and put it in the little drawing room. Duquesnel stayed with him, asking me to go back to the poet's guests. I went back into the banquet hall. Groups of people had formed. "Well?" they asked me as they saw me come back in.

"He is quite bad. The doctor has just arrived, and cannot say yet."

"It's indigestion!" pronounced Lafontaine (Ruy Blas), gulping down a little glass of brandy.

"It's cerebral anemia!" was the firm judgment of Talien (Don Guritan), who was always forgetting things.

Victor Hugo came up and said simply, "It's a fine death." Then he took me by the arm and led me to the end of the room where he turned my thoughts elsewhere by whispering poetic gallantries to me.

A little time passed, which was heavy with sadness. Then Duquesnel appeared. He was pale, but had composed his expression into that of a man of the world and answered all the questions, "Yes, they have just taken him back home . . . it is nothing apparently . . . two days of rest . . . Probably a cold in the feet during the meal."

"Yes," exclaimed one of the guests from *Ruy Blas*, "yes, there was a hell of a draft under the table!"

"Yes," replied Duquesnel to someone who was badgering him. "Yes, no doubt, too much heat in the head."

"In fact," added another guest, "our heads were on fire with this dratted gas." I could see the moment approaching when all these people were going to reproach Victor Hugo for the cold, the heat, the food, and the wine at the banquet.

Duquesnel, irritated by these ridiculous comments shrugged his shoulders and drawing me away from the crowd he said, "He's lost!" I had had a presentiment that it was so, but the certainty of it gripped me with poignant sorrow. "I want to leave!" I said to Duquesnel. "Be kind enough to call my carriage."

As I was making my way toward the little drawing room, which served as a cloakroom, I was jostled by old Lambquin who was a bit inebriated by the heat and the wine and was waltzing with Talien.

"Ah, excuse me my little madonna! I nearly knocked you over."

I drew her to me and without thinking said vehemently in her ear, "Don't dance any more mother Lambquin, Chilly is dying!" Purple as she was, her face turned white as chalk. Her teeth chattered without her saying a word. "Ah! My poor Lambquin! If I had known I would hurt you so much . . . !"

But she was no longer listening and as she put on her coat she said, "You're leaving?"

"Yes."

"Can you take me back? I will tell you something . . . " She wrapped a black scarf round her head and we left like that, led by Duquesnel and Paul Meurice who installed us in the carriage.

She lived in the district of Saint-Germain and I on the rue de Rome. As we going along the poor woman told me this: "You know, my little one, that I am crazy about somnambulists, Tarot card readers, and other kinds of fortune tellers. Well, last Friday—you know that I only ever consult them on Fridays—a Tarot card reader told me, 'You will die eight days after the death of a brown-haired man, who is not young, and who is linked to your life.' You can understand, my little one, that I thought she was pulling my leg, because there is no man in my life. I am a widow and have never had a relationship since my husband died. So I told her off, because after all I pay seven francs—she usually charges ten francs, but it's only seven for actors. She was furious that I did not believe her and took my two hands and said to me, 'You are yelling in vain, that's how it is! And if you want me to tell you the absolute truth, it's a man who provides your livelihood! And to be even more exact, there are two men who are responsible for your livelihood, a brown-haired one and a blonde one! It's a disgrace!' Before she could finish her 'It's a disgrace!' she received a slap like she's never received before, I swear! But afterward I racked my brains to figure out what the slut was saying, and I realized that the two men, one brown-haired, one blonde, who are responsible for my livelihood are our directors, Chilly and Duquesnel. And here you are telling me that Chilly . . . "

She stopped, out of breath from telling her story and gripped again by terror. "I'm suffocating," she said. In spite of the freezing cold we lowered the windows. I helped her climb up the four floors and asked the concierge to look after her, giving her, to be on the safe side, a *louis*. I went back home, feeling very shaken by these incidents, as dramatic as they were unexpected, at a party.

Three days afterwards, on June 14, 1872, Chilly died without having regained consciousness.

Twelve days later my poor Lambquin died, saying to the priest who absolved her, "I die because I believed in the Devil."

Chapter XXII

I left the Odéon with deep sorrow. I loved and still love this theater. It has the feeling of being a little provincial town all to itself—its welcoming arcades under which walk old and poor scholars coming to take the air sheltered from the sun; the great paving stones, in the cracks of which springs a yellow and microscopic weed; the high columns blackened by time, hands, and dirt from the street; the constant noise that surrounds them; the departure of omnibuses like the departure of the old stagecoaches; the fraternity of people who meet one another there; everything—even the railings of the Luxembourg— gives it the air of being a world unto itself, while yet in Paris. Besides, the atmosphere of school pervades it. The walls still harbor young hopes. People don't talk constantly about yesterday there as they do in other theaters. The young actors who come there talk about tomorrow.

I never think about these years of my life without childlike emotion, without recalling laughter, without my nostrils flaring to smell little bouquets, ordinary and clumsily assembled, and smelling of fresh windblown flowers; flowers offered by the hearts of twenty year olds, little bouquets paid for by student budgets.

I did not want to take anything away. I left my dressing-room furniture to a little actress. I left my costumes, my little trinkets. I gave away everything. I felt that my life of hope stopped there. I felt that the earth was ripe for the burgeoning of all my dreams, but that life's struggle was about to start. And I guessed right.

My first stint at the Comédie-Française had been a failure. I knew that I was entering into a cage of wild beasts. I had hardly any friends in this theater except Laroche,[1] Coquelin, and Mounet-Sully, the first two being friends from the Conservatoire, the latter from the Odéon. Among the women there were Marie Lloyd and Sophie Croizette, both friends from my childhood, nasty Jouassain,[2] who was only nice to me, and the lovable Madeleine Brohan.[3] Madeleine's goodness delighted one's soul and her wit one's mind, but her indifference chilled devotion.

173

M. Perrin decided that I would début in *Mademoiselle de Belle-Isle*,[4] in accordance with the wishes of Sarcey. The rehearsals started in the foyer, which bothered me. Madeleine Brohan was to play the role of the Marquise de Prie. At this time she was almost monstrously fat, and I was so thin, so thin that my thinness was food for the composers of satirical songs and the albums of caricaturists. So it was impossible for the Duc de Richelieu to mistake the Marquise de Prie (Madeleine Brohan) for Mlle. de Belle-Isle (Sarah Bernhardt), in the improper and conclusive nocturnal assignation given by the marchioness to the duke, who thought that he was embracing the chaste Mlle. de Belle-Isle. At each rehearsal, Bressant, who played the role of the Duc de Richelieu, would stop and say, "No, it's too stupid! I'll play the Duc de Richelieu without arms." And Madeleine would leave the rehearsal and go to the director's office to ask that her role be taken off her. This was in fact what Perrin wanted. In fact he had had Croizette in mind from the beginning, but he wanted to have his hand forced for some secret little reasons known only to himself and guessed at by others. Finally the change took place and serious rehearsals began. Then the first performance was announced for November 6 (1872).

I have always had and still have terrible stage fright, especially when I know that much is expected of me. I knew that the house had been sold out a long time in advance. I knew that the press was expecting a great success and that Perrin himself was counting on a succession of big receipts. Alas! All the hopes and predictions went down the drain; my new début at the Comédie was mediocre. This is what Francisque Sarcey—whom I did not know at the time, but who followed my career with very great interest—said in *Le Temps* of November 11, 1872:

> There was a dazzling audience, and this début had drawn all theater lovers. It must be said that aside from the personal merit of Mlle. Sarah Bernhardt there has formed about her person a host of legends, true or false, which hover around her name and pique the curiosity of the Parisian public. It was a disappointment when she appeared. By means of her costume she had ostentatiously exaggerated a slimness which is elegant under the wide pleated veils of Greek and Roman heroines, but displeasing in modern dress. Either because powder does not become her face, or because stage fright had made her terribly pale, it was not a particularly agreeable impression to see spring forth from this long black sheath— it gave me the impression of an ant's body—this long white face from which the sparkle of the eyes had disappeared and

in which showed only sparkling teeth. She spoke the three first acts while trembling convulsively, and we did not find the Sarah of *Ruy Blas* except in two couplets which she spun with her sorceress' voice and a marvellous grace. But she botched all the forceful passages. I doubt that Mlle. Sarah Bernhardt will ever find in her wonderful voice those thunderous and deep notes expressive of a paroxysm of violent passion, which transport an audience. If nature had given her this gift she would be a perfect artist, and there are none such in the theater. Annoyed by the coldness of the audience, Mlle. Sarah Bernhardt recovered herself completely in the fifth act. It was indeed our Sarah, the Sarah of *Ruy Blas* that we have so much admired at the Odéon. etc. etc.

Just as Sarcey said, I completely botched my début. My excuse was not stage fright but the anxiety into which I was plunged by the sudden departure of Mama from her place in the dress circle five minutes after I came on stage.

I had glimpsed, from the furtive glance I had thrown her as soon as I had come on stage, that she was deathly pale. I had the feeling when I saw her go out that she was going to have one of her attacks, which put her life in danger, and this first act seemed to be interminable to me. I threw one word after another, spluttering the phrases out haphazardly with only one idea in mind: to know what had happened.

The audience cannot imagine the torture endured by poor actors when they are there in front of them in body, making gestures, speaking words, while their anguished heart has flown off to be with a loved one who is suffering. Usually one can throw off the irritations and anxieties of life and for a few hours one sheds one's own personality to put on someone else's; one walks in the dream of another life, forgetting everything. But this is impossible when loved ones are suffering. Anxiety takes a grip on you, diminishing optimism, heightening pessimism, throwing into a turmoil the head that lives two lives, and tossing the heart that beats hard enough to break. These were the feelings I felt throughout the first act.

I left the stage. "Mama . . . what has happened to Mama?" Nobody knew anything.

Croizette came up to me and said, "What's the matter? I didn't recognize you. You weren't yourself on stage just now." I briefly told her what I had seen and felt.

Frédéric Febvre[5] quickly sent for news and the theater's doctor rushed up. "Your mother, Mademoiselle, has had a fainting fit but she has just been taken home."

I looked at him. "It's her heart isn't it, sir?"

"Yes," he said. "Her heart is very agitated."

"I know, she's very ill," and I could not restrain myself any longer. I burst into tears. Croizette helped me to go back to my dressing room. She was kind. We had known each other since childhood and we liked each other. Nothing had ever divided us, not even the nasty stories told by jealous people or little injuries to one's pride. My dear Mme. Guérard took a carriage and hurried to Mama's to bring me news.

I put on a little more powder. But the audience, not knowing what was happening, began to get annoyed and accuse me of some new caprice and received me even more coldly than before. That was fine by me: I was thinking about something else. I spoke the words of Mlle. de Belle-Isle—a stupid and deadly role—but I, Sarah, waited for news of Mama. I kept my eye open for the return of "my little lady" to whom I had said, "Open the door on the garden side a little as soon as you get back, and do this with your head if things are going better, and like this if they're going badly."

But by now I could not remember which sign meant what and when I saw Mme. Guérard at the end of the third act opening the door slightly and nodding her head up and down as though to say, "Yes," I became completely idiotic. It was during the great scene in the third act when Mlle. de Belle-Isle reproaches the Duc de Richelieu (Bressant) for losing her forever. The duke replies, "Wouldn't you say that someone was listening to us, someone who is hiding?" I cried out, "It's Guérard who is bringing me news!" The audience did not have time to understand, for Bressant skirted round the reply and saved the situation.

After some unenthusiastic applause, I received news of Mama. She was doing better but she had had a bad attack. Poor Mama! She had found me so ugly when I first went on stage that her wonderful indifference had collapsed under painful stupefaction, which turned into rage when she heard a big woman sitting near her say with a snigger, "She's a dry bone this little Bernhardt!" I was reassured and I played the last act with confidence. However the great success of the evening belonged to Croizette, who was delightful as the Marquise de Prie.

My success increased in the second performance however, grew firmer in the following performances, and became so great that I was accused of having paid for a claque. I laughed a lot at this and did not even defend myself as I cannot stand useless talk.

I went on to make a début in the role of Junie in *Britannicus*, with Mounet-Sully who was wonderful in the role of Nero. I received tremendous—incredible—acclaim in the delightful role of Junie. Then in 1873 I played Chérubin in *Le Mariage de Figaro*;[6] it was Croizette who played the role of Suzanne and it was a feast for the audience to see this delicious creature play a role of charm and gaiety. Chérubin was a role that brought me yet more success.

In March, 1873, Perrin had the idea of putting on *Dalila* by Octave Feuillet.[7] At that time I played young girls, young princesses, or young boys, as my slim body, pale face, and sickly aspect committed me for the time to victim roles. Seeing that victims gained the sympathy of the audience and thinking that it was because of my role that I aroused sympathy, Perrin suddenly decided to make the most ridiculous casting of parts. He gave me the role of Dalila, the spiteful brown-haired ferocious princess, and gave to Sophie Croizette the role of the blonde and idealized dying young girl. The play stumbled with this strange casting. I had to distort my nature to appear a haughty and voluptuous siren; I stuffed my bodice with cotton wool and the hips of my skirt with horsehair; but I still had my little thin and sorrowful visage. Croizette had to compress her bust, one of her best points, under bandages, which suffocated her; but she kept her pretty face full of pretty dimples. I was obliged to make my voice louder, she to quieten hers. In short, it was absurd. The play was only a partial success.

After this I played in *L'Absent*, a pretty piece in verse by Eugène Manuel,[8] and then *Chez l'avocat*, a very amusing one-act play in verse by Paul Ferrier in which Coquelin and I disputed delightfully. Then, on August 22, I played with immense success the role of Andromaque.[9] I will never forget this first performance in which Mounet-Sully was received with delirious acclaim. How fine Mounet-Sully was in the role of Oreste! His entry, his furies, his folly, and the visual beauty of this marvellous artist, how fine it all was! After Andromaque I played Aricie in *Phèdre*, and on that evening I was really the star of the performance although I was in a secondary role.

I took such a place in so short a time at the Comédie that some actors were worried and so was the director. M. Perrin, a man of superior intelligence whom I remember with great affection, was horribly dictatorial and so was I. There was perpetual war between us. He wanted to impose his will upon me and I did not want to submit. He would freely laugh at my caprice when it was directed against someone else, but he would get furious when it was directed against himself. It was a joy for me to send Perrin into a fury. I confess it. He would splutter out his words when he wanted to talk fast, when normally he weighed every word; his normally hesitant gaze would become quite grim and his pale and distinguished face would be blotched with red. Fury would make him take off his hat and put it back on fifteen times in fifteen minutes and his normally smooth hair would stand on end under the crazy stampede of the hat. Although I was old enough to be mature, I took pleasure in this childish mischief that I always regretted afterward and that I would always begin again; and still today, in spite of the days, weeks, months, and years that I have lived, I take tremendous pleasure in farce.

Nevertheless, life at the Comédie was becoming a little irritating for me. I wanted to play the role of Camille in *On ne badine pas avec l'amour*—the part was Croizette's. I wanted to play Célimène—the part was Croizette's. Perrin was very partial to Croizette. He admired her, and this young woman, who was very ambitious, showed a respect, consideration, and docility that charmed the old authoritarian. She got everything that she wanted and as Sophie Croizette was frank and straight, she would often say to me when I complained, "Do like I do, be more flexible. You spend your time rebelling. I give the impression of doing everything that Perrin wants, and, in fact, I make him do everything *I* want. Try it."

So I would take my courage in both hands and go up to see Perrin. Almost always he received me with this phrase, "Ah! Good day Mlle. Revolt, are you calm today?"

"Yes, very calm. But be kind, please give me what I want," and I would lay on the charm, putting on my pretty voice. He would purr, he would be witty (he had a lot of wit) and we were fine together for a quarter of an hour. Then I would blurt out my demand: "Let me play Camille in *On ne badine pas avec l'amour*."

"But that's impossible, my dear child. Croizette will not be happy."

"I've spoken to her about it and she doesn't mind."

"You were wrong to discuss it with her."

"Why?"

"Because casting is the business of the director and not the actors." He was no longer purring, he was growling. I would fly into a rage and in a moment I had gone out slamming the door.

In the meantime, I was beginning to wear myself out. I would spend nights crying. It was then that I rented a studio to do sculpture. As I could not expend my store of intelligence and creativity at the theater, I put them in the service of another art. I started to work at sculpture with tremendous enthusiasm. I quickly made great progress. I had become indifferent to the theater. I would get on my horse at eight o'clock and at ten o'clock I was in my sculpture studio at 11 boulevard de Clichy. My delicate health reacted to the pressure of this double endeavor. I vomited blood in a terrifying way and would spend hours unconscious.

I no longer went to the Comédie except when called there by duty. My friends were seriously worried. Perrin was informed of what was happening and as he was also under pressure from the press and the ministry he decided to give me a role in *Le Sphinx*[10] by Octave Feuillet. The main part was for Croizette; but when reading it over I found the part meant for me to be charming and I resolved that it would be the main part. There would be two main parts, that was all there was to it.

The rehearsals went quite well at the beginning, but as my part began to take on more importance than had been expected, irritation started to show itself. Croizette herself became irritable. Perrin was getting irritable, but this situation had the effect of making me all the calmer. Octave Feuillet, a subtle, charming, slightly ironic man of good breeding enjoyed these skirmishes tremendously.

However war was about to break out. The first act of hostility came from Sophie Croizette. I always wore three or four roses on my bodice which would lose their petals in the heat of the action. One day Sophie Croizette slipped full length on the stage and as she was tall and well built she fell without modesty and got up without grace. The stifled laughter of some subordinates stung her to the quick and she turned to me, "It's your fault! Your roses lose their petals and make everybody fall over!"

I began to laugh. "There are three petals missing from my roses and here they all are near the armchair on the court side, you fell on the garden side. So it's not my fault, but your clumsiness that's at fault."

The argument continued rather vehemently on one side and the other. Two clans formed: the Croizettistes and the Bernhardtistes. War was declared, not between Sophie and me, but between our respective admirers and detractors. These little quarrels spread beyond the stage, and the public itself began to form clans. Croizette had on her side all the bankers and the stuffy people; I had on my side all the artists and students, the dying and the losers. Once war was declared there was no more hesitation about going into combat. The first, the most bloody, and the most definitive battle took place over the question of the moon.

We were starting the last of the dress rehearsals. The third act took place in a clearing in a forest.[11] In the middle of the scene was a large rock on which Blanche (Croizette) gave a kiss to Savigny (Delaunay),[12] her husband. I (Berthe de Savigny) had to arrive by the little bridge, which crossed a stream. The moon bathed the whole clearing in its light. Croizette had just played her scene. Her kiss was applauded, daring as this was for the Comédie-Française at this time (what haven't we done since?!) Suddenly the bravos broke out again ... astonished faces. Perrin stood up terrified. I was crossing the bridge, pale and overwhelmed with sorrow, dragging with a drooping and discouraged arm the stole which was meant to cover my shoulders. I was bathed in the white light of the moon and the effect, it seems, was arresting and poignant.

A barbed nasal voice called out, "One moon effect is enough! Extinguish for Mlle. Bernhardt!"

I bounded out onto the front of the stage. "I beg your pardon, M. Perrin, but you have no right to take my moon away from me! It says in the script 'Berthe advances pale and convulsed under the rays of the moon.' I am pale and convulsed, I want my moon!"

"It's impossible!" roared Perrin. "The 'You love me then?' of Mlle. Croizette and her kiss have to be bathed in moonlight. She is playing the Sphinx, it's the main character, so you have to leave the main effects to her!"

"Well, sir, give a shining moon to Croizette and a little moon to me; I don't mind, but I want my moon!"

All the actors and stage hands and theater employees poked their heads through all the openings into the auditorium and onto the stage. The Croizettistes and the Bernhardtistes were giving their commentary on the dispute. When Octave Feuillet was called into the fray he got up too and said, "I agree that Mlle. Croizette is very beautiful with her moonlight effect and Mlle. Sarah Bernardt is perfect in rays from the moon! So I wish to have the moon for both of them!" Perrin could not contain his anger. There was discussion between the author and the director, between the actors, and between the doorkeeper and the journalists, who were asking him questions. The rehearsal was adjourned. I declared that I would not perform without my moon.

I did not receive any rehearsal notice for two days and I learned from Croizette that my role of Berthe was secretly being rehearsed by a young woman whom we had nicknamed "the Crocodile" because she followed all the rehearsals, just as this animal follows boats, hoping constantly to snap up a role tossed overboard. Octave Feuillet refused this substitution and came to see me with Delaunay who had patched things up. "It's agreed. The moon will shine on both of you," he said, kissing my hands. The première of Le Sphinx was a triumph for Croizette and me. The two clans were excited about the one outdoing the other, and this doubled our success and amused us very much, for Croizette has always been a wonderful friend and a loyal colleague. She worked for herself, but never against anyone else.

After Le Sphinx I played in a pretty one-act play by a student at the Ecole Polytechnique, called Louis Denayrouse, called La Belle Paule. This young author has since become an acclaimed scientist and has given up poetry. After this I begged Perrin to give me a month's leave, but he absolutely refused. He made me rehearse Zaïre during the painful months of June and July and announced, against my wishes, a première for August 6. That summer Paris was frightfully hot. I think that as Perrin could not master me he had the desire to master me by killing me, not out of any real ill will but out of sheer autocracy. Dr. Parrot had gone to see him and told him that my state of weakness was so great that it was dangerous to make me perform during the heat wave. He refused to listen. I was so furious at the ferocious stubborness of this bourgeois intellectual that I swore I would perform until it killed me.

It often happened to me as a child that I wanted to kill myself to annoy other people. I remember even having swallowed the contents of a big inkpot, after having been forced to eat a bread-soup in front of Mama, who fancied that bread-soups were necessary for our health. Our maid had revealed to her my horror of bread-soup, adding that each morning the bread-soup went into the slop pail. Of course I felt terribly sick and I cried from the torture in my stomach. I cried out to my horrified mother, "It's you who are making me die!" and my poor mother sobbed . . . She never knew the truth and she never forced me to eat anything ever again. So, after so many years, I found myself experiencing the same rancorous and childish feelings. "I don't care," I said to myself, "I'll surely faint and I'll vomit up blood and perhaps I will die! And that will serve Perrin right! He will be furious!" Yes, that's what I thought and that's how stupid I am sometimes. Why? I cannot explain, I merely describe it the way it is.

So on August 6, on an unbearably hot night, I played the part of Zaïre. The auditorium was completely full and all steamed up. I only glimpsed the spectators through a mist. The play was badly set up as far as the décor was concerned, but well costumed and especially very well performed by Mounet-Sully (Orosmane), Laroche (Nérestan), and myself (Zaïre) and it received enormous acclaim.

As I wanted to collapse in a faint, spit blood, and die, in order to enrage Perrin, I gave myself to the performance completely. I sobbed, loved, and suffered, and the cry that I gave as I was struck by the dagger of Orosmane was a real cry of pain. I had felt the steel penetrate my breast and then, as I fell breathless and dying on the oriental couch, I thought that I was indeed dying. Throughout the whole final act I hardly dared move an arm, convinced as I was of the reality of my languid agony, and a little scared, I confess, to see the naughty farce I had played to spite Perrin about to become a reality. But great was my surprise when after the curtain went down I rose briskly for the curtain call and acknowledged the audience without tiredness or weakness, ready in fact to begin the whole play again.

In my mind I put a special marker beside this performance, for, from this day, I realized that my physical energies were at the service of my intellect. I had always wanted to follow my mental instincts, but I had thought that it was beyond the power of my body to realize them. But here I was finding that even though I had physically given everything and more I was in a state of perfect equilibrium! Thus I glimpsed the possibility of the future that I had dreamed about. I had thought—until this performance of *Zaïre*—and I had heard it said, and I had read it in the newspapers, that my voice was pretty but frail; that my gestures were graceful but vague; that the way in which I carried myself was supple but lacking in authority; that the lost-in-the-clouds expression of my eyes did not subdue the beast (the audience). So now I reevaluated all of this. I had received proof that I could count on my physical strength, for I had begun the performance of *Zaïre* in such a state of weakness that it had seemed obvious that I could not finish the first act without fainting. Besides, although it is a gentle role, it requires two or three cries that could have provoked the vomiting of blood that happened to me so frequently at this time. Thus I ascertained this evening that I could count on the solidity of my vocal cords, for I had cried out with real rage and pain, hoping to break something in my inept desire to spite Perrin.

So the little comedy that I had contrived turned out to my advantage. As I could not die at will I changed my plans, and decided to be strong, solid, vivacious, and alive, and I carried it to such a point that some of my contemporaries, who had only supported me because I would surely soon die, hated me as soon as they were sure that I would perhaps live for a long time. I will give just one example as told by Alexandre Dumas *fils*[13] who was present at the death of his intimate friend Charles Narrey and recalled his last words: "I am happy to die, for I will hear no more talk of Sarah Bernhardt or of the great Frenchman (Ferdinand de Lesseps)."[14]

But this confirmation of my strength rendered more painful to me the life of idleness, as it were, to which Perrin condemned me. In fact, after *Zaïre* I went some months without major roles, performing in this, then in that. So, discouraged and disgusted by this theater, I gave myself up to my passion for sculpture.

When I had finished my horseback ride I would rest a little and then escape into my studio, where I would remain until the evening. Friends would come to see me and station themselves around me, playing the piano or singing. Then there would be fierce political arguments, for in this modest studio I received the most illustrious men of all political stripes. A few women would come for tea, which was always terrible and always badly served; but I didn't care. I was absorbed in this wonderful art and saw nothing, or rather, refused to see anything.

I was making the bust of a delightful girl, Mlle. Emily de ***. Her slow measured conversation was very charming. She was foreign, but spoke our language with a perfection that astonished me. She was never without a cigarette and was profoundly contemptuous of anyone who could not read her mind. I would make her sittings last as long as possible because I had the feeling that this sensitive spirit could imbue me with her ability to see into the beyond. Often at moments of crisis in my life I have said to myself, "What would Emmy have done?" or, "What would Emmy have said?"

I was a little taken aback one day when Adolphe Rothschild visited me to commission me to sculpt his bust. I set to work at once, but I had been mistaken in my estimate of this pleasant man. He had nothing of the aesthetic about him, quite the contrary. Nevertheless I tried, and I put all my will to succeed into this first commission of which I was so proud. Twice I threw the bust I had started onto the floor and, after a third try, I finally gave up, stammering foolish excuses which obviously did not convince my model for he never came back to visit me. When we met each other in the morning out riding he would greet me coldly and rather severely.

After this failure I undertook the bust of an adorable child, Miss Multon, a delicious little American girl whom I have since seen again in Denmark, now married and just as ravishingly pretty as a mother as she was as a child. After this I made the bust of Mlle. Hocquigny, a wonderful person who acted as overseer of the linen for the Supply Corps during the war and whose help was so invaluable to me and my wounded.

Then I undertook the bust of my youngest sister, Régina, who, alas, had already contracted tuberculosis. Never had a face more perfect been shaped by the hand of God! She had the eyes of a lioness fringed by the longest of eyelashes . . . a slim nose with delicate nostrils, a tiny little mouth, a determined chin, a pearly complexion. And all of this was crowned by hair like moonlight, for I have never seen on anyone else such pale blonde, shiny, silky hair. But this wonderful face was, nevertheless, lacking in charm. Her expression was hard and her mouth unsmiling. I tried as best I could to sculpt this beautiful marble face, but it would have taken a great artist to do justice to it and I was only a humble amateur.

When I exhibited the bust of my little sister she had been dead five months, after six months of slow agony punctuated by remissions. I had taken her in to live with me at 4 rue de Rome, in the little mezzanine apartment that I had rented after the terrible fire that had ruined my furniture, books, paintings, and, in fact, my whole small stock of possessions. This apartment on the rue de Rome was small. My bedroom was minute. The big bamboo bed took up all the room. By the window was my coffin in which I often lay to learn my parts. So, when I took my sister in to live with me I naturally took to sleeping each night in my little bed of white satin which was to be my last resting place, and to have my sister sleep in my big bamboo bed under its masses of lace. She too thought this was the best solution, since I did not want to leave her alone at night and it was impossible to put another bed in this little bedroom. Plus, she was used to my coffin.

One day when my manicurist was about to enter my room to do my nails she was stopped by my sister who asked her to go in quietly since I was still asleep. The woman turned to look at the armchair where she thought I was asleep and seeing me instead sleeping in the coffin she fled from the room shrieking. From this moment onward everyone in Paris knew that I slept in a coffin and rumours took flight in all directions.

I was so used to the kind of slander that was printed about me that I hardly worried about it. However, when my poor little sister died, a tragi-comic incident occurred. When the undertakers arrived at the room to take away the corpse they found themselves faced by two coffins. The master of ceremonies lost his head and sent for a second hearse at high speed. At the time I was with my mother who was unconscious and I arrived just in time to stop the men in black from carrying away my coffin. The second hearse was sent away, but the newspapers got hold of the incident and I was blamed and criticized. And yet it was not my fault.

Chapter XXIII

[*After the death of her sister Sarah falls ill from the stress and strain of caring for her day and night and the sorrow of losing her. To convalesce she is sent by her doctor to the south of France, but goes instead to Brittany with her little son, her manservant, Claude, and his wife. They stay for twelve days at Audierne. She spends the time making the dangerous ascent of the Pointe du Raz, swimming in the Baie des Trépassés, and then after a picnic lunch, painting till sunset. Her peace is somewhat marred by a band of local ragamuffin children begging for money. One day, driven by her "unbridled desire for danger," she descends a deep crevasse called the "Enfer du Plogoff" and is very afraid.*

After her return Sarah is given the role of Phèdre—hitherto she had played only Aricie—in part because Perrin wished to punish Rosélia Rousseil,[1] who normally played Phèdre. On the first night the theater is sold out. Mounet-Sully plays Hippolyte. Sarah is unnerved before the performance begins by her sense of the responsibility of the role, but regains her poise at the comic sight of Martel,[2] actor of Théramène, coming to comfort her with unfinished makeup on his nose. The performance is a great triumph for Sarah. The press is unanimously favorable except for the review of Paul de Saint-Victor, who upbraids her for what he interprets, erroneously, as her vying with Rachel. Sarah has never seen Rachel perform, but admires her and is surrounded by those who revere her memory.

After Phèdre *a new play by Bornier,[3]* La Fille de Roland, *is rehearsed with Sarah in the role of Berthe. At one rehearsal Emile Augier[4] demands that Berthe's only significant scene in the play—when as an anxious lover she describes a duel from her castle window—be cut, on the grounds that the audience will laugh at it. Bornier is afraid to ignore Augier since the latter is a member of the Academy to which Bornier is seeking admission. Sarah, nudged by Perrin, saves the situation for him, however, by threatening to drop the role if the scene is cut, and the scene turns out to be very successful on the first night.*

Later, Sarah plays Gabrielle *by Augier and Coquelin takes the part of her husband. But she finds her acting as mediocre as the play itself.*

Since January Sarah has been a sociétaire *of the Théâtre-Français, committed to perform for this theater for many years, an honor which she now already regrets seeking. She channels her discontent into supervision of a house, designed by Félix Escalier, which she is having built on the corner of the avenue*

185

de Villiers and the rue Fortuny, with money that she has inherited from her grandmother's sister. She has the interior of the house decorated with murals painted by her artist friends, Georges Clairin,[5] Duez, Picard, Butin, Jadin, Parrot, and Escalier himself.

One day she plays a trick on her aunt Betzy who is visiting from Holland. Sarah invites her to dine at the unfinished house where these painters are busy at work. Betzy is shocked to be welcomed by Sarah in her sculptor's outfit and even more shocked when Sarah seems to be inviting the "workmen" to dine with her. In the meantime Sarah and the artists change into formal dress, and it is only in the middle of lunch that Betzy realizes these elegant young gentlemen are the "workmen" she had previously spurned.]

Chapter XXIV

[*Alexandre Dumas* fils *creates the role of the Duchesse de Septmonts for Sarah in his new play* L'Etrangère, *but under pressure from Perrin it is given to Sophie Croizette instead, with Sarah playing the role of The Stranger. Later she receives an anonymous letter informing her that Perrin is exerting pressure on Dumas to change the play's title to* La Duchesse de Septmonts. *When Sarah angrily confronts Dumas with this he promises to keep the play's name unchanged. The play's* première *is a great success with the acclaim going to Coquelin, Febvre, and Sarah.*

Sarah becomes very absorbed in sculpting the figure of an old woman holding in her lap the body of a dead child, based on the story of an old woman she had seen in Brittany coming down to the sea each evening. This woman had lost all of her sons, three at sea and two at war. She had brought up a little grandson who had also drowned, and each night the woman would come down to the shore to throw bread into the sea for him. The sculpture is exhibited at the Salon of 1876 where it is awarded an honorable mention.

At the theater they begin to rehearse Rome vaincue *by Parodi.[1] With the old Bretonne woman in mind, Sarah refuses the part of Opimia, the young Vestal virgin, and requests the part of Posthumia, the old, blind, noble, Roman woman. Perrin agrees but is troubled by her potential disparity with Mounet-Sully, who is usually cast as her partner in love or suffering, until he hits upon the idea of casting him in the role of the old madman Vestaepor. The play, which is really rather mediocre, is very successful at its* première *of 27 September, 1876, and Sarah is acclaimed for her performance in the fourth act.*]

Chapter XXV

*O*ur production of *Hernani* completed my conquest of the public.
I already had experience of working with Victor Hugo and it was
a joy for me to find myself at his home almost every day. I had never
stopped seeing him, but I could never talk with him at his home. There
were always men with red ties there gesticulating, or tearful women
declaiming. He was good-natured and would listen with his eyes half
closed. I think he was actually asleep. Then the silence would wake him
up and he would say something complimentary, but he was clever enough
never to commit himself. Victor Hugo could not have promised anything since he liked to keep his promises.

I am not at all like that. I promise everything with the firm intention of keeping my promise, and then two hours later I have completely
forgotten about it. If someone around me reminds me of it I pull out
my hair and to patch things up for my forgetfulness I invent stories, buy
presents, in short complicate my life unnecessarily. I have been like that
since . . . forever. And it will always be like that till the end.

When I complained to Victor Hugo one day about never being
able to talk with him, he invited me to lunch and said that after lunch
we could chat together alone. I sallied forth in delighted expectation.
Paul Meurice, the poet Léon Cladel,[1] the communard Dupuis, a Russian lady whose name I have forgotten, Gustave Doré,[2] etc., were there
for lunch. Opposite Hugo was Mme. Drouet, his friend in times of
trouble. What a horrible lunch it was! God knows how awful the food
was and how badly served—plus my feet were chilled by the draft blowing under three doors and whistling under the table! Near me was M.
X, a German socialist, who is quite a man of substance these days. He
had such dirty hands and ate so ill-manneredly that I felt nauseous. I
have since seen him in Berlin. These days he is very clean, well man-
nered, and, I think, very much an imperialist. My uneasiness in the
company of this man, the cold on my feet, and the mortal weariness of
it all made a wreck of me. I fainted. When I came round I found myself
stretched out on a sofa with my hand in Mme. Drouet's. Opposite me,
sketching, was—Gustave Doré. "Oh! Don't move!" he cried, "You were

so pretty like that!" This totally inappropriate remark charmed me nonetheless and I did as he said. I left Victor Hugo's house without saying goodbye to him, feeling a little embarrassed. The next day he came to see me. I made up some story or other to explain why I was taken ill and I did not see him again until the rehearsals of *Hernani*.

The first performance of *Hernani* took place on 21 November, 1877. It was a triumph for the dramatist and all those who acted in it. *Hernani* had already been performed ten years previously but Delaunay was the exact opposite of what was required for Hernani. He was neither epic, nor romantic, nor poetic. His style was unsuited to the playing of great epics. He was charming, gracious, and perpetually smiling. He was of medium build and his gestures were restrained. He was ideal in Musset, perfect in Emile Augier, charming in Molière, but execrable in Victor Hugo. As for Bressant, who played Charles-Quint, he was the end. His pleasant, relaxed diction, his amused expression, and his wryly raised eyebrows robbed him of all dignity. His enormous feet, which were usually half hidden by his trousers, took on a ridiculous importance. Personally, I could see nothing but the feet. They were big, big, flat, and slightly pigeon-toed. They were frightful, nightmarish. Ah! The wonderful couplet to the shade of Charlemagne—what a travesty he made of it! The audience coughed and fidgeted. It was really painful.

In our production of 1877, on the other hand, it was handsome and talented Mounet-Sully who played Hernani and that wonderful actor Worms,[3] who played Charles-Quint—and with what largesse and impeccable delivery! The performance of 21 November, 1877, was a triumph, and the audience gave me my fair share of the credit for it. I played Doña Sol, and Victor Hugo sent me this letter:

Madame,

You were both charming and great. You moved me, the old soldier, and at one moment when the audience, touched and enchanted, applauded you, I wept. This tear that you caused to fall is yours and I put it at your feet.

Victor Hugo

Enclosed with the letter was a little box containing a bracelet with a teardrop diamond hanging from it. I lost this bracelet at the house of that richest of nabobs, Alfred Sassoon. He wanted to give me another, but I refused. He could not give me back the tear of Victor Hugo.

My success at the Comédie was affirmed and the audiences treated me as special pet. My colleagues held a grudge against me for this.

Perrin picked quarrels with me on any pretext. He felt a certain friendship toward me, but he could not allow that anyone might not need him; and as he regularly turned down whatever I requested I no longer appealed to him. I would send a note to the Minister and obtain his support.

Always thirsty for something new, I wanted to try painting. I knew a little about drawing and had a good eye for color. I did two or three little paintings first of all and then I started on the portrait of my dear Guérard. Alfred Stevens thought it was painted vigorously and Georges Clairin encouraged me to continue with painting. At that point I dived in, either courageously or foolishly, and undertook a painting nearly six feet long called *La Jeune Fille et la Mort.*[4]

Then there was a general outcry against me. Why do something other than acting when that was my career? Why should I have a need to make people talk about me? Perrin came to find me one day when I was very ill. He preached to me. "You're killing yourself, my dear child—why are you sculpting and painting? Is it to prove that you can do it?"

"Oh no!" I said. "It's to give myself a reason for staying here."

"I don't understand," said Perrin, suddenly attentive.

"Well, I have a great desire to travel, to see other things, to breathe other air, to see higher skies and taller trees—in other words, something different! So I create tasks in order to keep myself curbed. Without those I have a feeling that my desire to know and to see will carry me away and I'll do something silly!"

This conversation was to be used against me some years later during the suit that the Comédie brought against me.

The exhibition of 1878 had the effect of exasperating Perrin and some of the actors of the Théâtre-Français against me. They reproached me for everything: my painting, my sculpture, my health. Finally, I had a terrible scene with Perrin, which was the last, for henceforth we spoke to each other no more. Hardly even a stiff greeting passed between us.

This crisis blew up because of my trip in a balloon. I adored and I still adore balloons. I went up in the tethered balloon of M. Giffard every day. The scientist had noticed how often I did this and one day he introduced himself through a mutual friend.

"Ah, M. Giffard, how much I would like to go up in an untethered balloon!"

"Well, Mademoiselle, you may do so," the nice man said.

"When?"

"On whatever day suits you."

I would have liked to have done so right away, but he brought to my attention the fact that the balloon had to be equipped, and that he would be shouldering a great responsibility. An appointment was made for the following Tuesday, just a week later. I asked him to say nothing about it because if the newspapers got hold of the news my terrified family would not let me go up.

M. Tissandier, who was destined some time later, poor man, to crash while flying, promised to accompany me, but in the event he was unable to come, and I was deprived of his pleasant company. So it was young Godard who went up with me a week later in the Doña Sol, a pretty orange balloon specially prepared for our voyage. Prince Napoléon who had been with me when Giffard was introduced to me insisted that he wished to be one of the party; but he was heavy, a little clumsy, and I did not enjoy his conversation, in spite of his wonderful wit, because he was malicious and liked to run down Emperor Napoléon III whom I very much liked. Georges Clairin, Godard, and myself took off alone. The story had leaked out somehow anyway, but too late for the press to get hold of it.

I had been in the air for five minutes when one of my friends, Comte de Montesquiou, met Perrin on the pont des Saints-Pères.

"Look!" he said, "look up at the sky . . . there is your star taking off!" Perrin lifted his head and, pointing to the rising balloon said, "Who is in it?"

"Sarah Bernhardt!"

It seems that Perrin went purple and, grinding his teeth, murmured, "Another one of her games! But she's going to pay for this one!" and dashed off without even saying goodbye to my young friend, who was amazed at this irrational anger. And if he had known what tremendous joy it gave me to fly in the sky like that, Perrin would have been even more tormented.

Ah, our departure! It was five-thirty. I shook hands with some friends. My family, whom I had kept in complete ignorance, was not there. I felt a little nervous when I found myself a hundred and fifty feet in the air a second after the cry "Let go!" I could still hear some shouts—"Be careful! Come back! Don't kill her!"—and then nothing . . . nothing . . . the earth beneath, the sky above . . .

Then, suddenly, I find myself in the clouds. I have left misty Paris and instead I am breathing under a blue sky and see a radiant sun. Around us there are opaque mountains of clouds with iridescent crests. Our gondola plunges into a milky mist, all warm with the sun. It's wonderful! It's stupefying! Not a sound, not a gust!

But the balloon was making almost no movement. It was not until about six o'clock that the currents began to make themselves felt from the rear and we took flight toward the east. We were at an altitude of about five thousand feet. The spectacle was magical. Great white cumulus clouds were our carpet. Great orange draperies fringed with violet came down from the sun to lose themselves in the clouds of our carpet. At six-forty we were at an altitude of seventy-five hundred feet and the cold and our hunger were beginning to make themselves felt. Our dinner was plentiful with foie gras, fresh bread, and oranges. The champage cork shooting into the clouds gave a pretty little muted pop. We lifted our glasses in honor of M. Giffard.

We had talked a lot; night had covered our shoulders with a heavy brown mantle. It was very cold. The balloon was now at eighty-five hundred feet and the blood was humming loudly in my ears. My nose was bleeding. I felt very ill at ease and was dozing and unable to react. Georges Clairin got worried and young Godard cried out very loud, no doubt to wake me up, "Come on, we have to descend! Let's throw out the guide rope!"

This shout did in fact wake me up. I wanted to know what the guide rope was. I got up a bit dazed, and to shake me out of my torpor Godard put the guide rope in my hands. It was a strong cord, which rolled out to one hundred thirty yards, and on it were fixed at intervals little metal crampons. Clairin and I let out the rope laughing, while Godard leaned out of the gondola and looked through his binoculars. "Stop!" he shouted all of a sudden . . . Damn! There are a lot of trees down there!" In fact we were above the Ferrières forest. But in front of us a little plain invited our descent. "There's no time to waste!" Godard cried. "If we miss the plain we will come down in the Ferrières forest in the middle of the night. My God! That's dangerous!" Then turning to me he asked, "Will you open the pressure valve?" It was done, and the gas escaped from its prison whistling mockingly. The valve was closed again at the orders of the pilot and we descended rapidly.

Suddenly the silence of the night was broken by a trumpet call. I started. It was Louis Godard who had taken from his pocket (a veritable storehouse) a trumpet and he was blowing on it violently. A strident whistle responded to our call and we saw, fifteen hundred feet beneath us, a uniformed man who was shouting to us at the top of his lungs. As we were very close to a little train station we guessed that this man was the stationmaster.

"Where are we?" shouted Louis Godard in his trumpet.

"At En-en-en-ille!" the stationmaster replied. It was impossible to understand.

"Where are we?" thundered Georges Clairin with his most formidable voice. "At En-en-en-ille!" shouted back the stationmaster . . . and his crew. It was impossible to understand.

We had to weight the balloon. We went down at first a little too fast, and as the wind was chasing us toward the woods we had to rise back up again. However, after ten minutes, we opened the valve again and again descended. The balloon was now to the right of the station and very distant from its amiable master. "To anchor!" called out young Godard in a commanding tone. With the help of Georges Clairin he threw into space a different rope, on the end of which there was a formidable anchor. The cord was eighty yards long.

Beneath us a flock of children of all ages had been running after the balloon since we had stopped at the station. When we were a thousand feet from the ground Godard shouted in his trumpet, "Where are we?"

"At Verchère!" None of us knew Verchère.

"Well, we shall soon see. Let's keep descending. Come along everybody," cried the pilot, "take hold of the rope that's feeding out! But take care you don't pull too hard on it!"

Five men vigorously grabbed hold of the rope. We were four hundred feet from the ground and the spectacle was very strange. Darkness was dimming everything. I lifted my head to look at the sky but was flabbergasted to see that our half-deflated balloon was hanging around the base in a crumpled heap. It was very ugly.

We landed gently without the little hoo-ha that I had been hoping for and without the little drama that I had dreamed of. A torrential rain welcomed us in our descent. A young proprietor of a neighbouring château ran up like the peasants to see us. He offered me his umbrella. "Oh sir, I'm so slim that I can't get wet, I pass between the raindrops." This remark was repeated and became legendary.

"What time is the train?" asked Clairin.

"Oh, you've got time," replied a newcomer with a deep hoarse voice. "You can only take the ten o'clock train, as the station is an hour from here, and as there's no carriage, with the weather it's going to mean a two-hour walk for Madame."

I felt overwhelmed, and looked around for the young proprietor and his umbrella to use as a cane, as neither Clairin nor Godard had brought one. But just as I was mentally accusing him he jumped out lightly from a carriage, which I had not heard draw up. "Here," he said, "a carriage for you and these gentlemen, and another for the corpse of the balloon."

"My word, you're a savior!" said Clairin. "It seems that the roads are plowed up."

"Oh," the young man cried, "it would have been impossible for the feet of a Parisian lady to cover even half the distance!" Then he waved goodbye and wished us a good journey.

A little more than an hour later we arrived at the station at Emerainville. When the stationmaster realized who we were he welcomed us very warmly. He apologized for not having been able to make himself heard when we had called to him an hour earlier from our floating vehicle. He gave us a little frugal meal: some cheese, bread, and cider. I hated cheese and had never wanted to eat it as I thought it was not poetic, but I was dying of hunger. "Taste it, taste it," Georges Clairin kept saying. I tasted it ever so warily and found it excellent.

We got back very very late at night and I found everybody in a state of extreme anxiety. My friends who had come to learn the news had stayed. There was a crowd at my place. I was a little annoyed as I was dead tired. I sent away all these people a little irritably and went up to my bedroom. As I was getting undressed, my maid told me that someone had come several times from the Comédie-Française.

"Oh my God!" I cried out. I was very worried. "Has the play been changed?"

"No, I don't think so," replied the young woman. "But it seems that M. Perrin is furious and that they are all enraged with you. Anyway, here is the letter that was left."

I opened the letter. I was summoned to the director's office on the following day at two o'clock.

When I arrived at Perrin's office at the appointed time, I was received with exaggerated but severe politeness. Then commenced a string of recriminations concerning my whims, my caprices, my eccentricities. He finished his speech by saying that I had to pay a thousand-franc fine for having travelled without the authorization of the administration.

I snorted with laughter. "The balloon incident," I told him, "was not premeditated and I assure you that I will not pay the fine. I do what I please outside the theater and it is none of your business, M. Perrin, as long as it has no negative effect on the performance of my duties! Plus . . . you bore me stiff! . . . I am giving you my resignation. Be content!" I left him contrite and worried.

The next day I sent my written resignation to M. Perrin. A few hours later I was summoned by M. Turquet, Minister of Fine Arts. I refused to go. They sent a mutual friend who told me that M. Perrin had exceeded his brief, that the penalty was lifted and that I should withdraw my resignation; and so it happened.

But the situation was tense. My celebrity had become irritating for my enemies and a little too resounding, I admit, for my friends. But at the time all the acclaim amused me tremendously. I did nothing to attract attention. I was set apart by my rather strange tastes, my thinness, my pallor, my individualistic way of dressing, my disdain for fashion, and my couldn't-care-less attitude. I was not conscious of it. I did not read and never read the newspapers. So I was unaware of everything that was said about me, whether good or bad. Surrounded by a court of male and female worshipers, I lived in my own sunny dream.

All the royalty and celebrities who were guests of France at the Exhibition of 1878 visited me. This procession amused me very much. The Comédie was the first theatrical stop for all these illustrious visitors and Croizette and I performed almost every evening.

I fell quite seriously ill while performing in *Amphitryon* and I was sent to the Côte d'Azur. I stayed there two months. I lived in Menton but I had made my headquarters at Cap Martin. I had had a tent put up on the spot on which the Empress Eugénie later chose to build a magnificent villa. I did not want to see anybody and thought that if I spent all day in a tent far from any town no visitor would hazard the journey. Wrong! One day while I was eating with my little boy, I heard the tinkling bells of two horses that were pulling a carriage suddenly fall silent. The road overhung our tent, which was half hidden under some bushes. Suddenly a voice that sounded familiar, although I could not put a name to it, cried out in heraldic tones, "Is it here that Mme. Sarah Bernhardt lives, *sociétaire* of the Comédie-Française?" We did not move. The question was shouted again. Same silence. But we heard the sound of breaking branches and bushes pushed aside and two yards away from the tent, the voice which had now taken on a mocking tone, started again.

We had been discovered. So I went out, a little irritated. Facing me was a man dressed in a greatcoat of tussore,[5] with a lorgnette strung on a shoulder strap, a grey bowler hat, a red happy face with a horseshoe shaped goatee. I looked in annoyance at this character who was neither distinguished nor coarse, but looked the picture of a social upstart. He took off his hat.

"Mme. Sarah Bernhardt is here?"

"What do you want, sir?"

"Here is my card, Madame . . . " I read "Gambard, Nice, villa de Palmiers." I looked at him nonplussed, and he was even more so when he saw that his name meant nothing to me. He had a foreign accent. "Well, Madame, I have come to ask you to sell me your piece *Après la tempête.*"[6]

I started to laugh. "I'm in the process of negotiating with Susse. They are offering me six thousand francs. If you give me ten, I'll let you have it."

"Perfect!" he said. "Here is ten thousand francs! Do you have something to write with?"

"No, sir."

"Ah, excuse me!" He took out a little writing case in which he had pen and ink. I gave him a receipt and a note to say that he could pick up the piece at my studio in Paris. He took his leave and I heard the jingling bells start up and disappear into the distance.

After this I was often invited to the home of this character, who was one of the petty moguls of Nice.

Chapter XXVI

$\mathscr{W}$e returned shortly afterward to Paris. We were rehearsing a benefit performance for Bressant who was retiring. It was agreed that Mounet-Sully and I would perform one act of the *Othello* by Jean Aicard.[1]

The audience was very well disposed as it always is on such occasions. After the song of Saul I had stretched out on the bed of Desdemona when, suddenly, I heard the audience laugh—quietly at first and then uproariously. Othello had just entered in the darkness, dressed in a shirt and very little else with a lantern in his hand, and was heading for a door hidden under some drapery. An audience, an impersonal mass, will abandon itself without reserve to rather gross behavior like this, when each member of this mass taken individually would be ashamed to have his or her thoughts revealed. The ridicule thrown on this act by the exaggerated pantomime of the actor precluded rehearsals for performance of the play in its entirety, and it was not until twenty long years later that *Othello* was performed in full at the Théâtre-Français. I personally never appeared in it again.

After performing the role of Bérénice in *Mithridate*[2] with success, I took up again my role of the queen in *Ruy Blas*. The play was just as long-running a success as it had been at the Odéon, and the public showered perhaps even more acclaim on me. It was Mounet-Sully who played Ruy Blas. He was wonderful and a hundred times superior to Lafontaine who had played it at the Odéon. Frédéric Febvre's costume was very good and his performance was interesting, but he was nevertheless not as good as Geffroy, who had been the most distinguished and horrifying Don Salluste that one could have imagined.

My relationship with Perrin grew cooler and cooler. He was glad for the sake of the House of my great success. He was overjoyed at the magnificent receipts for *Ruy Blas*. But he would have liked it to have been someone other than I who benefited from all the acclaim. My independence and horror of submission, even feigned, annoyed him prodigiously.

199

One day my manservant came to tell me that an old Englishman was demanding to see me so insistently that he thought he had best come and tell me, in spite of orders.

"Send away this man and let me work." I had just begun a painting of a subject that enthralled me: a little girl holding some palms in her arms on Palm Sunday. The little Italian model who was posing was a ravishing little eight year old girl.

Suddenly she told me, "The Englishman's arguing . . . "

Indeed, I too could hear coming from the antechamber raised voices that were becoming more and more quarrelsome. I went out with my palette in my hand, determined to chase away the intruder. But at the very moment that I opened the door of my studio a tall man approached so close to me that I had to step back, and in this way he found his way into my studio. He had clear hard eyes, silver hair, a well-groomed beard. He apologized very correctly, admired my painting, my studio—so much and so well that I still did not know his name.

When, after ten minutes, I asked him to sit down to tell me the reason for his visit, he started to speak in measured tones and with a heavy accent. "I am Mr. Jarrett, an impresario. I can make your fortune. Do you want to go to America?"

"Never on my life!" I exclaimed vehemently, "Never, never!"

"Oh well, don't get upset. Here's my address. Don't lose it." Then just as he was leaving he said, "Ah! You're going to London with the Comédie-Française—do you want to make yourself lots of money in London?"

"Yes, how?"

"By performing in people's drawing rooms. I could help you make yourself a small fortune."

"Oh, certainly, I would like that if I go to London, but I have not made up my mind."

"So would you like to sign a little contract with me to which we could append a clause?"

I signed a contract with this man who immediately inspired total confidence in me, a confidence in which I was never betrayed.

The Committee and M. Perrin had entered into an agreement with John Hollingshead, the director of the Gaiety Theatre[3] in London. No one had been consulted and I found that a little rude. So when I was made a part of the contract accepted by the Committee and the director I did not say a word.

Perrin, a little worried, took me aside, "What are you brooding about?"

"I'm brooding about this: I don't want to go to London with a status inferior to anybody. I want to be a full *sociétaire*[4] for the whole duration of our contract."

This demand caused great excitement among the Committee. Perrin told me the next day that my proposition had been rejected. "Well, then I won't go to London, that's all. Nothing in my contract compels me to make this journey."

The Committee met again and Got[5] exclaimed, "Let her not come then! She annoys us!"

So it was decided that I would not go to London. But Hollingshead and Mayer, his associate, did not accept this and declared that the contract would be void if Croizette, Coquelin, Mounet-Sully, or I did not come. The agents who had purchased two hundred thousand francs worth of seats in advance refused to accept the deal without our names. Mayer came to see me in deep despair and informed me of what was happening. "We're going to break our contract with the Comédie if you don't come, the whole affair no longer seems possible."

Scared about the consequences of my bad temper, I ran to Perrin and told him that after the consultation I had just had with Mayer I understood that I had unintentionally damaged the interests of the Comédie and of my friends and I declared that I was ready to leave no matter what the conditions. The Committee was in session. Perrin asked me to wait and he came back shortly afterward. Croizette and I had been appointed full *sociétaires*, not only for London, but forever. Each of us had done what we had to do. Perrin was very moved and put out his arms to draw me to him, "Oh, what a good, uncontrollable little creature you are!" We embraced and peace was made between us once again.

But it could not last long. Five days after this reconciliation around nine o'clock in the evening, M. Emile Perrin was announced. I had company to dinner. Nevertheless, I went out to see him in the hall. Handing me a paper he said, "Read that!" and I read in an English paper, the *Times*, the following paragraph, which I translate:

> Comedies at the salon of Mlle. Sarah Bernhardt,
> under the direction of Sir... Benedict.

The repertoire of Mlle. Sarah Bernhardt is composed of comedies, proverbs, playlets, and monologues especially written for her and one or two actors, who are also members of the Comédie-Française. These comedies are performed without scenery or props and adapt themselves, in London as in Paris, to afternoons and evenings in high society. For further details and conditions please contact Mr. Jarrett (secretary of Mlle. Bernhardt) at the Majesty Theatre.

When I read these lines I realized that Jarrett knew I was definitely coming to London and had started his little advertising campaign. I explained it to Perrin very frankly.

"Why should you begrudge me the opportunity to use my evenings to earn money?"

"It's not me, it's the Committee."

"Oh, that beats everything!" I exclaimed. I called my secretary and said to him, "Give me the letter from Delaunay that I gave you to keep yesterday."

"Here it is," he said, taking it from one of his innumerable pockets. Perrin could read:

> Would you like to perform *La Nuit d'Octobre*[6] at Lady Dudley's house on Thursday, June 5? They will give us five thousand francs for the two of us.
>
> > Sincerely,
> > Delaunay

"Can I have this letter?" asked the vexed director.

"No, I don't want to do that. But you can tell Delaunay that I told you of his offer."

For three or four days there was talk of nothing else in Paris, in the newspapers and in discussion, but of the scandalous announcement in the *Times*. The French, who were very little anglicized at that time, were unaware of the customs of England. Finally the uproar irritated me to such a point that I begged Perrin to put a stop to it. The next day the following passage appeared in *Le National* of May 29:

> A lot of noise about nothing. In a friendly discussion it was agreed that beyond the rehearsals and performances of the Comédie-Française each actor was free to use his time as he wished. There is thus absolutely no truth to the allegation that the Comédie-Française is in dispute with Mlle. Sarah Bernhardt. This actress has only laid claim to an absolute right that nobody would dream of denying her, and from which all her colleagues intend to profit equally. The director of the Comédie-Française has simply requested that the *sociétaires* should not perform as a group.

This article emanated from the Comédie and the members of the Committee had benefited from it by making themselves a little advertisement announcing that they too were available for drawing-room performances. The notice was sent to Mayer with the request that he should place it in the English newspapers. I know this from Mayer himself.

Now that all the quarrels were over we began preparations for our departure. I had never made even the smallest journey by sea when the trip to London was arranged for the actors of the Comédie-Française. The wilful ignorance of the French of everything foreign was much more obvious at that time that it is today. So I had had made a very warm coat. I had been told that the crossing was freezing cold, even in the summer, and I believed it. I was presented on all sides with pastilles for seasickness, with painkillers for headaches, with tissue paper to put on my back, with little compress poultices to put on the diaphragm, and with rubber insoles to put in my shoes since, whatever happened, one must not get cold in the feet. Oh, how funny and amusing it all was! And I took everything. I listened to all the recommendations and I believed them all.

But what was the most incredible of all was an enormous but very light chest that appeared on the boat five minutes before we sailed. It was held by a tall young man, who is today a remarkable person with all the medals and honors one could imagine, a colossal fortune, and an overwheening vanity. At that time he was a timid inventor—young, melancholy, and poor. He always had his nose in books on abstract subjects, and he knew nothing of life. He had a great admiration for me, mingled with a little fear. My little court had nicknamed him "the Sausage Roll." He was long, flabby, and colorless, and looked like the filling in a sausage roll.

He approached me with a face even more deadpan than usual as the boat was rocking a little. My departure terrified him and the wind was making him oscillate from left to right. He beckoned me mysteriously. I followed with "my little lady," my friends watching ironically. He opened the chest and took out an enormous lifebelt, which he himself had invented. I was astounded, for although I was a novice at voyages, the idea had not entered my head that there was a danger of shipwreck in the course of a one-hour crossing. Very composedly the Sausage Roll unrolled the lifebelt and put it on to show me how to operate it. Nothing could have looked more foolish than this man, in a top hat and morning coat with his serious and melancholy face, putting on this contraption. Hanging around it were a dozen containers the size of eggs. In eleven of these inflated eggs there was a piece of sugar; in the twelfth there was a tiny little bottle containing ten drops of brandy. In the middle of the belt there was a little pincushion with some pins in it.

"You understand . . . " he said to me, "you fall in the water—splash!—you stay like this," and he crouched down raising and lowering himself to follow the movement of the waves, his two hands in front of him floating on imaginary water, while he stretched his neck like a turtle to hold his head out of the water. "You see, you have been in the water for two hours and you have to restore your strength. So you take a pin and prick an egg. In this way you take your piece of sugar, you eat it, and that's worth as much as half a pound of meat." Throwing the little deflated vessel overboard he plunged into the chest, took out another egg, and attached it to the belt. He had thought of everything.

I was transfixed. Some of my friends had approached hoping for some crazy scheme from the Sausage Roll, but they had not anticipated this one. Mr. Mayer, one of our impresarios, was afraid of a comic story and drove away the crowd. I did not know whether to be angry or to laugh; but a derisive and unfair outburst from one of my friends aroused my pity for poor Sausage Roll. I had a vision of the hours spent researching, designing, and finally making this ridiculous machine. I felt a tenderness for the anxious love that had presided over the birth of this engine of rescue. I held out my hand to poor Sausage Roll and said to him, "Run, the boat is about to sail!" He kissed this friendly hand and fled. I called my manservant. "Please, Claude, as soon as land is out of sight throw the chest and its contents into the sea."

The departure of the boat was accompanied by hurrahs, goodbyes, good luck wishes, upraised arms, waving handkerchiefs, kisses sent at random into the crowd. But what was really wonderful, and an unforgettable spectacle, was our disembarkment at Folkestone. There were thousands of people there and this was the first time that I heard the cry, "Long live Sarah Bernhardt!" I turned to find myself face to face with a pale young man—the ideal head for Hamlet—who gave me a gardenia. Later I would admire him as Forbes Robertson playing Hamlet.[7]

We were passing through the midst of a hedge of proffered flowers and outstretched hands. I saw immediately that I was more favored than the others, which embarrassed me a little, but charmed me at the same time. A colleague, who was near me, and who did not like me said nastily, "Soon they'll be making you a carpet of flowers."

"Here it is!" cried a young man throwing down in front of me an armful of lilies. I stopped in confusion, not daring to walk on these white flowers, but the crowd pressing behind me forced me to go on. I had to crush these poor lilies.

"Hip, hip, hooray for Sarah Bernhardt!" cried out the fiery young man. He was taller by a head than everyone else, his eyes were luminous, his hair was long; he looked like a German student. He was, however, an English poet, one of the greatest of this century, a poet full of genius but—alas!—tormented since and vanquished by folly: it was Oscar Wilde.[8] The crowd responded to his call and we got into the train pursued by cries of "Hip, hip, hooray for Sarah Bernhardt! Hip, hip, hooray for the other French actors!"

When the train stopped at about nine o'clock at Charing Cross, we were more than an hour behind schedule. Sadness took hold of me. The sky was overcast. And I had thought we would be acclaimed again on our arrival in London. I was ready for some more hip, hip, hooray's. There were some people there, a great many people, but nobody seemed to know us. I had seen a fine carpet as we arrived in the station. I thought it was for us. Oh, I was ready for anything, our welcome at Folkestone had gone to my head! But the carpet had just been used by Their Royal Highnesses the Prince and Princess of Wales who had just gone to Paris! This news upset me, even personally annoyed me. I had been told that the whole of London was moved to the quick by the idea of receiving the Comédie-Française and I found London to be very indifferent. The crowd was large, compact, but very cold.

"Why are the Prince and Princess of Wales leaving today?" I asked Mayer.

"Because they have decided to go to Paris."

"Oh! So they will not be at our première?"

"No. The Prince took a box for the season and paid ten thousand francs for it, but it will be occupied by the Duke of Connaught."[9]

I was desperate. I don't know why, but I was desperate. I felt that everything was going badly. A porter led me to my carriage. I crossed London with a heavy heart. Everything seemed black. When I arrived in front of the house at 77 Chester Square I did not want to get out. But the wide-open door showed me a lighted hallway, in which stood all the flowers of the earth in baskets, bouquets, and sprays. I got out and went into the house that I was to inhabit for six weeks. All the branches seemed to be stretching out their flowers to me.

"You have the cards for all these bouquets?" I asked my servant.

"Yes," he replied.

"I put them on the tray, as all the flowers arrived yesterday from Paris, sent by the friends of Madame. There is only this one bouquet which is from here," and he gave me an enormous bouquet. I took the card. It said "Welcome!—Henry Irving."[10]

I made a tour of the house. I found it gloomy. I wanted to go out into the garden, but the damp was penetrating. I went back inside with my teeth chattering and went to sleep with an anguished heart, as though on the eve of a misfortune.

The next day was dedicated to receiving the journalists. I wanted to receive them all together, but Mr. Jarrett was opposed to that. This man was a real genius at publicity but I didn't realize it at the time. He had made me a very fine offer for America and although I had refused he had become a guiding force with me because of his intelligence, his sense of humor, and my own need to be guided in this unfamiliar country. "No," he said, "if you receive them all together they will all be furious, and you will have bad press. You must receive them one after another."

Thirty-seven came that day and Jarrett did not spare me from a single one. He stayed with me and saved the situation every time I said something stupid. I spoke English very badly, some of them spoke French very badly, and Jarrett translated my replies. I remember clearly that all of them said to me first of all, "Well, Mademoiselle, what do you think of London?" I had arrived at nine o'clock in the evening and the first journalist to whom I spoke asked me this question at ten o'clock in the morning. I had pulled aside the curtain when I got up and all I knew of London was Chester Square, that is to say a little square of somber greenery in the middle of which there was a black statue, and on the horizon an ugly church. I could not reply to this question. But Jarrett had foreseen the situation and the next day I learned that I was enthusiastic about the beauty of London and that I was already familiar with a whole pile of monuments, etc. etc. . . .

At about five o'clock the charming Hortense Damain, who was very popular with English high society, came to tell me that the Duchess of *** and Lady R*** would visit me at five-thirty. "Oh stay with me!" I said, "You know how wild I am. I have a feeling that I'll do something stupid." At the appointed time the visitors were announced. This was my first contact with the English aristocracy and I have a charming memory of it. Lady R*** was a perfect beauty and the duchess had a grace, distinction, and kindness that moved me. Lord Dudley came a few minutes later. I knew him very well. He had been introduced to me by Maréchal Canrobert, one of my dearest friends. He asked me if I would ride the next morning. There was a very nice lady's horse for my use. I thanked him, but I wanted to go first to Rotten Row[11] by carriage.

At seven o'clock Hortense Damain came to take me to dinner at the house of Baroness M. of ***. She lived in a pretty house at Princess Gate. There were about twenty people there, including the painter Millet. I had been told that the food was very bad in England: I found the dinner perfect. I had been told that the English were cold and stiff: I found them charming and full of wit. Everybody spoke French very well. I was ashamed of my ignorance of the English language.

After dinner there was music and recitation. I was very touched by the good grace and tact of my hosts who did not ask me to recite any verse. I took great interest in examining the people around me. They were not at all like a typical French group. The young ladies enjoyed themselves in their own right and very sincerely so. They were not there to find husbands. What surprised me a little were the low necklines worn by ladies who were ravaged by time. I discussed it with Hortense Damain. "It's frightful!" I said. "Yes, but it's chic!" She was charming, my friend Damain, but the only thing she knew about was what was "chic." She had sent me the Commandments of Chic a few days after I left Paris.

> You will live at Chester Square.
> You will ride at Rotten Row.
> You will visit the Houses of Parliament.
> You will be seen at garden parties.
> You will return every visit you receive.
> You will reply to every letter.
> You will sign your photographs.
> You will listen to Hortense Damain.
> And you will follow all her advice.

I had laughed at these commandments, but I quickly realized that, teasing aside, she took them seriously. Alas! My poor friend's advice was less than welcome. I hated paying visits, writing, signing photographs, and following advice that I was given. I love receiving visitors, but I hate paying visits. I love receiving letters, reading them, commenting on them, but I hate writing them. I hate going for walks in crowded places, I love deserted roads, and solitary places. I love giving advice, I hate receiving it, and I never immediately follow a good piece of advice that I am given. I have to make an effort of will to recognize the value of the advice and an intellectual effort to be grateful for it; my first reaction is to be annoyed by it.

So I took no notice of the advice of Hortense Damain nor of Jarrett's advice; and I was very wrong for I made many people unhappy. In another country I would have made myself some enemies. During my first visit to London, there were so many invitations I did not reply to, so many charming women whose visits I did not return, so many times that I accepted an invitation to dinner and then did not go, without informing the hosts. It was terrible. And yet I always accept invitations with pleasure, promising myself that I will be on time; but when the time comes I am overtaken by fatigue, by a need to dream, or to fulfill an obligation. Then when I finally make up my mind to go anyway, the time has passed, it is too late to notify the hosts, too late to go, and I am left dissatisfied with myself, with them, with everything.

Chapter XXVII

The talent for hospitality possesses a primitive flavor and an antique grandeur. The English people, in my opinion, are the most hospitable in the world, and they *are* so simply and generously. Once he has opened his door, the Englishman never closes it again. He excuses your faults and accepts your shortcomings. It is thanks to this generous attitude that, in England, I have remained for twenty-five years a beloved and spoiled actress. I was delighted by my first evening in London. I went back home very gay and a fan of the English. I met some friends, Parisians who had just arrived in England, and they were infuriated and exasperated by my enthusiasm. We sat up arguing about it until two o'clock in the morning.

The next day I went to Rotten Row. It was a beautiful day. The whole of Hyde Park seemed scattered with enormous bouquets, by the flowers marvellously grouped by the gardeners and by the clusters of parasols, blue, pink, red, white, yellow, which sheltered pale hats covered with flowers, under which shone the pretty faces of babies and women. On the riding path there was the vertiginous gallop of elegant thoroughbreds, carrying hundreds of fine, supple, and daring Amazons, and there were cavaliers too. Then there were children on large Irish ponies, while other children galloped on Shetland ponies with their long shaggy manes. The hair of the children and the horses' manes lifted in the wind as they rode. The carriage path, holding the middle between the riders and the pedestrians, was plowed by dog carts, barouches, four-in-hands, eight-springs, and very elegant cabs. There were footmen in powdered wigs, horses decorated with flowers, "sportsmen" drivers, and ladies stylishly driving wonderful trotters.

All this elegance, this scent of luxury, all this *joie de vivre*, called up in my mind's eye the evocative memory of our Bois de Boulogne, so elegant, so alive a few years previously, when Napoléon III, nonchalant and smiling, used to drive through it *en daumont*.[1] How pretty our Bois de Boulogne[2] used to be! The officers used to caper about in the avenue des Acacias watched by beautiful socialites! *Joie de vivre* was evident everywhere at that time: love of love enveloped life with infinite charm! I closed my eyes and felt a deep pang of sorrow as the frightful memory of the year 1870 suddenly gripped me. The gentle emperor with the subtle smile had died, vanquished by arms, betrayed by fortune, devastated by grief. Life had regained its intensity in France. But elegance, charm, and luxury were still in mourning. It was barely eight years since the war had cut down our soldiers, ruined our hopes, and humiliated us. Three presidents had already succeeded one another. That little rascal Thiers, with the perverse bourgeois soul, who had worn down his teeth gnawing on all the different régimes—the royalty of Louis-Philippe, the empire of Napoléon III, and the executive power of the French Republic—had hardly thought about raising up our dear Paris, bowed under so much ruin. He had been replaced by Mac-Mahon, a good but insignificant man. Grévy[3] had succeeded him. But Grévy was stingy and found all expense unnecessary, whether for himself, for others, or for the country. Paris remained sad and peeling with the leprosy contracted from the kiss of the inferno of the Commune. Our charming Bois de Boulogne still bore the scars of the wounds inflicted on it by the National Defense, and the avenue des Acacias was still deserted.

I opened my eyes, which were full of tears, and through their mist I saw again the triumphant vitality that surrounded me. I wanted to go home right away for I was performing in the evening for the first time and I felt ill at ease and desperate. People were waiting for me at Chester Square. I did not want to see anybody. I had a cup of tea and went to the Gaiety Theatre where we were going to confront the British public for the first time.

I knew already that I was the Chosen One and that terrified me, for I am what is called a "*traqueuse*," that is to say I suffer from stage fright, terrible stage fright. When I first started on the stage I was shy, but I did not suffer from stage fright. Sometimes I would flush bright red if my eye met that of someone in the audience and I was embarrassed to talk so loudly in front of silent people—that came from my convent education; but I felt no kind of fear.

The first time that I really experienced stage fright was in January, 1869, during the seventh or maybe the eighth performance of *Le Passant*. The success of this little masterpiece had been tremendous, and my interpretation of Zanetto had charmed the audience and especially the students. When I made my entrance on this particular day I was suddenly cheered. I turned toward the imperial box thinking that the emperor had just entered the theater. But no, the box was empty, and I was confronted with the reality that all these cheers were for me. I was seized by a nervous trembling, and a crazy desire to cry stung my eyes.

I was a tremendous success that night. Agar and I had five curtain calls, and, as I was leaving, the students lined up on either side gave me three rounds of applause. Once I was back home I threw myself into the arms of my blind grandmother who lived with me.

"What's the matter, my little one?"

"Grandma, I am lost; they want to make a star out of me and I don't yet have the talent for that. You'll see, they'll throw me down and defeat me with their bravos."

My grandmother took my head and fixed the emptiness of her big clear eyes on my face. "You told me, my little one, that you would be number one in your career, and now that the chance presents itself are you afraid? You seem to be a very bad soldier to me!"

I fought back my tears and promised myself that I would try to support courageously the success that was disturbing my tranquillity, my happy-go-lucky nature, and my "couldn't give a damn" attitude. But from this time onward fear took hold of me, and stage fright made a martyr out of me.

It was in this frame of mind that I got ready for the second act of *Phèdre*, in which I was to appear for the first time in front of an English audience. Three times I put rouge on my cheeks and shadow on my eyes; three times I wiped it all off with a sponge. I found myself ugly. I seemed thinner and shorter. I closed my eyes to listen to my voice. My own personal tuning-fork is the word "*le bal*" which I pronounce low by opening the "a": "*le baaaal*," or high by closing the "a" and emphasizing the "l": "*le balll*." Ah, yes! I could not pronounce "*le bal*" either high or low. My voice was hoarse when I pronounced the low notes and husky in the soprano notes. I wept with rage. Someone came to tell me that the second act of *Phèdre* was about to begin. I went crazy. I did not have my veil. I did not have my rings. My cameo belt was not attached. I murmured:

> *Le voici. Vers mon coeur tout mon sang se retire.*
> *J'oublie, en le voyant . . .* [4]

But the words "*J'oublie*" struck me—what if I forgot what I had to say? As a matter of fact, what did I have to say? I couldn't remember any more. What did I say after "*en le voyant*"? Nobody answered. I frightened everybody with my nervous state. I heard Got murmur, "She's going crazy!"

Mlle. Thénard,[5] who played Oenone, my old nurse, told me, "Calm down, all the English have left for Paris, there are only Belgians left in the theater!"

This ridiculous comment rallied my anxious spirit. "You're stupid!" I told her. "You know very well how frightened I was at Brussels."

"Oh, quite unnecessarily," she replied coldly, "there were only English people present on that day."

It was time to go on stage. I did not have time to reply, but she had altered my state of mind. I had stage fright, but not the kind that paralyses you, rather the kind that makes you crazy. That was bad enough but preferable to the other kind. One overacts, but at least one can do something. The entire theater had applauded my entrance for a few moments. As I bent in a bow I said to myself, "Yes, yes . . . you'll see . . . I'm going to give you my blood . . . my life . . . my soul." When I began my scene, as I was still not in full possession of myself, I started at rather too high a pitch. Impossible to bring it down once started. I was off. Nothing could stop me now.

I suffered, I wept, I implored, I cried out; and it was all real. My suffering was horrible, my tears flowed hot and bitter. I implored Hippolyte for the love that was killing me and the arms I stretched out to Mounet-Sully were the arms of Phèdre, twisted by the cruel desire for an embrace. The divine spirit had possessed me. When the curtain fell, Mounet-Sully picked me up unconscious and carried me to my dressing room. The audience, not realizing what was happening, wanted me to come back for a curtain call. I also wanted to go back to thank the audience for their attentiveness, their goodwill, their emotion. I went back.

This is what John Murray said in *Le Gaulois* of June 5, 1879:

> When Mlle. Bernhardt was called back with loud cheers, exhausted by her efforts and supported by Mounet-Sully, she was given a reception that I believe to be unique in the annals of the theatre in England.

The next day the *Daily Telegraph* finished its wonderful critique with these lines:

> Clearly Mlle. Sarah Bernhardt exerted every nerve and fibre and her passion grew with the excitement of the spectators, for when, after a recall that could not be resisted the curtain drew up, M. Mounet-Sully was seen supporting the exhausted figure of the actress, who had won her triumph only after tremendous physical exertion—and triumph it was, however short and sudden.

The *Standard* finished its article with these words:

The subdued passion, repressed for a time until at length it burst its bonds, and the despairing, heart-broken woman who is revealed to Hippolyte, was shown with so [sic—Translator] vivid reality that a scene of enthusiasm such as is rarely witnessed in a theatre followed the fall of the curtain. Mlle. Sarah Bernhardt in the few minutes that she was upon the stage (and coming on, it must be remembered, to plunge into the middle of a stirring tragedy) yet contrived to make an impression which will not soon be effaced from those who were present.

The *Morning Post* said:

Very brief are the words spoken before Phèdre rushes into the room to commence tremblingly and nervously, with struggles which rend and tear and convulse the system, the secret of her shameful love. As her passion mastered what remained of modesty or reserve in her nature, the woman sprang forward and recoiled again with the movements of a panther, striving, as it seemed to tear from her bosom the heart which stifled her with its unholy longings, until in the end, when terrified at the horror her breathings have provoked in Hippolyte, she strove to pull his sword from its sheath and plunge it in her own breast, she fell back in complete and absolute collapse. This exhibition marvellous in beauty of pose, in febrile force, in intensity, and in purity of delivery, is the more remarkable as the passion had to be reached, so to speak, at a bound, no performance of the first act having roused the actress to the requisite heat. It proves Mlle. Bernhardt worthy of her reputation, and shows what may be expected from her by the public which has eagerly expected her coming.[6]

This first night in London was a definitive one for my career.

Chapter XXVIII

$\mathcal{M}$y violent desire to conquer the English public had overtaxed my strength. I had given everything on the first night. I had not handled myself sufficiently carefully, and in the night I began to vomit blood to such an extent that a doctor was hurriedly sought at the embassy. Dr. Vintras, the chief doctor at the French hospital in London, found me stretched out in my bed drained, and seemingly dead. He was alarmed and demanded that my family be fetched. I signaled to him that there was no point. As I could not speak, a pencil was brought to me and I wrote "Telegraph Dr. Parrot." Vintras stayed with me for part of the night, slipping crushed ice between my lips every five minutes. Finally, around five o'clock in the morning, the vomiting of blood stopped and I went to sleep, thanks to the potion of Dr. Vintras.

The next night I was meant to perform in *L'Etrangère* at the Gaiety Theatre. As it was not a very tiring role, I wanted to perform *"quand même,"*[1] but Dr. Parrot formally opposed this. He had arrived by boat at four o'clock. He had been my doctor for a long time. However, I felt better. My fever had disappeared. I wanted to get up. Parrot was against it. Dr. Vintras and Mr. Mayer, the impresario of the Comédie-Française, were announced. Hollingshead, the director of the Gaiety Theatre, was in his carriage waiting to find out whether or not I would perform in *L'Etrangère*, as advertised. I asked Dr. Parrot to go and join Dr. Vintras in the drawing room, and I ordered that Mr. Mayer be brought into my room. I said to him quickly, "I feel better. I am very weak, but I will perform. Ssh! Not a word here, tell Hollingshead and wait for me in the smoking room; but don't say anything to anybody."

I threw myself out of bed. I dressed in a wink, helped by my chambermaid who had guessed my plan and was much amused by it. Wrapped in my coat and wearing a lace shawl over my head, I went to Mayer in the smoking room and got into the hansom cab with him. "Come to me in an hour," I whispered to my maid.

Amazed, Mayer said, "Where are we going?"

"To the theater, quick, quick!"

The carriage moved off and I explained to him that if I had stayed at the house neither Parrot nor Vintras would ever have let me perform. "Now," I said, "the die is cast. We shall see what happens."

At the theater I hid myself in the director's office to avoid the fury of Dr. Parrot, whom I adored. I felt keenly the wrong that I was doing him—he had so generously responded to my initial appeal—but I could never have made him understand that I really felt better and that by risking my life I was only risking my own property. Half an hour later my chambermaid came to me with a letter from Parrot, full of tender reproaches and furious advice and finishing with a prescription in case of a relapse. He was to sail an hour later, not wanting to come and shake hands with me. But I was sure that we would be friends again on my return.

I got ready to perform in L'Etrangère. Three times I lost consciousness as I got dressed, but I wanted to perform all the same. The opium that I had been given in the potion had left me with rather a heavy head. I went on stage oblivious, charmed by the welcome that I was accorded. I walked in a dream. I could hardly make out my surroundings. I saw the auditorium through a shining haze. My feet glided without effort across the carpet, and the sound of my voice seemed far away, very far away. I was under the wonderful spell that is created by chloroform, morphine, opium, or hashish. The first act went very well. But during the third, when I had to tell the Duchesse de Septmonts (Croizette) about all the misfortunes that I, Mistress Clarkson, had experienced in my life—just as I was about to begin on my interminable account—I forgot everything. Croizette whispered the line to me, but I saw her lips move and heard nothing. So I said calmly to her, "I brought you here, Madame, to tell you of the reasons for my actions . . . but on reflection, I will not tell you them today." Sophie Croizette looked at me in terror, got up, and left the stage, her lips trembling, all the time fixing me with her eyes.

"What's the matter?" she was asked as she fell almost lifeless into an armchair.

"Sarah has gone crazy! I tell you she has gone crazy! She has cut her entire scene with me."

"How's that?"

"She cut out two hundred lines!"

"But why?"

"I don't know. She looks very calm."

This whole conversation, which was recounted to me later, took less time that it takes to write it down. Coquelin was alerted and went on stage to finish the act.

The curtain fell, and I remained confused and desperate about what I had been told. I had noticed nothing and it seemed to me that I had played my role as usual. I was in fact under the control of the opium. There were only a few things left for me to say in the fifth act and I executed them perfectly.

Next day the reviews praised our company highly but the play itself was criticized. I feared for a moment that my involuntary suppression of the big scene in Act III might have contributed to the severity of the press. But no, all the critics had read and reread the play, they discussed its content but made no mention of my error. Only *Le Figaro*, which was at that time badly disposed toward me expressed itself in these terms:

> *Le Figaro*, June 3. *L'Etrangère* is not to the taste of the English, but Mlle. Croizette was enthusiastically applauded along with Coquelin and Febvre; but Mlle. Sarah Bernhardt, still nervous, lost her memory.

The good Johnson knew very well that I was ill. He had come to my house, he had seen Dr. Parrot, he knew that I had performed against doctors' orders to save the Comédie's receipts. However, the English audience had shown me such sympathy that the Comédie had been rather troubled by it and as *Le Figaro* was the mouthpiece of the Théâtre-Français, they had asked Johnson to moderate his praises in my regard. So he did, all the time that we were in London.

I have insisted on recounting this trivial incident about my forgetfulness, which has no importance in itself, to show how wrong authors are, to be preoccupied with character. It is certain that Alexandre Dumas was anxious to demonstrate the rationale for the strange actions of Mistress Clarkson. He created an interesting character, vibrant, integral to the plot, and immediately revealed to the audience in the first act in the words that Mistress Clarkson says to Mme. de Septmonts: "I would be very happy, Madame, if you would pay me a visit. We could talk about one of our friends, M. Gérard, whom I like perhaps as much as you like him, although he does not like me, perhaps, as much as he likes you." That was enough to interest the audience in these two women. It was the eternal struggle of Good and Evil. The combat between Virtue and Vice. But that seemed a bit bourgeois to Dumas, rather old hat, and he wanted to rejuvenate the old theme by trying to orchestrate together the organ and the banjo, with the result that he obtained a horrible cacophony. He created a terrific play, which could perhaps have been beautiful, for his original style, his honesty, and his brutal humor were enough in themselves to rejuvenate old ideas which are, after all, the eternal basis of all tragedies, comedies, novels, paintings, poems and pamphlets: love torn between Vice and Virtue.

No one among the audience at the performance of *L'Etrangère*—and there were as many French as English—no one said, "Hm, something is missing . . . I do not understand this character very well."

I questioned a learned Frenchman, "You didn't see that there was a gap in the third act?"

"No."

"In my big scene with Croizette?"

"No."

"Well, read what I missed."

After reading it, my friend exclaimed, "Well, so much the better! It's boring, it's history, and it's pointless. I understood the character very well without this rambling fable."

Later, when I apologized to Dumas *fils* for cutting the text he said, "Ah, my dear child, when I write a play I think it's good, when I see it performed I think it's stupid, and when it is told to me I think it's perfect, because one always forgets the half of it!"

The performances of the Comédie-Française always attracted a large audience to the Gaiety Theatre, and I remained the favorite. I say this here with pride, but without vanity. I was very happy and grateful for my success, but my colleagues begrudged me it, and war started tacitly and treacherously.

Mr. Jarrett, my adviser and agent, had assured me that I would be able to sell some of my work, whether it be painting or sculpture. So I had brought with me six pieces of sculpture and ten paintings and I held an exhibition in Piccadilly. I sent out invitations—about a hundred of them. His Royal Highness, the Prince of Wales, told me that he would be coming with the Princess. All the top English aristocracy and all the celebrities of London came to this opening. I had sent out a hundred invitations and twelve hundred people came. I was delighted, I enjoyed myself tremendously.

Mr. Gladstone[2] did me the great honor of talking with me for more than ten minutes. This man of genius talked about everything with a particular grace. He asked for my opinion on the attacks that some clergy were making against the Comédie-Française and against the damnable profession of acting. I replied that our art was just as profitable to morality as the sermon of a Catholic or Protestant preacher.

"But explain to me, Mademoiselle, what is the moral lesson that one might draw from *Phèdre*?"

"Oh, Mr. Gladstone, you surprise me a little! As *Phèdre* is an ancient tragedy the customs and morality arise from a different point of view from our own and from the morality of our society. However, in the play there is the punishment of the old nurse Oenone, who commits the atrocious crime of accusing an innocent person. The love of Phèdre is excused by the fatality that weighs on the family and falls unmercifully upon her. Today this fatality would be called atavism, for Phèdre is the daughter of Minos and Pasiphae. As for Thésée, his arbitrary and monstrous verdict without appeal is punished by the death of the son he loves so much, the only and last hope of his life. One should never create an irreparable situation!"

"Ah!" the great man said gravely, "You're against the death penalty?"

"Yes, Mr. Gladstone."

"You are right, Mademoiselle."

Frederick Leighton[3] came to join us and very kindly paid me some compliments on my painting representing a girl carrying palms. This painting was bought by Prince Leopold.

My little exhibition was very successful and I had no doubt that it would be the cause of a lot of fuss and cowardly attacks, and that it would bring about my definitive break with the Comédie-Française. I had no pretentions as a painter or sculptor. I exhibited my work in order to sell it, because I wanted to buy two lion cubs. I did not have enough money to buy them. I sold my paintings for what they were worth, which is to say at very modest prices.

An English lady, Lady H***, bought my group entitled *Après la tempête*. This group was a reduction of the large scene that I had exhibited two years earlier at the Salon de Paris and had sold. I wanted to sell it for four thousand francs, but Lady H*** sent me ten thousand, with such a delightful note that I permit myself to reproduce it here.

Do me the honor, Madame, of accepting the enclosed four hundred pounds for your wonderful painting *Après la tempête*, and do me the honor of coming to dine with me. After dinner you will choose yourself the place where it will be best lit.

Ethel H.

I received this on a Tuesday. I was performing in *Zaïre* in the evening, but I had no performance on Wednesday, Thursday, or Friday. I had enough money to buy my lions. Without saying anything to anyone at the theater, I slipped off to Liverpool the next day. I knew that there was a big zoo there called the Cross Zoo and that I would find some lions there.

The journey was very amusing. Although I was traveling incognito I was recognized throughout the journey and I was pampered and cosseted. Three male friends accompanied me. It was a real adventure. I knew that I could not possibly be neglecting my duties for the Comédie because I was not to perform until Saturday and it was only Wednesday. We left at ten-thirty in the morning and arrived at Liverpool at two-thirty. We went straight to Cross's house.

It was impossible to find an entrance to the house. We asked a shopkeeper on the corner. He pointed to a little door that we had already opened and closed twice, hardly believing that that was the entrance. I caught a glimpse of a large ironwork gate through which one could see a large courtyard. We found ourselves in front of a tiny little door opening into a tiny little bare room, where a tiny little man was standing.

"Mr. Cross?"

"That's me."

"I would like to buy some lions."

He started to laugh. "So, it's true, Mademoiselle, you like animals as much as that? I went to London last week to see the Comédie-Française perform, and I saw you in *Hernani*."

"But that's not how you discovered I like animals?"

"No. A man who sells dogs in St. Andrews Street told me that you had bought two dogs from him and that, if it had not been for a gentleman who was with you, you would have bought five." He said all this in very bad French but with a lot of humor.

"Well, Mr. Cross, today I want two lions."

"I'll show you what I have."

We went out into the courtyard where the animals were. Magnificent beasts! Two superb African lions with shining coat, and powerful tails sweeping the air. They had just arrived. They were still in full health and full of the courage to rebel. They did not know the spirit of resignation, which is the stigma that dominates domesticated creatures.

"Oh, Mr. Cross, those are too big. I want cubs."

"I don't have any, Mademoiselle."

"Well, show me all your animals then!"

I saw the tigers, the leopards, the jackals, the cheetahs, the pumas, and stopped in front of the elephants. I adore elephants! But I would have liked a dwarf elephant. This is a persistent dream of mine. Perhaps it will be realized some day. Cross did not have any, so I bought a cheetah. He was very young and amusing, he looked like a medieval gargoyle. I bought a completely white wolfhound with a thickset coat, fiery eyes, and teeth as sharp as a lance. He was frightening to look at. Mr. Cross made me a present of six miniature chameleons that looked like lizards, and gave me one other wonderful chameleon, a prehistoric animal with an air of the fabulous, a real Chinese trinket who changed his colors through the spectrum from pale green to black-bronze, svelte and elongated like a lily leaf and then suddenly inflated and squat like a toad. His bulbous eyes, like those of a lobster, functioned separately from one another. He could look forward with his right eye and backward with his left. I was immediately delighted and enthused with this present. I called my chameleon "Cross-çi, Cross-ça" in honor and appreciation of Cross.

We went back to London with the cheetah in a cage, the wolfhound on a leash, my six miniature chameleons in a box, and "Cross-çi, Cross-ça" on my shoulder on a gold chain that we had just bought at a jeweller's. I had not found a lion, but I was content.

My staff was less so. There were already three dogs in the house: Minuccio whom I had brought with me from Paris, and Bull and Fly bought in London. Then there were also Bizibouzou, my parrot, and my monkey Darwin. The intrusion of these new guests provoked shrieks from Mme. Guérard. My butler hesitated to approach the wolfhound. It was in vain that I assured everyone that the cheetah was not dangerous, nobody wanted to open the cage, which had been carried into the garden. I asked for a hammer and some pliers to prise open the nailed door, which was holding the poor cheetah prisoner. Seeing this, my servants decided to open it. Mme. Guérard and the female domestics watched from the windows. The door flew open and the cheetah, overjoyed, bounded out like a tiger from its cage, drunk with liberty, boxing at the trees, and aiming straight for the dogs who began to howl with terror; there were four of them however. The parrot shrieked stridently with excitement and the monkey shook its cage and let out some ear-splitting squeals.

This concert in the silent square had a prodigious effect. All the windows opened, and above the wall of my garden more than twenty heads appeared, curious, trembling, furious. Hysterical laughter took hold of me, my friends Louise Abbéma,[4] the painter Nittis, who had come to visit me, and Gustave Doré, who had been waiting for me for two hours. Georges Deschamps, a talented amateur musician, tried to note down this Hoffmannesque symphony, while my friend Georges Clairin, his back shaking with laughter, sketched this unforgettable scene.

The next day in London the talk was all of the row at 77 Chester Square, and it grew to such proportions that our *doyen*, M. Got, came to ask me not to create a scandal which would reflect on the Comédie-

Française. I listened to him in silence and then I took his hand and said, "Come, I am going to show you the scandal." I led him into the garden, followed by my visitors and friends. "Release the cheetah!" I cried, standing on the steps like a captain of his vessel crying, "Take in the reefs!" The cheetah was released and the same mad scene of the day before took place again. "You see, *doyen*, this is my row."

"You're crazy!" he said kissing me, "But it's incredibly funny," and he laughed till he cried when he saw the heads appear over the wall.

However the hostilities continued, with the gossip passed on from one mouth to another, from one environment to another, just as much in the French press as in the English press. In spite of my good humor and my contempt for rumors, I was beginning to feel irritated. Injustice has always deeply outraged me and Injustice was indulging herself to her heart's content. I could do nothing that was not immediately judged and criticized.

One day when I was complaining to Madeleine Brohan, whom I loved, the adorable actress took my head and looked in my eyes and said, "My poor darling, you can't help it. You are original without trying. You have a formidable mane of rebellious naturally curly hair, your slimness is extreme, your vocal chords are a natural harp. All of this makes of you a being apart, which is a crime against mediocrity. So much for your physique. As for your morality, you cannot conceal your thoughts, you cannot bow down, you accept no compromise, you submit to no hypocrisy—all of which is a crime against society. So how do you expect not to arouse jealousy, cause offense, excite rancor? If you despair under attacks you'll be lost, for you'll be without the strength to fight. If this should happen, I advise you to brush your hair and put oil on it to make it as flat as the Corsican's. But, on second thoughts, no—Napoléon's hair was so flat it was original! Let's see ... flat like Prudhon's hair, that will be no risk (Prudhon was an actor with the Comédie-Française).[5] I also advise you," she continued, "to put on some weight and to make your voice a little rougher. Then you will offend nobody. But if you want to stay yourself, my darling, be prepared to mount a little pedestal built of calumny, gossip, injustice, adulation, flattery, lies, and truth. Just make sure, once you are up there, that you cement yourself well with your talent, your work, and your kindness. Then all the spiteful people who, without meaning to, furnished the building materials for the edifice, will try to kick it down. But if you so wish, they will be powerless, and this is what I hope for you, my dear Sarah, for you are thirsty for Glory. I personally don't understand that, I like only shade and repose."

I looked at her with envy. She was so beautiful with her moist eyes, her face with its pure and reposeful lines, and her tired smile. I asked myself anxiously if happiness resided in this tranquillity and disdain for all things. I gently questioned her to try to find out. She told me that the theater bored her, that she had had so many disappointments. Her marriage? She was still shuddering over it. Motherhood gave her nothing but sorrow. Love had left her with a broken heart and a crippled body. Her beautiful eyes were in danger of going blind. Her legs were swollen and only carried her reluctantly. She told me all this in the same calm, slightly tired, tone. What had just now charmed me now chilled me, for her hatred of movement was caused by her weak eyes and legs, and her love of the shade was only the necessary treatment for wounds already received in life.

Love of life took hold of me more violently than ever. I thanked my beautiful friend and benefited from her advice. For, from this day, I armed myself for the struggle, preferring to die in combat rather than to perish full of regret for what I had missed in life. I no longer wanted to cry over the insults hurled at me. I would no longer suffer from injustice. I took it upon myself to mount my own defense. I did not have to wait long for an opportunity to do so.

We were performing *L'Etrangère* for a second time (June 24, 1879, as a matinée). The day before I had informed Mayer that I was not well and as I was also performing *Hernani* in the evening, I asked him to change the play in the afternoon if possible. But the revenue from the ticket sales amounted to more than four hundred pounds, and the Comédie would not hear of it. "Well," said Got to Mayer, "we'll find a substitute for Sarah Bernhardt if she cannot perform. There are Croizette, Madeleine Brohan, Coquelin, Febvre, and I, in the play, and, goddamn it, we are certainly together the equal of Mlle. Bernhardt!" Coquelin was given the job of asking Lloyd to substitute for me, for she had already played the role at the Comédie when I was ill. But Lloyd was afraid and refused. The play was changed and *Le Tartuffe*[6] was put on instead of *L'Etrangère*. But the audience, almost in its entirety, asked for their money back, and the takings which should have been five hundred pounds, were only eighty-four.

This brought about a great surge of rancor and jealousy against me. The whole Comédie (especially the men, except for one, M. Worms) mounted a frontal attack against me. Francisque Sarcey, transformed into a drum-major, beat the rhythm, his formidable pen in hand. The craziest inventions, the most stupid calumnies, the most odious lies, took flight like a cloud of wild ducks coming down to land in all the enemy publications. They said there that I could be seen wearing men's clothes for a shilling, that I smoked large cigars, leaning on the balustrade of my house, that when I performed in playlets at social evenings my chambermaid acted as my respondent, that I fenced in my garden dressed as a white pierrot, that I was taking boxing lessons and had knocked out two of my unfortunate teacher's teeth!

Some of my friends advised me to pay no attention to these insults, saying that the public would not believe them. But they were wrong. The public loves to believe what is bad. It is more amusing than the good, and I had proof that the English public was beginning to believe what the French newspapers said. I received a letter from a tailor asking me to wear one of his suits when I dressed as a man, and saying that not only would he not charge me for it, but he would give me a hundred pounds if I would wear it. This man was a coarse character, but he was sincere. I received several boxes of cigars, and boxing teachers offered me their services at no charge. All of this irritated me to such a degree that I resolved to put an end to it. It was an article by Albert Wolff in *Le Figaro* that made me decide to take measures to stop those who were hounding me. Here is the response that I sent following the article that appeared in *Le Figaro* on June 27, 1879:

Albert Wolff, *Le Figaro*, Paris

And you too, my dear M. Wolff, believe such crazy lies? Who could have informed you so badly? Yes, you are my friend, since, in spite of all the infamy that has been passed onto you, you still have some kindness. Well, I give you my word of honor that I have never dressed as a man here in London! I did not even bring my sculptor's suit. I formally deny this allegation. I have only been once to the little exhibition that I held, once only, and it was a day on which I had issued only private invitations for the opening. So nobody paid a shilling to see me. I perform privately at social gatherings, that is true. But you do not realize that I am one of the lowest-paid *sociétaires* at the Comédie-Française. I therefore have the right to make up the difference a little bit.

I am exhibiting ten paintings and eight pieces of sculpture. That is true. But as I brought them in order to sell them, I have to exhibit them.

As far as respect due to the House of Molière is concerned, dear M. Wolff, I maintain that I have this more than anybody as *I* would never be capable of inventing such calumnies in order to kill one of its standard-bearers.

Now, if the foolish things that are being said about me have made Parisians tire of me, and if they are decided to give me a poor welcome on my return, since I do not want to provide anyone with an excuse for base behavior I shall give my resignation to the Comédie-Française. If the London public is tired of all this noise and wants to turn its kindness into spite, I beg the Comédie to allow me to leave England to save it the misery of seeing a *sociétaire* whistled and booed.

I am sending you this letter by cable. The esteem in which I hold public opinion gives me the right to do this foolish thing and I beg you, M. Wolff, to accord the same honor to my letter as you have done to the calumny of my enemies.

Kind regards,
Sarah Bernhardt

This letter caused a lot of ink to flow. I was generally acknowledged as being in the right, while I was also treated as a spoiled child. The Comédie became a little kinder. Perrin wrote me an affectionate letter, asking me to give up any plan to leave the Comédie. The women acted very friendly. Croizette came to see me and took me in her arms saying, "You won't do that, will you, my mad darling? You're not seriously going to send in your resignation? In any case, they would not accept it, I can assure you!" Mounet-Sully talked to me about art and morality. His whole conversation was imbued with Protestantism. There were several Protestant ministers in his family and he was unconsciously influenced by them. Delaunay, nicknamed "Father Outspokenness," came to tell me solemnly of the bad impression made by my letter. He told me that the Comédie-Française was a ministry in which there was a minister, a secretary, the deputies, and the employees, and that each had to obey the regulations and contribute either his talent or his work, and so on and so forth. I saw Coquelin in the evening at the theater. He came to me with outstretched hands. "You know that I won't praise you for what you've rushed into; fortunately we can change your mind. When one has the happiness and honor of being at the Comédie-Française, one must stay there till the end of one's career." Frédéric Febvre observed to me that I should stay at the Comédie because it was accumulating some savings for me, which I was incapable of doing myself. "Believe me," he said, "when you're at the Comédie, you must stay there—it guarantees you've got something to live on later on."

Finally Got, our *doyen*, came to see me. "You know what that's called when you give your resignation?"

"No."

"Deserting!"

"You're mistaken, I'm not deserting. I'm changing barracks!" I replied.

And there were others, and they each gave me advice according to their personality: Mounet as an inspired believer, Delaunay with the soul of a bureaucrat, Coquelin as a politician, condemning someone else's idea only to preach it later for his own profit, Febvre as a lover of respectability, Got as a grumbling old egotist, recognizing only orders and advancement through the hierarchy. Worms said to me in his melancholy way, "Are people any better elsewhere?" Worms had the dreamiest soul and the most frank personality of our illustrious company. I loved him.

We were about to return to Paris, and I did not want to think about anything for a while. I hesitated, and put off until later a final decision. The uproar around me—the good spoken in my favor and the bad written against me—all of that had created a warlike atmosphere in our artistic world. We were about to return to Paris. Some of my friends were worried about the reception that I would be given. In its sweet ignorance the public imagines that the noise surrounding famous artists is consciously caused by the latter; and in its irritation at seeing the same name constantly brought up on every occasion, it declares that the actor who is being attacked or spoiled is infatuated with publicity. Alas, three times alas! In fact, we are *victims* of publicity. Those who taste the joys and sadness of celebrity when they have passed the age of forty know how to defend themselves. They know the blind corners and the potholes hidden under the flowers, and they know how to bridle this monster of publicity, an octopus with innumerable tentacles which throws out its viscous arms to the left and right, forward and backward, picking up with its thousand little suction pumps whatever gossip, calumny, or praise lies there, and then vomiting it out in a stream of black bile. But those who are confronted with publicity at the age of twenty have no idea what to do.

I remember that the first time a reporter came to my home I strutted like a cock. I was seventeen. I had played a little Duc de Richelieu[7] in society drawing rooms with tremendous success. This gentleman came to find me at my mother's house and asked me this, and that, and then this again. I replied, talked . . . I was overcome with pride and emotion. He took notes. I looked at Mama. I felt as though I was growing taller. I had to kiss Mama in order to compose my expression. I hid my face in her neck to conceal my joy. Finally this gentleman got up, gave me his hand, and left. I was jumping up and down in the room and turning in circles saying, "*Trois petits pâtés, ma chemise brûle,*"[8] when all of a sudden the door opened and the gentleman said to Mama, "Ah! Madame, I forgot. Here is the little bill for the magazine subscription. It's nothing, just sixteen francs a year." Mama did not understand immediately. I stood there, open-mouthed, unable to swallow my "*petits pâtés.*" Mama paid the sixteen francs, and gently stroked my hair with pity as I cried.

Since then I have been at the mercy of the monster, bound hand and foot. And yet I have been, and still am, accused of loving publicity. My first title to publicity was my extraordinary slimness and fragile health. I had hardly made my début when epigrams, puns, and caricatures began to appear in great quantities. Was it really to gain publicity that I was so slim, small, and weak? That I spent six months in bed, laid low by illness? My name became famous before I was really so myself. One day we were performing in a première, at the Odéon, of *Mademoiselle Aïssé*. Flaubert,[9] a close friend of Louis Bouilhet, the author of the play, introduced an attaché from the English embassy. "Oh! I have known you for a long time, Mademoiselle! You are the little stick with a sponge on top!" There had in fact appeared such a caricature of me which had been the joy of mindless people.

At this time I was still a child and I did not suffer over anything or concern myself with anything. In any case, I had been condemned by the doctors. So it was all the same to me. But the doctors were wrong, and twenty years later I would have to do battle with this monster.

Chapter XXIX

The return of the Comédie to its home was an event, but rather a subdued one. Our departure from Paris had been noisy, gay, and public. Our return was clandestine for many: a sad one for those actors who had been unappreciated and an angry one for the failures.

I had not been at home for an hour when our director, Perrin, was announced. He started to reproach me gently for being so careless about my health and he said that I was creating too much of an uproar around myself.

"But," I exclaimed, "is it my fault if I am too thin, if I have too much hair, if it is too frizzy, and if I don't think like other people? Imagine if I took arsenic for a month to blow me up like a barrel, if I shaved my head like an Arab, and if I said yes to everything you say. People would still say that I did it for the publicity."

"But, my dear child," replied Perrin, "there are people neither fat nor thin nor shaved nor hairy who say both yes and no."

I was struck dumb by his reasonableness. I was confronted with the "because" that went with all the "why's" that I had asked for so many years. I was not average; I was made up of "too much" and "too little" and I felt that there was nothing I could do about that. I admitted it to Perrin, and told him he was right. He took advantage of my docility to preach to me, and, finally, to advise me not to appear at the return ceremony at the Comédie-Française. He was afraid of a cabal against me. Feelings were running high, rightly or wrongly—probably a bit of both he said, with the air of breeding and courtesy that he always had. I listened to him without interrupting him, which embarrassed him a little, for Perrin was a quibbler, not an orator.

When he had finished I said, "You have said too many things that excite me, dear M. Perrin. I love a battle. I will appear at the ceremony. Look, I have already been warned. Here are three anonymous letters. Read this one, it's the prettiest!"

He unfolded the amber perfumed paper and read:

229

My poor skeleton, you would do well not to show your horrible Jewish nose at the ceremony the day after tomorrow. I
am afraid that it might serve as a target for all the apples that
we are cooking for you in your good city of Paris. Spread a
rumor that you have been spitting up blood, and stay in bed
to reflect on the consequences of extreme publicity.

A SUBSCRIBER

Perrin pushed the letter away in disgust.

"And here are two others," I told him, "but they are too vulgar, I
will spare you them. I will go to the ceremony."

"Fine! We are rehearsing tomorrow," said Perrin, "will you be there?"

"I'll be there."

The next day at the rehearsal the actors were not very eager to
come onstage to bow or curtsey with me. I must say that they all did it,
nevertheless, with good grace. However, I declared that I would break
the rule and go on alone, because I wanted to be subjected alone to the
ill will and the cabal.

The theater was as full as could be. When the curtain went up the
ceremony started with cheering from the audience. The audience was
happy to see their beloved actors. They went forward two at a time, one
going off to the left, the other to the right, holding the palm or the
crown to decorate the bust of Molière.

When my turn came I went forward alone. I was conscious of
being pale and I was determined to conquer. I advanced slowly toward
the footlights and, instead of curtseying like my colleagues, I remained
standing, looking straight into all the eyes, which converged on me.
War had been declared. I did not want to provoke it, but neither did
I want to flee from it. I waited a second, I could feel the theater trembling with tension. Then, suddenly, uplifted by a feeling of tender
generosity, the audience broke out into a fanfare of bravos and cheers.
The audience so loved and so loving was inebriated with joy. This was
certainly one of the finest triumphs of my career.

Some actors were very happy, especially the women, for this is a
notable thing about our art: the men are jealous of the women much
more than the women are jealous of each other. I have encountered
many enemies among male actors, and very few among actresses. I
think that acting is essentially a feminine art. Indeed, to make up one's
face, hide one's true feelings, try to please, wish to attract attention,
these are the faults of which women are often accused, and for which
they are forgiven. These same faults are odious in a man.

And yet the male actor has to make himself as attractive as possible, whether it be by means of makeup, fake beards or toupees. If he

is a republican, he must uphold with warmth and conviction royalist theories, and if he is conservative, anarchist theories, if such is the wish of the playwright. Poor Maubant at the Théâtre-Français was an extreme radical, and yet his stature and good looks condemned him to play the parts of kings, emperors, and tyrants, and throughout rehearsals one would hear Charlemagne or Caesar cursing tyrants and conquerors and demanding the harshest punishments for them. I reveled to see the struggle between the man and the actor.

Perhaps the perpetual suppression of himself gives the actor a more feminine nature. In any case, it is certainly true that the male actor is jealous of the actress. The courtesy of the well-bred man evaporates in front of the footlights. The actor, who would help a woman in trouble in private life, will pick a quarrel with her on stage. He will risk his life to save her from danger by road, rail, or sea, but on the planks of the stage he will do nothing to save her from embarrassment if she forgets her lines, or will willingly push her a little further if she makes a false step. I am perhaps exaggerating a little, but not as much as one might think.

I have performed with famous actors who have done me bad turns. On the other hand, some of them are wonderful people, remaining more men than actors on-stage: Pierre Berton,[1] Worms, and Guitry[2] are and will remain for the actress the archetype of friendly and protective courtesy. I have performed in many plays with each of them and suffering from stage fright as I do, I felt at ease with them. I knew that they were highly intelligent, sympathetic toward this condition, and alert to the nervousness that it produced in me.

Pierre Berton and Worms, both great, great, actors retired from the stage at their physical and artistic prime—Pierre Berton to devote himself to literature, Worms I don't know why . . . as for Guitry, by far the youngest, he is the greatest actor on the French stage, for he is both a very good actor and an artist at the same time, which is very rare. I know very few actors in France or abroad who combine these two qualities. Henry Irving is a wonderful artist, but not an actor. Coquelin is a wonderful actor but not an artist. Mounet-Sully has genius, which he puts in service sometimes to the artist and sometimes to the actor, but, on the other hand, he has some tendencies toward hyperbole as an artist and actor which grate on lovers of the Beautiful and the True.

Bartet[3] is a perfect actress with a very delicate artistic sense. Réjane, the most actressy of the actresses, is an artist when she wants to be. Eleonora Duse[4] is more of an actress than an artist. She walks in the tracks left by others. She does not imitate them, to be sure, since she plants flowers where there were trees, and trees where there were flowers, but no personality emerges from her art that can be identified with her name. She has not created a being, a vision, that will evoke her memory. She puts on the gloves of others, but inside out, and she does so with infinite grace and nonchalance. She is a great, very great, actress, but she is not a great artist. Novelli is an actor of the old school in which one paid little attention to the artistic side. He is perfect at laughter and tears. Beatrice Patrick-Campbell is above all an artist and her talent is made up of charm and thoughtfulness. She detests the beaten track. She wants to create, and she creates. Antoine is often betrayed by his methods, for his voice is somber and his appearance is a little ordinary, and he also often leaves something to be desired as an actor. But he is always an extraordinary artist and our art owes a great deal to him in its evolution towards truth; and he too is not jealous of actresses.

Chapter XXX

The days that followed this return of the Comédie to its home were very tense ones for me. Our director wanted to curb me, and to do that he made me suffer a thousand little pinpricks, which were more painful for someone of my nature than blows with a knife. (At least this is what I think, never having experienced any!) I became ill, irritable, and in a bad mood about everything. Normally so gay, I became melancholy. My health, which was always fragile, was more and more threatened by this situation.

Perrin gave me the role of the Adventuress. I did not like this role, I hated the play, and I thought the poetry of *L'Aventurière* was bad, very bad. As I am not good at dissimulating, I said this openly in a fit of temper to Emile Augier. He took his revenge for this in a rude way at the first opportunity that presented itself. This opportunity was my definitive break with the Comédie-Française, the day after the first performance of *L'Aventurière*, which took place on Saturday, April 17, 1880.

I was not ready to play this role. I had been very sick and the proof is in this letter, which I wrote to M. Perrin on April 14, 1880:

I am sorry M. Perrin, but my throat is so sore that I cannot speak and am obliged to stay in bed. Please excuse me. It was at the blessed Trocadéro on Sunday that I caught cold. I am very worried as I know that this puts you in a spot. No matter what I will be ready for Saturday. A thousand apologies and kind regards.

Sarah Bernhardt

I was in fact ready to perform as I had cured my sore throat. But I had not been able to rehearse for three days as I had not been able to speak; I had not been able to try on my costumes as I could not get out of bed. I went on the Friday to ask Perrin to put off until the following week the performance of *L'Aventurière*. He told me that that was impossible, the reservations had been made and the play had to be performed on that coming Tuesday, the season ticket day. I allowed myself to be persuaded, trusting in my star. "I'll manage 'no matter what,' " I told myself.

But I did not manage, or rather I managed very badly. My costume was a failure and did not suit me. I, who was constantly criticized for being too thin, looked like an English teapot. My voice was still slightly hoarse, which disturbed me a little. I performed very badly in the first part of the play and better in the second. During a violent scene I was standing with my two hands on a table on which there was a lighted candle. There were shouts in the theater because my hair was close to the flame. The next day one of the papers said that, as I was aware of having performed badly, I had wanted to set fire to my hair so as to put an end to the performance by bowing out completely. It was the most stupid allegation imaginable.

The reviews were not good and the reviews were right. I had been inferior, ugly, and in a bad mood, but I thought that they were lacking in courtesy and kindness toward me. Auguste Vitu in *Le Figaro* of April 18, 1880, finished his review with this sentence: "The new Clorinde (the Adventuress) moved during the last two acts with bodily gestures that would seem, most unfortunately, to have been borrowed from big Virginie in *L'Assommoir*[1] and introduced into the Comédie-Française." The only fault that I have never had and could never have is that of vulgarity. It was an unjust criticism and one deliberately made to insult me. Besides, Vitu was not one of my friends.

I realized from this way of attacking me that little hatreds were raising their heads like rattlesnakes. I had been aware for a long time of the venomous low life that slithered underneath my flowers and laurels. Sometimes I heard their tails rattling off-stage. I wanted to give myself the joy of hearing them sound all together, so I threw my laurels and flowers to the winds. I broke off my contract with the Comédie-Française, and in so doing I also severed my connection with Paris.

I locked myself up all morning and after a thousand and one discussions with myself I resolved to send my resignation to the Comédie-Française. So I wrote this letter to M. Perrin, dated April 18, 1880:

Dear Sir,

You forced me to perform when I was not ready. You allowed me only eight rehearsals on the stage, and the play was only rehearsed three times in its entirety. I could not wish to perform in such circumstances. But you absolutely demanded it.

What I foresaw came to pass. The consequences of my performance have surpassed even my predictions. A critic has claimed that I performed Virginie in *L'Assommoir* rather than Doña Clorinde in *L'Aventurière*. May Zola and Emile Augier forgive me. It is my first failure with the Comédie-Française, it will also be my last. I warned you on the day of the general rehearsal, but you carried on regardless. I abide by my word. By the time you receive this letter I will have left Paris.

> Yours faithfully,
> Sarah Bernhardt

So that this resignation could not be discussed by the Committee, I sent a copy of the letter to the newspapers *Le Figaro* and *Le Gaulois*, where it appeared as Perrin received it.

Having decided not to let myself be influenced, I left immediately with my chambermaid for Le Havre. I had given orders that nobody should know where I was, and I spent the evening of my arrival in the strictest incognito. But by the next morning people had recognized me and telegraphed Paris. I was assailed by reporters. I fled in the direction of La Hève where I stayed the whole day, stretched out on the shingle, in spite of the cold rain which fell unceasingly. I went back to the Hotel Frascati feeling frozen. That night I had a fever so violent that Dr. Gilbert had to be called. Mme. Guérard, called by my panicked chambermaid, came to stay with me and for two days I had a high temperature. During this time the newspapers continued to spill torrents of ink about me. This ink changed into gall and I was accused of the worst misdeeds.

The Comédie had a sherriff knock on my door at the avenue de Villiers. This man declared that having knocked on my door three times and having received no response, he had left a copy of a summons, etc. etc. He was lying. There were living at my house my son and his tutor, my manservant who was the husband of my chambermaid, my butler, the cook, the cook's help, the second chambermaid, and five dogs. But it was pointless to argue against the word of this man, who represented the Law. According to its regulations the Comédie had to give me three warnings. They were not issued, but nevertheless a suit was filed against me. My cause was lost from the start.

Maître Allou, lawyer for the Comédie-Française, invented some spiteful little stories. He took pleasure in making me look ever so slightly ridiculous. He had an impressive file of letters from me to Perrin, letters that had all been written either in a moment of tenderness or anger. Perrin had kept all my letters, even the shortest notes. I had not kept any of his, and the few letters from Perrin to me that had been published had been provided by Perrin himself, after he had had them recorded in his copy book. Of course, he had only released those which would give the public an impression of his paternal kindness in my regard etc.

The suit of Maître Allou was very successful. He sued for three hundred thousand francs in damages and interest, plus the confiscation—to the profit of the Comédie—of forty-three thousand francs that it owed me. My lawyer was Maître Barboux, a close friend of Perrin. He defended me lamely. I was ordered to pay a penalty of one hundred thousand francs to the Comédie-Française, plus the forty-three thousand francs that I had in trust with the administration.

I must say that I hardly paid any attention to the suit.

Three days after my resignation, Jarrett appeared. For the third time he proposed a contract to tour America. This time I listened to his propositions. We had never discussed figures and this is what he proposed: five thousand francs for each performance and half of the ticket sales beyond fifteen thousand francs; that is to say that on a day when the receipts reached twenty thousand francs I would make seven thousand five hundred francs. In addition, a thousand francs a week for my hotel expenses, a special train for my travels containing a bedroom, a drawing room with a piano, four beds for my staff, and two chefs to cook for me on the road. Mr. Jarrett would make ten percent of all my profits. I accepted everything. I was eager to leave Paris.

Jarrett immediately sent a telegram to Mr. Abbey, the great American impresario, and he arrived thirteen days later. I signed the contract drawn up by Jarrett and through him discussed every clause with the American director. In exchange for the contract I was paid a hundred thousand francs in advance for the expenses connected with departure.

I was to perform in eight plays: *Hernani, Phèdre, Adrienne Lecouvreur, Froufrou,*[2] *La Dame aux camélias, Le Sphinx, L'Etrangère, La Princesse George.*[3] I ordered twenty-five outfits for city wear from Laferrière, who was my designer at the time. I ordered from Baron six costumes for *Adrienne Lecouvreur* and four costumes for *Hernani.* I ordered from a young costume designer called Lepaul my costume for *Phèdre.* Altogether these thirty-six outfits cost me sixty-one thousand francs. It is true that the costume for *Phèdre* created by young

Lepaul cost in itself four thousand francs. This unfortunate artist embroidered it himself.

The costume was a marvel. It was delivered to me two days before my departure, and I cannot think about the moment of its delivery without deep emotion. Unnerved by the wait, I was writing an angry note to the costume designer when the latter was announced. I received him coldly at first, but I found him so changed, the poor man, that I asked him to sit down so that I could find out why he looked so ill.

"Yes, I am quite sick," he said in a voice so shaky that I was overcome. "I wanted to finish this work and I spent three nights on it. But see how beautiful your costume is!"—and he spread it out with respect and love in front of me.

"Oh, look!" said Guérard, "a little spot!"

"Oh, I pricked myself," said the poor artist quickly.

But I had just noticed a drop of blood on his lips. He wiped it away quickly so that it would not fall on the beautiful costume like the other drop. I gave the artist the four thousand francs, which he took with a trembling hand. He murmured some unintelligible words and disappeared. "Take this costume away! Take it away!" I cried to "my little lady" and my chambermaid. I sobbed with such deep sorrow that I had the hiccups all evening. Nobody understood my sorrow. I cursed myself for having harrassed the poor man so. It was obvious that he was going to die, and I felt that I had forged the first link in a chain of circumstances that made me an accomplice in the death of this man, this child of twenty-two, this artist of the future. I never wanted to put on this costume. It is still in its yellowed box. Its gold embroidery has turned brown with time and the little spot of blood has slightly eaten away the fabric. As for the poor artist, I learned of his death during my stay in London in the month of May, for before leaving for America I signed with Hollingshead and Mayer, the agents for the Comédie, a contract to perform in London from May 24 to June 27 (1880).

It was during this period that the trial was held for the suit brought against me by the Comédie-Française. Maître Barboux never consulted with me, and my success in London without the Comédie had the effect of irritating the Committee, the press, and the public. Maître Allou, in his speech for the prosecution, claimed that the London public had very quickly tired of me and no longer wished to come to the performances given by the Comédie in which I appeared. Here is the best refutation of this allegation of Maître Allou:

PERFORMANCES GIVEN BY THE COMÉDIE-FRANÇAISE
AT THE GAIETY THEATRE

(The asterisks indicate the performances in which I appeared.)

1879   Revenue (Francs)

June

  2 Prologue, *Le Misanthrope, Phèdre*, Act II,
     Les Précieuses ridicules[4] *13,080
  3 *L'Etrangère* *12,565
  4 *Le Fils naturel*[5] 9,300
  5 *Les Caprices de Marianne*,[6] *La Joie fait peur*[7] 10,100
  6 *Le Menteur*,[8] *Le Médecin malgré lui*[9] 9,530
  7 *Le Marquis de Villemer* 9,960
  7 Matinée: *Tartuffe, La Joie fait peur* 8,700
  9 *Hernani* *13,600
 10 *Le Demi-Monde*[10] 11,425
 11 *Mademoiselle de Belle-Isle, Il faut qu'une porte soit
     ouverte ou fermée*[11] 10,420
 12 *Le Post-Scriptum*,[12] *Le Gendre de Monsieur Poirier*[13] 10,445
 13 *Phèdre* *13,920
 14 *Le Luthier de Crémone*,[14] *Le Sphinx* *13,350
 14 Matinée: *Le Misanthrope, Les Plaideurs*[15] 8,800
 16 *L'Ami Fritz*[16] 9,375
 17 *Zaïre, Les Précieuses ridicules* *13,075
 18 *Le Jeu de l'amour et du hasard, Il ne faut jurer de rien*[17] ... 11,550
 19 *Le Demi-Monde* 12,160
 20 *Les Fourchambault*[18] 11,200
 21 *Hernani* *13,375
 21 Matinée: *Tartuffe, Il faut qu'une porte soit
     ouverte ou fermée* 2,215
 23 *Gringoire*,[19] *On ne badine pas avec l'amour* 11,080
 24 *Chez l'avocat, Mademoiselle de la Seiglière*[20] 9,960
 25 Matinée: *L'Etrangère*............................. *11,710
 25 *Le Barbier de Séville*[21] 9,180
 26 *Andromaque*,[22] *Les Plaideurs* *13,350
 27 *L'Avare*,[23] *L'Etincelle*[24] 11,775
 28 *Le Sphinx, Le Dépit amoureux*[25] *12,860
 28 Matinée: *Hernani*............................... *13,730
 30 *Ruy Blas* *13,660

July

1 *Mercadet,*[26] *L'Eté de la Saint-Martin*[27] 9,850

2 *Ruy Blas* *13,660

3 *Le Mariage de Victorine,*[28] *Les Fourberies de Scapin*[29] 10,165

4 *Les Femmes savantes, L'Etincelle* 11,960

5 *Les Fourchambault* *10,700

5 Matinée: *Phèdre, La Joie fait peur* 14,275

7 *Le Marquis de Villemer* 10,565

8 *L'Ami Fritz* 11,005

9 *Hernani* *14,275

10 *Le Sphinx* *13,775

11 *Philiberte,*[30] *L'Etourdi*[31] 11,500

12 *Ruy Blas* *12,660

12 Matinée: *Gringoire, Hernani* Act V, *La Bénédiction,*
Davenant,[32] *L'Etincelle* *13,725

Total receipts 492,150

The average of these receipts was approximately 11,175 francs. These figures show that out of the forty-three performances given by the Comédie-Française, the eighteen performances in which I took part yielded an average of 13,350 francs per performance, whereas the twenty-five other performances yielded an average of 10,000 francs.

It was in London that I learned that I had lost the suit and was informed of its long-winded whys and wherefores. "On these grounds Mlle. Sarah Bernhardt is hereby deprived of all the rights, privileges, and advantages issuing from the engagement which she contracted with the Comédie-Française by notarial deed on March 24, 1875. She is required to pay the prosecution the sum of one hundred thousand francs as damages and interest." I was giving my last performance in London on the day when the papers announced this unjust verdict. I was acclaimed and the audience showered me with flowers.

∞∞

[In the remainder of the chapter: *Sarah has brought with her to London the actors Mme. Devoyod, Mary Jullien,*[33] *Kalb, Sarah's sister, Jeanne, Pierre Berton, Train,*[34] *Talbot,*[35] *and Dieudonné, and has presented the repertoire she intends to take to America. She is surprised to find that the critics Vitu, Sarcey, and Lapommeraye have followed her to London to see her perform and that, although they have recently criticized her in Paris, their reviews of her London performances are full of praise. Moreover, her success in* Froufou *is so great that it makes up for the defection of Coquelin who had originally agreed to act with her (with Perrin's permission)—a defection that Sarah believes has been deliberately engineered by Perrin to injure her chances of success in London. Perrin also sends Got to try to persuade her to go back to the Comédie-Française, but Got irritates Sarah and he is unsuccessful.*

She leaves London with great regret. As a Frenchwoman she did not find London immediately lovable because of its houses with curtainless sash windows, its dirty, ugly monuments, its sad and shabby flower girls, the black mud in the streets and overcast skies, its drunken couples staggering about, and everywhere groups of skinny, ragged, little girls dancing wildly to the music of street organs. However, Sarah finds that the elegance of London's aristocracy, the beauty of the women, and the respectful gallantry of the men, compensate for its more dreary side.

Two things, however, which Sarah could never like are the black mud of the streets (as opposed to the pale mud of Paris), and the sash windows that can never be completely opened.

Nevertheless, she loves London, and since her first visit with the Comédie-Française has returned twenty-one times.]

Chapter XXXI

[*Sarah spends a few days in Paris on her return from London and then goes to Brussels to perform* Adrienne Lecouvreur *and* Froufrou. *She then takes these two plays to Copenhagen and is intimidated by the huge crowd that greets her at the station. She performs at the Royal Theatre before royalty and is received in the royal box. She makes a visit to Elsinore and visits the tomb of Hamlet and Ophelia's spring and the castles of Kronborg and Marienlyst. She is disappointed by this visit, finding her imagination to have been better than the reality. On the boat back, however, there is a beautiful moment at sunset, when some young people in a sailboat sing old Danish songs and throw roses into the water for her.*

On the eve of her departure a banquet is held in her honor, attended by numerous dignitaries. When Baron Magnus, a Prussian minister, proposes a toast to France, Sarah's painful memories of the Franco-Prussian war just ten years previously prompt her to reply, "So be it! But let us drink to France in her entirety, Mr. Prussian minister!" Sarah is asked to retract her remark because of the embarrassment it has caused Magnus with Bismarck, but Sarah, although she respects and likes Magnus, refuses.

Sarah returns to Paris and makes preparations for her departure for America on October 15. One August afternoon, when she is entertaining her usual five o'clock circle of friends (Girardin, Comte Kapenist, Maréchal Canrobert, Georges Clairin, Arthur Meyer, Duquesnel, Augusta Holmès, Raymond de Montbel, Nordenskjold, O'Connor, etc.), Duquesnel proposes for fifty thousand francs a tour of twenty-five French cities in twenty-eight days. She agrees, and is visited in turn by her friends who draw lottery tickets for the place and date of their "assignation."

After her return to Paris she is engaged by Eugène Bertrand to perform after her return from America in a play by Victorien Sardou at the Vaudeville.

Just before her departure for America there is an outpouring of vituperation as well as praise in the press. Laudatory articles are written about her by J.-J. Weiss, Zola, Emile de Girardin, Jules Vallès,[1] Jules Lemaître,[2] etc., and poetry in her honor by Victor Hugo, François Coppée, Richepin,[3] Haraucourt,[4] Henri de Bornier, Catulle Mendès,[5] Parodi, and later Edmond Rostand.[6] She leaves for America with regret for the loved ones she leaves behind, but also with desire for wider spaces and different horizons.]

241

Chapter XXXII

$\mathcal{T}$he ship that was to carry me toward other hopes, experiences, and triumphs was called the *Amérique*. It was a cursed ship. A haunted ship. It had been its lot to experience every possible misfortune, accident, and storm.

It had been stranded for months with its keel out of water. It had been rammed in the stern by an Icelandic boat. It had also, I believe, foundered on some shoals in Newfoundland and then been refloated. It had also caught fire right in the harbor at Le Havre, although it did not sustain very great damage. This poor ship was also notorious for a misadventure that had cast some ridicule over it. In 1876 or 1877 a new pumping system had been installed, of a type which had been in use for a long time on English ships, but was then unknown in the French navy. The captain had had the very sensible idea of trying out the pumps in order that his crew would know how to use them in an emergency. The trial run had been going on some minutes when the captain was informed that the hold was filling with water, but that no one knew why. "To the alert everybody! Pump! Pump!" was the captain's response. And the pumps worked away harder than ever—so hard that the hold filled up completely with water and the captain had to abandon the ship, after putting the passengers out in the lifeboats. An English whaler came across the ship two days later. He set the pumps to work and they worked very well—but the reverse of what the French captain had ordered. This little mistake cost the shipping company two hundred thousand francs to salvage. When they tried to relaunch the ship no one wanted to travel on it, so they offered my impresario, Mr. Abbey, very favorable terms. He accepted them and was right to do so, in spite of the ship's reputation, for the ship had paid its dues.

I had traveled very little until this time and I was wild with delight. On October 15, 1880, at six o'clock in the morning, I took possession of my cabin. It was a large cabin hung with pale garnet rep decorated with my initials. What a profusion of SB's! There was a big shiny brass bed and flowers everywhere. There was another very comfortable cabin opening off on one side which was for "my little lady," and another one *en suite* with that for my maid and her husband. The rest of my staff were at the other end of the ship.

It was foggy. The sea was grey with no visible horizon. I was going over there, beyond this fog, which joined the sea to the sky to form one mysterious rampart. The hustle and bustle of our departure threw everything and everyone into confusion. The rumbling of the engine, the sounds of whistling, sobbing, laughing, creaking ropes, shrill orders, shrieking passengers afraid of missing the boat, and the cries of men hurling packages into the hold, the laughing slapping of the water against the side of the ship—all of this mingled together into one dreadful uproar that tired one's brain, and made one uncertain what one's real feelings were.

I am one of those people who are happy right up to the last minute, saying goodbye, shaking hands, making plans for the return, giving farewell hugs and kisses, and then as soon as it is all over, throw themselves lost and sobbing onto the bed. I remained in a state of frightful despair for three days, crying big burning tears. Then I calmed down and my will overrode my pain.

I got up on the fourth day at about seven o'clock in the morning to go and take the air on deck. It was bitterly cold. As I walked I kept passing a lady dressed in black, whose face wore an expression of pained resignation. The sea was sullen looking, colorless and motionless. All of a sudden a large wave crashed so violently against our ship that we were both knocked over. I immediately grabbed hold of a bench leg. But the poor lady was thrown forward. I jumped up and was just in time to grab hold of her skirt. With the help of my maid and a sailor, I stopped the unfortunate lady from plunging down a staircase head first. In pain, and a little confused, she thanked me in a voice so soft and far away that my heart began to beat with emotion.

"You could have killed yourself, Madame, on those horrible stairs."

"Yes," she said with a regretful sigh, "God did not wish it." Then, looking at me more closely, she said, "Aren't you Mme. Hessler?"

"No, Madame. My name is Sarah Bernhardt."

She recoiled and stood straight, her face white and frowning. In a pained deathly voice she snapped, "I am Lincoln's widow."[1]

I also recoiled and felt a sudden wave of sorrow, for I realized that I had just done this unhappy woman the one favor that I ought not to have done her—I had saved her from death. Her husband, President Lincoln, had been assassinated by the actor Booth,[2] and it was an actress who had prevented her from joining her beloved in death. I went back to my cabin and stayed there for two days. I did not have the courage to encounter this person with whom I felt such sympathy again. I would not have dared to speak to her a second time.

On October 22 we were buffeted by a terrible snow storm. I was hastily summoned by Captain Jouclas. I put on a great fur overcoat and went up onto the bridge. It was deafening, stunning, and yet like something out of a fairy-tale, to hear the crash of the hardened ice flakes as they clashed with one another in a wild dance stirred up by the wind. Suddenly the sky was hidden by whiteness, which fell about us in avalanches and sealed us off from the rest of the world. I was facing the sea, and Captain Jouclas pointed out to me that we could not see more than a hundred yards in front of us. Then I turned around and saw that the ship was as white as a seagull: the rigging, the ropes, the rails, the scuttles, the shrouds, the whaling boats, the deck, the sails, the ladders, the chimneys, the air inlets—all were white! The sea was white, the sky was black. All alone the white boat floated in this immensity. There was a struggle between the high chimney, spluttering its smoke out with difficulty through the wind whirling in its large maw, and the prolonged wailing of the siren. There was such an extraordinary contrast between the virginal whiteness of the ship and the infernal noise it was making that I felt as though I were looking at an angel suffering an attack of hysterics.

In the evening of this strange day the doctor informed me that one of the emigrant women, whom I had taken under my wing, was in labor. I was soon at her side and helped the poor little being as best I could to enter this world. Oh, what mournful noises in this mournful night in the midst of all this misery! Oh, the first piercing cry of this child as it affirmed its will to live, in the midst of all this suffering, all this anguish, all this hope!

Everything was jumbled together in this human muddle: men, women, children, rags and conserves, oranges and basins, heads with hair and bald heads, the half-open mouths of virgins and the pinched lips of shrews, white bonnets and red scarves, hands stretched out toward Hope, and fists clenched against Adversity. I saw revolvers half hidden under tatters, knives in belts. A sudden roll caused a package to fall from the hands of a determined looking rascal and disgorge an axe and a club. A sailor immediately seized them to take to the purser. I will never forget the attentive look that the man gave him. He had certainly noted the sailor's features exactly, and I prayed that there would never be a lone encounter between these two men.

I remember with remorse the disgust I felt when the doctor gave me the child to wash. This little dirty, red, moving, sticky thing was a human being, a soul, an intelligence. I felt sick, and I was never able to see this child, whose godmother I became, without reliving this first impression.

When the young mother was asleep I decided to go back to my cabin with the help of the doctor. But the sea was so rough that we made difficult progress amidst the bundles and the emigrants. Some crouching on the floor watched us silently, as we stumbled and swayed like drunkards. I was irritated to feel myself being watched by these malevolent and impertinent eyes.

One man accosted us, "So, doctor—you can get as drunk on sea water as on wine? You and the lady look like you're on your way back from a revel!"

An old lady clung to me, "I say, Madame, are we going to be shipwrecked with it rocking like that? My God! My God!"

Then a tall red-headed and bearded devil approached the poor old woman and said, as he put her back down on the floor, "Sleep well, old woman! If there's a shipwreck I promise you more'll be saved down here than up there!" Then he came up to me and said defiantly, "The rich'll be the first . . . in the water! The emigrants the second . . . in the boats!" I heard sly stifled laughter, which seemed to come from every-where—in front of me, behind me, next to me, even under my feet, echoing in the distance like laughter "off" in the theater. I kept close to the doctor. He realized that I was worried.

"Ach! We would defend ourselves!" he said, laughing.

"But how many passengers could be saved, doctor, if we were in real danger?"

"Two hundred . . . maybe two hundred and fifty . . . assuming that all the life boats were used and that they all reached port safely."

"But there are seven hundred and sixty emigrants, the purser told me; we first- and second-class passengers barely number a hundred and twenty; how many officers, crew members, and other staff do you reckon there are?"

"A hundred and seventy," the doctor replied.

"So there are a thousand and fifty of us all together, and you could save only two hundred and fifty of them?"

"Yes."

"Well, in that case, I understand the hatred of these emigrants that you bring onboard like animals and treat like negroes and who are absolutely certain that in a crisis it would be them that you would sacrifice!"

"But they would be saved in their turn."

I looked in horror at the man I was talking with. He had an air of integrity and he believed what he said. So, these poor creatures, be-trayed by life and maltreated by society, would have a right to live only after others who were more fortunate? Oh! Now I understood the poor rascal with the hatchet and the club! Now I really sympathized with the revolvers and the knives hidden in their belts! Yes, he was right, that tall red-headed devil—since we wanted first place, always first place, then we would have first place—heave ho! Into the water!

"So, are you happy?" asked the captain who was coming out of his cabin. "Did it all go well?"

"Very well, captain. But I am disgusted!"

Jouclas recoiled. "Oh! My God! What about?"

"Disgusted by the way you treat your passengers." He tried to speak, but I broke in, "How is it that you expose us, in the case of a shipwreck . . . "

"We never have a shipwreck!"

"Alright. But in the case of a fire . . . "

"There's never a fire on board!"

"Alright. In the case of a flood, then . . . "

He started to laugh. "I give in. To what are you being exposed, Madame?"

"To the worst kind of death: a hatchet blow over the head, a knife in the back, or simply a good punch of the fist that would send one flying into the water." He tried to speak, but I continued. "There are seven hundred and fifty emigrants in steerage, while there are barely three hundred first- and second-class passengers and crew. The life boats can save two hundred people . . . if that."

"So?"

"So, what about the emigrants?"

"We will save them before we save the crew!"

"And after us?"

"Yes, after . . . you!"

"And you think they will allow that?"

"There are guns to keep them in order!"

"Guns . . . guns against women and children?"

"No, the women and children leave first!"

"But that's crazy! Absurd! Why save women and children if you make widows and orphans of them? And do you really think that these young men will give up in the face of your guns? They are in the majority! They are armed! Life owes them this revenge! They have the same right as we, to fight for themselves at the last moment! Moreover, they have the courage that comes from having nothing to lose and everything to gain by the struggle! And I find it vile and shameful that you should expose *us* to certain death, and *them* to a forced and justifiable crime." The captain tried to speak . . . "And even without going as far as supposing a shipwreck—imagine the kind of situation that has happened before—that we could be tossed around for months on high seas . . . You surely don't have provisions for a thousand mouths for two months . . . or three?"

"No, certainly not," said the purser dryly. He was a very nice, but very touchy, man.

"So what would you do?"

"Well, what would *you* do?" interrupted Captain Jouclas, who was very amused by the purser's starchy reaction.

"I would make one boat for emigrants and one for the other passengers, and I think that would be fair!"

"Yes, but it would also be financially disastrous."

"No. The one for the wealthy would be a steamer like this one, and the one for the emigrants would be a sailboat."

"But, my dear Madame, that would also be unfair, since the steamer would go much faster than the sailboat."

"That doesn't matter, captain. Rich people are always in a hurry and poor people never are. And then think what is waiting for them . . . there where they are going."

"It's the Promised Land!"

"Oh the poor things! The poor things! The Promised Land . . . Dakota or Colorado! During the day the sun addles the brain, scorches the earth, dries up the springs, and brings forth countless mosquitoes to harass them in body and mind! The Promised Land! At night the cold is so extreme that it's painful to the eyes and joints and ruinous for the lungs! The Promised Land . . . death in some godforsaken corner, after vain appeals to their countrymen's sense of justice—death amidst tears and imprecations! And all of them will surely be welcomed by God, for it is pitiful to think of all these poor creatures being handed over with their feet chained by suffering, and their hands chained by hope, to slave traders who trade in whites! And when I think, Purser, sir, you have in your coffers the money that the slave trader has brought you for the transport of all these poor beings! Money acquired by calloused and trembling hands! Pitiful money saved a penny and a tear at a time! When I think of that I wish that we *would* be shipwrecked and that we were all killed, and they were all saved!" I went off to my cabin to cry, feeling overwhelmed by great love for humanity and by great sorrow at not being able to do anything . . . anything at all.

The next morning I woke up late, having gone to sleep late. My cabin was full of visitors, each of them holding a little package behind their backs. I rubbed my sleepy eyes, still puzzled as to the reason for this invasion. Mme. Guérard kissed me.

"My dear little Sarah, don't think that those who love you could forget your birthday!"

"Ah! Today's the twenty-third?" I exclaimed.

"Yes. And first of all here are the remembrances of those who are not with us."

My eyes filled with tears and through a mist I glimpsed the portrait of a young being, who was the dearest creature in the world to me, with some words in his own handwriting ... Then there were some presents from friends ... little pieces of handiwork from humble admirers. My little godson born the night before was presented to me in a basket, surrounded by oranges, apples, and mandarin oranges. He had a golden star on his forehead, a little star made of gold chocolate wrapping paper. My maid Félicie and her husband Claude, two good-hearted devoted people, gave me some other little ingenious surprises.

There was a knock at the door.

"Come in!"

To my surprise I saw three sailors come in with a superb bouquet, which they gave me on behalf of the crew. I was amazed. How could flowers have been kept in such good condition? The bouquet was enormous. I took it and then let it fall as I burst out laughing. It was a bouquet of flowers made from vegetables—with such consummate skill that even from ten feet away they looked real. Magnificent yellow roses had been carved out of carrots, camelias had been made from turnips, little radishes had been made into rose buds stuck on the end of green leek stems, and the whole thing was set off by carrot leaves artistically sprinkled throughout, in imitation of the leaf sprays in the most elegant bouquets. The stems were bound together with a tricolored ribbon.

An emotional little speech by one of the sailors on behalf of his fellows, who wished to thank me for a little service that I had rendered them, and a cordial handshake and affectionate thank you on my part, were the signal for a concert organized in the cabin of "my little lady." Two violinists and a flutist had rehearsed in secret and I found myself soothed for an hour by delightful music which carried me back to my loved ones in my home so far away. This almost "family" birthday and this music called up something tender and reposeful in me and I cried— without sorrow, without bitterness, without regret for crying. I cried because I was touched, tired, tense, and longed to rest. I fell asleep amidst my tears, my breast still heaving with sighs and sobs ...

Chapter XXXIII

The ship finally came to a halt on October 27 at half past six in the morning. I was asleep, still tired by the three days and nights of furious storms. My maid had some difficulty waking me. I refused to believe that we had actually arrived and I wanted to continue sleeping right up until the last minute. I had, however, to accept the evidence. The ship was coming to a halt and I could hear an endless series of dull thuds.

I put my head out of my porthole and caught sight of some men, busy cutting us a passage down the river. The Hudson was frozen. The surface of the river was completely frozen over and the heavy vessel only advanced as the ice broke up in blocks under the workmen's pickaxes. This completely unexpected arrival filled me with transports of joy. In the space of one minute all was transformed. I forgot my sickness and boredom during the twelve-day crossing. A pale pink sun was rising, dissipating the mist and gleaming on the ice as the workmen's efforts sent a thousand icy sparks flying into the air. I was entering the New World in the midst of an icy firework display. Our mode of entrance was fairy-like and a little mad, but I felt it boded well.

I am so superstitious that, if I had arrived on a day without sun, I would have been sad and uneasy until my first performance. It is really a torture to be superstitious to such a degree, and I am now ten times more so than I was at that time; for, besides the superstitions of my own country, I have burdened myself with the superstitions of all the other many countries to which I have traveled. I have all of them— all of them! At serious moments in my life they raise themselves in legions either for me or against me! I cannot take a step, make a movement or gesture, sit down, go out, go to bed, get up, look at the sky or the ground, without finding a reason to hope or despair—until I reach a point where, in exasperation at all these self-imposed constraints on my actions, I defy all my superstitions and do what I want.

Happy with what seemed to me to be a good omen, I gaily set about getting myself dressed.

251

Mr. Jarrett knocked on my door. "Madame, I beg you to get ready quickly. Several boats flying the French flag are approaching."

I glanced out of my porthole and saw a steamer, which looked dark with all the people on it. There were also two other little boats no less loaded than the first one. A multitude of French flags were quite visible in the sunshine.

My heart thumped a little. I had been without news from France for twelve days—for the *Amérique* had taken that long, despite the best efforts of our good captain. A man jumped onto the bridge. I ran up to him and held out my hand, unable to say a single word. He gave me a packet of telegrams. I neither saw nor heard anything. I wanted to know. Amongst all the telegrams I was looking, above all, for one signature. Finally, there it was—the telegram I had expected and hoped for, and dreaded that I might not find! Signed—"Maurice!" There it was! I closed my eyes for a moment, seeing and savoring in this instant all that was dear and sweet to me.

I was a little confused when I opened my eyes. I was surrounded by a crowd of strangers, silent and kindly, but very curious. Wanting to extricate myself, I took Jarrett's arm and he led me to the lounge. As I came through the doorway the *Marseillaise* struck up and our consul said some words of welcome as he presented me with some flowers. A group representing the French settlers gave me a very nice plaque. Then M. Mercier, the editor in chief of *Le Courrier des Etats-Unis*, made a very French speech in which wit and emotion were equally mingled. Then came the terrible moment of the introductions. Oh! What a tiring time! How I struggled to understand the names!

"Pemberst . . . "

"Madame, pronounce the 'h,' Harthtem . . . "

I would only just have the first syllable, when the second would trail off into a jumble of muffled vowels or whistling consonants. By the time we reached the twentieth name I was no longer listening, I just kept my little Santorini's risorius[1] going, glancing in the right direction, holding out my hand mechanically, on the end of which was to be found another hand shaking and being shaken, and repeating, "I'm delighted to meet you . . . Madame . . . Oh! Certainly . . . Oh! Yes . . . Oh! No . . . Ah! . . . Ah! . . . Oh! . . . Oh! . . . " I was becoming dazed, idiotic, and exhausted with standing. There was only one thing on my mind: I had to take my rings off, as my fingers were swelling with the pressure of so many handshakes. My eyes boggled as I saw a never-ending crowd pouring through the door to meet me . . . still so many names to hear . . . still so many hands to shake . . . still so many times to work my Santorini's risorius. I felt myself beginning to sweat. I began to feel terribly tense. My teeth were chattering and I started stuttering, "Oh!

Madame . . . Oh! . . . I am char . . . cha . . . a . . . a . . . " I could take no more. I knew that I was either going to fly into a rage or start crying . . . in a word that I was going to make a fool of myself.

I decided to faint. I put out my hand as though I couldn't quite . . . I opened my mouth . . . I closed my eyes . . . and let myself collapse ever so gently into Jarrett's arms.

"Quick, give her some air!" "A doctor!" "Poor young woman!" "How pale she is!" "Take her hat off!" "Her corset!" "She's not wearing one . . . " "Unhook her dress."

I began to panic. But "my little lady" and my servant Félicie, who had been hastily summoned, both said no to the idea of undressing me. The doctor came with a bottle of ether.

Félicie grabbed the bottle. "Oh no, doctor, no ether! When Madame is well the smell of ether makes her faint!" And that was true.

I felt it was time to come round. The reporters approached. There were more than twenty of them. But Jarrett, who felt very sorry for me, asked them to come to the Albemarle Hotel, where I was going to be staying. I saw each of the reporters take Jarrett aside. When I asked him the secret of all these asides he replied phlegmatically, "I gave them appointments starting at one o'clock. A new one will arrive every ten minutes." I looked at him petrified. He looked back steadily and said, "Oh yes. It has to be done!"

When I arrived at the Albemarle Hotel I was tired and very much in need of solitude. I made haste to lock myself up in one of the bedrooms, in the suite of rooms reserved for me. I closed all the doors. One of them had neither lock nor key, so I pushed a piece of furniture up against it and forcefully refused to open any door.

In the drawing room there were about fifty people, but I was overcome by the kind of extreme fatigue that will drive you to violent extremes to obtain an hour of rest. I wanted to stretch out on the carpet with my arms folded, my head back, and my eyes closed. I did not want to talk any more, smile any more, or look any more. I threw myself down on the floor and made no response to the knocking on my door and Jarrett's pleas. I did not want to enter into any discussion. I did not say a word. I heard the buzzing of visitors outside and the muttering of Jarrett as he tried to hold them back. I heard a piece of paper being slid under the door and then the whispering of Mme. Guérard.

"You don't know her, Mr. Jarrett. If you force the door that she has jammed, she is quite likely to jump out of the window."

"No, Madame," Félicie was saying to a Frenchwoman who was very insistent. "It's impossible! Madame would have a fit of hysterics! She needs an hour of rest. We must wait!"

Further in the distance I heard a confusion of other words and then I fell into a delicious and slightly merry sleep, for my gaiety rose to the fore as I thought about the enraged and discomforted faces of my tormentors . . . sorry . . . of my *visitors*. An hour later I woke up, for I have the precious gift of being able to sleep for ten minutes, a quarter of an hour, an hour, at will. And nothing is better for me than this voluntary and measured rest of body and soul. Often, amongst close friends at home, I have stretched out on the bearskins by the hearth and asked them to continue their conversation without me, while I have slept for an hour. Sometimes, on waking, I have found two or three newly arrived guests joining in the general conversation, and waiting until I woke up to give me their respects. Nowadays I still stretch out on the heavy plush sofa in the little Empire drawing room that is attached to my dressing room, and sleep, while friends and actors with whom I have appointments are brought in. And when I open my eyes I am surrounded by kind friendly faces, delighted at the rest that I have taken, as they offer me their hands affectionately. Calmed and rested in this way, my spirit can be receptive to fine ideas and brush off good-humoredly all the absurdity that it encounters.

So I woke up an hour later on the carpet of the Albemarle Hotel. I opened the door and found my dear Guérard and Félicie sitting on a trunk.

"Are the people still here?"

"Oh, Madame, there are a hundred now!" said Félicie.

"Quick! Help me to get undressed and give me a white dress."

This was done in five minutes and I felt pretty from head to foot. I was heading for the drawing room where all these strangers were waiting for me, when Jarrett ran up to me, but seeing that I was well-dressed and smiling, he put off till later the sermon that he intended to deliver.

I want to describe Jarrett to my readers, for he was an extraordinary man. At this time he was between sixty-five and seventy. He was tall. He had a face like King Agamemnon's crowned with white hair—the most beautiful hair that I have ever seen on a man. His eyes were of a blue so pale that when anger made them shine he seemed blind. When he was relaxed and calmly admiring nature his face was really handsome; but when he was gay his upper lip curled up to show his teeth in a ferocious grimace, while his pointed ears twitched like those of an animal stalking its prey.

He was a formidable man. He was gifted with superior intelligence and since childhood he had had to do battle with life, with the result that he had conceived a deep contempt for humanity. Since he himself had greatly suffered, he had no pity for anyone else who suffered, saying that all males were equipped to defend themselves. He pitied women without liking them, but he was always ready to assist them. He was very rich and very thrifty, but not greedy.

He often used to say to me, "I have made my way in life with the aid of two weapons—moral integrity and a revolver. In business, moral integrity is the most powerful weapon against rogues and tricksters. The former are not acquainted with it, and the latter do not believe in it; and the revolver is a wonderful invention for forcing rascals to stand by their word."

He would tell me stories of wonderful and terrifying adventures. He had a deep scar under his right eye. During a violent discussion concerning the signing of a contract for Jenny Lind, the famous singer, Jarrett said to his interlocutor, "Look at this eye, sir," and he pointed to his right eye. "It reads in your thoughts everything that you do not say!"

"It reads badly then," said the other, "as it has not foreseen this!"— and he shot him with his revolver intending to put out his right eye.

"Sir," replied Jarrett, "this is the way you should have fired to close it for ever!" and he lodged a bullet between the man's eyes, killing him.

When Jarrett told this story his lip curled back, his two incisors seemed to gnaw pleasurably at his words, and his bursts of suppressed laughter sounded like snapping jaws. But he was a man of honesty and integrity. I liked him very much and I have good memories of him.

My reaction, on seeing the drawing room for the first time, was one of delight. I clapped my hands as I went in. Busts of Racine, Molière, and Victor Hugo were on pedestals surrounded by flowers. Against the walls of the spacious room there were sofas laden with cushions, and there were tall palm trees overhanging them to remind me of my Parisian home.

Jarrett introduced me to Knoedler, who was the likable instigator of this piece of gallantry. I shook the hand of this very charming man and we were friends immediately and forever.

The visitors left gradually, but the reporters did not. They were sitting, some on the arms of chairs, others on cushions. One of them was sitting cross-legged on a bearskin, his back against the burning "steam." He was pale and thin and coughed frequently. I went up to him and just as I opened my mouth to speak to him—a little shocked to see that he did not stand up—he interrupted me in a deep voice, "Madame, which is your favorite role?"

"That's none of your business!" I said, turning my back on him. I bumped into another reporter who was more polite.

"What do you eat when you get up, Madame?"

I was going to make the same reply as I had to the first reporter, but Jarrett, who had had great trouble calming the fury of the man who was sitting cross-legged, replied quickly, "Oatmeal!" I didn't know what that was.

"And during the day?" the ferocious reporter asked.

"Mussels!" I cried.

He wrote down phlegmatically, "Mussels all day . . . "

I headed toward the door. A female reporter, with short hair and a mannish tailored skirt, said to me in a soft clear voice, "Are you JewishCatholicProtestantMuslimBuddhistatheistZoroastrian or a deist?"

I stood nailed to the spot, dumbfounded. She had said all of this in one breath, stressing the words at random and making the whole thing into one crazily incoherent word, so that I felt rather nervous in the presence of this gentle and strange person. My worried look fell on an elderly woman who was gaily conversing with a little group.

She came to my aid and said to me in very good French, "This young lady is asking you, Madame, whether you are Jewish, Catholic, Protestant, Muslim, Buddhist, or an atheist, theist or deist."

I fell onto a sofa. "My God! Will it be like this in all the cities that I visit?"

"Oh no," replied the placid Jarrett, "your interviews are going to be telegraphed to the whole of America."

"And the mussels?" I wondered. "I am Catholic, Mademoiselle!" I replied absent mindedly.

"Roman or Orthodox?"

I leaped up, she was really too annoying! A very young man approached timidly. "Would you permit me to finish my drawing, Madame?"

I stood there, my face in profile, as he wished. When he had finished I asked to see it. Without embarrassment he showed me a horrible drawing: a skeleton wearing a frizzy wig. I tore up the drawing and threw it in his face. The next day the horror appeared in the newspapers with a nasty caption.

Fortunately, there were a few journalists of integrity and intelligence with whom I could speak seriously about my art. But in America, twenty-seven years ago, sensational journalism was much more appreciated than articles of depth, and the public, which was much less educated than today, unquestioningly accepted the scandal invented by a desperate reporter. I do not think that there has been anyone in the world, since the invention of reporting, who has suffered more from it than I did during this first tour. There was all the basest libel, hurled by my enemies long before my arrival in America, and all the perfidy of friends of the Comédie-Française, and even of my own fans, who were set on my failing during my trip so that I would return all the quicker to the nest, diminished, calmed, and subdued. There were all the outrageous and ridiculous claims made by my impresario, Abbey, and Jarrett, my agent, the source of which I did not know until a long time later, when it was too late—oh, very much too late!—to rob the public of the conviction that I was the prime instigator of all these inventions. So I gave up trying. It matters little to me whether one believes this or that! Life is short, even for those who live a long time. One must live for those who know you, appreciate you, judge and forgive you, and for whom one feels the same tenderness and indulgence. The rest is the "mob," pleased or displeased, loyal or perverse, from which one has nothing to expect except fleeting emotions, good or bad, that leave no trace. One must hate very little, for it is very tiring. One must have a great deal of contempt, often forgive, and never forget. Forgiving does not mean forgetting, at least not for me. I will not reproduce here any of these outrageous and infamous attacks; this would be to do too great an honor to the rascals who fabricated these things from start to finish, by dipping their pens in the gall of their souls. But one thing I can affirm—and that is that nothing kills except death, and anyone who wishes to defend himself against calumny can do so just by living! However, it is not given to everybody to be able to do this. It depends on the will of God who sees and judges.

I rested for two days before going to the theater. I felt as though I were still at sea. I was slightly dizzy, and I still saw the ceiling rising and falling. Those twelve days of sea voyage had unbalanced me. I sent a note to the stage manager to advise him that we would rehearse on Wednesday. As soon as lunch was finished I went to Booth's Theatre,[2] in which our performances were to take place. At the stage door I saw a dense swarming crowd of busy gesturing people. These strange beings did not belong to the world of the arts and were not reporters. *They*, alas, I knew too well to mistake. They were not there out of curiosity, for they seemed too purposeful. And, besides, there were only men. My carriage stopped. One of them dashed toward the door and went back to the swarming group. "There she is! It's her!"

All of these common-looking men with white tie and grubby hands, wearing unbuttoned morning coats and trousers worn and dirty at the knees, poured behind me into the narrow corridor leading to the stairs. I felt uneasy and climbed the stairs quickly. Several people were waiting for me at the top of the stairs: Mr. Abbey, Mr. Jarrett, some reporters (alas!), and two gentlemen and a charming and distinguished lady, with whom I have since maintained a friendship (although she does not much care for the French). I saw the cold and haughty Abbey go up graciously and courteously to one of these men who were following me. Both of them tipped their hats, then made for the middle of the stage followed by the strange and brutal gang.

Then I became a spectator of the strangest of spectacles. In the middle of the stage were arranged my forty-two trunks. At a sign twenty men detached themselves from the group and positioned themselves, one man between two trunks each. Then with a quick movement they lifted up the lids of the trunks, one in the right hand and one in the left. Jarrett, with furrowed brow and a nasty grimace, was holding the keys. He had asked me for them in the morning for the formalities of customs. "Oh, it's nothing," he had said, "don't worry." And I was reassured by the fact that I had encountered perfect respect for my luggage in all the other countries that I had visited. Now the most important person of the ugly group approached me, led by Abbey. Jarrett had just informed me what was going on. It was "the Customs," an abominable institution in any country, and more so in this one than in any other. I prepared myself and put on a pleasant face for this executioner of the traveler's patience. He lifted the bowler hat which served as headgear, and without removing the cigar from his mouth, said something incomprehensible to me. Then, turning to his gang, he made a brusque gesture underlined by a curt word, and the forty dirty hands of these twenty men fell on my satin, my velvet, and my lace. I leaped forward to save my poor dresses from this outrageous violation. I ordered our wardrobe mistress to take out my dresses one at a time, which she did with the help of my chambermaid, who was in tears at the way these yokels were treating all these graceful and fragile costumes with so little respect.

Two noisy and bustling ladies arrived. One was fat and short, with a nose which took root at the hair line, round, placid eyes, and a mouth like a muzzle. Her arms hid themselves timidly behind her soft, heavy bust, and her immodest knees seemed to emerge directly from the groin. She reminded me of a cow sitting down. The other one looked like a terrapin. Her little head, black and spiteful, was perched on the end of a neck that was too long and very twisted, and which she drew in or extended from her boa with remarkable rapidity. The rest of her body bulged outward . . .

These two delightful characters were the dressmakers hired by Customs to estimate the value of our costumes. They threw me a fleeting glance and a little gesture of greeting, which was full of gall and jealous rage at the sight of my dresses, and I realized that two more enemies had just entered the arena. These two odious butcher-birds began to fiddle and diddle with my dresses and coats, all the time jabbering away.

They let out shrieks of emphatic admiration. "Oh! How *beautiful* it is! Oh! What *magnificence*! What *luxury*! *All* our clients are going to want dresses like *this*! We will *never* be able to make them for them! This is going to *ruin* us poor American dressmakers!!" They were working up the judges in this trial of the wardrobe. They lamented, went into ecstasies, and demanded "justice" against the foreign invasion. And the ugly group opined with their heads, and spat on the floor to affirm their independence.

Suddenly the terrapin dashed toward one of the inquisitors. "Oh! How *beautiful* it is! . . . Let's see, let's see!" and she took hold of a dress from *La Dame aux camélias* all embroidered with pearls. "This dress is worth at *least* ten thousand dollars!" she cried. Coming up to me she said, "How much did you pay for this dress, Madame?" I ground my teeth and refused to reply, for at this moment I would have liked to see the terrapin at the bottom of one of the saucepans in the kitchen of the Albemarle Hotel. It was half past five. My feet were frozen. I was numb with fatigue and repressed fury.

The rest of the appraisal was put off until the next day. The ugly bunch offered to put everything back in the trunks, but I said no. I sent out for five hundred yards of blue tarlatan to cover the mountain of dresses, hats, coats, shoes, lace, linen, stockings, furs, gloves, etc. They made me swear that nothing would be removed (charming trust!), and I charged my butler, Félicie's husband, to stand guard over everything. He set up a bed in the theater.

I felt so tense that I wanted to go far away and take some air. A friend offered to take me to see the Brooklyn Bridge. "This masterpiece of American genius will make you forget the petty meanness of our bureaucrats," he told me kindly. So we left for the Brooklyn Bridge. It was not yet finished. We needed a special permit to visit it, but carriages were already venturing onto it. Oh, the Brooklyn Bridge! It's crazy, wonderful, grandiose, something to be proud of. Yes, one is proud to be a human being when one thinks that a mind created this awesome machine, suspended in the air one hundred fifty feet above the ground, and that it is able to support ten trains jam-packed with passengers, ten or twelve tramways, a hundred carriages, cabs, wagons, and thousands of pedestrians, all of them whirling together in the din of the music of metals that cry, grind, groan, and grumble under the enormous weight of people and things. This formidable to-ing and fro-ing of machines, tramways, and wagons that were being tried out on the bridge created a tempestuous wind, which made me dizzy and took my breath away. I signaled the carriage to stop and closed my eyes. I had the strange and indefinable sensation that I was perceiving the Chaos of the universe. I opened my eyes, my mind a little calmer, and I saw New York stretched

out along the river putting on its nighttime jewelry, as sparkling under
its dress of a thousand lights as the firmament under its tunic of stars.
I went back to the hotel, feeling reconciled with this great people.

I went to sleep, physically tired but mentally rested. I had some
wonderful dreams, which put me in a good mood the next day, for I
love dreaming. Days that follow dreamless nights are painful and depressing for me. One great sorrow is the fact that I cannot choose my
dreams. How many times have I done my utmost to prolong the happy
time that I am having in a dream! How many times have I spoken to
loved ones that I saw as I slept! But my mind always eventually takes a
turn and transports me elsewhere. I very much prefer to dream, even
if the dream is unpleasant, than to experience a complete negation of
thought. When I am asleep my body is in a very pleasurable state, but
it is torture for me to have thought stop altogether. This negation of
life outrages my life forces. I accept that I have to die one day, but I
reject the little deaths of dreamless nights.

When I awoke my maid told me that Jarrett was waiting for me to
go to the theater, so that the evaluation of the costumes could be
completed. I told Jarrett that I had seen enough of the gang of customs
officers and I asked him to finish off without me with Mme. Guérard
in my place. For two days more the terrapin, the seated cow, and the
black band took notes for the taxes, made sketches for the newspapers,
and designs for clients.

I was getting impatient because we needed to rehearse. Finally, I
found out on Thursday morning that the work was finished, and that
I would not get my trunks until I had paid twenty-eight thousand francs
to the Customs. I was overtaken by such hysterical laughter that it
affected the terrified Abbey and even Jarrett, who showed his vicious
incisors. "My dear Abbey," I cried, "please sort it out! I have to give my
first performance on Monday, November 8. Today is Thursday. I will be
at the theater, Monday, to get dressed. Make sure I have my trunks. The
duties were not included in my contract, nevertheless, I will pay half of
them." The twenty-eight thousand francs were put into the hands of an
attorney who initiated a suit on my behalf against the Board of Customs. My trunks were returned against this deposit and the rehearsals
started at Booth's Theater.

On Monday, November 8, at eight thirty, the curtain went up for
the first performance of *Adrienne Lecouvreur*. The theater was jam-packed
full. All the tickets had been bought at exorbitant prices, as they had
been bought at auctions or from touts. The audience waited for my
entrance with impatience and curiosity, but without affection. There
were no *young* ladies in the theater, as the play was considered too

immoral (poor Adrienne Lecouvreur!). The audience was very polite toward the actors in my company, but a little impatient to see the strange person that they had heard about. Adrienne does not appear in the first act. A disgruntled member of the audience demanded to see Mr. Henry Abbey. "I want my money back because Bernhardt is not in all the acts!" Abbey refused to return the money to this strange individual and, when the curtain went up for the second act, he ran back to take possession of his seat.

My entry was greeted by several rounds of applause that had been paid for, I believe, by Abbey and Jarrett. I started; and the sweetness of my voice (such as I had shown in the fable of *Les Deux Pigeons*) worked a miracle. The whole theater, this time, burst into cheers. A current of sympathy had just been established between the audience and me. Instead of the hysterical skeleton that had been described to them, and whose arrival they expected, they had in front of them a frail being with a very sweet voice. The fourth act was loudly applauded. The revolt of Adrienne against the Princesse de Bouillon brought the audience to its feet. Then finally the fifth act, in which the unhappy actress is seen in the throes of death after having been poisoned by her rival, caused a show of great emotion.

It seems that after the third act the young men were sent by the ladies to seek out every available musician. What was my surprise and joy when I arrived at the hotel to hear a wonderful serenade during my supper! A crowd had grown under the windows of the Albemarle Hotel and I had to go out several times to greet and thank the public, who, I had been warned, was cold as a matter of course, and prejudiced against me in particular. So I thanked from the bottom of my heart all my detractors and libelers, who had given me the joy of fighting, along with an assured victory, which was even finer than I had dared to expect.

I gave twenty-seven performances in New York. The plays were *Adrienne Lecouvreur, Froufrou, Hernani, La Dame aux camélias, Phèdre, Le Sphinx,* and *L'Etrangère.* The average receipt for a performance, including the matinée, was 20,342 francs. The last performance was given on Saturday, December 4, as a matinée, as my company was leaving that same night for Boston, and I had reserved the evening for a visit with Edison at Menlo Park, where I was to receive a most fairy-tale welcome.

Oh, this matinée on Saturday, December 4—I'll never forget it! When I arrived at the theater to dress, it was midday, for the matinée started at one thirty. My carriage stopped, unable to advance any further for the road was cluttered with seated ladies, some on chairs borrowed from stores nearby, some on folding chairs that they had brought themselves. We were putting on *La Dame aux camélias.* I had to get out of my carriage and walk twenty yards to get to the artists' entrance. It took me twenty-five minutes to get to this door. They shook my hand, they begged me to return. A lady took off her brooch and pinned it on my coat. It was a modest brooch made of an amethyst surrounded by small pearls, but surely for this woman it was worth a small fortune.

I was held back at every step. One lady had the idea of having me sign her appointment book. The idea caught on like wild fire. Some children with their parents made me sign my name on their cuffs. I could take no more. My arms were loaded up with little bouquets and sprays. I felt someone behind me pulling on the feather in my hat. I turned round sharply. A woman with a pair of scissors had tried to cut off a lock of my hair, but she had cut my feather instead. Jarrett vainly made large gestures and loud appeals; I could not move forward. Some security guards were fetched to rescue me, which they did without courtesy either toward my fans or myself. They were real brutes; and it was time that I got there as I was beginning to get annoyed.

I performed *La Dame aux camélias*. I counted seventeen curtain-calls after the third act and twenty-nine after the fifth. Because of the applause and the curtain-calls the play had lasted an hour longer than usual. I was dead with fatigue. I was just about to get into my carriage to go back to the hotel when Jarrett came to warn me that there were more than five thousand people outside. I fell onto a sofa, tired and discouraged. "Ah! I'll wait till the crowd has dispersed. I can't take any more . . . I can't take any more."

However, Henry Abbey had an ingenious idea. "Here," he said to my sister. "Put on Madame's hat and her boa, and take my arm. Oh yes! Take these bouquets as well, and give those to me . . . I'll take the rest. Now, let's get into your sister's carriage and wave to everybody." He said all that in English, and Jarrett translated it for my sister who threw herself into the little comedy with good grace. During this time, Jarrett and I were getting into Abbey's carriage, which was waiting at the front of the theater, where no one was expecting to see me. And it was lucky that we were able to do this, as my sister did not get back to the Albemarle Hotel till an hour after me, very tired, but very amused. The resemblance between us, plus my hat, boa, and the twilight, had all conspired to bring off the little comedy offered to my fans.

We were to leave at nine o'clock for Menlo Park. We had to wear our traveling clothes because the next day (Sunday) we were leaving for Boston; our trunks were leaving that very evening along with my company, which was to precede me by a few hours to this city. Our meal was, as always, terrible, as in this era American food was the horror of horrors. At ten o'clock we boarded the train. It was a special pretty train, all garlanded with flowers and decorated with flags that had been kindly made for me. But it was a tedious journey nevertheless, as we had to stop for every little thing—for a train to pass, an engine to manoeuver, or to wait for the switching of the points.

It was two o'clock in the morning when the train finally stopped at the station at Menlo Park, the place where Thomas Edison lived. The night was a deep black. Snow was falling silently and heavily. A carriage was waiting, and the single lantern of this vehicle lit up the station, as the electric light had been put out purposely. I oriented myself with my arm in Jarrett's and was helped by some friends who had accompanied us from New York. The intense cold was causing the falling snow to freeze, and we were walking over veritable icicles, which were spiky, cutting, and brittle. Behind the light cabriolet was a heavier vehicle hitched to one horse and without a lantern. This vehicle could hold five or six people at a squeeze; there were ten of us. Jarrett, Abbey, my sister, and I took places in the first carriage and the other people piled into the second. We looked like conspirators. The dark night, the two mysterious carriages, the silence imposed by the freezing cold, us, all muffled up in furs and throwing worried looks here and there—all of this gave our visit to the great Edison the atmosphere of a scene from an operetta.

The carriages set off, sticking in the snow and jolting terribly. The jolts made us fear at every moment some tragi-comic accident. How long had we been going? I cannot say. Rocked by the movement of the carriage and buried in the warmth of my furs I was gently dozing, when a loud "Hip, hip, hooray!" made us all jump—my companions, the driver, the horses, and me; and, faster than one could take it in, the countryside suddenly lit up. Everywhere—under the trees, above the trees, in the bushes, along the paths—lights flashed into life triumphantly.

The carriage went a few more yards and we found ourselves in front of the house of the illustrious Thomas Edison. A group of people were waiting for us in front of the porch: four men, two ladies, and a girl. My heart was thumping. Which of these men was Edison? I had not seen his photograph, but I had a great admiration for this genius.

I sprang out of the carriage. The dazzling electric light created an impression of full daylight. I took the bouquet that Mrs. Edison presented to me, and as I thanked her, I tried to figure out which of these men was the great man. All four had moved toward me, but one of them blushed slightly, and his blue eyes expressed such discomfort that I realized it was Edison. I became confused and embarrassed myself, for I realized that I was bothering him. He saw in my visit only the banal curiosity of a foreigner drunk on publicity. He already foresaw the interviews the day after, and the stupid remarks that would be put in his mouth. He suffered in advance for the ignorant questions that I was going to put to him, and the explanations that politeness would force him to give me; and for a minute Thomas Edison disliked me. His marvellous blue eyes, which were more luminous than his incandescent lamps, made it possible for me to read all his thoughts. Realizing then that I must win him over, my combative spirit drew on the full force of my seductive power to conquer this wonderful shy scientist.

I succeeded so well that half an hour later we were the best friends in the world. I followed him quickly as he climbed staircases narrow and vertical like ladders, and crossed bridges suspended over veritable furnaces. He explained everything to me. I understood everything and my admiration increased yet further, for this King of Light was simple and charming. While we were both leaning over the flimsy bridge that swayed above the frightful abyss in which there turned, swung, and shrieked enormous wheels within wide belts, he gave various orders in a voice clearly audible above the din; and light sprang up in all directions, some in crackling greenish jets, some in rapid flashes, some in serpentine trails like rivers of fire.

I looked at this man of average height, with a rather strong head and a noble profile, and I thought of Napoleon I. There was certainly a great physical resemblance between these two men, and I am certain that they shared certain physical characteristics of the brain in common. Of course, I am not comparing their geniuses. The one was destructive and the other creative. But, although I detest battles, I love victories, and in spite of his errors, there is an altar in my heart to Napoleon, the god of death, the god of glory! So as I looked at Edison, this imaginative spirit, I compared his image to that of the great dead man.

The numbing noise of the engines and the blindingly rapid changes of light made me dizzy. Forgetting where I was I leaned on the flimsy guard rail that separated me from the abyss, with so little consciousness of danger, that before I could even recover from my surprise, I found myself swept by Edison into an adjoining room and installed in an armchair, without having any memory of what had happened. He told me a little later that I had had an attack of vertigo.

After he had done us the honor of demonstrating to us his inventions, the telephone and the astonishing phonograph, Edison offered me his arm to take me into the dining room where we found his family assembled. I was very tired and did honor to the supper that had been prepared with as much grace as I could.

I left Menlo Park at four o'clock in the morning. This time, the countryside, the roads, and the station were lit up *à giorno* by the thousand lights of this good scientist. A strange illusion created by the darkness—I had thought that we had traveled a long way coming over very rough roads. In fact, it was only a short distance and the road was fine, although it was covered by snow. Imagination had played a big part in the journey that had taken us to Edison's house, but reality played a yet bigger one in the same journey back to the station.

I was carried away with admiration for the inventions of this man. I continue to be charmed by the memory of his shy and courteous grace, and by his deep love for Shakespeare.

Chapter XXXIV

$\mathcal{T}$he next day, or actually on the same day, as it was four o'clock in the morning, I left for Boston. Mr. Abbey, my impresario, had arranged to have a delightful car set up for me. This was not yet the wonderful Pullman, as I would not pick that up until after leaving Philadelphia for the continuation of my tour. Nevertheless I was delighted when I entered the compartment that had been reserved for me: a real brass bed, wide and soft, stood in the middle of the little room, there was an armchair, a pretty dresser, a beribboned basket for my dog, and flowers everywhere with a delicate, not a harsh, scent. My personal staff were comfortably installed in a compartment adjoining mine.

I went to bed happy and woke up when we reached Boston. A large crowd was waiting for us at the station: reporters and many curiosity seekers, people who were more interested than friendly, without malice but without enthusiasm. I had been the talk of the town in New York for a month. I had been criticized and glorified. So much negative gossip had circulated on my account—stupid, disgusting, ridiculous, and odious! Some criticized and others admired the disdain with which I had responded to this slander, but they were not unaware that I had won in the end and had triumphed over my slanderers. Boston knew too that the clergy had mounted their pulpits to declare that I had been sent by the Old World to corrupt the New, and that I had learned my art from the Devil. All of this was known, and the public wanted to see me for themselves.

Boston belongs particularly to its women. Legend has it that it was a woman's foot that first trod the soil of Boston. Women are in the majority there. Their characters are a combination of puritanism and intelligence, independence and grace.

I made my way through the crowd formed by these strange, courteous, cold people. Just as I was about to get into my carriage a lady approached me and said, "Welcome to Boston, Ma'am! Welcome to Boston, Ma'am!" as she held out to me her little tiny soft hand—American women in general have charming hands and feet. Other people approached and smiled at me. I had to shake numerous hands.

267

I immediately took a liking to this city. However, I was furious when I saw a reporter, who was even more bold and pressing than the others, jump onto the running board of the carriage. That really went beyond the bounds of decency. I angrily pushed the horrible man away, but Jarrett had the foresight to hold onto his collar, otherwise he would have a bad fall onto the pavement—which was exactly what he deserved.

"What time are you going on the whale?" this strange person intoned.

I looked at him in bewilderment. He spoke French perfectly. "He's crazy," I whispered to Jarrett.

"No, Madame, I'm not crazy, but I would like to know what time tomorrow you are going to go on the whale. Perhaps it would be better to go there this evening, because there's a fear that it might die tonight, and it would really be a pity if you didn't visit him while he's still alive." So he spoke, and as he did so he crouched next to Jarrett, who was still holding him by the collar, afraid that he was going to fall off the carriage.

"But, Monsieur," I cried, "what's this about a whale?"

"Ah Madame, it's wonderful! It's enormous! It's in the harbor! Men have been hired to break the ice around it day and night!" Then, suddenly, standing up on the running board, he leaned over to shout to the coach driver, "Stop! Stop! Hey, Henry, come here! Look, here's Madame!"

The carriage stopped, and without more ado he jumped down and pushed into my landau a short thickset man, his eyes hidden under a thick fur hat, an enormous diamond in his necktie—in a word the strangest sort of oldtime Yankee. He could not speak a word of French, but happily installed himself next to Jarrett, while the reporter continued to hang onto the side of the carriage. Three of us had left the station. Five now arrived at the Hotel Vendôme.

There were a lot of people waiting for us to arrive, and I felt most ashamed of my new companion. He talked loudly, addressing himself to everybody, laughed, coughed, spat, issued invitations. Everyone seemed delighted.

A young girl threw her arms round her father's neck. "Oh yes, Daddy, please, let's go there!"

"But," he replied, "we have to ask Madame," and he approached me with an elegant and courteous manner. "Madame, is it your pleasure that we should be among your guests when you go to see the whale tomorrow?"

"But Monsieur," I replied, glad to be talking finally with a well-mannered man, "I don't know anything about this. It's only a quarter of an hour since this reporter and this strange man have spoken about a whale and declared with authority that I must visit it, but I know nothing about it. These two gentlemen besieged my carriage, sat themselves in it without my permission, and, as you can see, are making invitations in my name to people with whom I am unacquainted, to go with me to a place that I don't know, to visit a whale that must be introduced to me, and which is looking forward to seeing me so that it can die in peace."

The nice gentleman gestured to his daughter to follow and I went up with them, Jarrett, and Mme. Guérard in the elevator, which stopped outside my suite.

My suite was decorated with precious paintings, magnificent ornaments, and wonderful statues. I was even a little worried, for amongst the objets d'art were two or three objects that were very beautiful, very rare, and priceless in value. I was afraid that one of them might be stolen, and I shared my fear with the proprietor of the hotel who replied, "Monsieur ***, to whom these objects belong, wants you to be able to look at them all the time that you are here, Mademoiselle, and when I conveyed to him the same fear that you have just mentioned, he said that he was unconcerned!"

It turned out that the paintings belonged to two rich landowners in Boston. One of them was a superb Millet, that I would have liked to own myself. After having expressed my thanks and marvelled at these wonders, I asked for an explanation of the story of the whale. Mr. Max Gordon, the little girl's father, translated for me the words of the short man in the fur hat. He was the owner of a cod fishing fleet. One of his boats had caught an enormous whale, which had two harpoons stuck in its flank. The unfortunate beast was struggling, exhausted, several miles off shore and was easily caught and taken in triumph to the owner of the fleet, Henry Smith.

By what twist of logic or mental path had this man come to consider the combination of his whale and my name as a source of fortune? I don't know. But, in any case, he was so amusingly, so authoritatively, and so violently insistent, that there we were at the harbor, fifty of us, the following morning, at seven o'clock in freezing rain. Mr. Gordon himself drove his carriage pulled by four very beautiful horses. His little daughter, Jarrett, my sister, Mme. Guérard, and another elder lady, whose name I have forgotten, traveled with us. Seven other carriages followed. It was very very amusing.

We were welcomed on arriving at the quay by the comical Henry, this time clad in fur from head to foot, his hands in great woollen mittens. Only his eyes and the big diamond were visible twinkling under the fur. I went to the edge of the quay, very intrigued. There were some rubberneckers and—alas, alas!—some reporters!

Then Henry's woollen paw took me by the hand and dragged me off toward the steps, I in imminent danger of breaking my neck. He pushed me stumbling down the ten steps and I found myself on the back of the whale which, they said, was still breathing . . . really I could not swear to it. But as the waves broke against the poor whale they made it move slightly. It was covered with a thin coating of ice. Twice I found myself spreadeagled on its back. I laugh about it now, but I was furious then. All around me they were insisting that I pull off a whale-bone from the poor captive, one of those little whalebones that are used in women's corsets. That worried me. I was afraid I would hurt it. It was so wretched I thought—this poor great beast on top of which three people—Henry, the little Gordon girl, and myself—had been skidding about for the last ten minutes! Finally I made up my mind. I pulled off a little whalebone and went back up on the quay carrying my sad trophy, surrounded, harrassed, irritated.

I was angry with Henry Smith. I did not want to get back in the carriage. I wanted to hide my bad temper in one of those deep and dark landaus that had been following us; but charming Miss Gordon asked me why, so nicely, that I felt this child's smile dissolve my anger.

"Do you want to drive?" her father asked me.

"Oh yes! With pleasure!"

But Jarrett started to get out with as much haste as his age and corpulence would permit. "If you're driving, I prefer to get out," and he got into another carriage.

I boldly took Mr. Gordon's place to drive, but we had hardly gone a hundred yards when I drove the horses into a drugstore on the quay, crashing the carriage up onto the sidewalk. Without the rapid response of Mr. Gordon we would all have been killed. Back at the hotel I went to bed until it was time for the performance.

In the evening we performed *Hernani* to a full theater. The seats had been auctioned and had reached quite high prices. We gave fifteen performances at Boston with average receipts of nineteen thousand francs per performance.

I left this city regretfully. I had spent two weeks there filled with charm and a sense of affinity with the Bostonian women. They are puritans from head to toe, but indulgently, and without bitterness. What most struck me about them was their harmonious gestures and the pleasant timbre of their voices. With its severe and ascetic background the Bostonian race seems to be the most refined and mysterious of the American people. Since the women are in the majority in Boston, many of them remain spinsters. Thus all the life force, that they might otherwise expend in love or maternity, is spent in toning up and strengthening the beauty of their bodies by physical activities in which there is no lack of grace. The reserves of their hearts overflow into intellectuality: they adore music, the theater, literature, painting, poetry. They know everything, understand everything, remain chaste and reserved, and neither laugh very much nor talk very loud. They are as far removed from the Latin race as the North Pole is from the South; but they are interesting, delightful, and captivating.

So it was with rather a heavy heart that I left Boston to go to New Haven. Imagine my surprise, on arriving at the hotel in New Haven, at finding Henry Smith there, the man with the whale. "Oh my God!" I exclaimed, throwing myself into an armchair. "What does this man want with me now?" It was not long before I found out. A frightful cacophony of brass, drums, trumpets (and saucepans too I think), drew me to the window. I saw an enormous float surrounded by an escort of negro minstrels and, on the float, a horrible colored poster, monstrous in size, representing me standing on the whale, which reared up as I ripped a whale bone from its back. Sandwich-men followed carrying placards saying

COME AND SEE
The Enormous Cetacean that Sarah Bernhardt
Killed Ripping from It Whalebones for her Corsets
Which Are Made by Mrs. Lily Noë
Who Lives etc. etc.

Then on other placards carried by other sandwich-men it said

The Whale is Just as Flourishing (Sic)
As in Its Lifetime
It has $500 of Salt in Its Stomach
The Salt on Which It Rests Is Renewed Daily
At a Cost of $100!

I went deathly pale. My teeth chattered with fury. I could not utter a word. Henry Smith came toward me. I slapped him and fled into my bedroom where I sobbed with disgust and fatigue.

I wanted to leave for Europe immediately, but Jarrett showed me my contract. I wanted to have this odious exhibition prohibited and promises were made to placate me, but in fact I got nowhere. Two days later I was at Hartford and the same whale was there again; it made its tour at the same time as I made mine. Its salt was replenished, its ice was replenished, but it continued to travel, and I met up with it wherever I went. Each time I started all over again a suit that had to be

begun again in another state, the laws not being the same from one
state to another. Every time that I arrived at a hotel I found an immense bouquet of flowers with the horrible card of the whale show-
man. I would throw down the flowers and stamp on the them—I, who
love flowers so much—I took an aversion to them. Jarrett went to see
this man to beg him not to send me any more bouquets. It was no
good. This was the man's revenge for the slap I had given him. Besides
he did not understand my anger. He was making money like crazy and
had even offered me a percentage of his profits. I would have happily
killed the execrable Smith! He was poisoning my life and he was all I
saw in the cities I went to. I would not go out, except from the hotel
to the theater with my eyes closed. When I heard the minstrels, I started,
and turned green. Luckily I was able to rest at Montreal where he did
not follow me. I think I would have fallen ill. I could see nothing
besides him nor think of anything else. I was haunted and obsessed by
this perpetual nightmare. Finally I left Hartford after visiting the big
factory where the famous Colts are manufactured. I purchased two of
them. Jarrett assured me that Henry Smith would not be at Montreal:
he had fallen suddenly ill. I suspect that Jarrett had given him some
kind of violent purgative to stop him in his tracks. He was laughing too
much about it on the journey, ferocious gentleman that he was. Nevertheless, I was infinitely grateful to him for having rid me of this man for
the moment.

Chapter XXXV

[*Sarah arrives at Montreal*[1] *on an exceptionally cold winter's night and is welcomed by a vast crowd of people, among them Louis Fréchette,*[2] *a poet who recites a poem in her honor at the station, whereupon Sarah faints from cold and fatigue. She is rescued, as her sister Jeanne later tells her, by a herculean young man who comes next morning to see her at her hotel. As he is leaving he begs Sarah to promise that if she ever learns who he is she will remember him only for the service he has done her. At this moment Jarrett enters and Sarah hears only the words "detective . . . door. . . assassination . . . impossibility . . . New Orleans." The young man is led away and later Sarah hears that he has been hanged.*

The Bishop of Montreal inveighs against the immorality of French literature and of Sarah's company and the plays they perform, with the result that audiences flock to their performances.

Sarah is taken to visit the Iroquois at Canghnanwaga along with her sister, Jarrett, and Angelo (strong and brave but without talent as an actor).[3] *The chief, Sun of Nights, son of Great White Wing, is a pathetic sight in European clothing peddling various goods, including brandy in which he finds oblivion. Sarah is disgusted by the Indian reservation as a symbol of the crimes committed in the name of civilization.*

The extraordinary success of Sarah's company in Montreal is due in part to the great enthusiasm of the students in the audience, who sing songs and transport bouquets to the stage by pulleys and messages by doves. Sarah notices the courtesy with which the Marquess of Lorne, governor of Canada, stands for the enthusiastic singing of the Marseillaise, *but the pride with which he stifles its last notes as he gestures to the orchestra to play* God Save the King.

Sarah's last performance is Hernani *on Christmas Day. Next day she and her sister take a walk beside the St. Lawrence and are nearly swept away on a piece of ice, onto which they climb as a prank. They are finally rescued but upbraided by Jarrett, who points out that if Sarah had died she would have been in breach of contract. They reach the station just in time for the train to Springfield and are given a rapturous send-off.*]

273

Chapter XXXVI

$\mathcal{A}$fter the great noisy success of our visit to Montreal, we were a little surprised by the icy welcome afforded us by the people of Springfield.

We were doing *La Dame aux camélias*, called in America *"Camille"*— why? No one has ever been able to tell me. This play, which the public flocked to see, outraged the extreme puritanism of the small towns of America. The critics in the big cities discussed this modern Mary Magdalene, but those in the little towns threw stones at her. From time to time in the small towns we found people primly prejudiced against the impurity of Marguerite Gautier, and Springfield at that time had hardly thirty thousand inhabitants.

During the day that I spent at Springfield I went to a gunsmith to buy a hunting rifle. The dealer took me into a long and very narrow yard where I tried out several. When I turned round I was surprised and embarrassed to see two gentlemen, who were taking an interest in my shooting. I wanted to leave immediately, but one of them came up to me and said, "Would you like to fire a cannon, Ma'am?" I nearly fell over with surprise and could not reply for a second. Then I exclaimed, "I would love to!" I made an appointment with the man, who turned out to be the manager of the Colt weapons factory. An hour later I went there as arranged. More than thirty people hastily invited were already waiting, which annoyed me a little. I shot the newly invented canon-mitrailleuse.[1] I found it a very amusing experience, but not one which affected me emotionally.

In the evening, after the chilly reception given to our performance, we left for Baltimore at a dizzy pace, as the performance had finished after the Baltimore train had left. We had to catch up with this, come what may. The three enormous cars that made up my own personal train set off at full steam. As there were two locomotives pulling us we kept making great leaps only to fall back, God only knows how, onto the rails. We finally managed to catch up with the express train, which had been telegraphed to say we were on its heels and therefore made a short stop—just long enough for us to jump on somehow or other, and in this way we arrived at Baltimore where I stayed four days and gave five performances.

Two things struck me in this city—the mortal cold of the hotels and the theater, and the beauty of the women. I felt very sad at Baltimore because I spent New Year's Day far away from the one who was so dear to me. I cried all night and felt for a while the kind of unhappiness that makes one wish one could die. However we received colossal acclaim in this city and I left it with regret for Philadelphia, where we were to spend a week.

This city was very beautiful but I did not like it. I received an enthusiastic welcome there, in spite of the fact that we had to switch the play on the first evening. Two of the actors had missed the train, so we could not put on *Adrienne Lecouvreur*. I had to substitute *Phèdre*, the only play in which the two late-comers did not appear. Our receipts for the seven performances given over six days averaged twenty thousand francs.

My stay in Philadelphia was marred by a letter which informed me of the death of my friend Gustave Flaubert, the writer who is most sensitive to the beauty of our language.

From Philadelphia we went to Chicago. At the station I was welcomed by a delegation representing the women of Chicago, and a bouquet of rare flowers was presented to me by a gorgeous young woman called Mrs. Lily B ***. Then Jarrett steered me into one of the station waiting rooms, where the French delegation was waiting for me. A very short but emotional speech by our consul conveyed to us the friendship and confidence of the French population of Chicago. After thanking him wholeheartedly I was on the point of leaving the station, when, all of a sudden, I felt myself turned to stone—and it appears that my face took on such an expression of intense suffering that everybody rushed up to help me. A sudden anger had electrified my whole being, and I walked straight toward the horrible vision that had just risen up before me—the man with the whale! So the horrible Smith was alive! He was covered with furs and had diamonds on every finger. The horrible brute was there with a bouquet in his hand! I refused his flowers and pushed him away with all my strength, a strength that my anger rendered ten times stronger than usual. A stream of crazed words issued from my pale lips. But this scene delighted him because it was retold, hawked about, and amplified, and the whale received even more visitors than usual.

I went to Palmer House, one of the most magnificent hotels at this time, the proprietor of which, Mr. Palmer, was a perfect gentleman—courteous, amiable, and generous. He filled the enormous suite that I had with the rarest of flowers and he took pains to have me served in French style—a difficult thing at that time.

We were to stay two weeks in Chicago. Our success surpassed everyone's expectations. I found these two weeks the most pleasant ones we had spent since we had arrived in America. This city takes its vitality from the constant hustle and bustle of men whose knitted brows denote only one thing: reaching the "goal." They go and go, and no cry or appeal for caution can make them turn back. What goes on behind them matters little. They do not wish to know the reason for the cry and they do not have time to be cautious: the goal awaits them. The women here, as in the rest of America, do not work. But they do not stroll down the streets as they do in other cities: they walk quickly. They also are in a hurry, in a hurry to amuse themselves.

Each day I went out some distance into the surrounding countryside in order not to meet the sandwich-men advertising the whale.

One day I went to the slaughterhouse where pigs were slaughtered. What a horrible yet magnificent spectacle! There were three of us—my sister and I, and an Englishman friend of mine. When we arrived we saw hundreds of pigs, jostled and squeezed together, grunting and jibbing, as they filed out onto a narrow elevated bridge. Our carriage passed under this bridge and stopped in front of a group of men who were waiting for us. The manager of the stockyard welcomed us and led us into his slaughterhouse.

As you go into the enormous shed, which is feebly lit by windows with greasy reddened panes, a disgusting smell hits you and makes you retch, a smell that will not leave you for several days afterward. A bloody mist rises up everywhere, like a light cloud floating on a mountainside illuminated by the setting sun. An infernal din rings in your ears: the almost human shrieks of the slaughtered pigs, the violent thudding of the hatchet chopping off the legs, the successive grunts of the ripper who, with a superbly sweeping gesture, lifts the heavy axe, and with a single blow splits open the unfortunate beast from top to bottom as it struggles on a hook; perceived also in the swift glimpse of this horrifying moment is the continual grinding of the revolving razor, which instantaneously removes the bristles from the trunk thrown to it by the machine which had cut off the four trotters; the whistle as the steam escapes from the hot water in which the head of the animal is scalded; the cascading of waste water; the rumble of little trains, carrying away under wide arches wagons loaded with ham, sausage etc. etc. . . . All of this against the background of the locomotive bell warning of the train's approach which, in this place of frightful massacre, sounds like a perpetual knell, tolling for all these death agonies.

Nothing was more Hoffmannesque[2] than this pork slaughterhouse at the time I visited it, although since then a more humane concern has infiltrated (albeit rather timidly) this temple of porcine hecatombs.

I returned from this visit feeling quite ill. In the evening I performed in *Phèdre*. I went on stage feeling very tense, and with a will to do whatever I could to chase away the horrible vision of a short time previously. I threw my whole heart and soul into the character, so much so that, at the end of the fourth scene, I fell down on the stage in a dead faint.

On the day of my last performance I was presented with a magnificent diamond necklace from the ladies of Chicago. I left this city loving everything about it: its people, its lake as big as an inland sea, its enthusiastic audiences—everything, yes everything, but not its stockyards. I even bore no ill will toward the bishop who, like those in the other cities, had inveighed against my art and against French literature. Besides, the vehemence of his sermons had given us so much free publicity that our manager, Mr. Abbey, wrote him the following letter:

Your Grace,

When I come to your city I am in the habit of spending four hundred dollars on publicity. But as you have created the publicity for me I am sending you two hundred dollars for the poor.

Henry Abbey

We left Chicago to go to Saint Louis, which we reached after traveling two hundred eighty-three miles in fourteen hours. In my drawing room on the train Abbey and Jarrett showed me the grand total for the sixty-two performances we had given since we had left France: 227,459 dollars—i.e. 1,37,284 francs—an average of 18,343 francs for each performance. This gave me great pleasure on behalf of Henry Abbey, who had lost everything in his previous tour with a wonderful opera company, and it gave me even greater pleasure for myself, since I was to receive a large share of the receipts.

We stayed at Saint Louis for a whole week from January 24 to 31. I must say that this city, which was particularly French, pleased me less than the other American cities. It was dirty and the hotels were not very comfortable. Since then it has made great progress, but it is because of the Germans that it now bears the mark of progress. At the time that I am talking about, in 1881, the city was really revoltingly dirty. Alas, we were hardly colonizers at that time, and all the cities in which French influence was preponderant were behind the times and poor.

I was mortally bored at Saint Louis and wanted to leave immediately after paying an indemnity to the theater manager. But the ferocious Jarrett, a man of integrity and duty, said to me with the contract in his hand, "No, Madame. You must stay, die with boredom if you wish, but you must stay." To entertain me, he took me to a famous cave in which live millions of fish without eyes, for light has never penetrated into this cave. It seems that as they did not need their eyes these primitive fish bred offspring without eyes. We went to see this cave. It was far away, very far away. Taking a thousand precautions we crawled on all fours down into the cave like cats. We went along like this for what seemed an interminable amount of time. Finally the guide said, "It's here." We were able to stand up, as the cave had a higher roof. I could not see anything. I heard a match being struck and the guide lit a little lantern. I made out in front of me, almost at my feet, a natural basin that was quite deep. "You see," said the guide in a deadpan tone, "here is the basin. But at the moment there is no water and no fish. You must come back in three months." Jarrett made such a frightful grimace that crazy laughter took hold of me, laughter that was close to madness. I hiccuped, cried, and choked. I went down into the basin to look for a piece of flotsam, a little bone from a dead fish, a little something . . . there was nothing, nothing. We had to go back on all fours again. I made Jarrett go in front of me, and the sight of his great furry back, as he crawled along on his hands and knees grumbling and swearing, gave me such great joy that I no longer regretted anything. I gave ten dollars to our guide to his great surprise and incredulity.

We go back to the hotel and I am told that there is a jeweler there who has been waiting for me for two hours. "A jeweler? But I have no intention of buying any jewels, I have too many already!" But Jarrett gives a look to Abbey who is there, and we go in. I notice immediately that there is some connivance between the jeweler and my two impresarios. They explain to me that my jewels very much need to be cleaned, that this jeweler will take it upon himself to clean them like new, repair them, and, in a word, exhibit them! I rebel, but it is no use. Jarrett assures me that the ladies of Saint Louis are partial to this kind of spectacle; that this would be very good publicity; that my jewelry is very tarnished; that some stones are missing that the jeweler will replace for nothing. What a saving! Think about it! And I give in, for this kind of discussion bores me.

Two days later the jeweler's dazzling window was receiving visits from the ladies of the city, come to admire my jewels. But my poor

Guérard, who had wanted to go and see them, came back horrified. "They have added to your jewels six pairs of earrings, two necklaces, and thirty rings; there is also a lorgnette all in diamonds and rubies, a gold cigarette holder set with turquoise, a little pipe with an amber end set with diamonds, sixteen bracelets, a toothpick set with a sapphire, and a pair of glasses with the side-pieces in gold and a little pearl teardrop at the end of each! They must have made them especially," said my poor Guérard, "because no one wears glasses like that! And it says above them 'Study glasses of Mme. Sarah Bernhardt'!" Really! I felt this exceeded the limits of desirable publicity to have me smoking a pipe and wearing glasses, it was really too much! I got into a carriage and went to the jeweler's. I arrived just in time to knock my head against closed doors. It was five o'clock on Saturday, all was dark, the lights were out, the shop was closed! I went back to the hotel and shared my discontent with Jarrett who said calmly, "What does it matter, Madame? Tons of girls wear glasses. As for the pipe, the jeweler told me that he had received five orders and that it was going to become a fashion. Besides, there is no point in getting annoyed. The exhibition is over, your jewels are being returned this evening, and we are leaving the day after tomorrow." Indeed, that same evening the jeweler gave me back my jewelry, restored to look like new, brilliant, flashy, and re-paired. There was a gold cigarette holder with it decorated with tur-quoise, the same one that he had exhibited. I could not get this man to understand anything I said, and my anger melted at his good grace and his joy.

But this publicity nearly cost us our lives, for, lured by so many jewels—most of which did not belong to me—some crooks banded together to steal my jewels, which they thought were in the big bag always carried by my manservant. On Sunday, January 30, at eight o'clock in the morning, we were leaving Saint Louis for Cincinnati. I was in my magnificently appointed Pullman car. I had asked that my car be at the back of our special little train so that I could enjoy from the observa-tion platform the beauty of nature, which unfolded before me in an ever-changing, living, wonderful panorama. We had hardly been travel-ing for ten minutes when the conductor suddenly leaned over the rail of the little balcony, then, quickly standing up straight, he took my hand and, looking very pale and anxious, said to me in English, "Ma-dame, I beg you, go back in!" I realized that a real danger threatened me and I went in quickly. He pulled the alarm, and even before the train had completely stopped he signaled to another conductor and both of them rushed to the end of the train. He had fired a shot to alert everybody. Jarrett, Abbey, and the actors were squeezed in the narrow corridor. I found myself in their midst, and we were amazed to see the two conductors dragging from underneath my carriage a man armed to the teeth.

He finished by confessing the truth as he had a revolver clamped against each temple. He had been charged by the gang at Saint Louis to steal my jewelry, for the jeweler's publicity had excited the whole world of thieves. The plan was to disconnect my carriage from the rest of the train between Saint Louis and Cincinnati, at a place called Petite-Montée. This was to happen at night. As my carriage was at the end, it was very easy. All he had to do was lift the enormous hook and take it out of its ring. This man, who was a real young colossus, had clung to the underside of my carriage. We went to look at his setup: huge belts a foot and a half wide held him as he clung to the underside of the train between the wheels, and his hands were free to manoeuver. The courage and sangfroid of this man were admirable. He told us that seven armed men were waiting for us at Petite-Montée, and that they did not intend to harm us if we did not defend ourselves. They only wanted to take my jewelry and the twenty-three hundred dollars that the secretary was carrying on him. Oh, he knew everything! He knew everybody's name and he spoke to me in garbled French, "Oh, *you*, Madame, we wouldn't have done any harm to you, in spite of your pretty revolver. We would even have let you keep it." This man and his band knew that the secretary slept in my carriage and that he was hardly formidable (poor Chatterton!), that he was carrying twenty-three hundred dollars, and that I had a very pretty engraved revolver decorated with cat's eyes. The man was firmly tied up and held at bay by the two conductors and we reversed all the way to Saint Louis. We had not been gone more than a quarter of an hour. The police, who had been alerted, sent us five detectives, and a freight train was sent ahead of us to precede us by half an hour. Eight detectives were put on the freight train who had orders to get out at Petite-Montée. Our colossus was put into the hands of the law, and I was promised that he would be treated leniently in view of the confession that he had made. I learned later that this promise was kept and that the man was sent back to Ireland, his native country.

From this time onward my car was put between two other cars at night; during the day I was permitted to have my carriage at the rear, on condition that I accept an armed detective on the platform, for whom I nevertheless had to pay.

We left approximately twenty-five minutes after the freight train. Our dinner was very gay for the excitement had infected everybody. As for the conductor who had discovered the colossus hidden under the train, Abbey and I had so generously rewarded him that he got drunk and kept coming up to kiss my hand, crying drunkard's tears and endlessly repeating, "I saved the Frenchwoman! I am a gentleman!" Finally we began to approach Petite-Montée. Night had come and the engineer wanted to go at full steam. But we had hardly covered five miles when some detonators went off under the wheels and we had to slow down. What was the new danger threatening us? Anxiety took hold of us. The women were getting nervous. Some of them were crying. We were moving forward slowly, groping in the dark, trying to make out from the light of a detonator the silhouette of a man or several men. Abbey thought that we should go ahead anyway at full speed, because, he said, these detonators had been placed there by the bandits, who had foreseen that the colossus might not have been able to disconnect the wagon and were trying to stop the train by another method. The engineer refused to move saying that these were in fact a sign from the railway administration, and that he could not risk everybody's life on the basis of a mere conjecture.

The man was in the right and he was very brave. "We will always get the better of a bunch of rogues, but I cannot answer for the life of anyone if the train derails, collides, or falls into a precipice." We went forward slowly. We had put out all the lights so that we could see as much as possible without being seen. The truth had been hidden as much as possible from the actors, except for three men whom I had called to my side. The actors had nothing to fear from the thieves. I, alone, was their target. To avoid giving evasive and worrying answers to their questions we had sent the secretary to tell them that there was a mechanical holdup and we had to slow down. They were also told that repairs were being made to a gas pipe, and that the lights would be on again in a few minutes. Then the connection between their carriage and mine was cut off.

We had been going along for perhaps ten minutes when every-thing was lit up by a great light that made us stop. We saw running toward us a crew of railway workers. I still shudder to think that these people were nearly killed. We had been in such a state of nerves for several hours that at first we thought we saw running toward us the colossus's roguish band of friends. A first shot went off and if the brave engineer had not shouted, "Halt!" along with a terrible oath, two or three of these people would have been wounded. I had taken up my revolver. But before I had pulled off the ring which served as a safety catch one could have had, a hundred times over, the time to seize me, tie me up, and kill me.

And just imagine that every time I go to a place where I fear some danger I always take along my pistol, for it is not a revolver, it is a pistol. I always say "revolver," but in truth it is a pistol, an old-fashioned pistol with a ring and a trigger, which is so stiff that I have to use both hands. I do not shoot badly for a woman, as long as I can take my time, which is really not very convenient if one wants to shoot a thief. And yet I always have it with me. It is there on my table, I can see it at this very moment as I write. It is in its holster, which is rather tight, so that I have to pull it out with some force and patience. If an assassin were to arrive at this moment, I should have to undo the stud which sticks, pull off the holster which is too tight, pull off the ring which is a little stiff, and press with both hands on the trigger! Well, human beings are so strange that this little ridiculously useless thing in front of me seems to me to be an admirable defense. And I, who am unfortunately so prone to fear, feel secure near this little friend, who must be laughing in his holster from which I can never get him out.

Finally, we were given an explanation. The freight train that had gone on ahead of us had derailed without great damage and with no loss of life. The gang from Saint Louis had thought of everything and had prepared a little derailment two miles from Petite-Montée, in case their friend clinging under my carriage had been unable to disconnect it. The derailment had taken place, but, when the rogues hurled themselves at the train that they thought was mine, they had found themselves surrounded by the group of detectives. It seems they had put up a fierce fight. One of them was killed on the spot, two others were wounded, the rest were taken prisoner.

A few days later the ringleader was hanged. He was a boy of twenty-five, named Albert Wirtz, a native of Belgium. I did everything I could to save this man, for it seemed that I was the unintentional cause of his evil plan. If Abbey and Jarrett had not been thirsty for publicity, if more than six hundred thousand francs worth of jewels had not been added to mine, this man, this poor child, would not have had the stupid idea of stealing them. Who can say what ideas were germinating in this young and hungry mind, a mind perhaps inebriated with intelligent schemes? Perhaps, as he stopped in front of the jeweler's window, he said to himself, "There is a million francs' worth of jewels. If I had them I could sell them, go back to Belgium, give joy to my poor mother wearing her eyes out in the lamplight, and marry off my sister." Perhaps he was an inventor and said to himself, "Ah! If I had all the money that these jewels represent I could market my inventions myself, instead of selling my patent to some highly esteemed rogue, who would buy me out for a mouthful of bread. What can it matter to this actress? Ah, if only *I* had this money!" Perhaps he cried with rage at the sight of all these riches belonging to one individual! Perhaps the idea of the crime germinated in a mind pure of any previous offense!

It is hard to know what hope can breed in a young mind. A wonderful dream can end up in a mad desire to see it realized. To steal someone else's property is not good, but it does not merit the death penalty. Oh no! To kill a man of twenty-five is a much greater crime than to steal jewels, even if armed; and the society that bands together to hold the sword of justice is much more cowardly when it kills, than the one who steals and assassinates all alone, with all its risks and perils! I cried for this man that I did not know, who was perhaps a rascal, perhaps a hero, perhaps a simpleton who had become a brigand, but who was twenty-five years old and had a right to life.

I hate the death penalty! It is a vestige of cowardly barbarism. It is a disgrace for civilized countries still to be raising guillotines and gallows! Every human being has a moment of tenderness, a sorrowful tear, and this tear can fertilize the generous thoughts that lead to repentance! I would not for anything in the world wish to be one of those who condemns a man to death. And yet many of them are good men, who go home and tenderly kiss their wives and scold baby for breaking dolly's head.

I have seen four executions: one in London, one in Spain, and two in Paris.

In London it was a hanging, which seems to me more hideous, repugnant, and deceitful, than any other form of execution. It was a man in his thirties, with a virile, willful face. I saw him for a second. He shrugged his shoulders as he looked at me, and his eyes were full of disdain for my curiosity. At that moment I felt that the thoughts of this man were much superior to mine, and he seemed much greater than those who were watching, perhaps because he was much closer than all of us to the great mystery. I thought I saw him smile at the moment when they covered his face with the hood, and I fled, feeling completely overwhelmed.

At Madrid I saw a man garroted, and the barbarity of this punishment left me with a feeling of horror that lasted several weeks. It was said that he had killed his mother, but no real evidence had been laid against this unfortunate. While he was being held seated, before the garrote was put on him, he cried out, "Mother, I am going to join you and you will say to me that they have lied!" These words uttered in vibrant tones in Spanish were translated for me by an attaché at the English embassy, with whom I had gone to see this hideous spectacle. The unfortunate man cried out in a voice so sincere and heartbreaking that I felt it was impossible that he was not innocent. This was also the opinion of my companions.

The two other executions that I witnessed took place in Paris in the place de la Roquette. One of the executions was of a young medical student, I think, who had killed an old newspaper seller with the help of a friend. It was an odious and stupid crime; but this man was crazy rather than guilty. He was of superior intelligence and had taken his examinations at an early age. He had worked too much. His mind was deranged. He ought to have been put out to pasture, cared for like an invalid until he was better, and returned to science. He was a superior being. I can still see him. He was pale, with his eyes lost in infinity. This poor child's eyes were so sad! Yes, I know very well that he had cut the throat of a poor old defenseless woman. That's odious! But he was twenty-three years old, and his mind had been derailed by too much study and ambition, and by the habitual amputation of arms and legs and the dissection of the corpses of men, women, and children. None of that is an excuse for the abominable action of this man, but it could all have contributed to unbalance his sense of morality, which was perhaps very shaken by his studies, poverty, or heredity. In any case, I believe that it was an act of treason against humanity to extinguish this intellectual who, had he been brought back to his senses, could have rendered a service to science and humanity.

The last execution that I witnessed was that of Vaillant, the anarchist. He was an energetic and gentle man with very progressive ideas, but not much more progressive than those that have since gained ascendancy. He would often ask me for seats in my theater, which was then the Renaissance,[3] as he was too poor to indulge himself in the luxury of the arts. Ah, poverty! What a sad counselor it is! One must be very gentle to those who suffer from poverty.

One day Vaillant came to see me in my dressing room. I was performing in *Lorenzaccio*.[4] "This Florentine was an anarchist like me," he said, "but he killed the tyrant and not tyranny! That is not how I shall proceed." A few days later he threw a bomb in a public place: the Chamber of Deputies. The poor man was not as clever as the Florentine that he seemed to despise, as he did not kill anybody and did no real harm to anyone except himself.

I had asked to be informed of the day of the execution. One evening at the theater a friend came to tell me that the execution would be on the following day, a Monday, at seven o'clock in the morning. I left after the theater and went to rue Merlin, at the corner of the rue de la Roquette. The streets were still very busy because it was *Dimanche gras*.[5] People were singing, laughing, and dancing everywhere. I waited the whole night. I could not get permission to go into the prison. I sat on the balcony of the first floor apartment that I had rented. The cold misty night wrapped me in sadness, but I did not feel the cold because the blood was running rapidly in my veins. One hour slowly nudged the next as they chimed in the distance, "This hour is dead! Let the next hour live!" I could hear a vague muffled noise, footsteps, whisperings, wood cracking dully. I did not realize what these strange and mysterious sounds were, until the dawn allowed me to see that the gallows had gone up.

A man came to extinguish the lights illuminating the little place de la Roquette. An anemic sky spread its pale light above us. A crowd had gradually collected, standing in a compact group. The roads were blocked off. From time to time the crowd would part to allow through an indifferent and hurried man, who would present a card to a police officer and disappear again inside the prison building. It was a journalist. I counted more than ten of them. Then suddenly the Parisian Guards—double the usual number because there was fear that the anarchists might stage an attack—arranged themselves at the foot of that sad pedestal.

At a signal sabers were bared and the door of the prison opened. Vaillant appeared, pale, energetic, and brave. In a manly and confident voice he cried out, "Long live anarchy!" There was not a single answering cry. He was seized and pulled back over the plank. The blade fell with a muffled sound. The body toppled over. In a second the gallows were dismantled, the square swept up, the roads unblocked; and the crowd ran over the square, looking down at the ground, looking in vain for a drop of blood, sniffing with their noses in the air the odor of the drama that had just unfolded. Women, children, men of all ages, swarmed over this little square where a man had just expired in the ultimate agony. A man who had made himself the apostle of this people. A man who had claimed for this swarming race all liberties, all privileges, all rights!

On the arm of a male friend I mingled with the crowd, veiled and unrecognizable. I was sickened and in despair. Not a single word of recognition for this man . . . not a murmur of vengeance . . . not a feeling of revolt. I wanted to cry out, "You pile of brutes! Kiss the stones that the blood of this poor fool has reddened on *your* behalf!—for *you*—believing in *you*!" But I was preempted by a lout who shouted, "Read all about it! Read about the last moments of Vaillant! Read all about it! Read all about it!"

Oh poor Vaillant! His decapitated body was rolling toward Clamart. And the crowd for which he had wept, cried, and died, filtered away slowly, nonchalant and bored. Poor Vaillant! He had mad but generous ideas!

Chapter XXXVII

We arrived at Cincinnati safe and sound. We were to give three performances and leave for New Orleans. Finally, we were going to have some sun! We were going to warm our poor limbs pained by three months of mortal cold! We were going to breathe pure air through open windows instead of the suffocating and debilitating air of steam heat.

I fall asleep, and warm and perfumed dreams rock me in my sleep. Suddenly a knock on the door makes me start awake; my dog sniffs under the door with his ears pricked up, but he does not growl or bark. So it must be one of us.

I open the door and Jarrett, followed by Abbey, gestures to me not to speak. "Ssh!" He comes in on tiptoe and closes the door.

"What's happening?"

"Well," says Jarrett, "the continual rains of the last twelve days have made the water rise to such a height that the pontoon bridge, which crosses the bay of Saint Louis and which would allow us to get to New Orleans in one or two hours, is in danger of collapsing under the force of the water. Can you hear the gale that has just blown up? If we go back we have had it for three or four days."

I jumped up. "What? Three or four days? And we're going to have to go back into the snow? Oh no! No! Let's have some sun, some sun! But why can't we cross? Oh my God! What are we going to do?"

"Well, here is the plan. The engineer is here. He thinks that he can still cross, but he has just got married and he is willing to attempt the crossing only on condition that we give twenty-five hundred dollars (12,500 francs), which he will immediately send to Mobile where his father and wife live. If we get to the other side he will return this money, if not, he will have done right by his family."

I must say that I was speechless with admiration for this courageous man. I felt madly elated and cried out, "Yes, yes, give him the twelve thousand five hundred francs and let us go on!"

I have already said that I usually traveled in a special train. My train was made up of only three cars plus the locomotive. I did not doubt for a single moment the outcome of this criminal madness, and I did not inform anybody, neither my sister, nor my dear Guérard, nor my faithful servants Claude and Félicie. The actor Angelo, who was sleeping in Jarrett's sleeper during this trip, realized what was happening, but he was brave and had faith in my star. The money was given to the engineer who sent it forthwith to Mobile. Only as we started off did I have a vision of the responsibility I was shouldering, for I was risking the lives of thirty-two people without their consent. But it was too late. The train hurled itself at a terrifying speed onto the pontoon bridge. I was sitting on the observation platform. The bridge bent and swayed like a hammock under the dizzy strain of our passage. When we were halfway across the bridge it dipped so deeply into the water that my sister took my arm and whispered, "We're drowning . . . that's it . . . " and she closed her eyes and huddled close, nervous but brave. Like her I also thought that our final moment was come. And the terrible thing is that I did not think for a second about those who were full of trust and life, whom I was sacrificing and killing. I only thought about a certain young loved one who was going to cry.

And to think that we harbor within us our own worst enemy—"thought"—which, from time to time, raises its head, terrible, perfidious, and malicious. We try unsuccessfully to chase it away. We do not obey it all the time thank God! But it pursues us, torments us, and makes us suffer. How often the worst thoughts assail us, and what a struggle we must put up against these offspring of our own minds! Anger, ambition, vengeance, give birth to the most detestable thoughts for which one blushes as though for a defect. They do not belong to us, for we have not summoned them, but they soil us nevertheless and leave us despairing at our lack of mastery over our souls, our hearts, our bodies, and our brains.

It was not written in the book of Destiny that this should be my last moment. The train righted itself, and, half bounding, half rolling, we arrived on the other bank. Behind us we heard a frightful crash and saw a column of water, which fell back down in a noisy shower. The bridge had collapsed.

For more than eight days the trains coming from the east and the north could not enter the city. I let the brave engineer keep his twelve thousand five hundred francs; but I had an uneasy conscience. For a long time my nights were troubled by horrific nightmares. When an actor or actress spoke to me about a baby, mother, or spouse, and how nice it would be to see him or her again, I would feel a deep pang of emotion and realize that I was turning pale. I felt a great pity for the "I" that I was.

When I got out of the train I was more dead than alive from the effect of retrospective emotion. I had to endure the very kind but very tiring deputation of my compatriots. Then, loaded with flowers, I got into my carriage which was to take me to my hotel.

The roads were rivers and we were in an elevated area of the city. The coachman said with an accent typical of Marseilles, "The low-lying area of the city is flooded up to the top of the houses. The negroes have been drowned by the hundred!" he added, as he whipped up the horses.

The hotels were notorious at this time in New Orleans—dirty, uncomfortable, and black with cockroaches. As soon as the candles were lit the rooms filled with large buzzing June beetles that fell on our shoulders and got tangled in our hair. Oh, I still shudder to think of it!

There was an opera company in New Orleans at the same time that we were there, the star of which was a woman called Emilie Ambre, who once nearly became the queen of Holland. This part of the States was poor, like all territory in America where the French have preponderated. Yes, we are hardly colonizers! The opera's receipts were very poor and we did not do so well either. Six performances would have sufficed in this city and we gave eight.

Nevertheless, I enjoyed my stay very much. There was a tremendous charm about this city. All the people so different—both white and black—had smiling faces. All the women had grace. The shops attracted you with the gaiety of their displays, the merchants in the open air under the arcades interrupted one another with joyful repartee. And yet the sun did not show itself a single time. These people carried their own sun with them.

I did not understand why they did not use boats. The horses had water up to the hocks and it would have been impossible even to get into a carriage, if it had not been for the fact that the sidewalks were raised three feet above the road, and in some places even higher. The floods were as regular as the seasons, but no one had thought of solving the problem by damming the river or the sound. Instead, raised sidewalks and little fly-bridges had been built to make it easier to get around. The black children amused themselves by fishing for crawfish (where did they come from?) in the streams and they sold them to passersby. Occasionally we saw a whole family of water snakes gliding by with their heads held high and their bodies undulating, like long starry sapphires.

I went down into the low-lying area of the city. It was a distressing spectacle. All the blacks' shanties had subsided into the muddy water. They were there by the hundred, squatting on top of these shifting wrecks with feverish eyes and white teeth chattering with hunger. Right, left, and center, corpses with bloated bellies floated on the water and bumped against wooden piles. There were many ladies distributing provisions and trying to take these unfortunate people away. No. They wanted to stay there. With inane smiles they kept repeating slowly, "Water go away. House found. Me fix it." And their women would nod their heads in agreement. Some alligators had approached, carried in by the water, and two children had disappeared. A fourteen-year-old lad had just been taken to the hospital, his foot cut off at the ankle by one of these monsters. The family was howling with fury. They wanted to keep the little one. The black bonesetter claimed that he could have cured him in two days and that the white bonesetters (read "doctors") would keep him at least a month in bed.

I left this city with regret, for it was like no other city that we had visited until then. We were really surprised to find ourselves still in one piece, for we had, we told ourselves, encountered so many different dangers.

Only the hairdresser, a certain Ibé, who had been rendered half crazy with fear on the second day of our stay, failed to recover his equilibrium. He usually slept in the theater in his trunk of wigs—strange but true! The first night everything was normal, but on the second night he woke up the whole neighborhood with his screams. The poor man had fallen deeply asleep only to awake to feel his mattress being lifted above the wigs by some mysterious pushing. He thought that a cat or a dog had found its way into the trunk and he lifted the mattress, a feeble rampart. Two snakes were there . . . whether fighting or making love he could not say. Two snakes of a sufficiently imposing size to terrify the people that had been attracted by the cries of poor Figaro. He was still pale when I saw him get into the boat that was to take us to our train. I called him over and asked him to tell me the story of this terrible night. In the course of his story he showed me one of his sturdy legs and said, "They were as big as that, Madame, yes, like that," and he trembled with fear at the memory of the frightful size of the reptiles. I think that they were probably one quarter the size of his leg, but he was nevertheless justified in being frightened, for these were not inoffensive water snakes that bite out of spite but are not poisonous.

We arrived at Mobile rather late in the day. We had already stopped in this city on our way to New Orleans and I had had a fit of hysterics at the audacity of the inhabitants who, in spite of the fact that it was late at night, had sent me a deputation. I was dead tired and was just about to go to sleep in my bed on the train, so I adamantly refused to see anybody whoever they might be. But these people knocked on my windows and sang around my car, in short they exasperated me. So I flung open one of the windows and threw a jug of water on their heads. Men, women, and, among them, some journalists, were drenched. And great was their fury! So I was returning to this city preceded by this story, which the drenched reporters had embroidered for their own profit. On the other hand, there were other more courteous people who had refused to disturb a lady at such an unseasonable hour of night. In fact there were many such people and they defended me.

So it was in this warlike atmosphere that I appeared before the public of Mobile. I wanted to justify the good opinion of my defenders and confound my detractors. Yes, but a gnome was there who had decided otherwise. Mobile was a city that was generally much despised by impresarios. There was only one theater. It had been rented by the tragic actor Barrett,[1] who was to perform there six days after me, so all that was left was a wretched hall, so small that I knew of nothing to compare with it.

We were performing in *La Dame aux camélias*. At the moment when Marguerite Gautier orders dinner to be served, the servants tried to carry in the laid table through the door, but it was impossible. Nothing was more comic than the sight of these poor things trying it this way and that. The audience started to laugh, and amongst the laughter there was one laugh in particular that infected everybody. A black boy of twelve or fifteen years old, who had somehow managed to get in, was standing on a chair bending forward with his hands on his knees, his head thrust forward, and his mouth open. His laugh was so shrill, strident, and unremitting that I was seized by insane laughter myself. I had to go out while some scenery was removed at the back to allow the table to be brought in. I came back feeling calmer but still suffering from suppressed laughter. We had sat down around the table and the dinner had commenced in its usual way. But when the servants came in to remove the table one of them brushed up against the scenery. In their haste the scene-shifters had not secured it properly, and as a result the whole backdrop fell on our heads. Since, in this era, scenery was almost all made of paper, we were not "coiffed" but rather "collared" by the scenery, and we had to stay like this without moving. As our heads had gone through the paper we looked as comic and ridiculous as one could imagine. The black boy's laughter started up again even more stridently than before, and this time my suppressed laughter broke out into a fit of hysterics that left me utterly exhausted. The audience was given back its money, which totaled more than fifteen thousand francs. This city was fatal for me, and it was nearly literally so in my third visit in an incident that I shall relate in my second volume of memoirs.

We left Mobile the same night to go to Atlanta, where we put on *La Dame aux camélias*, and then left the same evening for Nashville. Then we stopped for a whole day in Memphis, where we gave two performances. Then we left at one o'clock in the morning to go to Louisville.

On the journey from Memphis to Louisville we were awakened by the noise of fighting, cursing, and screaming. I opened the door of my traveling bedroom and I recognized the voices. Jarrett came out at the same moment so we went in the direction of the noise. It was coming from an observation platform where the two combatants, Captain Hayné and Marcus Mayer, were fighting with revolver in hand. Marcus Mayer had an eye out of its socket, and blood covered the face of the captain. Without a thought I threw myself in between the two madmen who, seeing a woman, stopped fighting, with that brutal but touching courtesy typical of Northern Americans.

We began our whirlwind tour of the little towns. We would arrive at three or four in the afternoon, sometimes even at six, and then leave immediately after the performance. I never left the train except to go to the theater and I would come straight back after the performance to go to bed in my elegant but minuscule bedroom. I sleep very well in a train and I loved the sensation of speeding along. Sitting outside on the little observation platform, or rather stretched out in a rocking chair, I would watch the ever-changing spectacle of plains and American forests unfold before me.

We sped through Louisville, Cincinnati for the second time, Columbus, Dayton, Indianapolis, and Saint Joseph, where the beer is the best in the world. Here I was forced to go to a hotel so that a wheel on one of the cars could be fixed. I was carried off in the corridor leading to my room by a drunken dancer, who was taking part in a great ball being given at the hotel. This brute grabbed me just as I was coming out of the elevator and dragged me with the cries of a wild animal that had caught its prey after five days without anything to eat. My dog, excited by my screaming, bit him seriously on the legs thus maddening the drunkard even further. It was only with great difficulty that I was rescued from the paws of this fanatic. Supper was served. What a supper! Fortunately the beer, a fine, light, lager, enabled me to swallow the horrors that were served to eat. The ball, complete with intermittent gunfire, continued all night.

We set off again for Leavenworth, Quincy, and Springfield—not Springfield, Massachusetts, but Springfield, Illinois. During the journey from Springfield to Chicago we were stopped by snow in the middle of the night. The complaints of the engine, some shrill, some deep, had already woken me up some time before, when I called the faithful

Claude and found out that we had to stop and wait for some help. Helped by Félicie I got dressed at top speed and tried to get out. But it was impossible, the snow was as high as the observation platform. I remained there, wrapped up in furs, looking at this magnificent night.

The sky was hard, implacable, starless but yet translucent. Flares stretched out as far as the eye could see on the rails in front of me, as I had taken refuge on the platform at the rear of the train. These flares were to warn trains arriving behind us. Four of them came, and stopped as soon as they heard the detonators exploding under their wheels and moved slowly up to the first light, where a man was posted to explain what had happened to them. Immediately flares were lit behind that train as far back as possible and a man went in advance of the flares putting detonators on the rails. This was done with each train that arrived.

We were snowed in. I had the idea of lighting the kitchen fire and thus obtained enough boiling water to melt the top level of snow in the spot where I wanted to get out. After I had done this Claude and the negroes got out and cleared a little area as well as they could. I could thus get out in turn and I struggled to clear away some snow. My sister and I finished up by throwing snowballs at one other and full-scale war broke out: Abbey, Jarrett, the secretary, and some actors had joined us and we warmed ourselves up with this little battle of white cannonballs. The dawn found us firing revolvers at a target made from a champagne case. Finally a distant noise, greatly muffled by the snow, alerted us that help was coming. Indeed, there arrived at full steam, from the opposite direction to the one in which we were traveling, two locomotives loaded with men, picks, hoes, and shovels. They had to slow down when they got within half a mile of us, and the men got out and cleared the way in front of them. Eventually they managed to reach us. But we had to reverse and take the route westward.

The unhappy actors lamented, for they had been counting on dining in Chicago where we were to have stopped at eleven. With this new itinerary that had been forced upon us we would not reach Milwaukee until half past one, and we were supposed to be giving a matineé of *La Dame aux camélias* there at two o'clock. So I had a dinner made that was as acceptable as possible in the circumstances and my black servants took it to the company, who appreciated it very much. The performance did not start until three o'clock and finished at half past six. We started again at eight o'clock with *Froufrou*.

We left immediately after the performance for Grand Rapids, Detroit, Cleveland, and Pittsburgh, where I was to meet one of my American friends, who was going to help me to realize one of my dreams, at least so I thought. My friend owned, in partnership with his brother, a large steelworks and several oil wells. I had known him in Paris and had met him again in New York, where he had promised to take me to Buffalo so that I might visit—or be initiated into—Niagara Falls, for which he had the passion of a lover. He would suddenly leave, like a madman, at the most unexpected moments, to go and seek repose beside Niagara Falls. The deafening roar of the cataracts seemed like music to him compared with the harsh, pounding, strident sound of the steel mills; and the limpidity of the silvery cascades would rest his eyes and refresh his lungs saturated with oil and smoke.

My friend's phaeton, equipped with two magnificent trotters, carried us off in a vertiginous cloud of spattering mud and blinding snow. It had rained for two days and Pittsburgh in 1881 was not what it is today; but it was a city exhilarating in its commercial genius. Mud flowed black in the streets, and everywhere in the sky rose clouds of thick black oily smoke. But all of this had a certain grandeur because everywhere work was master. Trains crossed the streets filled with barrels of oil or piled to the brim with coal. The magnificent Ohio river carried along steamers, barges, and logs attached to one another forming enormous rafts, which descended the river on their own and would be stopped by the proprietor for whom they were intended. The wood was marked and nobody, in any case, thought of taking them. I am told that wood is not transported in this way any longer. It's a pity.

The carriage carries us across streets, squares, and railways underneath the unnerving buzzing of electric wires criss-crossing the sky above our heads. We start to cross a bridge, which sways under the light weight of the phaeton. It is a suspension bridge. Finally we stop. We are at my friend's factory. He introduces me to his brother, a charming man, cold, proper, and so uncommunicative that I am astonished. "My poor brother is deaf," says my companion. And I have been doing my best to put on my sweetest voice for the last five minutes! I look at this poor millionaire who lives amidst the most outlandish noise and cannot hear even a distant echo of this infernal uproar. He hears nothing, nothing, nothing. Should one envy him or pity him?

They take me to see the incandescent furnaces and the boiling tanks. They lead me into a room where steel disks, like setting suns, are cooling down. Their heat burns my lungs. I have the feeling that my hair is going to catch fire. We go across a long narrow street in which little trains go in opposite directions: some loaded with raw metals, the others with incandescent metals, which create iridescence in the air as they pass. We walk in single file along the narrow pedestrian pathway between the rails. I feel very uneasy, my heart is beating. Blown backward by the draft from the two trains as they pass one another in opposite directions, I press my skirts against me to prevent them being touched. Perched on my high heels, I fear with each step that I take that I am going to fall on this narrow, oily, coal-strewn path. In short, it is an unpleasant moment, and it is with great relief that I leave this interminable path, which ends in an enormous yard extending as far as the eye can see. There were rails lying about there everywhere which men polished, filed, etc.

But I had had enough. I asked to rest. All three of us went toward the house in which they lived. Valets in livery opened the doors, taking our furs, and walking on tiptoe. Everywhere there was silence. Why? It was incomprehensible. My friend's brother hardly spoke, and when he did it was so quietly that it was difficult to understand him. I noticed that when we asked him a question with sign language and then had to strain our ears to hear his reply, an imperceptible smile lit up his stony face. I realized later that this man hated humanity and that this was his way of taking revenge for his infirmity.

A lunch had been prepared in the conservatory, a magical corner of greenery and flowers. We had only just sat down at the table when a thousand birds burst into a fanfare of song. Everywhere under the broad leaves, invisible netting imprisoned families of canaries. They were in the air, down below, under my chair, under the table, behind me, everywhere! I wanted to dominate this shrill noise. I shook my napkin, I spoke loudly. But the feathered race started to sing their heads off. I saw the deaf man lying back in his rocking chair, and his face lit up as he burst into malicious and vengeful laughter. Just as anger was about to overtake me, I felt suddenly indulgent toward this man whose childish manner of vengeance touched me. I bravely tolerated the malice of my host and with the help of his brother I took my tea out into the hall, which lay at the other end of the conservatory.

I was dead with fatigue. When my friend proposed that we go and visit his oil wells which were some miles from the city I looked at him with such an air of wild desperation that he kindly and elegantly apologized. It was five o'clock. Night had come. I wanted to go back to my hotel. My host asked permission to take me back via the hills. It was a longer route but in this way I would have a bird's eye view of Pittsburgh, which was very worthwhile, he said.

We got back into the phaeton with new horses in the harness. Some minutes later I had the strange fantasy that my friend was Pluto, the god of the Underworld, and I was Proserpina! We were crossing his kingdom carried by winged horses! Everywhere there was fire and flame! The bloody sky was marked with long black bars like widows' veils! The earth was bristling with long metal arms stretched toward the sky in a supreme imprecation! These arms threw up smoke or flames or fireworks which fell back to earth in a shower of stars! The carriage carried us over the heights. The cold froze our bodies and the fire exalted our minds.

It was then that my friend told me about his love for Niagara Falls. He talked about the falls, not as an amateur but as a lover. He liked to go there alone. He would make an exception for me. He talked about the rapids with such intense passion that I worriedly asked myself if this man was crazy. And fear took hold of me as he drove the carriage, skimming over the tops of the hills and leaping over piles of stones. I kept looking at him furtively. His face was calm but his lower lip trembled slightly, which I had also noticed in his deaf brother. My nerves were on edge. The cold, the fire, the devilish road, the funereal and subterranean noise of the anvils, the whistling of the forges, which seemed like a desperate cry piercing the night, the chimneys that spat out their smoke in a perpetual death-rattle, and the wind that had just risen and was twisting the smoke plumes into spirals, which it hurled toward the sky or suddenly brought down upon us: this whole frenzied dance of natural and manmade elements affected my nerves. It was really time to get back to the hotel.

I got out of the carriage and made arrangements to see my friend at Buffalo. Alas! The poor man! I was not to see him again. On the day we had arranged he had caught a cold and could not join me. The following year I learned that he had been crushed against the rocks while navigating the rapids. He had died from his passion and for his passion.

The actors were waiting for me at the hotel. I had forgotten that there was to be a rehearsal of *La Princesse George* at half past four. I noticed among the actors an unfamiliar face. I inquired. It was an artist who had asked to do some sketches of me and was carrying a note from Jarrett. I put him in a corner and took no more notice of him. We had to hurry to rehearse in order to get to the theater in time for the performance of *Froufrou* that we were performing that evening. The rehearsal, muttered and botched, was over quickly and the stranger took his leave, refusing to let me see his sketches to which, he said, he wished to put the final touches.

Imagine my joy next day, however, when Jarrett furiously came in with Pittsburgh's biggest newspaper, in which the stranger (who was none other than a journalist), told the whole story of the rehearsal of *Froufrou*. This idiot wrote:

In the play *Froufrou* there is an important scene between two sisters. Mlle. Sarah Bernhardt did not surprise me. As for the actors of the company, I found them mediocre. The costumes are not very nice, and in the ball scene no one was wearing tails.

Jarrett was furious. I was overjoyed. He knew my horror of reporters and he had brought one in surreptitiously, hoping for some good publicity. But the journalist had thought that we were having a costume rehearsal for *Froufrou*, when in fact we were rehearsing the words to *La Princesse George* by Alexandre Dumas. He had taken the scene between Princesse George and the Comtesse de Terremonde for the scene in the third act between the two sisters in *Froufrou*. Each one of us was still wearing our traveling clothes, and he was surprised not to see the men in tails and the women in ball gowns! What hilarity this caused among the actors and in the city! And I must add it was a wonderful source of jokes for the rival newspapers.

I had to perform two days in Pittsburgh, then go on to Bradford, Erie, and Toronto. Finally, on the Sunday, we arrived at Buffalo. I had wanted to offer my company a whole day of enjoyment at the falls, but Abbey also wanted to act as host. There was a discussion between us during which we nearly fell out. He was authoritarian and so was I. For a moment we both felt we would rather not go there than give in to the other. But Jarrett made us realize that our "autocracy" was going to deprive the actors of a day of merrymaking that they had already heard about and were looking forward to. We gave in and as a compromise we agreed to go halves on this happy day.

The actors accepted our invitations with charming grace and we took the train to Buffalo where we arrived at ten past six in the morning. We had cabled ahead for carriages and coffee, and especially food; it would be absolute madness for thirty-two people to arrive in an English city on a Sunday without giving advance warning! The train was garlanded with flowers. It was a special train that traveled at high speed on the empty tracks this Sunday. The childlike joy of the young actors, the stories told by those who had already seen the falls, the loquaciousness of those who had heard about them, etc., the little bouquets of flowers distributed to the women, the cigarettes and cigars offered to the men— all of this put people in a good humor and everyone seemed happy.

When we got out of the train the carriages were there to take us to the Hôtel d'Angleterre, which had stayed open especially for us. There were flowers everywhere and lots of little tables on which there were coffee, chocolate, and tea. Every table was immediately surrounded by diners. I had at my table, along with my sister, Abbey, Jarrett, and the leading actors. The meal was short and full of joyful animation.

Then we went to the falls. I stayed for more than an hour on the lookout station hollowed in the rock; I had tears in my eyes and was moved to the depths of my being by the splendor of the spectacle and the beauty of its proportions. Radiant sunshine cast iridescence into the air around us. Everywhere rainbows illuminated the atmosphere with their soft silvery colors. The icicles that hung from rocks on both sides looked like enormous jewels. I was sorry to leave this lookout place. We went down in narrow cages that slid smoothly through a tunnel cut inside a fissure in the enormous rock. We arrived underneath the falls. There they were almost above our heads, showering us with blue, pink, and mauve drops!

Opposite us and shielding us from the falls is a mass of icicles that have fused to form one little mountain. We scale it as well as we can. My heavy fur coat tires me. I take it off in mid-climb and let it slide down the side of the mountain where I collect it at the bottom at the end. I continue wearing just my white dress and a light satin blouse. There is an outcry. Abbey takes off his cardigan and throws it over my shoulders. I quickly divest myself of that and Abbey's cardigan goes to join my fur coat at the bottom. The poor impresario's face is desperate. As he has had quite a lot of cocktails he stumbles, falls on the ice, gets up and falls down again, and everybody starts laughing. As for myself, I do not feel cold. I never feel cold in the open air. I only feel cold in houses when I am inactive. We reach the summit of the mountain of ice; the falls are really menacing us now, and we are drenched by the impalpable vapor that radiates from the uproar. I look, fascinated by the rapid movement of this water. It is like a wide unrolling silver curtain which then crashes violently in a mass which leaps and splashes with a din that is unlike any other noise I have ever heard. I easily get dizzy, and I am well aware of the fact that if I had been alone in this spot I would have stayed there for ever more, my mind lulled by the entrancing sound, my limbs numbed by the imperceptible but penetrating cold, my eyes fixed on the surface of the water as it moves along at full speed.

I had to be dragged away. I came to myself again when I found myself confronted with a problem. We had to go back down again, and it was much more difficult than it had been to go up. I took a cane from one of my companions and sat down on the ice. With the cane under my thighs I let myself slide to the bottom. Everybody copied me, and it was a comic spectacle to see thirty-two people going down this mountain of ice at full speed on their behinds. There were some tumbles, some collisions, and a lot of laughter. A quarter of an hour later everybody was back at the hotel where luncheon had been prepared. We were cold and hungry. It was warm in the hotel and the meal smelled good.

When the meal was over the proprietor of the hotel invited me into a little room where a surprise was waiting for me. There I saw on a table, under a long glass cover, Niagara Falls in miniature. The rocks were made of pebbles, a large mirror represented the expanse of water, and spun glass represented the falls. Then, here and there, there were little clumps of harsh green foliage, and standing on a hillock of ice was the figure of myself! It was all so ugly that it was enough to make one scream with horror. I gave a strained smile to the proprietor to congratulate him on his good taste, but I was transfixed to recognize the servant of the brothers Th***, my friends from Pittsburgh. They had sent me this monstrous caricature of the most beautiful thing in the world.

I read the letter that the servant gave to me and it melted my disdain. They had made such an effort to explain what they wanted and they were happy at the thought of giving me pleasure. I sent away the valet after having given him a letter for his masters. Then I asked the proprietor to send it to Paris for me with the greatest of care. I sincerely hoped that it would arrive in pieces. But I continued to ponder. How could my friend's passion for the falls be reconciled with such a present? Although his creative spirit may have wished to see the successful realization of his dream, how could he not have been repelled by the sight of this grotesque imitation? How had he had the courage to send it to me? What meaning did this grandiose marvel have for him? Since his death I have questioned his memory many a time, but he has never replied. He died for his beloved falls, swept away in their mass, broken by their caress; and yet I cannot believe that he actually saw them in their true beauty.

Very fortunately I was called to my carriage. Everybody was inside and they were waiting for me. The horses set off, carrying us along at that tired little trot which typifies tourists' horses. At the Canadian falls we had to go underground and deck ourselves in yellow and black rubber garments. We looked like squat and heavy sailors who had put on the abominable sou'wester for the first time.

There were two large cabins, one for men and one for women. Everybody got undressed, more or less in a jumble; we bundled up our rags and gave them into the care of the superintendent. Then we put on the rubber hood, which fastened under the chin and concealed the hair, the enormous blouse which enveloped the body, fur-lined boots which had studded soles to prevent broken legs and skulls . . . I am forgetting also the immense rubber pants cut on the Oriental pattern: all of this made even the prettiest and slimmest of women look like an enormous clumsy bear. A metal-tipped club in our hands completed the gracious ensemble.

I looked more ridiculous than the others because I had not wanted to hide my hair, and I had pretentiously pinned some roses to my rubber breast. Then I had gathered my blouse into pleats under my big silver belt. When they saw me the women went into ecstasies: "Oh, how pretty she looks like that! There's no one like her for chic, after all!" And the men gallantly kissed my bear's paw, bowing low and murmuring, "Always, no matter what, the queen, the fairy, the goddess, the divine one, etc., etc." And I went on my way, purring and content, when, passing the counter where the girl was selling tickets, I caught sight of myself in the mirror, enormous and ridiculous with my pretentious roses and my frizzy hair, which made a visor for my crude hood. I looked fatter than everybody because of my silver belt, which encircled my waist and bunched the rubber into stiff pleats around me. My thin face was eaten up by my hair, which was flattened by the hood. My eyes were no longer visible. Only my mouth, which is rather large, revealed that this barrel was a human being. Furious with my pretentious coquetterie, and ashamed of the weakness that had made me purr to hear base flattery and lies from people who were laughing at me, I resolved to stay like that to subdue my stupid pride. There were many strangers with us, who elbowed each other when they saw me and laughed under their hoods at my stupid get-up. It served me right.

We went down a staircase cut out of ice and found ourselves under the Canadian falls. There is the strangest and wildest of sights: above me an immense cupola of ice hanging in space, and attached on only one side to the rock. From this cupola there hang in the many different forms of a thousand icicles, dragons, arrows, crosses, tragic and comic masks, six-fingered hands, shapeless feet, unfinished torsoes, a woman's long hair. With half-closed eyes one can finish the sketch with the help of a little imagination. In less time than it takes to write it down the mind can evoke all the images of nature or of dream, all the crazy conceptions of a sick mind or the realities of a thoughtful one. Then in front of us there are some little steeples of ice. Some of them, proud and straight, leap toward the sky. Others, wrought by the wind, are like minarets ready to receive the muezzin.

On the right the cascade fell as noisily as on the other side; but the sun was beginning to decline and everything was taking on a tinge of pink. We were showered by water and little blades of silver rained down on us which, after a slight shake, stiffened on our rubber clothing. It was a shoal of tiny little fish that had had the misfortune to be drawn into the current and had just died in the breathtaking beauty of a setting sun.

On our left there was a block, which looked like a rhinoceros entering the water. "I would love to get on that!" I exclaimed.

"Yes, but it's impossible," replied one of my friends.

"Oh, impossible! Nothing's impossible! I shall risk it. The crevasse I have to cross isn't even a yard wide."

"No, but it's deep," replied a painter who was with us.

"Well, my dog has just died. I bet you a dog of my choice that I will get there!"

Abbey, who had been quickly fetched, arrived just in time to see me in the air. I was a hair breadth's away from falling into the crevasse. But once I got onto the rhinoceros' back I could not stand up. It was smooth and transparent like manufactured ice. I sat astride its back and leaned against the little lump sticking out from its head. I declared that if no one came to get me I would stay there, because I did not have the courage to take a step on its slippery back. Then I had the sensation that it was moving slightly. Then I lifted my head and felt myself getting dizzy. I had won my dog but was not longer excited. I was scared. Everybody was looking at me, terrified, and increasing my fear. My sister was overcome with hysteria, and my poor dear Guérard kept crying in a heart-rending way, "Ah, my God, my little Sarah! Ah, my God! etc. etc." The painter was sketching.

Luckily the company had gone back up in order to have time to see the rapids. Abbey was begging me . . . poor Jarrett was begging me . . . But no, I felt dizzy. I *was* dizzy, I neither wanted to nor could do anything further. So Angelo jumped across the crevasse and, standing on its edge, asked for a plank and an axe. "Bravo!" I cried from the top of my rhinoceros, "Bravo!" The plank was brought. It was an old, blackened, and rotten plank. I looked at it mistrustfully. The axe chipped off some of the tail of my rhinoceros and, once a hollow had been made, the plank was held in position on my side by Angelo, and held by Abbey, Jarrett, and Claude on the other side. I slid onto the rump of my rhinoceros and started, not without terror, to make my way across the rotten plank, which was so narrow that I had to put one foot in front of the other, toe to heel.

I went back to the hotel feeling feverish, and the painter brought me the funny sketches that he had made. After a snack I had to leave again for the train, which had been waiting for us for twenty minutes. Everybody had been sitting waiting in it for a long time. I left without seeing the rapids in which my poor friend from Pittsburgh was to meet his death.

Chapter XXXVIII

*O*ur big tour was coming to an end. I say "big" because it was my first tour. It lasted seven months. The other tours that I have made since have always been eleven to sixteen months in length.[1] We went from Buffalo to Rochester, Utica, Syracuse, Albany, Troy, Worcester, Providence, Newark, and then to stay for a short time in Washington, a wonderful city but a depressing one at that time. This was the last large city that I visited. After two excellent performances and a dinner at the embassy we left for Baltimore, Philadelphia, and New York, where our tour was to end.

I gave in this city a big matinée performance that had been requested by the artistic community of New York. The chosen play was *La Princesse George*. What a fine and unforgettable experience! Everything was noted by these artists. Nothing escaped the expert notice of this audience composed of actors, actresses, painters, and sculptors. At the end of the performance I was given a gold comb engraved with the date and the names of most of the people in my audience. I received from Salvini[2] a pretty casket of lapis lazuli, and from Mary Anderson,[3] who was then, at the age of nineteen, stunningly beautiful, a little medallion with a "Forget-me-not" in turquoises. I counted in my dressing room a hundred and thirty bouquets.

In the evening our last performance was to be *La Dame aux camélias*. I had fourteen curtain calls. For a moment I was confused because, amongst the tempest of cries and bravos, I could hear a strident cry coming from hundreds of mouths that I did not understand. I kept asking in the wings after each curtain call what this word meant that reached my ears over and over like a terrible fit of sneezing.

Jarrett arrived and helped me out. "They are asking for a speech." As I looked at him in astonishment he said, "Yes, they want you to make a little speech."

"Ah, no!" I cried as I went back for another curtain call, "No!" As I curtseyed to the audience I murmured in English, "I can't speak, but I can tell you 'thank you, thank you, with all my heart!'" I left the theater amidst thunderous applause with cries of, "Hip, hip, hooray! Long live France!"

On Wednesday May 4, I embarked on the same liner, the *Amérique,* the Flying Dutchman, to which my voyage had brought good luck. But it was not the same captain. The new one was called Santelli. He was as short and blonde as the other had been tall and dark. But he was just as charming and a good conversationalist. Captain Jouclas had blown off his head after a big loss at the gambling table.

My cabin had been refurbished to look like new. This time the paneling was upholstered in sky blue. As I went up the steps to embark I turned round to the friendly crowd and waved a last goodbye. They shouted to me, "Au revoir!" Then I headed for my cabin.

At the door, standing in an elegant steel-grey suit, wearing pointed shoes, a hat of the latest fashion, and gloves of dogskin, was Henry Smith, the whale trainer. I roared like a wild animal. He continued to smile happily and gave me a jewel-box, which I took with the intention of hurling it into the sea through my open porthole. But Jarrett stopped my arm and took possession of the box which he opened. "It's magnificent!" he exclaimed. But I had closed my eyes. I covered my ears and shouted to this man, "Go away! Rogue! Brute! Go away! I hope that you die with atrocious suffering! Go away!" I half opened my eyes. He had gone. Jarrett wanted to talk about the present, but I did not want to hear anything about it. "For the love of God, Mr. Jarrett, leave me alone! And since this is such a beautiful ornament give it to your daughter and don't talk to me about it again." And that is what he did.

On the eve of my departure from America I had received a long telegram signed by Grosos, President of the Association of Lifeguards of Le Havre, who asked me to give a performance for the families of the lifeguards when I arrived. I accepted this with unspeakable joy; as I returned to my beloved fatherland I was going to make the kind of gesture that comforts those in tears.

After the hustle and bustle of departure, our ship made a gentle lunge and we left New York on Thursday, May 5. I, who hate voyages by sea, embarked lightheartedly, smiling, and full of disdain for the horrible sickness that it causes.

We had not been gone from New York more than forty-eight hours when our ship stopped. I bounded out of my bunk and went to the bridge, fearing that our Flying Dutchman, as we had nicknamed it, had had an accident. Opposite us a French ship was raising, lowering, and raising again little flags. The captain who was replying to the signals called me to him and explained to me the handling and code of these signals. I must confess with shame that I do not remember anything of what he told me. Two sailors, and a very pale young man, whose dress showed he was poor, got into a lifeboat from this boat. Our captain lowered the ladder and when the lifeboat was up alongside ours the young man climbed up, accompanied by the two sailors. One of them gave a letter to the officer waiting at the top of the ladder. He read it. He looked at the young man and said to him gently, "Follow me." The lifeboat went back to its ship, the sailors got on board, the lifeboat was raised, a whistle was sounded, and our ship sounded one in return. After this customary salute the two boats continued on their way. The unfortunate young man was brought to the captain. I went back to my cabin and asked the purser to come and tell me the reason for this disembarkation and embarkation, if it was not a confidential matter. It was the captain himself who came.

The young man was a poor wood engraver who had slipped onto a liner leaving for New York, as he did not have a penny for his passage, not even at the steerage fare. He had hoped to pass unnoticed by hiding under bales of rags. Illness had betrayed him. Shivering with fever he had talked aloud in his sleep, babbling incoherently. He was taken to the infirmary and had confessed everything. The captain promised to make him accept what I sent him to pay for his voyage to America. The story got around and other passengers made a collection, and the young engraver found himself the owner of twelve hundred francs. He came three days later to bring me a little wooden coffer, which he had made and engraved himself.

This little coffer is almost full of flower petals, for each year, on May 7, I would receive a little bouquet with the two words, always the same—"Gratitude and devotion." I would put the petals of the bouquet in the little coffer. For the last seven years I have not received anything. Is it forgetfulness, or death that has stopped the artist's sweet gesture? I do not know. But the sight of this coffer always leaves me with a vague feeling of sadness, for forgetfulness and death are the most faithful companions of human beings. Oblivion creeps into our minds and hearts; Death is always there, creating pitfalls in front of us, spying on all our movements, and sniggering joyfully when we close our eyes in sleep, for then we show it a semblance of what it knows will one day be reality.

Apart from the incident described above, the voyage was uneventful. I spent every night on the bridge, staring at the horizon and hoping to draw toward me this land where my loved ones were to be found. I would go back to my cabin toward morning and sleep all day to kill time. Ships in those days did not make the crossing with the same speed as they do today. The hours seemed unfairly long. I was so violently impatient to be there that I called the doctor and begged him to make me sleep for eighteen hours! He made me sleep for twelve hours with a fairly strong dose of chloral and, as a result, I felt stronger and calmer and ready to withstand the shock of happiness.

Santelli had promised that we would arrive on the evening of the fourteenth. I was ready; I had been stamping the ground frenetically for an hour when an officer came to ask me if I wanted to go on the bridge, where the captain was waiting for me. I hastened there with my sister and quickly understood from the embarrassed circumlocutions of good Santelli, that we were still too far away to hope to dock that night. I started to sob. I felt that we would never arrive. I felt that the evil gnome had triumphed, and I cried. The captain did his best to make me see reason. I climbed down from the bridge with my body and mind in wet tatters.

I stretched out on a wicker *chaise longue,* and the dawn found me chilled and drowsy. It was five o'clock in the morning. We were still twenty miles away. However, the sun began joyfully to brighten up the little white clouds, light as snowflakes. The thought of my young loved one gave me courage. I ran to my cabin. I took a long time getting washed and dressed to kill time. At seven o'clock I made inquiries with the captain.

"We are twelve miles away," he said. "In two hours we will be on land."

"You swear?"

"I swear!" he said.

I returned to the bridge. Leaning on the rail I peered into the distance.

A little boat appears on the horizon. I see it without paying any attention to it. I am waiting for the cry, "Over there! Over there!" Suddenly I see masses of white flags waving on the little steamer. I take my binoculars . . . I let out a cry of joy that leaves me without strength or breath. I want to talk . . . I cannot . . . My face becomes so white it seems, that it scares those around me. My sister Jeanne cries as she waves toward the horizon. They want me to sit down. I don't want to . . . Clinging to the rails I smell the salts put under my nose! I let friendly hands dab my temples, but I watch that steamer approaching.

There is my happiness! My joy! My life! My everything! Dearer than all else!

The *Diamant,* as the steamer is called, comes close. A bridge of love is thrown from the little to the big ship. A bridge formed by the beating of our hearts, and by the kisses piled up during so many many days. Then there is the relief of tears when the rowboats, finally coming up alongside the big ship, allow the impatient to climb the ladder and throw themselves into outstretched arms. The *Amérique* is invaded. They are all there, my dear and faithful friends. They have brought my young son Maurice. Ah! The delicious moment! Replies forestall questions. Laughter is mingled with tears. Hands are pressed, embraces are given, and then we start again. We cannot tire of showing our love over and over again.

During this time our ship is making progress. The *Diamant* has disappeared, carrying the mail. But the more we advance the more the sea is furrowed by little boats decked with bunting. There are a hundred of them. Here are still more.

"So it's a holiday?" I ask Georges Boyer, a correspondent for *Le Figaro* who had come to meet me with my friends.

"Yes, Madame, there is a big holiday in Le Havre today, for they are waiting for the return of the fairy who left seven months ago."

"It's really to welcome me that all these little boats have unfurled their sails and decorated their masts? Ah! How happy I am!"

At this moment we come alongside the jetty. There are perhaps twenty thousand people there who shout together, "Long live Sarah Bernhardt!" I am confused. I had not expected a triumphant return. I know very well that the performance donated to the lifeguards has won the hearts of the people of Le Havre; but I also learn that packed trains have come from Paris to greet me on my return. I feel my pulse . . . it's really me . . . I am not dreaming.

The ship stops in front of a red velvet marquee and an invisible orchestra plays a tune from *Le Chalet*—*"Arrêtons-nous ici."*[4] I smile at this piece of typically French playfulness. I disembark and walk in the midst of kind smiling faces on both sides and sailors offering me flowers. Under the marquee all the lifeguards are waiting for me with their well-deserved medals on their wide chests. The president, M. Grosos, makes me this speech:

Madame,

As president, I have the honor of presenting to you a delegation from the Association of Lifeguards of Le Havre, who have come to welcome you and show you their gratitude for all the sympathy that you so warmly expressed in your transatlantic telegram. We come here to congratulate you on the immense acclaim that you have received everywhere that you have traveled during your daring voyage. You have now conquered in two worlds popularity and incontestable artistic celebrity, and your marvellous talent, joined to the charms of your person, have affirmed abroad that France is still the country of art and the cradle of elegance and beauty.

An already distant echo of the words you spoke in Denmark, evoking a grave and serious memory, still rings in our ears. It tells us that your heart is as French as your talent, for in the midst of your blazing theatrical success you have never forgotten to associate your patriotism with your artistic triumph.

Our lifeguards have asked me to express to you their admiration for the charming benefactress, whose generous hand has spontaneously stretched out toward their poor but noble association. They want to offer you these flowers plucked from the soil of the fatherland, from the earth of France, which you find beneath your feet. They deserve to be accepted with your favor, for they are presented to you by the bravest and most loyal of saviors.

My reply was, I am told, very eloquent, but I cannot confirm that this reply was really made by me. I had been living for several hours in a state of over-excitement made up of a succession of emotions. I had taken no food or sleep. My heart had not stopped beating with excitement and joy. My mind was full of a thousand things accumulated over seven months and recounted in the space of two hours.

I had been far from expecting this triumphant reception, in view of the way in which my departure had been so maligned by the Parisian press, and of how the incidents of my tour had been continually willfully misinterpreted by certain French newspapers! It was hard to understand how these contrasting reactions could exist at the same time.

The performance was a profitable one for the lifeguards. As for myself, I performed *La Dame aux camélias* for the first time in France. God had come! And I can affirm that those who saw this performance received the quintessence of my personal art.

I spent the night in my property at Sainte-Adresse.[5] The next day I was on my way to Paris. A most flattering ovation was waiting for me on my arrival.

Three days later, when I was settled into my house on the avenue de Villiers, I received Victorien Sardou[6] to hear him read his magnificent play *Fédora*. What a great artist! What a wonderful, marvellous actor! He read the whole play in one go, playing all the roles and giving me in an instant a vision of what I would do with it. "Ah," I exclaimed after the reading, "dear Master, thank you for this beautiful role! And thank you for the fine lesson you have just given me." Night came but found me sleepless, for I wanted to glimpse in the dark the little star in which

I had faith. I saw it at the beginning of the dawn, and I went to sleep, thinking about the new era on which it was going to shed light.

My tour lasted seven months. I visited fifty cities and gave one hundred fifty-six performances, distributed as follows:

La Dame aux camélias	65
Adrienne Lecouvreur	17
Froufrou	41
La Princesse George	3
Hernani	14
L' Etrangère	3
Phèdre	6
Le Sphinx	7

The grand total of receipts for all the performances was 2,667,600 francs, and the average receipt per performance was 17,100 francs.

I finish the first volume of my memoirs here, for this is really the first stage of my life: the real evolution of my physical and moral being. I had run away from the Comédie-Française, from Paris, from France, from my family and friends, with the intention of leaping, abracadabra, across mountain, sea, and space! I came back enamored of the distant horizon, but calmed by the experience of responsibility that had weighed on my shoulders for seven months. The terrible Jarrett had tamed my overly wild nature by his implacable and cruel wisdom and by constant appeals to my integrity. In these months I had matured in mind and tempered the crudity of my desires. My life, which I had at first expected to be very short, now seemed likely to be very very long; and it gave me great joy to think of the infernal displeasure that would cause my enemies.

I resolved to live.

I resolved to be the great artist that I wished to be.

And, from the time of my return onward, I dedicated myself to my life.

Notes

PREFACE

1. Much doubt surrounds the identity of Sarah Bernhardt's father, the nationality of her mother (Sarah says she was born in Holland but there is reason to believe that she was actually born in Berlin), and the exact date of her birth. For a good summary of the controversy see Ruth Brandon, *Being Divine: A Biography of Sarah Bernhardt* (London, 1991), pp. 5ff.

2. See Laurence Selnick, "Chekhov's Response to Bernhardt," in *Bernhardt and the Theatre of Her Time*, ed. Eric Salmon (Westport, Conn.: 1984).

3. George Bernard Shaw in "Sardoodledom," p. 75 in *Shaw's Dramatic Criticism (1895–98)* selected by John F. Matthews, (New York, 1959). Cf. also the criticism of Romain Rolland, a member of André-Léonard Antoine's *Théâtre libre*, who speaks of Sarah's "Byzantinized, or Americanized, neo-romanticism: stiff and congealed, without youth or vigor, weighed down with ornamanents, with jewels real or fake, bleak in its bluster, pallid in its outlook" (*Le Théâtre du peuple* [Paris, 1904]), as quoted and discussed by John Stokes in *Bernhardt, Terry, Duse: the Actress in Her Time* ed. John Stokes, Michael R. Booth, Susan Bassnett (Cambridge, 1988), pp. 28f.

4. Stage name of Elizabeth Félix (1820–1858), great tragic actress of Jewish descent who revived compellingly the drama of Corneille and Racine. Her reputation was an international one. She died at an early age from the tuberculosis from which she was already suffering when Sarah saw her at her school. On Rachel see Rachel Brownstein, *Tragic Muse: Rachel of the Comédie-Française* (New York, 1993).

5. For a detailed analysis of Sarah's voice see Gerda Taranow, *Sarah Bernhardt: The Art within the Legend* (Princeton, 1972), pp. 3ff.

6. *Ma double vie: mémoires de Sarah Bernhardt* (Paris: Charpentier et Fasquelle, 1907). According to Brandon (who does not give her source), p. 308, Bernhardt had originally contracted to bring out her memoirs in 1883 but had run into a dispute with her publisher which resulted in her withdrawing the manuscript. Brandon suggests that the fact that some episodes, corresponding closely to what would appear in the memoirs of 1907, were quoted by journalists and others years before this, indicates that the mem-

oirs existed, at least in part, long before they were finally published—Brandon, p. 309.

7. Max Beerbohm, "Sarah's Memoirs" in *Around Theatres* (New York, 1930).

8. Marie Colombier, *Le Voyage de Sarah Bernhardt en Amérique* (Paris, n.d.), p. 105.

9. *My Double Life. Memoirs of Sarah Bernhardt* (London: Heinemann, 1907). Published in America as *Memoires of My Life: Being My Personal, Professional, and Social Recollections as Woman and Artist* (New York: Benjamin Blom, 1908).

CHAPTER I

1. Former name of Oslo, Norway.

2. Baron Hippolyte Larrey (1808–1895), Napoléon III's doctor—see Arthur Gold and Robert Fizdale, *The Divine Sarah* (New York, 1991), p. 13—and son of Dominique Jean Larrey (1766–1842), surgeon to Napoléon's Imperial Guard.

CHAPTER II

1. Terry velvet.

2. A banker, it was rumored that he was the father of Régina, Sarah Bernhardt's sister. See Gold and Fizdale, pp. 28f.

3. Marie de Rabutin-Chantal, Marquise de Sévigné (1626–1696), famous for her letters describing the mores of high society.

4. George Sand, pseudonym of Aurore Dupin, Baronne Dudevant (1804–1876), novelist and dramatist.

5. The prestigious Comédie-Française, also known as La Maison de Molière, founded 1680. Stella Colas made her début at this theater in 1856 but later left for St. Petersburg, Russia, where she remained 1861–1875 (Lyonnet).

6. In Racine's (1639–1699) last play, *Athalie*, first performed 1691.

7. In Act II, scene 5 of *Athalie: "Tremble, m'a-t-elle dit, fille digne de moi"*— "Tremble," she said to me "tremble, daughter worthy of me!"

8. Gioacchino Antonio Rossini (1792–1868), the Italian composer, who spent much of his life in Paris.

CHAPTER IV

1. *Tobit Recovers His Sight.* The story is based on the one told in the *Book of Tobit* in the *Apocrypha.*

2. A thin cotton fabric similar to cambric.

3. A thin, stiff, gauze-like fabric.

CHAPTER V

1. Stage name of Sophie-Alexandrine Croisette (1847–1901), with whom Sarah would later meet up again at the Comédie Française where she was famed as an actress of great seductiveness.

CHAPTER VI

1. A semi-transparent fabric of silk and wool.

2. Fine linen or cotton fabric.

3. Charles-Auguste-Louis-Joseph, Duc de Morny (1811–1865). Illegitimate son of Queen Hortense (mother of Napoléon III) and the Comte de Flahaut. Ambassador to Russia (1856–1857), political figure, dandy, and speculator. He frequented courtesan circles and had many different lovers—see Joanna Richardson, *The Courtesans: The Demi-Monde in Nineteenth-Century France* (Cleveland, 1967), pp. 53f. A photograph of him appears in Richardson, p. 45.

4. More respectfully, "vous."

5. A wrapper worn over an underdress at home, especially in the mornings, or for informal occasions.

6. *The Life of St. Louis.* St. Louis = Louis IX (1215–1270), king of France.

7. The Conservatoire de Musique et Déclamation was founded at the end of the eighteenth century. It had close connections with the Comédie Française and had produced most of its great actors.

8. Tragedy based on Roman history by Racine, produced 1669.

9. 1668 comedy by Molière (Jean-Baptiste Poquelin, 1622–1673), based on *Amphitruo* of Plautus.

CHAPTER VII

1. Jean de La Fontaine (1621–1695), poet and author of the *Fables.*

2. Daniel-François-Esprit Auber (1782–1871), French operatic composer, who had a long and successful collaboration with the librettist Scribe.

3. Role in a tragedy by Racine of the same name. Produced 1677.

4. A tragedy by Corneille (1606–1684), produced 1637.

5. Tongue-twisting and somewhat nonsensical sentences composed for sound, not meaning: A very big rat in a very big hole / How much are these six sausages? / They're six cents these six sausages! / Six cents for these six sausages? / Six cents for these, six for those! Six cents for these six sausages! / Didon dined, they say, from the back of a plump goose / The littlest papa, little pipi, little popo, little pupu.

6. Princess loved by Hippolyte in *Phèdre*.

7. By Molière, the comedy *L'Ecole des femmes* was produced in 1662. Agnès is a character is this play who unwittingly cuckolds her husband-to-be, Arnolphe.

8. Line 578: "He has taken . . . he has taken the ribbon that you had given me."

CHAPTER VIII

1. A deep-falling collar, often of lace.

2. White linen or cambric eyelet in floral sprigs.

3. A sort of false bodice-front, made of white muslin, cambric, or tulle to cover the area of the bosom otherwise revealed by the décolleté neckline.

4. The fibers of raw silk are covered with silk-gum, a certain amount of which has to be removed by boiling off or "scouring" in order to process it into fabric. If too much is removed the silk loses its luster and strength and is "overscoured."

5. Stage name of Marie-Joséphine Déodica Petit (ca. 1841–1885). Made her début as an actress at the Odéon and then appeared at various "popular" theaters before finishing her career (brought to an end by her early death) in St. Petersburg, Russia.

6. *The Two Pigeons*, fable by La Fontaine.

7. Lines 1–2 of *Les Deux Pigeons:* Two pigeons loved each other with tender love / One of them growing bored at . . .

8. Pierre François Beauvallet (1801–1873). Beauvallet was short, ugly, and coarse in manners, but his acting ability, the timbre of his voice, and his enunciation qualified him often to play opposite Rachel in classical tragedy at the Comédie-Française—see Chevalley, p. 122. He was also a teacher at the Conservatoire.

9. J.-B. François Provost (1798–1865) was a teacher at the Conservatoire as well as a member of the Comédie-Française.

10. Augustine Brohan (1824–1893), also both a member of the Comédie-Française and teacher at the Conservatoire. She excelled particularly in com-

edy roles, but her witty jibes incurred her many enemies (Chevalley, pp. 126f.)

11. Two pigeons loved each other with tender love / One of them growing bored at home / Was sufficiently...

12. Joseph-Isidore Samson (1793–1871). A member of the Comédie-Française as well as a teacher at the Conservatoire, he taught Rachel. He was physically unprepossessing, his voice harsh, but he overcame his defects by sheer force of dramatic skill (Chevalley, p. 121).

13. Cheer up my lil' belly / Everything I earn is for you...

CHAPTER IX

1. By Voltaire (1694–1778), produced 1732.

2. Strike, I say! I love him! Line 832 of *Zaïre*.

3. In 1861 Rosélia Rousseil won in competition with Sarah the first prize for tragedy and the second prize for comedy (Lyonnet).

4. François-Joseph Philoclès Régnier de la Brière (1807–1885). A cheerful, unpretentious man who played leading roles in comedy at the Comédie-Française. A revered teacher at the Conservatoire (Chevalley, p. 122).

5. Members of the Comédie-Française are *pensionnaires* while on probation, and after that *sociétaires*, sharing in the management of the company and entitled to a pension on retirement.

6. A "popular" theater in Paris founded in the eighteenth century, dealing in light entertainment rather than the artistic or cultural fare of the Comédie-Française. See John McCormick, *Popular Theatres of Nineteenth-Century France* (London and New York, 1993), pp. 25ff.

7. My lil' belly isn't happy.

8. A *sou* was a coin of low value that is no longer in circulation.

9. For discussion of the curriculum and teaching methods at the Conservatoire, see Taranow, passim.

10. Constant-Benoit Coquelin (1841–1909), famous actor at the Comédie-Française, capable of playing a wide variety of roles (Chevalley, p. 163).

11. Casimir Delavigne (1793–1843), a now forgotten playwright and poet: *L'Ecole des vieillards* (1823) is his most famous comedy, *La Fille du Cid* (1839).

12. Stage name of Marie-Emilie Jolly (1842–1897), who, like Sarah, would later become a member of the Comédie-Française.

13. As spoken in the region of France known as the Auvergne.

14. "A small round sweet roll made with a light yeast dough." (Concise Oxford Dictionary).

15. Stage name of Gabrielle Charlotte Réju (1857–1920), famous actress especially of comic roles.

16. Character in Molière's *Le Misanthrope*. Produced 1666.

CHAPTER X

1. Edouard Thierry (1813–1894). Director, 1859–1871.

2. A sort of veil hanging down from the back edge of the hat and covering the nape of the neck.

3. Corded silk.

4. *Iphigénie en Aulide* by Racine. Produced 1674.

5. Pierrette Devoyod, born in 1838. Performed at the Comédie-Française from 1859 to 1872, but never became a *sociétaire* (Lyonnet).

6. Famous actress (1692–1730). Also 1849 play by Scribe and Legouvé. Mistress of Maurice de Saxe, she died shortly after he left her for the Duchesse de Bouillon, giving rise to rumors that the latter had poisoned her.

7. Stage name of Pierrette-Ignace-Maria Pingaud (1833–1908), whose lover, Mounet-Sully, Sarah would later steal from her—see Gold and Fizdale.

8. Act V, scene 3, the words are spoken by Iphigénie to Eurybate, a servant of Agamemnon's, telling him to take her to the altar for sacrifice: "Eurybate, conduct the victim to the altar."

9. A "popular" theater in Paris, originally founded in the eighteenth century. For its history see McCormick, pp. 23ff. According to Lyonnet, Léontine made her début at the Folies Marigny. She appeared at numerous popular theaters in Paris and led the life of a courtesan before going to Russia for a while. She died in 1901 (born in 1847).

CHAPTER XI

1. Anna-Stéphanie Coblentz, born ca. 1833, *pensionnaire* at the Comédie-Française 1862–1866.

2. 1822 comedy by Scribe (1791–1861) and Mélesville, pseudonym of Anne Honoré Joseph Duveyrier (1787–1865).

3. By Molière. Produced 1672.

4. Marie-Christine Royer (1841–1873).

5. Stage name of Zaïre-Nathalie Martel (1816–1885).

6. J.-B. Prosper Bressant (1815–1886). Described as handsome and graceful with a penetrating voice by Loliée, p. 283.

7. Rose Barretta, according to Lyonnet *pensionnaire* at the Comédie-Française 1864–1868, although this ceremony took place on 15 January, 1863 (see Gold and Fizdale, p. 52).

8. The French term is *émanciper*. "L'émancipation est un acte juridique qui donne aux mineurs certains des droits réservés aux majeurs"—see Claudine Herrman in her edition of *Ma double vie* (Paris, 1980), p. 309.

9. The Committee of the Comédie-Française was made up of fully tenured actors (*sociétaires à part entière*), who participated in the administration of the theater and received a share of its profits.

10. 1862 verse-drama of Louis-Hyacinthe Bouilhet (1822–1869).

CHAPTER XII

1. Round flat cake made of puff pastry.

2. A "popular" theater specializing in vaudeville and catering to a middle-class audience—see McCormick, passim.

3. Auguste-Adolphe Montigny, began his acting career at the Comédie-Française, but soon turned to writing plays for the popular theater and to management. He became director of the Gymnase in 1844 and died in 1880.

4. Victoria Lafontaine (1840–1918) became a member of the Comédie-Française in 1863, the year of Sarah's début at the Gymnase.

5. Blanche-Adeline Pierson (1842–1919). *Sociétaire* at the Comédie-Française from 1886 until her death. Her theatrical career spanned seventy years and all the female roles from child to grandmother (Chevalley, p. 191).

6. Céline Montaland (1843–1891) became a *sociétaire* at the Comédie-Française in 1888. She was the youngest actress ever to perform at this theater in the role of Camille in Augier's *Gabrielle* when she was six years old (Chevalley, p. 193).

7. *Un Mari qui lance sa femme* (1864): actually by Eugène Labiche (1815–1888) with the collaboration of Raymond Deslandes.

CHAPTER XIII

1. Sarah means Louis Josse who appeared at the Gaîté 1854–1858 and the Porte-Saint-Martin: 1859–1868, and died around 1868 (Lyonnet). Théâtre de la

Porte-Saint-Martin, a large theater suited to the spectacular genres of popular plays, such as the *féerie*, catering to a middle-class audience. See McCormick, p. 20.

2. "The nineteenth-century féerie is a form of the spectacular melodrama, distinguished by an emphasis on magic, the supernatural and the fantastic" (McCormick, p. 148), with lavish costumes and stage effects and considered suitable for children as well as adults. For more discussion see McCormick, chapter 10.

3. *La Biche au bois* (1845) by the Cogniard brothers, Théodore (1806–1872) and Hippolyte (1807–1882). They directed various popular theaters and wrote vaudeville and *féeries*—see McCormick, pp. 128, 155.

4. Venulie-Elise Debay, trained at the Conservatoire, described by Lyonnet as "intelligent and very pretty," appeared at the Odéon 1857–1868 and thereafter at the Ambigu.

5. Gabrielle-Delphine-Elizabeth Ugalde (1828–1911), made her début at the Opéra-Comique, became director of the Folies Marigny in 1872.

6. Founded in the eighteenth century as the home for light opera.

7. For a history of the Ambigu-Comique see McCormick, pp. 18ff. This theater, which was founded in the eighteenth century, originally dealt in "short comedies, often of a smutty nature, with songs" (McCormick, p. 18)—i.e., a hybrid-genre known as the "ambigu comique." Louis-François Faille (1825–1894), born to rural peasants, was manager of the the Ambigu 1864–1874 after which, financially ruined, he found himself having to return to the boards at the Porte-Saint-Martin and Châtelet.

8. An adaptation for the stage of Eugène Sue's (1804–1875) novel of that name. For a synopsis of the plot see McCormick, pp. 208f. Rodin is a Jesuit who pursues the Rennepont family's wealth, a role which gave Chilly "the opportunity for one of his greatest roles as the manipulative villain, who, when foiled at the level of physical violence, can switch to an even more diabolical plan to make the potential heirs destroy themselves" (McCormick, p. 209). Charles Marie de Chilly (1804–1872).

9. Made her début very young at the Odéon in 1865, appeared at several Parisian popular theaters (Lyonnet).

10. A three-act comedy by Alfred de Musset (1810–1857).

11. Charles de Chilly, director of the Odéon 1866–1872, Félix Duquesnel from 1872–1880.

12. Comedy written 1730 by Pierre Carlet de Chamblain de Marivaux (1688–1763).

13. The image in French involves a comparison between Sarah and a "flûte" (a long thin loaf of bread), lacking substance, which is offered to the ordinary people ("les gens du monde"). However the image is impossible to render effectively in English (translator).

14. A two-seated barouche (a four-wheeled carriage with a collapsible hood).

15. By George Sand. Written 1861, dramatized 1864.

16. By George Sand, dramatized 1849.

17. Prince Napoléon (1821–1891), patron of writers and artists and prominent in courtesan circles (former lover of Rachel)—see Richardson, pp. 54f., (photo p. 45).

18. Adolphe Thiers (1797–1877). First president of the Third Republic.

19. By Alexandre Dumas *père* (1802–1870), 1836.

20. A Republican, Victor-Marie Hugo (1802–1885) had gone into self-imposed exile after Napoleon III's coup d'état of 1851. *Ruy Blas* is the title of a tragedy by Hugo (1838).

21. Francisque Berton (1820–1874), father of Pierre Berton with whom Sarah also acted, married to Samson's daughter. An elegant, debonair, and distinguished actor (Lyonnet).

22. A "very mediocre" comedy by Jules Barbier about marriages arranged by matrimonial agency—Pronier, p. 44.

23. Stage name of Marie-Léonide Charvin (1836–1891), a *pensionnaire* of the Comédie-Française from 1863–1872, but never a *sociétaire*. She fell out of favor with the administration after declaiming *La Marseillaise* at a benefit concert for the widows and orphans of the Commune (Chevalley, p. 161).

24. François Coppée (1842–1908), soon-to-be-famed author of popular works focusing sympathetically on the lives of the humble.

CHAPTER XIV

1. The model for Swann in Proust's *A la recherche du temps perdu* and Sarah's lover for a while. See Gold and Fizdale, pp. 77ff.

2. This is Sarah's first mention of her illegitimate son, Maurice, born 22 December, 1854. His father was probably the Belgian prince, Charles Lamoral de Ligne.

3. A new play by a young Alfred Touroude from Le Havre, whose promising career as a dramatist was cut short by an early death—Pronier, p. 46.

4. A tragedy on a Roman theme by Latour de Saint-Ybars, now completely forgotten, but in whose plays Rachel also performed on occasion at the Comédie-Française—Pronier, p. 46.

5. *Jean-Marie* by Claude-Adhémar-André Theuriet (1833–1907), minor poet, novelist, and dramatist who excels in the celebration of provincial life.

CHAPTER XV

1. 19 July, 1870, the Franco-Prussian War.

2. Certain Canrobert (1808–1895), maréchal de France.

3. Achille François Bazaine (1811–1888). Bazaine's "second" act of treachery was diplomatic intriguing with the Prussians, which led to his defeat at Metz and conviction for treason in 1873.

4. Site of disastrous defeat of French on Meuse, near Belgian border, September 1, 1870. Napoléon III was captured by the enemy and, after some time in prison in Germany, joined his wife and son in exile in England, where he died.

5. Edmé-Patrice-Maurice Mac-Mahon (1808–1893), maréchal de France. President of France, 1873–1879.

6. Félix Faure (1841–1899). President of the French Republic, 1895–1899.

CHAPTER XVI

1. Similarly, a military hospital was set up in the Comédie-Française—see fig. 564, Chevalley.

2. Emile de Girardin (1806–1881), journalist and founder of *La Presse*, one of the first modern newspapers. Also a lover of Sarah's and a mover in courtesan circles—Richardson, pp. 65ff.

3. Head of the police générale and police judiciaire in the Ville-de-Paris, directly responsible to the Ministre de l'Intérieur.

4. Sic—translator.

5. This incident and the following are references to occurrences Sarah describes in chapter XIV when at the Tuileries Palace to perform for the Emperor and Empress.

6. Léon Gambetta (1838–1882). When the Prussians surrounded Paris (October, 1870) he left in a balloon and organized resistance from Tours and Bordeaux.

7. Antoine Eugène Alfred Chanzy (1823–1883). Commander of the Army of the Loire.

8. Charles Denis Sauter Bourbaki (1816–1897). Suffered a disastrous defeat as commander of the Army of the East.

9. Louis Jules Trochu (1815–1896). Severely criticized for his failure, as president of the Government of National Defense, to organize a more spirited defense of Paris after the rout of Sedan and the fall of the Second Empire.

10. Louise-Estelle Lambquin (1812–1872) acted at the Ambigu, Vaudeville, Comédie-Française, and Gaîté before moving to the Odéon in 1867.

11. On the left bank of the Seine in Paris. Site of a military hospital.

12. For an illustration see Lolliée, p. 389.

13. At the end of the Franco-Prussian War, rebels drawn mainly from the ranks of poor Parisians. Their resentment was directed against the monarchist National Assembly based in Versailles for its terms with Prussia and for the great hardships suffered by the poor during the war. The Commune was violently suppressed by an army commanded by MacMahon.

CHAPTER XVII

1. Jules Favre (1809–1880). Served briefly at the end of the Franco-Prussian War as minister in the provisional government.

CHAPTER XVIII

1. Gold coins in circulation until World War I.

2. Saint-Quentin (on the Somme) was the site of a battle between the Prussians and the French on 8 October, 1870. The Prussians were repulsed but the city was forced to surrender on October 21.

3. "A durable kind of cloth" (Oxford English Dictionary).

CHAPTER XIX

1. *Hernani* is a verse drama by Victor Hugo which attracted great attention because of its unconventionality when it was first performed in 1830.

2. Stage name of Jean-Sully Mounet (1841–1916). Great tragic actor, *sociétaire* of the Comédie-Française, famous for his interpretation of Hernani and many other roles. He often partnered Sarah on-stage and was her lover off. See Gold and Fizdale, pp. 97ff.

3. Henri de Rochefort (1830–1913), a journalist whose attacks on Napoléon III helped to undermine his regime.

4. Paul-Louis-Etienne de Rémusat (1831–1897), son of Charles de Rémusat. Politican and author of several books, one on Thiers (1889).

5. The nineteenth-century movement that supported the Orléans branch of the royal family.

6. See chapter XVI, n. 13.

7. Sarah has already mentioned performing in this play in chapter XIV.

8. Paul Porel was a fellow student of Sarah's at the Conservatoire. He later married Réjane.

CHAPTER XX

1. 1838 verse drama by Hugo.

2. Born in 1836. Besides the Odéon, Essler also performed at the Ambigu and Porte-Saint-Martin and other "popular" theaters.

3. Auguste Vacquerie (1819–1895). Hugo's daughter, Léopoldine, married Vacquerie's brother.

4. Edmond-Aimé-Florentin Geffroy (1804–1895) performed at the Comédie-Française from 1829 and was also well known for his paintings of actors and theater life.

5. A queen of Spain, honest and respectable / Should not in this way sit on the table.

6. One such painting by Geffroy can be seen in Chevalley, p. 125.

7. Louis-Henri-Marie Thomas, known as Lafontaine (1826–1898). *Sociétaire* at the Comédie-Française from 1863.

8. Stage name of Emile-Eugène Laurent, described by Lyonnet in the part of Guritan as "very remarkable." Later he was director of the Cluny and then performed at the Gaîté, returning to the Odéon in 1886. He died the year after.

CHAPTER XXI

1. Etienne Mélingue (1807–1875), a handsome swashbuckling actor, this was his last role. He was also a respected sculptor.

2. Prose drama by Victor Hugo (1835).

3. By Adolphe Belot based on a serialized novel that appeared in *Le Figaro* around 1860—Pronier, p. 44.

4. Juliette Drouet (1806–1883). Originally an actress, she became the devoted lifelong mistress of Victor Hugo.

5. William Busnach, a dramatist, dramatized Zola for the popular theater—see McCormick, p. 221.

6. Henri-Polidore Maubant (1821–1902) had a long career at the Comédie-Française extending from 1842 to 1888.

7. Emile Perrin was administrator of the Opéra-Comique and the Opéra before becoming administrator of the Comédie-Française in 1871. He held the position until 1885.

8. Théophile Gautier (1811–1872), journalist, novelist, and Romantic poet of the highest order.

9. Paul, Comte de Saint-Victor (1825–1881). Drama critic and author of *Les Deux Masques*, a three-volume study of the origins and development of drama.

CHAPTER XXII

1. Jules-Félix-Armand La Roche (1841–1925). First joined the Comédie-Française in 1860.

2. Cathérine-Julie-Clémentine Jouassain (1829–1902). Joined the Comédie-Française in 1851.

3. Madeleine-Emilie Brohan (1833–1900). Sister of Augustine Brohan mentioned earlier. Renowned for her beauty and acting ability when she first joined the Comédie-Française in 1850, but later gained a great deal of weight (Chevalley, p. 149).

4. Prose drama by Alexandre Dumas *père,* 1839.

5. Fréderic-Alexandre Febvre (1833–1916). Performed at the Comédie-Française 1866–1893.

6. Prose comedy by Beaumarchais (1732–1799), first produced 1784.

7. *Dalila* (1857) by Octave Feuillet (1821–1890), a very popular novelist and dramatist in his own day.

8. Eugène Manuel (1825–1901).

9. Tragedy of same name by Racine, produced 1667.

10. Prose drama. First performed 23 March, 1874.

11. There is an engraving of this scene in Lolliée, p. 339.

12. Louis-Arsène Delaunay (1826–1903). *Sociétaire* at the Comédie-Française from 1850, his son was also an actor and at the Comédie from 1896.

13. Alexandre Dumas *fils* (1824–1895). Illegitimate son of Dumas *père* and an extremely successful dramatist, especially with the dramatized version (1852) of his novel *La Dame aux camélias*, later to be a staple in Sarah's repertoire.

14. Ferdinand de Lesseps (1805–1894). Diplomat and engineer, famed for his supervision of the construction of the Suez Canal and later for his involvement in the scandal of the Panama Canal.

CHAPTER XXIII

1. Sarah says that Perrin was unhappy about the way in which Rousseil was aggressively seeking *sociétaire* status. According to F. Sarcey, *Comédiens et comédiennes: théâtres divers* (Paris, 1884) pp. 9f, 13f., Rosélia Rousseil (born 1840) spent two brief periods at the Comédie-Française, one under Thierry and a second under Perrin (1872–1874), but both periods were unhappy for her.

2. Stage name of Charles-Auguste Caristie. Made his début at the Odéon in 1850. Entered the Comédie-Française in 1872, and became the theater's oldest *pensionnaire* (Lyonnet).

3. Henri, Vicomte de Bornier (1825–1901).

4. Emile Augier (1820–1889). *Gabrielle*, like Bornier's *La Fille de Roland*, is a verse play.

5. A lover of Sarah's (and later lifelong friend) who painted a frequently reproduced portrait of her (as also did Parrot), reclining on a *chaise longue* with wolfhound at her feet.

CHAPTER XXIV

1. Alexandre Parodi (1840–1901).

CHAPTER XXV

1. Léon Cladel (1835–1892), also a novelist and writer of short stories about peasant life.

2. Gustave Doré (1832–1883), caricaturist and book illustrator, sculptor and painter and Sarah's lover—see Gold and Fizdale, pp. 130ff.

3. Gustave-Hippolyte Worms (1836–1910) joined the Comédie-Française in 1858 but performed in Russia for nine years before returning to this theater and becoming a *sociétaire* in 1870.

4. "The Young Girl and Death."

5. A type of silk.

6. "After the Storm."

CHAPTER XXVI

1. Adaptation by Jean Aicard (1848–1921) of Shakespeare.

2. By Racine, but Bérénice is a role in *Bérénice* (1670).

3. The Gaiety Theatre did not normally feature the kind of highbrow fare offered by the Comédie-Française, but rather extravaganza and burlesque—see J. C. Trewin, "Bernhardt on the London Stage," pp. 112f., in *Bernhardt and the Theatre of Her Time*, ed. Eric Salmon (Westport, Connecticut, 1984). For a full treatment of Sarah's experience on the London stage, see Elaine Aston, *Sarah Bernhardt: A French Actress on the English Stage* (Oxford, 1989).

4. *Sociétaire à part entière.*

5. Edmond-François-Jules Got (1822–1901). During his very long and distinguished careeer (1844–1894) at the Comédie-Française, Got was famed for his interpretation of comic roles. His opinion is quoted here since he was the *doyen* (or senior actor with responsibilities over the rest of the troupe) at the time.

6. By Alfred de Musset. One of the four lyrics called *Les Nuits* (1835–1837).

7. Sir Johnston Forbes-Robertson (1853–1937) as he later became, was one of the late nineteenth century's greatest English tragic actors, famous for his portrayal of Hamlet.

8. Oscar Wilde (1854–1900) Irish author, dramatist, and "personality," famed for his sententious wit, later emprisoned for homosexual offenses.

9. Duke of Connaught (1850–1942). English prince, son of Queen Victoria and Prince Albert, brother of Edward VII.

10. Sir Henry Irving (1838–1905). Famous English actor of the nineteenth century. Manager of the Lyceum where he staged spectacular plays with his leading lady, Ellen Terry.

11. In Hyde Park.

CHAPTER XXVII

1. Carriage and four with two postilions. For information about this and other carriages, mentioned here and elsewhere, consult Smith.

2. A park in Paris.

3. Jules Grévy (1807–1891). President of France 1879–1887.

4. Lines 581–82: Here he is. All my blood rushes towards my heart. / Seeing him I forget . . .

5. Stage name of Marie Vernin, born 1849. She left the Comédie-Française in 1882 to pursue an international career (Lyonnet).

6. I have corrected the spelling errors in these last two quotations, but I have not tampered with the English, which appears to have been misquoted in some places—Translator.

CHAPTER XXVIII

1. Sarah's motto "no matter what." See chapter XI.

2. William Ewart Gladstone (1808–1898). Served as prime minister of Britain four times (1868–1874, 1880–1885, 1886, 1892–1894).

3. Baron Frederick Leighton (1830–1896). English painter and sculptor, president of the Royal Academy from 1878 until his death.

4. Lifetime friend of Sarah, a painter who painted a well-known portrait of her. See Gold and Fizdale, pp. 133ff.

5. Charles-François-Joseph Prud'hon (1843–1930).

6. *Le Tartuffe*: verse comedy by Molière, produced 1667.

7. Character in *Mademoiselle de Belle-Isle* by Dumas *père*.

8. Three little pâtés, my shirt is burning.

9. Gustave Flaubert (1821–1880), renowned novelist, author of *Madame Bovary* etc. Flaubert staged Bouilhet's *Mademoiselle Aïssé* posthumously in 1872.

CHAPTER XXIX

1. Sarah met Pierre Berton at the Gymnase and when she arrived at the Odéon he was the leading actor there where he helped her cause and became her lover—see Brandon, passim.

2. Lucien Guitry (1860–1925). Actor, theater manager, playwright. Father of Sacha Guitry.

3. Stage name of Jeanne-Julia Regnault (1854–1941). Like Sarah before her, known as "la Divine." She was famed especially for her Racinian roles (Chevalley, p. 191).

4. Eleonora Duse (1859–1924). Great Italian actress and Bernhardt's rival for international stardom. See John Stokes et al.

CHAPTER XXX

1. *L'Assomoir*: 1877 novel by Emile Zola (1840–1902).

2. 1869 comedy by Henri Meilhac (1831–1897) and Ludovic Halévy (1834–1908), a partnership that produced many other successful works.

3. By Alexandre Dumas *fils*.

4. *Les Précieuses ridicules*. One-act prose comedy by Molière. Produced 1659.

5. *Le Fils naturel*: 1858 play by Alexandre Dumas *fils*.

6. *Les Caprices de Marianne*: by Alfred de Musset, 1834.

7. *La Joie fait peur*: by Delphine de Girardin (1804–1855), wife of Emile, 1854.

8. *Le Menteur*: comedy by Pierre Corneille, produced 1643.

9. *Le Médecin malgré lui*: 1666 comedy by Molière.

10. *Le Demi-Monde*: 1855 play by Alexandre Dumas *fils*.

11. *Il faut qu'une porte soit ouverte ou fermée*: 1848 comedy by Alfred de Musset.

12. *Le Post-Scriptum*: Emile Augier, 1869.

13. *Le Gendre de Monsieur Poirier*: 1854 comedy by Augier and Jules Sandeau (1811–1883).

14. *Le Luthier de Crémone*: an 1876 comedy by François Coppée.

15. *Les Plaideurs*: comedy by Racine based on Aristophanes' *Wasps*. First produced 1668.

16. *L'Ami Fritz*: 1876 prose comedy by Emile Erckmann (1822–1899) and Alexandre Chatrian (1826–1890), originally a novel.

17. *Il ne faut jurer de rien:* prose comedy by Alfred de Musset, published 1840, first produced 1848.

18. *Les Fourchambault*: 1878 comedy by Emile Augier.

19. *Gringoire*: 1866 one-act prose comedy by Théodore de Banville (1823–1891).

20. *Mademoiselle de la Seiglière*: this 1848 novel by Jules Sandeau was dramatized in 1851.

21. *Le Barbier de Séville*: prose comedy by Beaumarchais, first produced 1775.

22. *Andromaque*: tragedy by Racine, first produced 1667.

23. *L'Avare*: prose comedy by Molière based on Plautus' *Aulularia*, first produced 1668.

24. *L'Etincelle*: 1879 comedy by Edouard Pailleron (1834–1899).

25. *Le Dépit amoureux*: verse comedy by Molière first produced 1656.

26. *Mercadet*: produced 1851, adapted by d'Ennery from Balzac's comedy *Le Faiseur*, published 1851.

27. *L'Eté de la Saint-Martin*: 1873 comedy by Meilhac and Halévy.

28. *Le Mariage de Victorine*: comedy by George Sand, first produced 1861.

29. *Les Fourberies de Scapin*: 1671 prose comedy by Molière based on Terence's *Phormio.*

30. *Philiberte*: by Augier, 1853.

31. *L'Etourdi*: comedy by Molière, first produced 1655.

32. *Davenant*: by Jean Aicard.

33. Possibly identical with Marie Jullien, a young actress from the Odéon who joined the Gymnase in 1881 (Lyonnet).

34. Etienne Train, described by Lyonnet as "rather cold, but distinguished." He died at a young age in 1883.

35. Stage name of Denis-Stanislas Montalant (1824–1904), son-in-law of Geffroy. Performed at the Comédie-Française 1856–1879, *sociétaire* from 1859.

CHAPTER XXXI

1. Jules Vallès (1833–1885), journalist and novelist.

2. Jules Lemaître (1853–1914), drama critic and dramatist.

3. Jean Richepin (1849–1926), poet and dramatist and lover of Sarah's. See Gold and Fizdale, pp. 203ff.

4. Edmond Haraucourt (1856–1941), poet.

5. Catulle Mendès (1842–1909), *Parnassien* poet.

6. Edmond Rostand (1868–1918), dramatist, famed especially for his *Cyrano de Bergerac* (1897).

CHAPTER XXXII

1. Mary Todd Lincoln (1818–1882).

2. Abraham Lincoln (1809–1865), sixteenth president of the United States, was assassinated by John Wilkes Booth, an actor.

CHAPTER XXXIII

1. Muscle at the corners of the mouth used in the action of smiling.

2. Booth's Theatre was built for Edwin Booth (brother of Lincoln's assassin) on the southwest corner of the Avenue of the Americas and 23rd Street. It was demolished in 1883.

CHAPTER XXXV

1. For discussion of Sarah's trip to Montreal, see John Hare, "Sarah Bernhardt's Influence on the Theatrical Life of Montreal," in Salmon.

2. Louis Honoré Fréchette (1839–1908), French Canadian poet and politician.

3. Edouard Angelo was Sarah's lover and leading man on her American tour. See Gold and Fizdale, p. 161.

CHAPTER XXXVI

1. A rapid-firing cannon. The French term is used in American arms manuals of the time.

2. Of a gruesome or grotesque nature, as in the tales of Ernst Theodor Amadeus Hoffman (1766–1822), whose stories were translated into French as the *Contes fantastiques.*

3. Sarah acquired the Théâtre de la Renaissance in 1893 and kept it until 1899.

4. *Lorenzaccio*: a prose drama by Musset, written in 1834, in which Lorenzaccio (Lorenzo de' Medici) kills the despot Alessandro.

5. The Sunday before Lent.

CHAPTER XXXVII

1. Lawrence Barrett (1838–1891), American actor, famed especially for his portrayal of Cassius to Edwin Booth's Brutus.

CHAPTER XXXVIII

1. Sarah visited the United States nine times in all.

2. Tommaso Salvini (1829–1915), internationally famed Italian actor— especially for his playing of Othello. He performed in North and South America, Western Europe, and Russia.

3. Mary Anderson (1859–1940), American actress famed for her beauty and voice.

4. "Let's stop here"—a song from the comic opera *Le Chalet,* by Scribe and Mélesville (1834).

5. Sarah had a country house at Sainte-Adresse near Le Havre.

6. Victorien Sardou (1831–1908) wrote highly successful historical dramas. *Fédora* (1882) is a drama of revenge in a Russian setting.

Bibliography

EDITIONS AND TRANSLATIONS OF *MA DOUBLE VIE*

Ma double vie: mémoires de Sarah Bernhardt, ed. Claudine Herrmann. Paris: Editions des femmes, 1980.

Ma double vie: mémoires de Sarah Bernhardt. Paris: Charpentier et Fasquelle, 1907.

Memories of My Life: Being My Personal, Professional, and Social Recollections as an Artist. New York and London: Benjamin Blom, 1907. Reprinted 1968.

My Double Life: Memoirs of Sarah Bernhardt. London: Heinemann, 1907.

OTHER WORKS

Aston, Elaine. *Sarah Bernhardt: A French Actress on the English Stage*. Berg: Oxford, 1989.

Beerbohm, Max. *Around Theatres*. New York: Simon and Schuster, 1954.

Brandon, Ruth. *Being Divine: A Biography of Sarah Bernhardt*. London: Mandarin, 1992

Brownstein, Rachel M. *Tragic Muse: Rachel of the Comédie-Française*. New York: Alfred A. Knopf, 1993.

Chevalley, Sylvie, and Marie-Françoise Christout, Noëlle Guibert, Jacqueline Razgonnikoff. *La Comédie-Française: 1680–1980*. Paris: Bibliothèque Nationale, 1980.

Cunnington, C. Willett. *English Women's Clothing in the Nineteenth Century*. New York: Dover Publications, 1990.

Colombier, Marie. *Le Voyage de Sarah Bernhardt en Amérique*. Paris: Maurice Dreyfous, n.d.

Gold, Arthur, and Robert Fizdale. *The Divine Sarah: A Life of Sarah Bernhardt*. New York: Alfred A. Knopf, 1991.

Harvey, Paul, ed. *The Oxford Companion to French Literature*. Oxford: Clarendon Press, 1959.

Loliée, Frédéric. *La Comédie-Française: 1658–1907.* Paris: Lucien Laveur, 1907.

Levi, Anthony. *Guide to French Literature 1789 to the Present.* Chicago and London: St. James Press, 1992.

Lyonnet, Henry. *Dictionnaire des comédiens français (ceux d'hier).* Geneva: Revue Universelle Internationale Illustrée, n.d.

McCormick, John. *Popular Theatres of Nineteenth-Century France.* Routledge: London and New York, 1993.

Pronier, Ernest. *Sarah Bernhardt: une vie au théâtre.* Geneva: Alex. Jullien, n.d.

Richardson, Joanna. *The Courtesans: The Demi-Monde in Nineteenth-Century France.* Cleveland, Ohio: World Publishing, 1967.

Rolland, Romain. *Le Théâtre du peuple.* Paris: Librairie Fischbacher, 1904.

Sarcey, F. *Comédiens et comédiennes: théâtres divers.* Paris: Librairie des Bibliophiles, 1884.

Salmon, Eric, ed. *Bernhardt and the Theatre of Her Time.* Greenwood Press: Greenport, Connecticut, and London, 1984.

Selnick, Laurence. "Chekhov's Response to Bernhardt," in *Bernhardt and the Theatre of her Time.* Ed. Eric Salmon.

Shaw, George Bernard. *Shaw's Dramatic Criticism: From the* Saturday Review *(1895–98).* Selected by John F. Matthews. New York: Hill and Wang, 1959.

Smith, D. J. M. *A Dictionary of Horse-Drawn Vehicles.* London: J. A. Allen, 1988.

Stokes, John, Michael R. Booth, and Susan Bassnett. *Bernhardt, Terry, Duse: The Actress in Her Time.* Cambridge: Cambridge University Press, 1988.

Taranow, Gerda. *Sarah Bernhardt: The Art within the Legend.* Princeton, N.J.: Princeton University Press, 1972.

Trewin, J. C. "Bernhardt on the London Stage," in *Bernhardt and the Theatre of Her Time.* Ed. Eric Salmon.

Index